LUTON AT WAR

COMPILED BY
The Luton News

1947

HOME COUNTIES NEWSPAPERS, LTD
LUTON

To the People of Luton, who showed, not only that they could " take it," but that they could hit back . . . hard.

First published 1947

This reprint edition published in 1982

ISBN 0 901051 99 3

Bedfordshire County Library

Printed by White Crescent Press Limited, Luton, England

CONTENTS

Introduction

The war effort of the people of Luton is, to some extent, recorded in the files of the Luton newspapers between 1938 and 1946. Yet anyone who would seek the background to those years in the history of this thriving industrial town, who wished to measure its determination to play a full part in the onward struggle to final victory, could search those voluminous files in vain. Newspapers normally chronicle events as they pass. They could not, in 1940, speak of the grim events of that year from the viewpoint of 1946. They could not, in fact, record many events as they happened, because of a stringent war-time censorship, and much information had perforce to be filed away against the time when it could take its place in the broad canvas of an historical record.

The story of Luton at war, therefore, had to be written. It had to present the vivid picture of local war-time life in all completeness. More than 100,000 residents of Luton make up its community life, and those who in future years study the history of that community life must not find that a gap exists with little or no record of the effect of a great world upheaval on local life and habits.

It is appropriate, too, that wherever and in what form may be enshrined the Roll of Honour of Luton in this second world war, the names of those who gave their lives, whether in the Services or as civilians (for total war comes right into the homes of the people) should be attached to the story of their times.

The Roll has been compiled from particulars sent to the publishers, from inquiries made, and from records kept by *The Luton News* throughout the War. It is as complete as it has been possible to make it, but some who died may not have been recorded here. That does not diminish the honour they share with the host of the Fallen.

They paid the price—theirs is the Glory.

LEFT: *The entrance to the trench shelter on the Moor, which was completed in anticipation of war, in July 1939.*

BELOW: *As the threat of war drew nearer in August, volunteers help to fill sandbags, which were used for the protection of many public buildings in the town.*

The Uneasy Years

IN an obscure corner of its foreign news page one day in the early
twenties a *Times'* paragraph reported a political demonstration in a
small German town, " led," to quote *The Times'* own words, " by a
Herr Hittler." It was the cloud no bigger than a man's hand.

The years unfolded. Side by side the Fascist state of Italy and
National Socialist Germany, each under its fanatical dictator, began to
loom large in world affairs ; Abyssinia, Spain were the smoke wisps,
the smouldering of a new world conflagration.

Long before Munich anyone who travelled in Germany, and
listened, could sense that trouble was brewing for someone in the
future. At Nuremberg, just before it became the scene of the opening
of the Nazi campaign against the Jews, the writer was served an early
breakfast by a waiter, who in the absence of others to serve, felt
inclined to talk.

He produced some English newspapers, and by a question implied
that they were all alike. When told that although each might report
the same news, each was free to put forth distinctive views, he commented—" There is only one opinion in Germany."

Then he propounded this illuminating question, " Why can't
Germany and England get together—then we could whack the world?"

Asked in return why there should be any desire to whack the
world, he was at a loss for an effective answer.

That was typical of the German mind even in those days, and some
official spokesmen, in particular in the principal Ruhr cities, did not
attempt to veil their belief that Germany had undisputed right to
supremacy everywhere.

$$* \qquad * \qquad * \qquad *$$

The thunderclouds began to gather in Europe. Here in Britain
the masses of the people were undisturbed or, if they heard the
rumblings of the coming storm, they felt it was no concern of theirs.

Life had become easier after the troubled times of the early twenties.
Even the economic blizzard of 1931, so imperfectly understood by the
nation, had slipped into the past. A generation was growing up which
never knew 1914-18. They felt, as their elders did, that surely after
the devastation of one great war the world would not be so insane as
to embark on another. In any case, they said, foreign affairs and other
nations' troubles were not their concern.

Dancing, the cinema, cheap cars for joy-riding, tended to dominate
their lives. They became devotees of a new religion—swing. From
the light-of-heart came the cry : What does the future matter ? What
do we care about the past ? On with the dance ! The air was filled
with the throbbing rhythm of the jazz drums. Join the Territorials ?
Not likely, said many young men ; and none heard the approaching
drums of war.

Among many of the older generation, disarmament amounted to a creed. Remembering the horrors of 1914-18, believing that all nations with that experience had surely learned their lesson, they felt they had a panacea for peace for evermore. Even in their gradual disillusionment at the evident re-armament of other nations in the 1930's they felt that Britain should set an example and disarm, even if she disarmed alone. They would not realise, or admit, that there was an international parallel to the national necessity for a police force, not for the people who are peaceable, but to protect the peaceable against those who would break the peace.

Abroad, the feeling of impending catastrophe became more and more pronounced, so much so that in 1938 sensible travellers felt it wise to put the frontier between them and Germany. At home, however, even in 1938 there were still unbelievers, despite the fact that A.R.P. preparations were well advanced. These preparations were regarded very lightly by the people in general. Many looked on the early exercises of the personnel as a free entertainment for spectators and not as the prelude to something which, to themselves and their families, might become a matter of life or death.

*   *   *   *

Austria was annexed; Munich came. Prime Minister Neville Chamberlain, descending from the plane that brought him back to London, waved a scrap of paper above his head to the expectant crowds. " It is peace in our time . . . He has given me his promise."

How could there be peace ? Czechoslovakia had been " butchered to make a Roman holiday." Forced to surrender her natural bulwark, the Sudetenland, her independence was doomed. It was but the beginning of her years of tribulation. Yet still there were many in this country who continued to believe Hitler every time he made what he called his " last territorial demand." It was only the " last " until he was prepared to launch another, under circumstances of duress which made refusal by his victims well nigh impossible. Many Continental statesmen answered his summons to Berchtesgaden with dire results for them and their countries.

Christmas passed, and 1939, the fateful year, opened. Czechoslovakia, crippled already, was suddenly engulfed in the maw. Here in Britain uneasiness in high quarters intensified, and at last began to reveal itself among the ordinary people. Planning for the distribution of evacuees from London went on. A.R.P. training and civil defence preparations were pushed ahead, and the Government insisted that not even summer holidays should be allowed to interfere.

The Polish problem arose. Eastward thundered the armoured might of the Third Reich, to dispose of that problem by fire and sword. Peace lay dying. The drums of war rose in a deafening crescendo of sound.

And over the greater part of Europe the last lights flickered and went out . . .

10

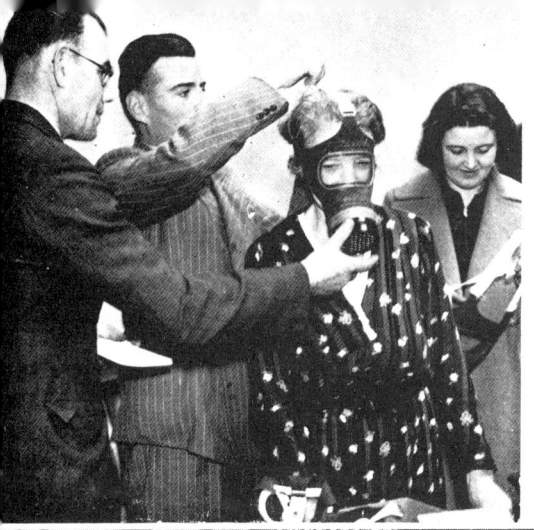

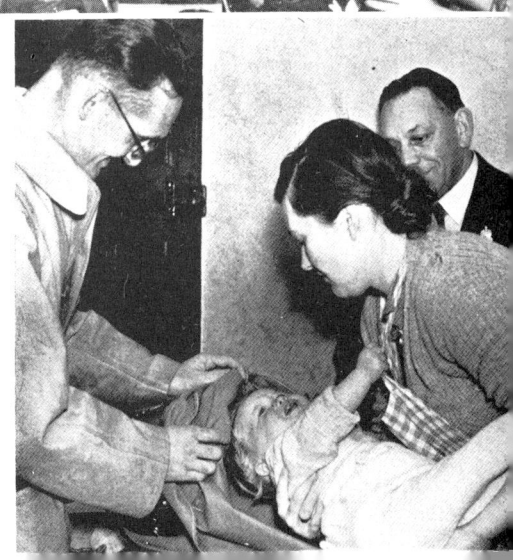

TOP LEFT: *As early as September, 1938, even before Munich, Luton people were being fitted with respirators.*

TOP RIGHT: *The tank in Wardown Park—a relic of the 1914—1918 war—is broken up for scrap metal.*

ABOVE: *Luton hat workers turn to a new type headdress, as they assist in the assembly of respirators.*

RIGHT: *Baby does not think very much of the idea of being put into his "gas mask."*

Zero Hour

Sunday morning and the Emergency Committee was in session. They had much to do, but as the hands of the clock crept closer to the hour of eleven, they leaned back in their chairs.

A member stretched across and flicked the knob of the radio. There was silence and they waited. Then, as the voice of the Prime Minister, Mr. Neville Chamberlain, low and grave in its tones, came over the air, each listened, and thought of the future.

There was a long pause, a click as the radio was turned off, then one moved forward in his chair.

" Well, gentlemen, it has come. I really didn't think it would."

The business of the Emergency Committee was resumed . . . It had definitely become more urgent.

End of an Era

BRITAIN was at war. And, as usual, Britain was not ready. We had not the men, the tanks, the planes for a war against Germany. Such men as we could put into the field immediately were the equal of any of their fighting predecessors. We had planes which were the best of their day, but woefully few when compared with Germany's vast numbers of perhaps older but quite serviceable types. Our tanks were hopelessly inadequate.

As usual, we had to start practically from scratch, against a war machine which for years had been preparing.

Hitler knew all this. What he did not know, or would not believe, was that " the effete, pleasure-mad youth of Britain," on whose decadence he relied for the downfall of their Empire, would in their unpredictable British way cast off the mask of their other selves and emerge as the fighting sons of a nation which could always fight when need be.

He was to learn that to his cost.

    *   *   *   *

What we were up against was not very apparent in that first winter of the war. The British and French sat behind an incomplete Maginot Line . . . incomplete in that it did not run to the sea. The Germans sat behind their hastily completed Siegfried Line. It was a war in which for months enemy forces looked at one another, but did not fight. It was incomprehensible. It was what the Americans called " a phoney war."

But the initiative lay with the aggressor. Overnight, in April, 1940, he struck. Denmark was occupied and simultaneously the citizens of Oslo and the main Norwegian ports woke to find Nazi transports in their harbours, Nazi planes overhead, Nazi troops in control. An expeditionary force sent from Britain got a footing and fought valiantly in the snow-covered mountains and forests, but without landing grounds and air cover it was a forlorn hope. The force had to be withdrawn.

Then in May the tornado struck in Western Europe. The enemy sidestepped the Maginot Line. They came round from the north. Holland was ruthlessly overrun. The King of the Belgians gave in and went into captivity. Churchill succeeded Chamberlain. Nazi armoured columns swept south to the Somme, taking the old battle-fields in their stride, and then swung round to envelop the Channel ports. The British Expeditionary Force, fighting like grim death, giving ground under the thrusts of overpowering enemy armour and ceaseless dive-bombing, found themselves in a tight corner, with their backs to the sea at Dunkirk.

Dunkirk was a miracle. In the first few days of June the greater part of the British Expeditionary Force, with some French and other troops, in all 335,000 men, were evacuated. 222 Naval vessels and 665 small craft, from paddle steamers down to rowing boats, and including many pleasure craft with volunteer crews, brought this vast part of the Army safely home to England. All equipment had to be left behind, but to have brought away safely so many of the men, when all had seemed lost, gave rise in itself to an intense feeling of relief and thankfulness. It was a deep but only a passing relief.

People were almost afraid to listen to the wireless. Disaster had piled on disaster. We dreaded what next would be announced. Norway and Denmark had been a shock, Holland and Belgium a catastrophe. Three weeks after Dunkirk the surrender of France, Britain's great and only remaining ally, seemed incredible.

Britain stood alone !

The one great question which was on everyone's lips was, What will happen now ? Only the Channel, 20 miles across at its narrowest, lay between England and the hordes of the enemy . . . an enemy whose bestiality in Poland and in the Low Countries had chilled all hearts. A.R.P. practice, gas exercises, siren tests, which to some had seemed almost comic in their early days, suddenly assumed a new significance.

And as the people faced the facts, the one great question became two. It was not merely, " What will happen *now* ? ", but also " What will happen *here* ? "

Strangers Within the Gates

MUNICH was three months past and the man in the street had begun to recover a sense of security. All was reasonably well. He had come to accept " Peace in our time " as a credible gospel and was beginning again to build his house of cards.

But though on the face of it the danger seemed to have receded, the government pushed ahead with certain preparations and in January, 1939, the chief Billeting Officer, Mr. E. O. Cutter, who was also Luton's Director of Education, began to probe quietly with a survey of the town.

The survey was for surplus accommodation ; special constables, school teachers, members of the women's auxiliary services and the schools' medical services got to work. They covered 29,000 houses, and, according to Ministry of Health standards, their survey showed that there were in Luton 32,000 surplus occupied rooms. That number was reduced later in the year to 22,000, but by the end of January the plan had been worked out, billeting arrangements were as complete as they could be, and Luton was ready to absorb her quota of evacuees.

For evacuation the Government had scheduled the whole country in terms of " danger areas," regarded as priority targets for enemy bombs ; " neutral areas " where the probable danger was not great ; and " reception areas " which, while not immune from danger, were regarded as improbable targets. Luton had the doubtful distinction of two designations from two different Government departments, but to the Ministry of Health who were responsible for evacuation, the town was a " reception area ", *i.e.*, it was suitable in all respects for the reception and billeting of children and mothers to be evacuated from more dangerous localities.

*　　*　　*　　*

The first great mass evacuation began on Friday, September 1st, 1939, and continued on the two following days, so that the original scheme was actually completed on the day that a state of war was announced. The first arrivals came from Walthamstow. They found the Mayor, the Town Clerk, the Chief Constable and the Medical Officer waiting on the L.M.S. Station to welcome them.

A main reception centre had been established at the Dunstable Road Junior Mixed School, and fifteen dispersal centres in other parts of the town—the Grammar and High Schools, the Technical College, and the following schools :—Beech Hill Senior Girls, Maidenhall Junior Boys, Stopsley Mixed, Norton Road Junior Mixed, Christ Church Junior Boys, Denbigh Road Senior Boys, Hart Hill Junior Mixed, Beechwood Junior Mixed, Hitchin Road Junior Mixed, Queen Square Junior Boys, Tennyson Road Junior Mixed and St. Matthews Junior Mixed.

At Dunstable Road the Chief Billeting Officers for the boroughs of Luton and Dunstable and the Luton Rural District, together with their staffs, received all the evacuees, who from this Centre went to various dispersal centres for classification and billeting. Those who were to be billeted in the borough underwent a medical examination before they left Dunstable Road.

*　　　*　　　*　　　*

According to official notifications which had been received, eleven trains were to arrive on each of three days, the total to be detrained at Luton being 25,866, of whom 22,000 were to be billeted in Luton, and the remainder passed on to Dunstable and the villages in the Rural District.

A few days before September 1st, however, it was notified that 500 adult blind and their helpers would come to Luton by road. So would all the expectant mothers.

The arrivals by the first train reached the Dunstable Road School at 10.45 a.m., and numbered 537. They were from three Walthamstow schools. Two of the schools were small, so the teachers and children from one were sent to Barton, and from the other to Dunstable. Those from the largest of the three schools were billeted in Luton.

This process went on throughout the day, and altogether 27 school parties were billeted, the last party leaving Dunstable Road School at 6.45 p.m. It was noticed that the numbers on the trains were considerably fewer than expected, and at the end of the day it was found that 4,887 children and 548 teachers had been received.

Throughout the day there were long " crocodiles " from the station to the main dispersal centre, and few people who witnessed them will ever forget the spectacle of the children. They carried their gas masks, bags of food, and their belongings, and although not a bit frightened, some looked a bit bewildered. Others were like happy youngsters on a Sunday School excursion. They waved out of the windows as their train drew in. Some were singing " It's a long way to Tipperary." They had a comfortable journey, and were as lively as crickets.

*　　　*　　　*　　　*

In the majority of cases it might be said that " they came, they saw, they conquered." It was not a martial victory. It was a triumph of human appeal. Few Luton women could resist the sight of the labelled little ones, loaded with their belongings. They opened their hearts as well as their homes to them, and set about making them feel that, if they had left behind a lot for which they cared, they had found some new friends.

The children came from the following London schools and colleges : George Gascoigne Central ; Edinburgh Road and St. Saviour's, Walthamstow ; St. John's and Napier Street, Hoxton ; Horley Crescent and St. Michael's, Camden Town ; Hampstead Parochial and

16

Christ Church, Hampstead; Margrave Park, Junction Road (2); Kingsdown Orphanage, Highgate; Haverstock Central Boys and Girls; St. Pancras C.E., Bath Street, St. Luke's Parochial, and Hugh Myddleton, Finsbury; St. Matthew's, South Islington; The Brecknock, Holloway; Lyulph Stanley Central; Netley Street and St. Dominic's, both from North-Western London; North London Collegiate; North-West Polytechnic; and St. George's College, Red Lion Square.

*   *   *   *

Next day the Dunstable Road School was literally besieged by mothers and children, expectant mothers, and blind people. It was at once apparent that train arrangements had been altered. In addition to train congestion, parties of blind arrived by road, and to make matters more difficult, streams of unofficial evacuees walked into the school, having made their own way from London. No more school units had arrived, and householders waiting to receive schoolchildren found themselves faced with crowds of mothers with children whom there was not the same inclination to take.

Billeting officers and their staffs worked unremittingly. They went without meals. Hour after hour at high pressure they worked while fatigue pressed inexorably on them and difficulties crowded on them. Some mothers were accompanied by five or six children from whom they refused to be parted. Blankets, towels and soap had to be bought, and food had to be provided for these parties until they could be billeted on the Sunday.

Arrangements had been made to billet all expectant mothers through Beech Hill School, so that they would be within easy reach of the Hospital, and in order that they might be specially registered by the Medical Department. Unfortunately these expectant mothers did not come together in distinct parties. They formed small groups in the larger parties, making it difficult to keep track of them.

It was afterwards learned that parties due to leave London on the Sunday had been advanced to Saturday. In consequence, instead of eleven trains stopping at Luton on the Sunday, only three were scheduled to do so, and even then the third was cancelled. In place of trainloads, however, there came individual cars carrying blind people. This respite enabled sectional billeting officers to carry out some redistribution of those who were billeted on the Friday and Saturday, and the billeting of some for whom accommodation could not be found on the Saturday night.

*   *   *   *

The total number passing through the Dunstable Road School on the three days was 12,285, of whom 8,091 were billeted in Luton and the remainder outside the town. There were 5,381 unaccompanied schoolchildren, 6,904 " other persons ", and 276 of the total were blind.

Original payments by the Government for billeting were :—Adults

17

with children, 5/- per week for adults and 3/- for each child, the only obligation on the householder being to take them in and give access to water and sanitary accommodation ; for unaccompanied children of school age, 10/6 where only one child was received, 8/6 each where more than one was billeted, the payment to cover full board and lodging and attendance.

In time the payment was found to be inadequate, and the amount rose according to the age of the child. Billeting rates for school-children became :—Age 10 to 14, 10/6 ; 14 to 16, 12/6 ; 16 and over, 15/-. There was a further revision in May, 1942, and from then onwards the payments were :—Under 5, 8/6, but 10/6 if only one ; 5 to 10, 10/6 ; 10 to 12, 11/- ; 12 to 14, 12/- ; 14 to 16, 13/- ; 16 to 17, 15/6 ; 17 and over, 16/6. The accommodation rates for children accompanied by adults remained unchanged.

* * * *

Where some large families that refused to be separated had to stay in a school for the night, billeting officials stayed with them, and some of the senior officials went the rounds during the night to see that all were as comfortably settled as they could be. On the Sunday special centres were opened for the payment of grants to mothers with children under five, or to others who had come in charge of such children, so that none who had to leave home without sufficient money for urgent needs should thereby be distressed. The money so paid out was an official gift, not a loan.

* * * *

The " wonderful way " in which Luton received the evacuees was the subject of an appreciative letter from Mrs. E. Baxter, one of the L.C.C. escorts, who accompanied a party of 400 mothers and children from the East End. Householders, she said, came out into the streets with cups of tea and milk for the children, and others carried the mothers' luggage, or the babies.

All the same, it was to be expected that in the settlement of all these strangers little difficulties would arise in some households. The Mayor obviously realised this, for, to a message of thanks to the people of Luton for so readily opening their homes and hearts in generous and friendly sympathy with the unfortunate refugees, he added :—

" Now just a friendly word from a heart that realises something of the strain that the coming months will impose on every one of us.

" Unselfish consideration for each other is a vital need.

" Remember, everybody has an extra burden to carry just now. Don't broadcast scares and rumours. Don't be a ' wet blanket.'

" To the best of your ability, be helpful.

" For such living, Heaven and your friends will bless you."

* * * *

For the part Luton had played in the evacuation scheme, a resolution of thanks passed by the L.C.C. the following month was forwarded to the Chief Billeting Officer. These sentiments were renewed on

LEFT: *Buses and cars wait outside Luton station to take London evacuees to their new "homes" in September, 1939.*

BELOW: *Tired out and nowhere to sleep, these little boys and girls could not find a home. This picture, taken in Alma Street, gives some indication of the difficulties with which billeting officials had to contend.*

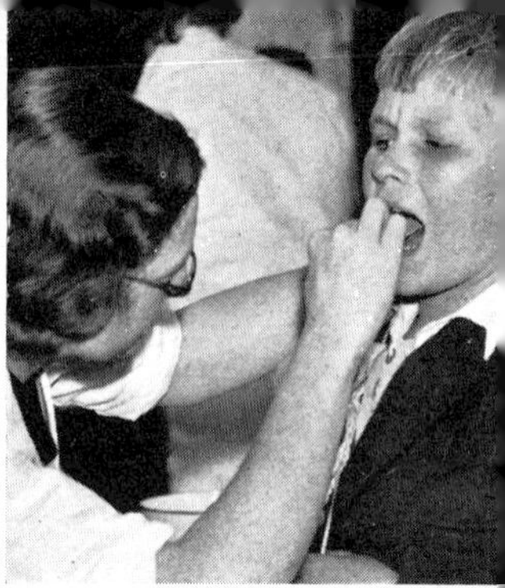

September 1939: *These young evacuees arrived in Luton with their kit-bags and waited their turn at the dispersal centre. A medical inspection was the next step before billeting. The young fellow (top right) is seen having his teeth inspected at Dunstable Road School.*

RIGHT: *"Yes, I'll have these three little girls." The billeting officer finds a willing Luton housewife ready to help.*

BELOW : *Evacuated to Luton High School, the girls of the North London Collegiate School soon settled down. This picture of a gymnastics class was taken soon after their arrival.*

February 13th, 1942, when the chairman of the L.C.C., the Rt. Hon. C. G. Ammon, M.P., (now Lord Ammon), expressed thanks to Luton foster-parents for their kindness and attention to the children of the evacuated schools in the town. Mr. Ammon was accompanied by the chairman of the L.C.C. Education Committee, Alderman Charles Robertson, and together they made a tour of the L.C.C. school units in Luton. Afterwards Mr. Ammon described the arrangements in Luton as equal to those he had seen anywhere.

Other official visitors, including Miss Florence Horsbrugh, then Parliamentary Secretary to the Ministry of Health, and Cardinal Hinsley, also expressed themselves as very satisfied with what Luton was doing, both in regard to billeting and social work among the mothers and children.

         *   *   *   *

Unaccompanied school-children received a medical card on arrival, and on registration with a local doctor they were entitled to free medical attention and drugs. Unfortunately there was no such provision for the mothers and the children accompanying them.

An emergency clinic service was put into operation, together with ante-natal clinics, and an appeal was made to the L.C.C. for a doctor and two nurses to relieve the strain on the local health services. Locally there was also an appeal for prams and push-chairs for the benefit of mothers who had been unable to bring such aids.

Wisely, the dispersal centres were kept open, and in time these became social centres as well as inquiry bureaux. The clergy also opened their own halls, so that mothers and young children could meet each day, and the arrival of two after-care workers from the L.C.C. extended the welfare work among mothers and children.

         *   *   *   *

By September 21st, however, about 50 per cent. of the mothers and children had returned to their homes. The main reasons given were inability to maintain themselves apart from their husbands; discontent at the loss of their neighbours and disturbance of their usual habits, and that London appeared to them to be as safe as, if not safer than, Luton.

Some found themselves landed among conditions better than those to which they had been accustomed, and found it irksome to try to live up to new standards. Others missed the old haunts and the old ties. There were some, in fact, who could not be happy out of their own street.

         *   *   *   *

Typical impressions were summed up by a London journalist who visited Luton, to see what was happening to the people from his own district.

" I hate the place and I hate the people," a London mother told him. " Heaven preserve me from ever becoming like Lutonians.

I never met such a snobbish, selfish, unfriendly, rude lot in all my life. All they think about is their houses. House-proud, that's their trouble."

That was certainly on the debit side. Fortunately there was a credit account. " We are so happy I'd hate to go anywhere else," said one contented mother. " Everyone I've met at Luton is the same—real good people."

*　　　*　　　*　　　*

After the first rush, evacuation was a matter of ebb and flow, varying according to the attention the enemy was paying to the London area. When he was troublesome there would be a rush of fresh evacuees, and some of the old ones would return. Many would find accommodation on their own, and there was seldom a day on which householders in the centre of the town did not have inquiries for rooms. When the bombardment slackened again, off would go the evacuees ; but there came a time when the lack of accommodation in London and the uncertainty of the flying bomb and rocket attacks made some of them fixtures in Luton.

Against the opinion of the mother who hated Luton and everything Lutonian, therefore, may be set the opinion of the father of a family that had experienced what it meant to be in the East End when the bombing was at its worst. They had stayed until they lost their home, considered themselves luckier than others in that they had saved some furniture, decided that Luton was good enough for them, and formed the conclusion that from the East End they had reached Paradise.

*　　　*　　　*　　　*

At first there were sufficient offers of accommodation to render billeting a voluntary affair. People were requested to billet, and in the majority of cases were willing. As time went on, it became necessary to require householders to provide billets, and a tribunal was set up to deal with difficulties arising between householders and evacuees.

Not unexpectedly some arose. In April, 1940, it was reported that Luton's call for householders to billet London school children, should the need arise for a second evacuation, had met with acceptance by only 2 per cent.

There were many reasons to account for this. The financial one probably weighed least in the balance, although many householders were out of pocket, for growing children have healthy appetites, and the keener air of Luton, while putting colour into their cheeks, also made catering for them a problem at times.

*　　　*　　　*　　　*

The condition of many of the children on arrival had come as a shock to local people, but it was afterwards pointed out that much of this was because the children came at the end of a holiday period and consequently had been away from medical supervision. Vigorous measures were taken locally to bring about an alteration, and these were so successful that soon 95 per cent. of the children were trouble-free in health.

In some cases uncleanliness was allied with a pitiful lack of clothing, and the Mayor felt it necessary to issue an appeal for footwear and clothes. What was known as the Mayor's Clothing Fund came into existence, with Waller Street School as the central depot, and under the leadership of the late Councillor Percy Mitchell an organisation was framed for collection and distribution of clothing and other requirements, such as prams and cots.

The response to the Mayor's appeal was immediate and generous. Women went through their wardrobes and sorted over their children's clothes, and all sorts of garments came along, from evening dresses and fur coats to shoes. These were dealt with by voluntary lady workers from various organisations in and around the town, and many an evacuee mother and child was made the happier through the transformation effected by gifts and adaptations.

*   *   *   *

Good work for some of the evacuees was also done at the Napier Centre at 52, Linden Road. This was run in connection with the Napier Street School from Shepherdess Walk, Hoxton, then at Beechwood School, and clothes were washed, mended, stored, and distributed.

While there was much that was pathetic about this sort of thing, the work was not without its lighter side. On the second morning the centre was open a girl walked in and asked, " Is this the house where they give out the clothes ? " calmly adding, " I'll take all that you don't want."

In many other ways the lot of the evacuees was eased, and it was astonishing how quickly links of affection were forged.

*   *   *   *

One of the most amazing demonstrations Luton has ever seen occurred on September 27th, 1939, when over 200 women from the Albert Road district marched to the Town Hall to present a petition to the Mayor against the removal of evacuee children from their homes. They were reinforced by the mothers of some of the children, who had come down specially from London and were determined, it appeared, to take their children home rather than have them moved to the Denbigh Road area.

The Mayor and the Chief Billeting Officer met the deputation, and the reason for the proposed move was explained. The meeting eventually broke up, but the deputation spokesman declared that a deputation would be sent to London before the end of the week.

Mr. Cutter's explanation was that all the children of the Hugh Myddelton School did not arrive together. The Council were instructed to educate the children as whole schools, the local authority had to find a place where they could all be billeted and sent to school together, and it was found that they could be billeted near, and sent to, Denbigh Road School.

Apparently, after further consideration among themselves, the demonstrators decided that the proposed move must take place, for no more was heard of the matter.

*   *   *   *

One of the problems created by the evacuees was their visitors. Eager to see their children and anxious, perhaps, to get away for a time to what was, in some respects, a safer area, fathers and mothers, not to mention other visitors, crowded into the town at week-ends. Special trains brought them, and a good many were made as welcome as the children; but quite a number of householders were worried by the demand made upon them by visiting relatives, for instance, demands for such things as accommodation for the night and meals.

In certain areas well-to-do parents supplemented the Government billeting allowance by gifts, a practice which sometimes caused discontent among neighbouring households.

*   *   *   *

Some parents had to be content with seeing their children out of doors, and Luton Rotary Club performed a useful bit of service at this time by opening a community centre at the Technical College. This enabled parents to meet their children away from the billets, and the provision of light refreshments at moderate cost was a feature that was appreciated.

Eventually, in 1942, a special centre for evacuees was opened in a disused hat factory in King Street. It was furnished for women and children, and became a cheery place for them, thanks to the vision and determination of the late Mrs. C. E. Chennells, who enlisted the aid of other W.V.S. members in staffing it. With its cooking arrangements, its " quiet room," and its amusement facilities for the children, the mothers found it " just what was wanted," and it did good work while the need for such work continued.

*   *   *   *

While the interest of some Londoners in Luton proved a trifle overwhelming, there was complaint on the other hand of lack of official interest by London. On October 18th, 1939, the Mayor indicted several London Boroughs for failure to provide after-care for their evacuees. He urged that there was a tremendous need among the evacuees for medical and general health services, with which the Luton services could not cope. This naturally brought denials from London, and a passing on of the responsibility. The borough councils said it was not their responsibility . . . that it rested with the L.C.C. Mr. Herbert Morrison, for the L.C.C., said he could understand the anxieties of Luton, but it was really a matter for the Government.

24

The late Cardinal Hinsley, Catholic Archbishop of Westminster, with Father O'Connor, of Leagrave Catholic Church, when the Cardinal came to Luton to visit evacuees.

Enemy bombers had driven them from their home, and one of Luton's shelters became their temporary abode . . . as safe as anywhere with death and destruction being dropped from the skies.

The return journey. These evacuees do not look very happy, as they wait for the "Evacuee Special" to take them back to London.

A statement was also issued by the chairman of the Education and Evacuation Committee of the L.C.C., in which it was claimed that much assistance had been given to the reception authorities. The fact remains that the first authority to send a woman worker was Walthamstow, a borough outside the area of the L.C.C.

To see for himself how matters stood, especially as regarded the Catholic children from his diocese, the Roman Catholic Archbishop of Westminster visited Luton on October 22nd, 1939—the first time a Cardinal had paid a visit to the town since the Reformation. Meeting the Mayor and the Chief Billeting Officer, Cardinal Hinsley expressed gratitude to Luton for its friendliness and for all it was doing for evacuees.

*   *   *   *

In Luton, as elsewhere, the influx of evacuees intensified the problem of school accommodation. It had been difficult before, in an ever-growing town ; it became more than ever impossible to try to squeeze " a quart into a pint pot." In an effort to overcome the difficulty, an "alternate days" scheme was put into operation. A Luton school occupied a building on one day, and a London school the next day. There was still the problem of the off day, but the head teachers had a plan for this. They arranged all sorts of things. Fortunately the weather was kind at first, and the children enjoyed excursions into the country, and lessons and games in the parks.

The question became more acute as the weather worsened, but with the return of many of the evacuees to London it was found possible between Christmas, 1939, and Easter, 1940, to absorb a number of the London children into the Luton classes. Double shifts were also put into operation, and 21 church halls were brought into use for school purposes.

*   *   *   *

It was, however, a disheartening time for educationists, and it was not surprising to find Luton's Director of Education declaring, when he addressed the Rotary Club in February, 1940, that evacuation had dealt education a death blow. Attention was called to the matter elsewhere, the President of the Board of Education instituted inquiries in Luton, and reports were called for.

Mr. Kenneth Lindsay, then Parliamentary Secretary to the Board of Education, undertook to see the Luton Education Authority, at the same time pointing out in the House of Commons that the difficulty arose only partly from evacuation. It was due in the main, he said, to an existing deficiency of accommodation, and he proposed to see the local education authority and the Regional authority with a view to remedying the position.

*   *   *   *

The arrival of many expectant mothers has been mentioned earlier. One result of evacuation was that scores of babies who would normally have been born " in town " first saw the light of day in Luton. All the time London was under bombardment parties of these expectant mothers were sent to Luton every week. Luton set aside the old Bute Hospital for them, and equipped it with 35 beds. There were births in the first few days, and by October 21st, 53 births which would otherwise have taken place in London had been " happy events " for the Bute.

The mothers were loud in their praise of the facilities provided, and many a father was to be seen striding towards the hospital, a bunch of flowers in hand, chest proudly expanded. When the mothers left hospital, there was the problem of billeting mother and child, many of whom could not have gone back to London had they so wished. Lists of sympathetically disposed people were obtained by the health visitors, and billets were kept available by payment of a small retaining fee.

*   *   *   *

With the end of the war in Europe there came the eagerly-anticipated code telegram from the Ministry of Health instructing the London return plan to be put into operation. By that time there were only about 200 official evacuees remaining in Luton. Some had been in the town since the beginning of the war, but the majority had been evacuated more than once. Special trains, catering for other districts as well, were put on to take them back. Mothers and children went first, and then unaccompanied children, the last evacuee special leaving Luton on June 23rd, 1945.

Scenes on the L.M.S. station were reminiscent of 1939, but now there were tears on both sides . . . tears on the part of the women who had cared for the children over such a lengthy period and were loth to part with them, and tears from the youngsters whose affection for them had grown with the years. Many gifts accompanied the children. Many took to London pets they had acquired, and many were the promises of visits to be made to Luton and London.

*   *   *   *

While there were tears, the homegoing was not without its humorous aspect. Some of the evacuees took their baggage to London earlier in the week, and then returned on purpose to travel on the special. One boy who had become apprenticed to a Luton firm went on one of the trains. The following day he returned to Luton to go into lodgings.

Even when evacuation had officially come to an end, there were still many evacuees remaining in Luton. Some were without homes to which to go, some were unclaimed. In the case of the latter, they eventually became de-billeted and were transferred to a new Government welfare scheme. There were also many other former evacuees who had found Luton so desirable a place that they had decided to remain.

There was another and unofficial aspect of evacuation which had a considerable effect on Luton. This was the exodus from London and elsewhere of firms who added an unusual variety to Luton's industrial activities.

*   *   *   *

The names of some famous London millinery wholesalers who had been blitzed, suddenly appeared on Luton buildings which they had managed to secure independently, or where trade friends had found them accommodation for the time being. Dozens of firms making hats or merchanting materials found accommodation here, and never before were Luton's smaller factories in such demand. More than one small man took the chance to sell out well in a very uncertain time. Some of the newcomers remained only a short time, and then re-established themselves in London. Others had to stay a considerable time before they could return. Still others seem likely to remain as a permanent addition to Luton's hat industry.

Hat people, of course, would obviously choose a hat centre like Luton when driven out of London, but there was no such predisposing influence affecting clothing factories. Yet for a time Luton became a centre of considerable importance for the manufacture of uniforms for the Services. All sorts of premises were acquired for the purpose. Some had been hat factories or warehouses. Durlers' big building in Guildford Street, which in its time had housed thousands, if not millions, of bales of plait from the Far East, in the days when men wore boaters, passed into the possession of one firm of clothing manufacturers. Part of a disused bleachworks accommodated another firm. Two roller skating rinks became uniform factories.

*   *   *   *

After a time much of this activity was directed elsewhere, to free local labour for other purposes, although not until after denims, battle dress, and caps, which must have totalled millions, had been produced. Some clothing firms, not concerned with uniforms, were permitted to carry on in Luton. Of those who had to move on, some have indicated that they propose to return and re-engage in the the civilian clothing trade as the premises they occupied again become available. It seems that in the years to come clothing manufacture will continue to be one of Luton's lighter industries.

*   *   *   *

Manufacturing furriers also came to Luton, and for a time the workers who came with them formed quite a distinct colony in one of the newer areas of the town which in the years immediately preceding the war had grown a bit faster than was warranted. Some comparatively small factories in Luton at times held almost fabulous values of skins in small compass, and precautions were taken to make uninvited entry out of hours practically impossible.

28

A tobacco and cigarette factory and a paint works were wartime additions. Other newcomers were producers of embroidery, artificial flowers, walking sticks, machinery belting, sweets, knitted gloves, waterproof clothing, and even carnival novelties. Some stayed. Some did not.

Luton even became a diamond cutting centre in a modest way—not gems, but industrial diamonds—and after this was given up in Luton it was continued in a neighbouring village.

The Local Authority

WAR caused an abrupt change in the municipal administration of Luton. For the time being it became a " Rule of Three." Even before the announcement that a state of war again existed it was clear that if war did come there would be many things requiring almost instant decision, and that normal Council procedure would be too cumbrous. The solution was to vest the necessary powers in an Emergency Committee of three, a triumvirate, who would have the backing of all the principal officials.

With an August vacation in prospect, and as a precautionary measure only, these powers were vested in Councillor John Burgoyne, then Mayor, the late Alderman C. C. Dillingham, then Deputy Mayor, and Councillor T. H. Knight. Events moved so rapidly that within the month this triumvirate found themselves shouldering practically the whole burden of the civil defence preparations, with an increasing sense of urgency and responsibility.

*   *   *   *

The schools were on holiday. Many Luton families were enjoying what was to be their last visit to the seaside for six years. The Chief Constable went away for a few days, but came back in a hurry. Many of the school teachers returned earlier than they would otherwise have done, to play their part in the reception of evacuees, and found they had returned not a day too soon.

The Emergency Committee met daily from the Thursday before the declaration of war. They met again on the Sunday morning, a fact sufficient in itself to indicate the seriousness of the business on hand. Daily they had been urging on the completion of Luton's civil defence preparations, but always with a lingering hope that the crisis might yet be averted. Suspending their discussion when Mr. Chamberlain came on the air, they listened to the broadcast. Then the business of the meeting was resumed. It had become even more urgent.

*   *   *   *

Already much had been done to prepare Luton for war. For nearly three years A.R.P. matters had figured with increasing frequency on Council agendas, an Air Raid Committee had been formed, and the Chief Constable, Mr. G. E. Scott, appointed as co-ordinating officer. It had been agreed that in the event of war he should combine with his police duties that of A.R.P. Controller.

War stopped practically all the ordinary work of the Town Council, and for a time they discontinued their twice-monthly meetings, while committee meetings were also suspended. Routine work had to go on, but some major projects which were in hand had received a severe jolt as early as the previous March. Some had to proceed, but without any publicity which would indicate a growth of population and therefore a growth of war industry. Land was acquired at Sundon for an entirely new electricity generating station, and it had to be assumed that this was merely a step preparatory to some future development. No mention could be made of the fact that it actually became the site of a new grid-tapping station, without which the power demands of the war factories in and around Luton could not have been met. The construction of the new sewage disposal works near Chiltern Green also went ahead. The clearance of slum areas had to be suspended, for in wartime even bad houses could not be spared. Defence measures had to take precedence over all work that could be deferred. Not even summer holidays could be allowed to interfere.

*   *   *   *

The Emergency Committee continued to meet daily, and sometimes twice daily, until September 14th. Then, everything being completed as far as was practicable, they reduced their meetings to three a week, although every Corporation department was working at full pressure on something connected with defence. Basements had to be shored up to provide shelters, trench shelters made in the less built-up areas. Camouflage of buildings, distribution of Anderson shelters, maintenance of food and fuel supplies . . . there were many important things to be watched.

A Food Control Committee had been appointed and held its first meeting even before the Board of Trade issued an Order that this should be done. A Fuel Advisory Committee was quickly set up. Then came National Registration.

*   *   *   *

Before the first month of war was out the Town Council were responsible for giving effect to some of the earliest wartime legislation

Luton Town Council in session. Councillor R. Colin Large is seen speaking in the Council chamber during the Mayor-making ceremony in November, 1945.

The white stonework of the Town Hall tower would have been an excellent pinpoint for the prying eyes of enemy airmen had it not been for the drab camouflage which covered it.

LEFT: *Members of Luton Town Council and Corporation officials inspecting the town's new sewage disposal plant at East Hyde, part of which was opened on 16th September, 1942.*

BELOW: *With the preparations for invasion, Wardown lake became a testing ground for Bedford trucks, fitted to take to the water as well as the road.* PHOTO: *Vauxhall Motors Limited.*

ABOVE: "Holidays at Home" became a familiar slogan during the war years. Here is a view of the fair in Wardown Park, taken across the lake, in August, 1944.

RIGHT: *Dr. F. Grundy, Miss H. K. Sheldon, Prof. C. E. M. Joad, Councillor A. W. Gregory, Dr. Leslie Burgin, and Sir Charles Bartlett, were the participants in this Brains Trust at Wardown Park Bandstand, in July, 1944.*

BELOW: *Spending a pleasant evening listening to the arguments of the "Brains Trusters."*

Alderman John Burgoyne, who for five of the war years was Mayor of Luton, receiving the Freedom of the Borough from Ald. Lady Keens, the town's first lady Mayor, in September, 1945.

The first four of Luton's post-war Council houses, which were completed and occupied in March, 1946.

—the National Registration Act. Although it involved the same " counting of heads " as a census, the effects were going to be much more far-reaching, When it became known that the appointed day was Friday, September 29th, 1939, and what was the extent of the information which would have to be placed on record, it caused quite a flutter in some domestic dovecotes.

The householder was responsible for ensuring that the form provided was filled in with accuracy. There was a code letter and number for each household, and a distinguishing number for each individual. Information which had to be given was the name, age, sex, and occupation of everyone in the house, whether they were single, married, divorced or widowed, and whether any of them were already in the Services. An unnamed baby had to be entered just as " Baby." Evacuees had to be included, and the particulars of night workers recorded when they returned the following morning. Hotels had to register their guests. Billeted soldiers were the only people exempt.

The object of registration was not only to obtain an accurate picture of the manpower of the nation at that particular date, but one which should remain accurate through the years. The Act made it a statutory duty to notify within seven days any change of address, even if only from one house to another in the same street. Where removal was from one registration area to another, details were sent to the Central Registration Office, and passed on to the new district. This had its particular value, as registration was also the basis of the subsequent issue of ration cards. It presumably made a " midnight flit " less easy. The experience was that an astonishing number of removals were reported even before the checking of the registration forms, on which a special staff worked twelve hours a day, had been completed.

Out of registration came not only ration cards, but also identity cards. Such cards had long been common in other countries. Here it was a new experience to have to carry one, and produce it on demand. There was also a subsequent limited issue of a personal identity card adorned with the photograph of the holder. Expected to have a special value under certain circumstances, it was rather more difficult to secure than a passport, in that it had to be applied for in person, and the applicant underwent a mild cross-examination before being relieved of his ordinary identity card and given a receipt which was valid until the special card came along from the seaside fastness of the department concerned.

*   *   *   *

The increase in the strength of the Fire Service, the large number of people who immediately became involved in full-time civil defence duty, and their long hours of duty at the start, created a feeding problem. This was met by the Corporation opening a canteen in Waller Street. Lady Keens took charge, and the need for this service was soon evident, for during the second week no fewer than 2,918 dinners and suppers and 2,632 teas were served. The canteen rendered a useful service for a long period. Throughout it was run entirely by voluntary helpers, except for one woman to assist in washing up, and a man to do the cleaning and heavy work.

* * * *

During September some members of the Council began to think they should have a little inside information as to what the Emergency Committee was doing, and a deputation went to the Mayor to advocate a special meeting of the Council. This was met to the extent of holding a meeting of the Council-in-Committee, at which the chief officers submitted detailed reports of what had been done. There was a plea that ordinary committee meetings should be resumed, but this had to be turned down in view of the amount of other work still on hand. The Emergency Committee was therefore left to carry on in its own sphere, any urgent ordinary business going to the chairman of the committee concerned, and the appropriate officials.

Council meetings were in fact resumed in the October, but on a monthly basis. With all ordinary business slowed down or suspended however, discussions continued to centre round Emergency Committee activities, and in the following February there was a move to have their business made the subject of a full monthly report to Council-in-Committee. It was not successful at that time. The Mayor was convinced of the desirability of a great deal of the work remaining as secret as possible. He told the Council he did not enjoy the responsibility imposed on the Committee, but realised its necessity.

* * * *

About this time conscientious objectors were pretty numerous, and they became the subject of keen debates, but a proposal submitted in May, 1940, that Council employees who were in this category should be given leave of absence for the duration of the war, without salary or wages, was rejected.

* * * *

Towards the end of 1940 the blackout caused the Council to change the time of their meeting from the Tuesday evening of long custom to Saturday afternoons, but it was only a passing change, and they afterwards reverted to Tuesday evenings, although not to the twice-a-month meetings of pre-war days. The " Rule of Three " was enlarged by the addition of Alderman W. F. Mullett and Councillor W. G. Roberts, and the five became six the following May, Councillor Percy Mitchell being added. Emphasis was being laid on the fact that the Emergency Committee would in that year alone be spending well over a quarter of a million on A.R.P. alone, and that, of the total, the Council would have to bear over £41,000. The next month there was an effort to get the Emergency Committee to report in open Council, but such publicity was still held to be unwise.

Compulsory firewatch, the employment of women to help in the collection of refuse and salvage, and the establishment of day nurseries to help more mothers engage in war work, were other things which came along. Having regard to the limited amount of extra labour which these day nurseries made available, they were regarded as an expensive experiment. The first were at Linden Road and Manor Road. Others were established later, but equipment and staffing were always problems. One built at Chaul End was, in fact, never used, and eventually became an annexe to the Maternity Hospital.

*　　　*　　　*　　　*

Seaside local authorities regularly engage in the entertainment industry, and so do some inland towns possessing amenities which make them popular resorts. In 1942 local authorities in general were directed to follow suit. The Government's idea was that if people were provided with entertainment at home there would be less holiday travel, and railway congestion would be relieved. So the Town Council became amusement caterers for " Holidays at Home," passing on the actual job to the Parks Committee, with some outside helpers. What effect, if any, this had on reducing railway travel is open to question, but there can be no doubt about the popularity of some of the events which were arranged.

The 1942 plan was necessarily experimental. There was no basis on which to assess the amount of public support which would be forthcoming. Some mistakes were inevitable. Actually it proved unwise to split the outdoor attractions between Wardown Park, Pope's Meadow, and the Moor, and in subsequent seasons all such shows were centred in Wardown Park. There was some grumbling, of course, when the ratepayers were later called on to subsidise the scheme, but the amount they had to pay was really small when compared with the enjoyment derived by many thousands of people, and particularly those with families. They found they could get through travel-restricted holidays much more cheerfully than would otherwise have been the case.

The other grumble which arose over Home Holiday entertainments was the use of Wardown Park year after year for a big fun fair, which stayed for some weeks. Maybe the grumble would have been justified in normal times, but in the war the Park was no longer what it had been. Buses and Army lorries parked there, the lake was used for testing waterproofed Army vehicles, and the N.F.S. built ugly pump houses and laid pipelines across the greensward. What did it matter if in the part allotted to the fair the ground was worn bare ? It recovered, was again worn bare, and again recovered before the next season came round.

But the fair, into which many who were not fair fans drifted when they left the band enclosure or some other attraction, will not be there again. " Holidays at Home " programmes will no longer be organised, the Park will be quieter, and the fairground will now be the Moor. There, in April, 1946, people saw what was as nearly as possible a revival of the April Fair which used to fill part of George Street, Park Square and Park Street, before street fairs became a thing of the past.

These Home Holiday programmes have left one good legacy. This was the discovery of a band enclosure as nearly ideal as possible. The old bandstand and surroundings lacked many desirable features. Possibly, even without a war, something better would have come. With a circus, complete with band, on one side, and a huge fun fair on the other, something had to be done for the notable bands which were engaged. The first move was an improvement, but not an adequate improvement. Then a tree-lined site near the upper bowling green was tried. With a temporary bandstand it immediately became a popular enclosure, where people sat in deck chairs for which a seaside resort had no current use, and walked over seaside shingle as they approached their seats. There was no sea or sea breeze to complete the transformation, but the right place had been found. By the next season a permanent bandstand of very modern design had been provided, with flowers blossoming in the foreground. And there bands will in future play. The only thing now lacking is cover for the audience, so that bands can play wet or fine.

*   *   *   *

Council work in time became almost routine. It was found practicable to begin consideration of things which could be done after the war. The Corporation was appointed leader of a group of ten local authorities, joined to deal with the advance preparation of housing schemes so that between adjoining areas there should be some co-ordination of planning. The Council also went ahead with planning extensive sites in Luton. Principal schemes centred on Hart Hill and Farley Hill. The scheme for the latter is the most comprehensive, for it visualises ultimate development as a complete neighbourhood unit. To this end the plan includes provision, not only for houses, but also shops and flats, a community building, reservation of a church site, and infants', junior, and senior schools. When building again became possible, however, the earliest progress was made on a Leagrave site where, because of the war, some houses had to be left unfinished.

In the meantime, to meet particularly pressing needs for accommodation, local authorities were given requisitioning powers. The object was to prevent houses remaining empty for an unreasonable time pending sale at an inflated price. Where a house became vacant a requisitioning notice was served immediately, sometimes on the very day it was vacated. Then it was up to interested parties to convince the Council that the new occupier was taking possession within a reasonable time. A fortnight was the usual period of grace. In some big houses more than one family was put under requisitioning powers. The material gain by requisitioning, however, was not great, and it is doubtful whether it offset the considerable resentment often created.

*   *   *   *

In the autumn of 1943, the curtain of the municipal stage rose to reveal the county borough status question.

Stockwood became the war-time home of the Alexandra Orthopaedic Hospital evacuated from London. The mansion, together with 263 acres of the estate, was purchased by Luton Town Council in September, 1945.

It was a revival of a thorny subject. Years ago Luton's application in this direction was unsuccessful, and in the years between it had continued to be a sore point that Luton did not have full control of its own affairs.

The Council appointed a special committee to take the necessary steps preliminary to another application. It was urged that Luton could submit an excellent case and was quite capable of shouldering the extra responsibilities consequent upon becoming a county borough.

When the matter was raised, the procedure to be followed was still unchanged, and a special Act of Parliament would have been necessary. But later a change in the law brought into existence the Local Government Boundary Commission, which did not adjudicate on claim and counter-claim as between local authorities, but was empowered to collect its own evidence and make its own proposals for status and boundary revision. The Council therefore issued a plan showing suggested extension of boundaries. The plan showed first what was regarded as the minimum necessary expansion. It showed by progressive stages additional areas which would be acceptable if the Commissioners thought proper to allot them to Luton. The maximum area visualised as a possible county borough of Luton was shown as extending southwards to the Hertfordshire border. Towards Bedford, it included the village of Barton. Only part of Harlington appeared within the " acceptable " boundary, which extended well beyond Toddington, crossed the Watling Street well north of Hockliffe, included Heath and Reach, on the Leighton Buzzard boundary, and then went to the Buckinghamshire boundary so that Eaton Bray would be included. It brought in Studham, Whipsnade, Kensworth and Caddington. The problem of the neighbouring borough of Dunstable, said the explanatory note issued with the plan, was for Dunstable itself to solve, by considering whether it wished to retain its individuality or throw in its lot with Luton.

The publication of the plan, however, brought fierce opposition from Bedfordshire County Council, who objected to Luton becoming a county borough with or without extension. They had opposed Luton's previous application. For a long time they had opposed the Leagrave and Limbury incorporation, only withdrawing when the public inquiry stage was reached. Had that opposition been pursued successfully, Beechwood Road and many other roads in the old parishes of Leagrave and Limbury would have continued in a state akin to Bunyan's Slough of Despond.

The position was complicated by changes due to new legislation, and other centralisation proposals which were in the air. Higher education in Luton had always been a county affair. The Education Act of 1945, transferred Luton's elementary schools to the county authority, although a local committee was given some limited delegated powers. To retain even these powers Luton had to fight, and it cannot be said that this transfer improved the relations between town and county.   In addition had come the proposal that non-county boroughs should no longer be independent police authorities, and that their police forces should be merged into the county constabularies.   Similarly there was the proposal that Fire Brigades, taken away from the control of local authorities and combined in the National Fire Service for the war period, should not return to the local authorities which previously maintained them, which was the understanding, but should also be handed over to the county.   As a county borough, Luton felt it would have a right to resume control of these services, though the sorting out promised to be a pretty business.

*   *   *   *

Another notable wartime decision of the Council was one not concerned with the problems of the time or even with utilitarian matters, but one which aimed solely at catering for the pleasure of generations yet to come.   In 1945 the Council had an opportunity to buy Stockwood Park and mansion for £100,000.   They took the opportunity.   The park of 263 acres was laid out, and the mansion completed just 200 years earlier by John Crawley, member of a family identified with Luton for 500 years.   Until the war began it was still the home of a direct descendant, Mrs. Crawley Ross Skinner, but then it became the wartime home of the Alexandra Hospital for Crippled Children, evacuated from Swanley, Kent, and it was understood early on that Lieut.-Col. and Mrs. Ross Skinner did not propose to occupy the mansion again.

There were critics, of course, who asked, " Can Luton, in these times, afford to spend £100,000 on another park, when there are so many other and more urgent requirements ? "   There had been much more vigorous opposition years ago when the Council of the time decided to buy the property now known as Wardown Park.   To buy even that 50 acres for a park was an extravagance, they argued at that time, and one that Luton could not afford.   Luton, however, decided to afford it, and for many years now the wisdom of the purchase has been recognised.   Had the Council not bought Wardown at the time the speculative builder would before long have got busy.   Luton, like other towns, will always be peopled by two classes—those who blame past authorities for the present shortcomings of the town, and those who will raise their voices in protest and ask, " Can we afford it ? " when an opportunity occurs to do something for the future.

The use to be made of the mansion when the Alexandra Hospital has found other accommodation has, at the time of writing, still to be decided.   The one thing made clear when the purchase was announced was that the Park was not intended for housing, as for this purpose the Council had also bought 105 acres of Farley Farm, a neighbouring part of the Crawley estate.   Nor was the net cost to be £100,000, for part of this was offset by the sale of land on the Brache Estate, never developed as planned, and the allotments known as the Marsletts. It was this latter feature which caused something approaching a bitter

41

controversy. The plotholders could not be convinced that the purpose to which the land was to be put justified their disturbance, or that if they were re-established on permanent allotments at Stockwood they would not still be the losers. These things, however, settle themselves in time. What is quite certain is that there will grow up generations of Lutonians who will be satisfied that the authorities of our day, however much they may have failed in other things, " backed a winner " when they decided that Stockwood should belong to the town.

*   *   *   *

In another direction the Council also took steps to provide for an unknown future. For years they have provided wards in which babies can be born. Now they provide graves in which people can be buried. They have yet to follow the example of some other countries in making the Town Hall a popular marriage centre, but in taking over the Luton General Cemetery as a going concern, they had in mind that in time to come it may be desirable to establish a crematorium, to which a necessary preliminary is that the Council shall already be a burial authority.

*   *   *   *

Suspension of local elections throughout the war meant that there were few changes in the personnel of the Council during those years. An outstanding record of service was that of Alderman John Burgoyne —he became an alderman in 1943—who successfully shouldered the responsibilities and duties of mayor for six successive years. This was a record for Luton and made at a time when the Mayoralty could be little short of a full-time job. Succeeded in November, 1945, by Lady Keens, he afterwards received the honorary freedom of the borough, and in the New Year honours of 1945 was awarded the O.B.E.

Councillor F. C. Ellingham died in February, 1940, and Mr. A. C. Richardson was co-opted to the Council. Councillor Jack Harrison was granted leave of absence on joining the R.A.F. in 1941, and at the end of that year the Council received the resignation of Alderman Harry Arnold, " Father " of the Council, whose service had extended over forty years. An honorary freeman since 1935, he was followed on the aldermanic bench by Councillor Harry Brooker, and Mr. H. C. Janes joined the Council. Councillor H. G. Day, who had taken an appointment under the Ministry of Supply in November, 1939, resigned from the Council in 1942. This created a vacancy in the High Town Ward, where a second was caused by Lady Keens becoming an Alderman following the resignation of Alderman P. W. Currant. Their successors were Messrs. E. K. Hickman and R. R. Hunter. Councillor Percy Mitchell died in June, 1942, and was succeeded by Mr. G. L. Hey. Alderman C. C. Dillingham, Deputy Mayor throughout the war until he died in 1943, was succeeded as alderman by Councillor John Burgoyne, and Mrs. Bart Milner joined the Council.

Another vacancy, caused by the death of Councillor Peter Mitchell in January, 1945, was filled by Mr. A. E. Meeks.

Others who served during the war were Aldermen A. E. Ansell, S. H. Godfrey, O. E. Hart, W. F. Mullett and A. E. Nicholls ; Councillors G. Bavister, W. J. Edwards, P. G. Gladwell, A. W. Gregory, H. S. Hewson, T. H. Knight, W. J. Lane, R. C. Large, H. C. Lawrence, R. C. Oakley, F. J. Randall, W. G. Roberts, G. F. Seaward, C. A. Sinfield, T. Skelton, S. Smith, S. B. J. Snoxell, W. G. Veals and P. R. Williams.

Chief officials who served throughout the war were the Town Clerk, Mr. W. H. Robinson ; Borough Treasurer, Mr. F. Bunting ; Borough Engineer, Mr. F. Oliver ; Medical Officer of Health, Dr. F. Grundy ; Director of Education, Mr. E. O. Cutter ; Librarian, Mr. F. Gardner ; Transport Manager, Mr. C. S. A. Wickens ; Director of Parks, Mr. R. J. English ; Sewage Farm Manager, Mr. C. Hamlin, and Aerodrome Manager, Mr. H. T. Rushton.

Chief Officer A. Andrew retired from the Fire Brigade early in 1941, and from February of the following year Mr. J. Stephen, Director of Public Cleansing, was lent to the Ministry of Supply to act as Deputy Assistant Director of Salvage, Mr. C. V. Roberts taking over his duties. The Borough Electrical Engineer, Mr. Rennie Dean, died in March, 1943, and was succeeded by Mr. C. T. Melling. In the autumn of 1944, Mr. G. E. Scott left to become Chief Constable of Newcastle-on-Tyne, and Mr. Ronald Alderson came from Macclesfield to succeed him in the combined posts of Chief Constable and A.R.P. Controller.

Wardens on the Watch

JOE and Ben, Shorty and Jack, were four very ordinary Luton individuals who during the war got to know quite a great deal about each other and about their part of the town.

They met every fourth night in a stuffy little room and—according to the weather or the Luftwaffe's immediate plans—they made tea, swapped yarns and played cards, or walked the streets wearing tin hats and carrying rattles and first aid kits.

They were air raid wardens on the look-out for trouble. Sometimes it came. More often it did not, but they were always ready for it.

They knew all there was to be known about the game of solo. They could also tell you how many people there were in any given house, whether those people sheltered under the stairs or in an outdoor

Anderson, where the nearest fire hydrant was, how to treat a Potts fracture, whether a hole in the road was made by a small bomb that had gone off or a large bomb that hadn't ; and at a pinch they might have made quite useful midwives.

They were the smallest unit of one of the many branches of Luton's Civil Defence services. Every night for five years they and their counterparts stood by—human cogs in a vast and complicated organisation slowly built up, improved and extended to cover every possible contingency that might follow air attack.

To shelter the people from bomb and splinter, to rescue the injured, to house the homeless, to clear up the mess, to keep the life of the town going—these were the main aims of A.R.P., as it was first called, and it covered an immense range, from mending shattered gas mains to finding out what happened to the pet kitten of little Maisie Smith-Jones who, homeless after the raid, refused to be comforted without it.

*   *   *   *

There had been many portents of the storm that was to come, and many who refused to heed these portents. It was well for the town that some were more weatherwise, and insisted on preparations. For what they would have to prepare was largely guesswork. The experiences of 1914-18 were no real guide. That there would be no Zeppelins coming over Luton again was small comfort. The air held vastly greater potential risks. It was natural that all precautionary plans in the early days should have as their basis the perils which might come from above in the form of high explosive or gas. Even as early as 1935 consideration was being given as to how best the people could be given protection against bombs. One of the earliest suggestions was that tunnels should be driven into the hills around Luton. Mr. G. E. Scott, as A.R.P. Controller, with the then Borough Engineer, Mr. J. W. Tomlinson, went to Dover to see the tunnels driven into similar chalk hills during the previous war, and were very much impressed. In fact, Mr. Scott said they were the finest tunnels he had ever seen. But the four tunnels which did become an important feature of Luton's safety provision were not tunnels into the outside hills. The main reason why that idea was abandoned was that few people would be able to reach them quickly, and such people could be equally well provided for, at much less cost, by giving them the Anderson steel domestic shelters for each family which had been developed before the construction of tunnels had become practical politics.

The basic idea of tunnels was to give shelter to the thousands of people who might want it suddenly if caught in the streets, although in experience they proved to have a more practical value as sleeping quarters, and were later adapted for this purpose by the provision of bunks. To assess how many were likely to be put in need of sudden shelter, counts were made of the number of people in George Street and other central streets at peak periods like Saturday afternoons. The maximum was found to be in the region of 15,000. For these busy areas tunnels, supplemented by reinforced basements, were decided upon. Test borings were made for five tunnels, but the one projected for Park Street, which later suffered more damage than any other area, had to be abandoned because of the high water level in the ground.

The four which were constructed were known as the Upper George Street, High Town, Beech Hill, and Albert Road tunnels. In each case their ramifications underground extended into other streets, so that in all they had many points of approach. Those at High Town and Beech Hill were the deepest. The four cost over £70,000, and chief constructional troubles were experienced in the tunnel which ran from Upper George Street under Gordon Street and Alma Street to Inkerman Street. There was some fault in the strata, with the result that, following a heavy storm, there were two collapses while only temporary supports were in use, and before the tunnel was lined. It caused delay in opening this tunnel, and there was a minor repercussion when a building in Gordon Street, adjoining the Union Cinema, was affected by subsidence. The tunnel could not be proved responsible. It was equally difficult to prove that it was not a contributory factor. The Corporation compromised by contributing to the cost of underpinning the building.

When Luton was having its nightly alarms and occasional bombs the tunnels were used by thousands of people, and they were not always the people who lived in the immediate neighbourhood. Some came in from the outskirts, and it was rumoured that among these there were people who were rather particular with whom they associated, and that they did not go to the handiest tunnel, but to the one where they thought they would be among the best people.

Apart from those who only dived underground when danger threatened, there were others who made it a nightly practice, siren or no siren, to be on the safe side. They seemed to consider security for the night outweighed any discomforts. In the mornings they could be seen moving homewards with their blankets or rugs, and sometimes deck chairs, looking a bit dishevelled, but content with having had one more night in safety.

The shelterers created some problems. Steps had to be taken to ensure that the tunnels were used only for the purpose for which they were intended, and that they did not become the haunts of undesirables who were seeking to escape notice elsewhere. There were some of these, but they found the tunnels less attractive when the police decided to make occasional visitations. For the real shelterers, tunnel marshals did some very good service in seeing to the well-being of the people in their charge.

Additional shelter in the central area was provided for about 4,000 people in shop and warehouse basements, specially shored up by the Borough Engineer's Department. Originally more than twice the number were selected, but in all they would have provided accommodation for only a few hundred more people, and the number was revised at the instigation of the Home Office. Those actually used were selected from a great number offered by firms and individuals during the critical time just before the war began.

For the outer areas trench shelters had been dug when the Munich crisis was at its height. Digging and sandbagging was then an unusually popular pastime. The trenches, somewhat hasty constructions at the time, were considerably improved and strengthened later. Except in the early stages, when people in the open were directed to take cover if the sirens sounded, the trenches were not much used ; but at that time, when there was utter uncertainty as to what might happen, they created a certain amount of public confidence. The trench shelters at the schools did far more to justify their cost, and in one instance at least, when a raider did heavy damage opposite Old Bedford Road School, the children owed their complete safety to their shelters, plus the fact that there had been ample warning time for teachers to take the children to safety.

*　　*　　*　　*

Many individual families came to have cause to bless the fact that they agreed to bury an Anderson steel shelter in the garden. Over 10,000 were supplied. Fewer availed themselves of the Morrison indoor shelter which was a later idea. Brick surface shelters, generally built in the roadway, but often in front or back gardens, were another development, the value of which, as it happened, was never severely tested in Luton.

Now basements and cellars have been cleared and restored to their normal purpose. Some, but not all, of the trenches have been filled in. Digging up Anderson shelters was a job nobody seemed inclined to tackle with the hurry they showed in burying them. Brick shelters continue to obstruct some streets. The tunnels remain, in a state of disuse which will probably continue, for it is difficult to see to what useful purpose they can be put. If in process of time their entrances and exits disappear, so that there is no visible reminder of these underground burrowings, and they join the things that are forgotten ; if, in some future age remnants of them are discovered, the historians of that age will have more reliable data about the original purpose than had those wise men who pondered over holes on the hills round Luton, and affirmed that they were made by Neolithic man for safety from a known or unknown enemy, or simply as a quick and cheap solution of an early housing problem.

*　　*　　*　　*

It may be asked, if A.R.P. had been under consideration since about 1935, why so little seemed to have been done, why so much had to be done in a frantic hurry in the end, and what would have been the position if Munich had not staved off things for a year. Everybody was in the dark about what ought to be done. Even higher authority dallied in settling a defined policy and, until that was done, what

Vauxhall employees in cheerful mood as they dig trench shelters near their works in October, 1938.

Many hands make light work as the health centre at the corner of Dunstable Road and Beechwood Road is barricaded with sandbags.

ABOVE: *A scene reminiscent of a coal mine, as workmen hack away at the chalk face inside one of Luton's tunnel shelters.*

BELOW: *Some of the brick and concrete surface shelters which gave confidence to thousands of Luton people during the raids.*

In October, 1939, Luton's first consignment of Anderson shelters arrived, and the public were shown how they should be erected.

Pupils of Denbigh Road School file to their shelter in an orderly manner during an A.R.P. practice.

A home built dug-out becomes flooded after heavy rain.

Beneath the symbol of Peace, Luton's memorial to the dead of World War I, weirdly-clad members of an anti-gas squad of World War II carry out a demonstration.

should have been everybody's business was in fact nobody's business. It was a long time before Luton secured freedom to do as it thought best, but when that stage was reached, everything was pushed ahead with vigour. It has also to be remembered that while there seemed no imminent danger there was no rush of volunteers to lend a hand in any scheme of communal security, although there were plenty when the need was obvious.

All that could be done was to lay the foundations of a Civil Defence scheme, designed to permit of rapid expansion. The attitude of the time was clearly shown in connection with the issue of gas masks. There had been no rush to train in anti-gas measures, possibly because people were hard to convince that a gas attack from the air could be sufficiently concentrated to be effective. But with the public issue of gas masks at the time of Munich, a lot of people were not quite so certain, and 67,000 of these uncertain people in Luton promptly collected a gas mask each. That wasn't by any means all the people, of course, and although another 17,000 did likewise in a subsequent " special week," there were many who waited until a state of war had been declared before admitting to themselves that a respirator " might" be useful.

*　　　*　　　*　　　*

Enrolment of wardens began in 1937. The late Alderman C. C. Dillingham, in addition to being Mayor at the time, was also chairman of the A.R.P. Committee, and became chief warden. He continued as chief warden until ill-health caused him to resign late in 1942, and he lived only a few months longer. With the Chief Constable also being A.R.P. Controller, it was natural that a lot of organising work should be done by the police, and quite early on Sgt. John Thomson, who later became an inspector, was assigned to A.R.P. work, his services in this capacity being ultimately recognised by the award of the B.E.M. Eventually three officers were devoting full time to the work, which grew enormously as time went on, and particularly when incendiary bombs made it necessary to institute the fire-watching scheme. Of this Sgt. Whiffin, who also became an inspector, had charge.

For a time, however, the scheme had to remain in skeleton form. Its principal value was that it produced people prepared to go away for specialised training, so that they could be instructors when the rush of volunteers came, and that there was time to make careful plans for the co-ordination and co-operation of other services which would be in action in raids.

In one of the earliest forms of the A.R.P. scheme the town was divided into four groups, each with head and deputy head warden. The groups were divided into 84 sectors. The scheme needed 650 air raid wardens. That was considered on the low side, but that was as many volunteers as it had been possible to secure apart from those associated with works schemes. This scheme was greatly expanded when volunteers became plentiful, in a manner referred to later on.

Based from the beginning on part-time, unpaid volunteers, the scheme was found to need a leavening of paid personnel for some day duties, and particularly in the early stages of the war, when it was considered desirable that some wardens' posts should be open the whole 24 hours. In time the number was reduced from over 200 to 160. The wage bill was considerable, but it was not a local liability. Then Sir John Anderson, to save the country five millions a year, ordered a further general cut, and Luton's 160 came down to 60. It meant that some posts could no longer be kept open continuously, although they were always opened immediately a raid warning was sounded.

*　　*　　*　　*

An effective system of siren warnings of impending raids was not without its problems. At first there was a test of the factory hooters which were no longer permitted to warn men to hurry to work, but it was found that there were " dead spots " where not one of these was audible. The question of whether electricity could be relied on had to be considered, for the possibility of bombing causing an interruption of supply could not be ignored. In the end electric, steam, and compressed air sirens were all used. There were fourteen, so distributed that every area received a clear warning. Eventually all were operated from Central Control by remote control which also operated the Dunstable sirens.

First tests somewhat startled the people, but after they had heard many genuine warnings they hardly seemed to notice the brief Monday morning tests which became routine to ensure that all were in working order.

When the sirens were first sounded in earnest the majority of the part-time personnel were mobilised in a few minutes, and were on patrol with their rattles and handbells. There was no bombing, no gas. As a contrast, Luton's first attack from the air came without warning, but the whole service was quickly in action. It was a pretty heavy raid, although it did not last long, and next day there were many volunteers for the large amount of work still to be done, while not a few neglected their normal work for some days. When warnings became very frequent, key personnel remained at headquarters or their posts all night, while from the beginning of 1941 until February, 1945, six wardens reported for sleeping duty each night at the larger posts, and three at the smaller ones. They had some unusual experiences, even when there was no air activity.

The story is told of one agitated householder who dashed into a post and declared that a bomb had fallen in his garden, but not exploded. The wardens were sceptical. The householder would not be satisfied, so the wardens went to search the garden. It was a very dark night. The part of the garden where the bomb was supposed to have fallen was in a somewhat wild state, with grass, and wet grass at that, about two feet long. The wardens toiled all night, and found

52

nothing. No bomb has since exploded in that area, so it can be assumed that there was no bomb. It was just one of the things the wardens had to do as part of their job.

There is also the story of the lady who returned home one day to find what looked like a " butterfly bomb " in the garden. She told her neighbours, who promptly cleared all their children out and took cover while someone went to fetch the Warden. The warden took one look and sent for the bomb disposal squad. The bomb disposal squad took one look, picked up the alleged butterfly bomb and dropped it into the dustbin. It was a discarded ball cock and valve from a lavatory cistern.

*   *   *   *

Having regard to the almost lighthearted way in which people seemed to ignore the sound of the sirens in daylight during the later stages of the war—although up to the last they gave most people a creepy feeling at night—it is interesting to recall an eve-of-war statement. This was :—" Luton's defence preparations are being pushed ahead. The public may rest assured that everything is being done to safeguard them in the event of war. The elaborate A.R.P. scheme is moving smoothly, and all arrangements are progressing rapidly. Some trenches are ready, and work on the remainder is proceeding rapidly.

" *People will be urged to get off the streets immediately on the sounding of a raid warning. Those near their own homes should stay in their own shelter or house. The same applies to people at or near their work.*"

*   *   *   *

People did not have long to wait. The first siren sounded in Luton as a raid warning on September 6th, when the war was only three days old. It was at a time before most business of the day had started, although workers were going to the factories. People were told to take cover. They took cover. The whole town came to a standstill and in practically every street one could have heard a pin drop. Not until the warning was over did police or wardens look kindly on anyone who was out in the streets. People did not seem to realise that after all only advice, and not an order, to take cover could be given. Even so, it was one of the many things in which during wartime it was advisable to adopt a helpful rather than obstructive attitude. Nobody knew what was likely to happen. In fact, nothing did happen on that first occasion, except to prove the promptness with which those with duties to perform could be about those duties.

The start of war caused a last-minute flurry for gas masks. There was some dissatisfaction because the special respirators for babies and small children were not available, and this caused a spate of inquiries from anxious parents before the little Mickey Mouse respirators arrived for issue. Then contex filters had to be added to all adults' respirators as a further precaution, and when evacuee children arrived there had to be house-to-house enquiries to check up what was wanted.

An issue of ear-plugs followed, leaving people to think that Luton was to have heavy A.A. guns, but it had no guns. When a large-scale inspection of civilian masks was carried out some of the early issues already proved to be sadly in need of repair. The only container issued officially for the civilian mask was a cardboard carton. There was no haversack or satchel of any kind for carrying convenience. Many immediately came on to the market or were made by those who had the facilities. A metal cylinder seemed most popular. They weren't all so well made that they could be exempt from suspicion of causing some of the damage.

The gas which was so much feared did not come to worry anyone, and wardens and other defence volunteers who might have had to wear anti-gas clothing, even for a short time, were profoundly grateful. It was not nice to wear even when inactive.

Instead, the wardens found one of their chief responsibilities in the quiet periods was in helping to enforce the blackout regulations. These were not without seeming anomalies. Vehicles could show lights, but light must not be allowed to escape from a " roofed building," a term which figured prominently in summonses against the fairly numerous offenders.

The story is told of a badly-fitting front door near the Luton stream which is dignified by the name of the River Lea. Two inches of light showed under the door. Zealous patrolling wardens promptly knocked, and the householder, who prided himself on his blackout, did not like it.

" What," he snorted, " are they coming up the adjectival river in submarines now ? "

Maybe this was an extreme case of adhering to the letter of the law, but there was plenty of need for watchfulness. Blackout at front windows might be perfect, but not that at the back, and often there was good reason for wardens to go on the prowl, especially as a night reconnaissance of Luton from the air led to an official report that far too much light was to be seen. Some offending lights were elusive. They could not be located at close quarters, or from ground level. There was one in particular which caused a lot of trouble, and it only ceased to offend after, according to the story told in court, bearings had been carefully taken so that the building from which the light emanated could be identified in daylight.

*   *   *   *

Training for the Civil Defence services was both intensive and thorough. It was constantly being brought up to date in the light of experience gained in Luton and elsewhere, and in answer to new methods of enemy attack and new weapons. One of the chief centres of training in Luton was a piece of ground at Stopsley, most of which was left in its rough state, with numerous hollows and clumps of bushes.

Wardens would be taken there, and sent round in small parties in search of various signs and objects. These they had to recognise and identify, and then shape their actions accordingly.

It was a favourite trick at this training ground for an instructor, conveniently hidden up wind behind some bushes, to release tear gas on the unsuspecting wardens as they stood grouped round another instructor or diligently carried on their search. Someone would shout a warning, or sound a rattle if he had one, respirators would be out of haversacks and on in a space of time that would shame any parade ground respirator drill, and the party would carry on.

Another note of realism would be struck when—without warning— the whine of a falling bomb would be heard. Done on a sort of tin whistle, it would sound enough like the real thing to make the wardens flatten themselves before the resultant explosion—the firing of a bomb already on the ground.

A half-built house, specially erected for the purpose, was also used at Stopsley for staging realistic incidents, and a " house front " of corrugated iron, with a window and sill at first floor level, was used to teach the gentle art of lowering people to safety from burning buildings. The art lay in manipulating the rope, and the largest member of the party was generally chosen to make the first descent. It never looked very safe, especially when he was lowered by a man only half his size, but science always won.

Other training was carried out at intervals by staging large-scale " incidents " in the streets and in various buildings. At one of these " incidents " a warden grimly struggled up to the flat roof of a high building in search of casualties which the narrative informed him were there. They were soldiers, and according to the labels setting out their injuries, they were in a bad way. They were also down wind from a gas bomb crater, so the warden dutifully started to put on the respirators they conveniently carried. He got a shock. " Have a heart, mate," they said: " We were just all set for a quiet smoke up here out of the way."

*   *   *   *

By the time they were called upon to function in earnest, the Civil Defence Services had been strengthened very considerably. The town was regarded as two divisions, each with five air raid wardens' groups ; ten new head and deputy wardens had been chosen, and the post warden had come into existence. There were 165 sectors, with the parish of Hyde tacked on as a separate unit. Some of the re-planning came into effect after an official deputation had been to Paris to study what was being done there. They found the Parisian muni-cipal authorities very helpful and hospitable, and were glad they went while there was yet time.

As part of the policy to secure co-ordinated effort among all services a technical committee was a very useful help. It included the Chief Constable, as A.R.P. Controller, the Town Clerk, the Borough Engineer, the Medical Officer, the Electrical Engineer, the Fire Brigade

Chief, the Transport Manager, Mr. W. Phillips for the Gas Company, and Mr. P. C. Phillips for the Water Company.

*   *   *   *

The sort of thing Luton might have to expect had been demonstrated just about the time of the Munich crisis. To facilitate a big-scale, practical test of Luton's A.R.P. organisation, planes swooped over the Marston Gardens area, bombs exploded, " houses " were damaged, and one partly demolished. Within twenty minutes there was a second dive-bombing raid, with incendiaries being used. It was a really good experience for A.R.P. personnel. The one disappointing feature was that enough of the public did not bother to attend, so it did not cause the desired influx of recruits. If the display did not have this effect, the Munich crisis did. It also set a lot of people digging their own shelters. They had begun to take the threat of war seriously.

So that they should not, and could not, ignore it, there was another demonstration. This was held right in the centre of the town, when the streets were at their fullest on a Saturday evening. Air raid effects were repeated, " casualties " had to be cleared, and gas decontamination of the street carried out. Thousands of people then saw an effective demonstration of what was being practised for their protection, and who was practising, for it brought into operation not only air raid wardens but also St. John Ambulance and Red Cross detachments, the W.V.S., the Fire Brigade (as it still was), regular and special police, rescue squads, ambulances, the medical services, and even the messenger services. Holding the demonstration held up everything else in the heart of the town. It had some useful effect on recruiting.

When sirens became available there was another big-scale exercise, to test the speed with which A.R.P. would function when a wailing warning was given.

*   *   *   *

A gas test was staged in some of Luton's central streets, with George Street as the main scene of operations. Quite a number of people were caught without their masks, and they were advised to keep clear of the area, from which traffic was diverted. People who had masks were not allowed to approach the area without first putting them on, and in several instances the wardens put children's masks on for them, to ensure that they were worn properly. That was in the days when everybody was expected to carry a mask, when there were gas indicator boards dotted about the town, and when employees who had not brought them were refused admittance to some of the big works.

What a difference there was as time went on. Eventually no-one carried a mask, or was expected to do so !

*   *   *   *

The secret of success in dealing with an " incident " was prompt work and the close dovetailing of all the branches of Civil Defence that were in action, both on the spot and way back at depots and centres.

56

ABOVE: *Two young ladies receive expert attention as they have their respirators fitted.*

LEFT: *Fully covered by his anti-gas clothing, a police officer uses a portable loud speaker to give warning of gas in a mock attack.*

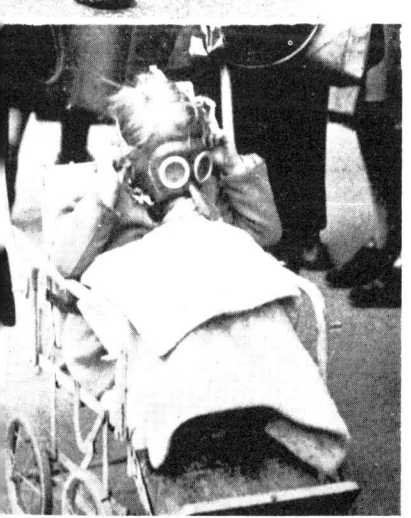

little girl who took heed of the warning . . .

and the man who didn't.

ABOVE: *With his binoculars at the ready, one of the roof spotters, who were employed by many Luton firms, to watch and listen for enemy aircraft.*

LEFT: *A member of an anti-gas squad dons the cumbersome protective clothing at an A.R.P. display.*

Schoolchildren being taught by an air raid warden the correct method of handling a stirrup pump.

Bombs were intended as much to cause confusion and chaos as they were to inflict damage and cause loss of life. It was the task of the Civil Defence services to defeat both of these aims, and to this end the A.R.P. Controller laid great emphasis on what was called " incident control." He trained many Incident Officers, whose job it was to direct operations on the spot. It was no easy job, for the smallest incident covered a fairly large area, and it meant sizing up a situation not only from what one could see but from what one was told by contact men. It meant deploying different services in their right order and to the maximum effect, usually in darkness, and always (at first) in confusion.

Civil Defence workers will not easily forget some of the scenes in which they took part. The one that looked the worst—although from the point of view of casualties it was not the worst—was that in Park Street caused by a parachute mine on a Sunday night late in September, 1940.

Houses turned into piles of rubble and splintered woodwork, houses with their fronts gone, houses with naked rafters and shattered chimney stacks showing gauntly against a moonlit sky, streets thickly covered with wreckage over which it was difficult to pick one's way— this was Park Street on the night when services from all over the town concentrated on the spot. Devastation was great and widespread. It looked as though a battle had swept through the place.

Against this background the work of rescue began, and it went on all through the night.

There were other incidents, most of them not so large, but the setting was always the same—rubble, brickdust, shattered glass, blood-stained casualties, and toiling rescuers. And always there was the most dramatic of all moments, when the shout, " Quiet ! " would go up and be passed along until a deathly silence had settled on the grim scene. Then in the stillness a rescue party would listen for the sound of any people trapped under debris. A cry, or a faint knocking, and the suspense would be broken, the digging, the human chain passing the bricks and timber piece by piece, would start again, desperately fighting against time, trying to get to the injured, trying to get them out while they still had a hold on life.

*   *   *   *

" Jim Crows " were a development of the period when raid warnings were so frequent that much time was being lost in the big factories through employees having to go to the shelters even though a threatened raid did not materialise. The outcome was the develop‌ment of a system of " roof spotters," the aim being to give confidence that work could continue safely after an " alert," and that there would be an " imminent danger " warning if necessary. To start the system, P.c. Davey attended a special course for spotters at Hendon. On his return instructional courses were organised, including visits to posts of the Royal Observer Corps, to Luton Airport, and to Hatfield, for height judging and recognition tests. All firms in Bedfordshire and Huntingdonshire had opportunity to send representatives, and 158 did so within a few weeks. Those qualified returned to train other spotters. Soon spotters could be seen perched on most of the big buildings, generally with some useful protection for themselves, and those barrels on poles appeared as an adjunct to the spotters' posts. With a barrel still at the top of the pole, there was nothing to worry about. If the barrel dropped, then it was a case of take cover, and quickly. It saved a lot of works' time which would otherwise have been lost.

Complementary to this scheme was a further warning system by which imminent danger could be indicated from observation posts. Key posts were proposed, and it was suggested that these should be linked with Royal Observer Corps posts, a direct approach being made to Lord Beaverbrook and Fighter Command. Then came a national scheme under which an alarms controller was stationed at each Royal Observer Corps centre, and warnings were given to Luton whenever a hostile plane was within 15 miles. " Release " messages were circulated in the same way. All firms included in the Luton scheme were linked to Central Control by bell circuits, which repeated the alarm throughout the works, and in the first six months of working 130 hours' working time, representing 20,000 man-hours were saved in one factory alone. The alarms were also transmitted to key wardens' posts, and later the scheme was extended to include loud speakers over which the plottings of enemy planes were broadcast, so that the work could continue until the enemy turned towards the town.

Luton was one of the few places in the country where this broadcast system was installed, and it was further adapted for the Fighter Priority message system, subsequently introduced. Under this system brief details were at once transmitted to Regional Headquarters of the fall of any bombs or flares.

Some of the Luton observation posts were also the means of giving bearings of bomb or flare incidents before police or wardens could send the information. First information, of course, was scanty, and had to be supplemented by reports from other sources to assess the amount of help required, but when Luton had its one rocket bomb the system enabled ambulances to be dispatched within one minute.

*   *   *   *

Mutual aid between neighbouring authorities was expected to play an important part in Civil Defence, and in fact did so. Luton, Bedfordshire and Hertfordshire joined in a very early scheme for help to be sent to raided areas from areas not attacked, but although regional headquarters were notified, the scheme remained for a long time without regional backing. The scheme was worked out in great detail, with departure points on the main roads out of the town, and rendezvous points where incoming services could expect to meet guides. Twice parties came to Luton under this mutual aid scheme, and once Luton sent assistance as far as Norwich, after the "Baedeker" raid on that city.

Before these emergencies arose the scheme had been thoroughly tested. Luton had sent parties in answer to test calls from elsewhere, and once called for five other districts to join in a comprehensive mutual aid exercise. The call brought a rescue party from Welwyn, ambulances, first aid parties and a mobile canteen from Hemel Hempstead, and other ambulances and first aid parties from Harpenden, Hitchin and Letchworth. It was considered well worth while, for it revealed some weaknesses which otherwise might not have shown themselves in time to be remedied.

In connection with mutual aid the foresight of another early Luton move was demonstrated. Some six months before the war began, Luton began to build up a branch of the Civil Defence service devoted solely to communications. It originated in the offer by Mr. T. I. Pabst, secretary of Luton and District Motor Cycling Club, to place the services of the club at the disposal of the town in case of emergency. When the war started there were many volunteers for this service, and although it had to be augmented by full-time messengers, with their own headquarters in Waller Street, those early volunteers showed a public spirit which was much appreciated.

After the first experience of enemy attack the scheme was extended to include depots in the Memorial Park, at Chaul End, and at Round Green, the distribution of anti-tetanus serum to first aid posts on the fall of bombs or even warnings of an impending raid, and other duties. The withdrawal of the basic petrol ration was a handicap to the scheme which was never entirely overcome, but that was not the fault of the motor-cycle volunteers.

The anti-tetanus serum was in charge of the borough pathologist, who was attached to Luton and Dunstable Hospital in an honorary capacity, and the co-operation of public and private medicine made the municipal laboratory an asset to the town throughout the war.

The Public Health department was also responsible for instituting a casualty bureau. This was an essential service at a time when rapid collation of civilian casualties was in demand by all the other branches. It required accurate on-the-spot work, generally at a time when the resources of the department were already strained to the limit.

*　　*　　*　　*

Changes in enemy tactics affected A.R.P. as it did other services. Following experience elsewhere that huge numbers of incendiary bombs, by the very chance that some could lodge on roofs and not be tackled until too late, were causing far more material damage than high explosive bombs, the Fire Guard (Business Premises) Order came into force early in 1941. Luton was made an area in which its application was compulsory, and everybody not exempt by other service had to register for this new duty. The door to part-time service was open wider than ever. " Eighteen to sixty," all came within the net.

It meant that many more people had to be watchers by night, even if as fire guards they were only expected to be awake during " alerts," when they were expected to patrol the premises which they were guarding. It meant such an increased demand for part-timers that wardens, like men in other voluntary services, could no longer resign unless there were very exceptional circumstances. For other reasons this had become a very necessary step. There had been constant losses, especially among the younger and more active men. The older men were doing wonders, but could not be expected to carry all the burden.

The wardens' service helped in the establishment of the Fire Guard organisation, and as the two branches were bound to be very closely linked, the wardens' headquarters became fire guard headquarters also, and Mr. H. Brandon, who had succeeded Alderman C. C. Dillingham as Head Warden, doubled with this post that of Chief Fire Guard.

Owners of business premises had to make their own plans, and submit them for approval or otherwise. It cannot be said that the Fire Guard was an altogether popular form of service, particularly among people who were allotted duties at premises in which they had no personal interest. They sometimes felt that they would be better occupied looking after the welfare of their own families. The position arose because enrolment over the town was somewhat irregular. There were areas with a surplus of Fire Guards, areas where there was a definite shortage which had to be made good. Sometimes this was because staffs of business premises were so reduced that an adequate rota could not be maintained without outside assistance. Actually the centre of the town was for a short time without any volunteers, and this brought the pointed official comment that there were still many people sleeping comfortably in their beds and doing nothing at all, quite prepared to let others stand by for the general safety.

There was also dissatisfaction because, while Fire Guard as a Civil Defence duty was an unpaid job, some big firms were paying substantial sums to watchers. The compromise suggested was a substantial meal and out-of-pocket expenses, but it was not every place which had facilities for supplying meals, and a subsistence allowance, spendable at discretion, became the more general practice. Patrolling also gave place to a block system—special centres where a group of Fire Guards reported for duty, and had a defined area as their special responsibility.

A number of inspectors were appointed to pay surprise visits and see that those supposed to be doing duty were in fact doing it. Unfortunately there was sometimes justification for such visits. The reasons given were various, and sometimes perhaps better justified than the authorities seemed inclined to believe.

Later the Fire Guard system extended to residential areas. Every road had its rota, and gate signs indicated where stirrup pumps, ladders, water, sand, etc., were available. Some street parties took their duties so seriously that they had everything possible painted fire brigade red, and marshalled almost like a Guards' parade. The stirrup pumps had their tricks, and for a time " pumping parties " enjoyed a certain popularity. Most of these later developments proved not really necessary here, Luton by this time having suffered most of its damage from the air. But these additional safeguards were considered a necessary feature of our wartime life, and if the street parties did nothing else they certainly helped to broaden one's knowledge of others who lived in the same street and who had hitherto remained comparative strangers. One reason was that more women took a hand in fire watching in their own streets than in other Civil Defence activities, some of which were necessarily closed to them. In fact, although the Home Office scale of wardens for Luton envisaged the inclusion of a number of women, Mr. G. E. Scott from the first took the view that there could be no proper sphere for women as air raid wardens, however useful they could be, and were, as ambulance drivers and in other special capacities.

*   *   *   *

If more has been written about the Wardens and Fire Guards than the people who served in the many other ramifications of Civil Defence, it is because they were the most numerous, while the early wardens were also the longest on the job, and from the start of the war were on a more or less active job every night, whereas some other personnel, although standing by, only became really active when there were incidents. It may be that, having no patrolling to do, and no contacts to make, their job was all the more monotonous. Certainly Civil Defence could not have functioned so effectively without its casualty services. These included fixed first aid posts, each with a medical officer, trained nurses, dispensers, messengers, and a clerk in attendance ; mobile first aid posts—vehicles with windows boarded up, and equipped with drugs, dressings and splints, ready to go at a moment's notice to any point where there happened to be a large number of casualties and give treatment on the spot before ambulances removed the casualties to hospital ; stretcher party stations with a number of wholetime personnel, and part-time volunteers trained in first aid and anti-gas measures ; first aid parties which in time became light rescue parties because it was often found that people had to be rescued from a damaged building before they could be treated for injuries ; heavy rescue parties, with vehicles equipped with gear to lift even girders in order to free some unfortunate ; and cleansing stations with air locks and every equipment for neutralising the effects of gas.

And right on their heels came the first aid repair parties to do a wonderful job. Wherever houses had suffered damage, up rolled these men from the Borough Engineer's department, with tarpaulins for roofs which were no longer guaranteed to keep out the rain, glass substitute for the windows from which all the glass had gone, and generally to make a quick job of the things needed to keep a house watertight and reasonably habitable. The very quickness with which they set about the job was in itself a great comfort to distressed people who might otherwise have been forced to leave their homes.

*   *   *   *

The big works and the public utility undertakings had their own A.R.P. arrangements, and when those undertakings were not affected there was always personnel ready to lend a hand elsewhere to back up the work of the town A.R.P. organisation, which included in its branches groups of people specifically responsible for gas identification, a mortuary service for the civilian war dead, cleansing of shelters, trenches and tunnels, emergency rest centres and feeding stations, and many other duties which the times made necessary, or might have done. The police, the Fire Service, and a lot of other people had a place in the general scheme. All played their part well. All helped to earn the tribute of Sir Will Spens when, paying his final visit to Luton as Regional Commissioner, he met about 1,000 of Luton's 2,500 volunteers at the Odeon, and told them they had all helped Luton to be " a Civil Defence model to the Eastern Region and the country." In this he was in full agreement with Wing-Commander E. J. Hodsoll, Inspector-General of Civil Defence, who had been similarly complimentary at a somewhat earlier inspection on the Town Ground.

It was truly written at that time, " In its war memories the town will forever have a grateful thought for those men and women who were about the first to enter the great army of passive defenders and about the last to leave it. Some of their work was most spectacular. They toiled amid scenes of ruin and desolation, and their aid was given to people who were in most urgent need of it. At many an incident a minute or two lost in searching the rubble, a second or two lost in applying first aid, meant all the difference between life and death. And when the casualties were got away to clearing station or hospital there were still many jobs to be done . . . people to be accounted for, belongings put in safe keeping, many human problems brought about by the sudden upheaval to be settled.

" It was on these occasions that the real spirit of the people of Luton was to be seen. Tragedy, loss and suffering, or just an acute mental upset—all these things were present in greater or lesser degree. It was the privilege of Civil Defence to give their help at these trying times, and the work brought its own reward, for never did a people show more spirit in the face of adversity."

*   *   *   *

War or no war, some skeleton form of Civil Defence is to be kept in being. When this became known, the spirit which animated some of Luton's wartime volunteers found new expression, for 200 of them volunteered to carry on.

Security Service

ALL sorts of rumours are apt to fly about in war time. Some are started by enemy agents or sympathisers, some by mischief makers with a personal grudge, some are misconstructions of over-heard conversations. Quite a number have some basis in fact but they become so elaborated on their travels that the ultimate rumour is almost entirely false.

From 1939 the public was ceaselessly enjoined not to indulge in " careless talk." So well publicised was the campaign that before long secrecy became a habit of mind of the British people. No one talked about his war job, every man and woman in every Luton factory engaged on the production of any sort of war material made it a point of honour that no one should glean what that factory was doing. In effect every man and woman not only kept " mum " but acted as a Security Officer and woe betide any casual acquaintance who let his tongue wag too freely.

In the places where the Services foregather the investigations of the source of careless talk were a matter for the security sections of those services, but on the civilian side, the responsibility of investigation fell on the police. Luton Borough Police investigated not only careless talk but every brand of rumour that saw the light of day in Luton.

Experienced officers were detailed for this work. Some of it came within the sphere of every officer, but, in wartime, security work is so important, and covers such a wide field, that obviously it must receive the full attention of specialists. Little imagination is needed to realise the difficulty of tracing the source of some rumours, though occasion-ally the puzzle proves easy, and the answer interesting and possibly amusing.

Did you hear that spies had landed in the Streatley district ? Some of the enemy had in fact landed there, but they were merely enemy airmen who had been forced to bale out. They had no further interest in the war, but they were not the type of enemy in which security police were particularly interested.

A very similar report arose when an aircraft jettisoned some of its gear when passing over Luton.

One night, however, it did look as if Luton would have a chance to catch a spy. Information came that a hostile plane would pass over at a stated time, signal, and drop an enemy agent by parachute. Every-thing happened as expected, except that the spy landed in a neighbour-ing district, where he was quickly rounded up.

But for his capture a big comb-out in Luton might have been necessary. There were, in fact, a number of systematic checks always going on although they did not necessarily cover the whole town. Much work of this kind was handled by a department dealing solely

E

with the considerable number of aliens living in the town, but routine checks had to be made at hotels, boarding houses, and elsewhere, and when there was a very general check of identity cards the military also took a hand. The identity cards issued after national registration, apparently simple but holding pitfalls for the forger, were among the difficulties facing spies landed here. They became a ready means of checking a person's identity, and were of particular value in identifying deserters, absentees, and people evading national service.

In this, and on many other matters, there was close liaison between Luton Police and the military, and there was constant revision of plans to meet possible new war emergencies, all involving extra work for the available man-power.

*   *   *   *

Regularly there came to the police hosts of new regulations. Every officer had to be familiar with them, even with those where the responsibility lay elsewhere, for police co-operation always had to be available.

Immediately on the outbreak of war there came the blackout regulations. Everyone had to be impressed with the need for the greatest care, reports of elusive lights that had aroused suspicions had to be investigated, and sometimes houses had to be forcibly entered to put out lights that had been left on. A.R.P. personnel were often able to help, but the blackout regulations probably caused more continuous trouble than any. Even though prosecutions began quite early on, and public warning was given that inspection from the air had shown that far too many lights were visible at night, people continued to be careless, and some began to earn quite a bad name in court. The regulations were all-embracing, restricted the amount of lighting permissible on vehicles, and also had particular reference to hand torches.

In fact, wartime regulations provided quite a number of new opportunities for people to become officially " known to the police." Breach of the blackout regulations in respect of buildings was only one. A garden bonfire which, apparently burnt out, decided to flare up again in the night, was just as disastrous. While it was still an offence not to have the usual obligatory lights on a car, it was possible to offend by having too much light, and special masks for headlamps were introduced. Cyclists offended if their front light was too bright, or if they failed to carry the red rear lamp which the war made compulsory. Absence of two thicknesses of tissue paper over a torch bulb invited prosecution, and so did parking on the wrong side of the road in the hours of darkness, during which a lower speed limit also applied. Aliens who stayed out after their curfew without a special permit were liable to penalties. To be unable to produce one's identity card on demand, to lend it to another person or to be found in possession of another person's, were punishable offences, and so was registering for accommodation in an assumed name. The motorist who, after basic petrol disappeared, had a petrol ration for a specific purpose and who used it for another purpose, or even deviated from his shortest route, invited a lot of trouble, and there were all sorts of other possible offences in wartime, even if it was not up to the police directly to deal with them.

*   *   *   *

These extra duties had to be tackled while the regular force was steadily decreasing through members joining the Services, and although it was augmented by the Special Constabulary, the War Reserve, the Women's Auxiliary Police Corps, and in other ways, there was never strength to spare.

In one way it was fortunate that the shadow of things to come was cast long before war became imminent. Local developments in connection with air raid precautions, dealt with elsewhere, were from the beginning largely the responsibility of the police, and as the Chief Constable was also A.R.P. Controller, it was natural that he should expect considerable help from the force in general, and not only from those officers who eventually became entirely occupied with the duties. A.R.P. began to be a matter of importance as early as 1935, and by 1937 had become one of very great importance. Men went for instruction at Home Office schools, some going to Easingwold, Yorks., others to Fallowfield, Gloucestershire, and still others to Preston. Passed out as qualified, they returned to instruct others. Senior officers and sergeants attended a course at a bomb reconnaissance school at Bury St. Edmunds, and there were other courses at Norwich and Southend. The Munich crisis gave point to all this training, and, as a result, by 1939 the police were fully trained in every phase at that time thought necessary. Right through the war, however, there were new developments coming along; when piloted planes ceased to be so troublesome, there came the flying bombs and rockets. One of the latter provided the last real test of the A.R.P. service, but it was not until the end of the war in Europe that it could be said there could be nothing more for which to prepare.

Long before that time, however, although the police were always in control at incidents, the organisation had so developed that it covered a huge number of full-time and part-time personnel; but for the police it continued to be just something which had to be done in addition to normal police duties. So also was the work which had to be done in co-operation with the military as preparation for possible emergencies of a different character, and these involved joint exercises to ensure that plans were as near perfection as possible, although there was never any need to operate the scheme. If Luton had been affected by enemy invasion, an enormous number of important new duties would have fallen to the police, even down to killing pigeons, so they had to be well versed in the elaborate plan which was prepared.

Never throughout the war, therefore, could they anticipate a time which would be free from new training, re-organisation, or changes of some kind, and from the time these developments began the full period covered was over ten years.

*   *   *   *

Adequate discharge of all police duties would have been impossible without the great expansion of the Special Constabulary. Its re-organisation began quite early. Re-organisation is rather an under-statement, for though the Specials rendered such good service in World War I, in most places it was a force which had been, for all practical purposes, allowed to die out. Luton was one of the few places which still had a shadow force—only about 30 old stalwarts, it is true—but this nucleus quickly claimed the attention of Mr. G. E. Scott, after his appointment as Chief Constable in 1936. As his successor Mr. Ronald Alderson remarked at the " Stand Down " of the Specials in 1945, it seemed that Mr. Scott even in 1936 foresaw the world conflict which was approaching. It was a foresight to which Luton was to owe much, for in the war years the Specials not only did many hours of training and many hours of routine duty, but when occasion arose faced situations of danger with courage and resource.

While tribute should be paid to the work as Chief Special Constable of Alderman J. T. Harrison, who died during his Mayoralty a year before the war started, much credit must also go to his successor, Mr. W. R. I. Dandy, for the standard of efficiency the force had attained by the time the war started, and for the way in which it carried out its duties throughout the subsequent years. Mr. Dandy, who had been Commander of No. 1 Company, was awarded the M.B.E. for his work. He built up the force to a maximum of about 300, despite an increasing drain through the call-up of members and other unavoidable losses.

There was rapid progress right from the time re-organisation began. At the outset most of the old brigade intimated a desire to continue, and in 1937 members already numbered 120—a notable achievement when war still seemed unlikely, and when peace propaganda discouraged preparedness of any kind. All the members knew that, without pay, they must serve their town wholeheartedly if occasion made it necessary. Later, as often happens when people seek to decry the work of a voluntary body, there were rumours that they were paid ; in fairness to them, steps were taken to give wide publicity to a denial.

Numbers went on increasing, and as war approached the authorised strength of 250 was rapidly approached. When war began, Luton had a splendid force almost fully trained. Then came a slight setback. The formation of the Police War Reserve took from the Specials some who were willing to do full-time duty, but more volunteers came along, and it is noteworthy that throughout the whole of the war every special was a volunteer, not one man having been " directed " into the force. The Specials had their own headquarters, first at 9, Gordon Street, and then in larger premises at 15, Gordon Street.

In 1940 strength reached 260, but by the end of that year 33 members

68

George Street in the black-out! This time-exposure photograph taken from Luton Town Hull one moonlit night shows more of the town centre than would be good for any Hun to see. The white streaks are the lights of passing vehicles during the time the photo-graphic plate remained exposed.

RIGHT: *A little girl's respirator is tested for leaks while two Luton police officers look on during a mock gas attack in the town.*

ABOVE: *Colonel J. d'Ewes Coke, H.M. Inspector of Constabulary, taking the salute on Wardown Sports Ground as Luton Special Constables march past after an inspection on May 30th, 1943.*

LEFT: *Some of Luton's War Reserve policemen get down to a spell of classwork during their training.*

had been lost to the Services, the Military Police sometimes being the gainers. In addition to attending drills and lectures and turning out on sirens, every man did at least three hours' duty every third night, and during the year, 18,845 police duties were carried out, in addition to manning headquarters day and night. In 1941 duties rose to 21,186, and the issue of efficiency chevrons began, a good percentage of the members becoming entitled to them.

With authorised strength increased in 1942 to 300, and actual numbers to 295, duties increased to 23,575, and the following year, although numbers were slightly fewer, total duties reached 26,250. Then came the last complete year of the war. Ordinary duties decreased, but with special duties included, the total was still well over 20,000. At the time of the Order releasing personnel in July, 1945, the force still numbered 247, of whom 218 had earned the long service medal, to which three members were able to add two bars, and several one bar. Many had done duties far in excess of the prescribed minimum, despite being overworked on their own jobs, increasing difficulties through restricted bus services, laid-up cars, and, despite many of their wives being drafted into industry or working long hours on their own voluntary jobs.

As a fitting climax the Specials almost to a man volunteered to carry on after the Stand-Down. Most people were then freeing themselves of war duties as quickly as possible. The offer of the Specials to carry on was all the more valuable because War Reserve constables were released while the regular forces was still waiting the return of many men from the Services. So reliable were they, in fact, that there were times when they policed the town without the aid of regulars, and perhaps the most striking evidence of their spirit as a body was that many former members, on return from the Services, applied to rejoin.

In conjunction with some social activity at their headquarters outstanding work was done by a savings group, which from the outset to the end of 1944 raised over £20,000.

* * * *

In addition to the great help they received from the Specials and the War Reserves, the regular Police were also assisted by the First Reserve. Started in 1937, but always a very small body, they were all ex-members of Luton or other police forces. Supplied with uniform and equipment they were paid a small retaining fee, plus payment for attending drills and training instruction. When the war started they were able to go on patrol duty at once ; throughout the war their experienced assistance was always valuable, and particularly so when younger men had left the regular police for the Services. The number of First Reserves who could be obtained was necessarily limited, so the War Reserve had to have its numbers maintained by the " direction " of men under the National Service Acts. They had to be physically fit, and to express a preference for this form of service.

Contrary to popular impression, the members of the Women's Auxiliary Police Corps were not women constables. Although in uniform, they were not attested. Their work was limited to driving, telephone operating, and similar duties from which they could release men. The Corps was started in the latter part of 1941, the members all proved very efficient in their duties, and many will remember their smart appearance. One eventually transferred to Leicester City Police as a policewoman.

*　　*　　*　　*

All this added strength was not a bit too much in view of the reduced size of the regular force, and the many extra duties arising out of the war. In 1939, the regulars numbered 112, including one inspector responsible for war duties and a sergeant and two constables delegated to general A.R.P. work. The Services took away 45, not counting ten cadet clerks, and there were losses through other causes, including the retirement of Supt. Wood, who, though anxious to see the war through, found himself compelled to give up.

Towards the end of the war, Chief Constable Scott went in a similar capacity to Newcastle-on-Tyne. A man with a high sense of duty, he had been a tower of strength. At the slightest sign of danger he would be at the police station, or elsewhere if need be, and at one period he was not infrequently at the police station all or most of the night. He had a forthright way, and did not hesitate to tell leading citizens that he expected them to set an example.

Luton, however, was fortunate in the successors to both positions. Insp. Sear, who had been awarded the George Medal for his work in connection with a parachute mine incident, became Superintendent, and, having deputised as Chief Constable in the interim between the departure of Mr. Scott and the arrival of Mr. Alderson, he was formally appointed Deputy Chief Constable. Like his predecessor, Mr. Alderson was appointed A.R.P. Controller.

*　　*　　*　　*

As another close link between the police and civil defence, Central Control was at the police station, and at one time senior officers and other ranks did duty there every third night, while for a long time a number of officers regularly slept there. It was the distributing point for raid warnings on which Dunstable, Hitchin and Letchworth eventually relied.

At the police station there were preparations for many eventualities. There was an auxiliary lighting installation in case electricity failed, all offices had oil lamps available, telephone operators were trained to work while wearing specially adapted gas masks, and when the " Jim Crow " system of " spotters " was introduced, a spotters' post was established on the roof. Fire-watching duty had to be done at the police station, just as elsewhere.

Incidentally, people may like to know what would have happened if there had been a direct hit on the police station. They would not have escaped being " run in," if necessary, but would have been " entitled to admission " to the Town Football Ground, where suitable accommodation had been arranged.

Because it is unusual with our police it is also a point to record that for certain duties during the war years they were armed. All were trained to use rifle or revolver, and most people will recall that their headquarters were protected by pillboxes.

As though they had not enough on their hands already, they had the extra troubles caused by trying to check the wave of destruction which seemed to sweep over the town when salvage had resulted in the removal of so many fences and gates. This destruction was aided, if not made wholly possible, by the blackout. It can only be attributed to gangs of hooligans. Single individuals not only would not have dared, but would have found it impossible, to do some of the damage. In Wardown Park, for example, iron seats were thrown bodily into the lake. Others had their heavy frames smashed. When, after many protests about the danger to little children caused by the removal of the dwarf fencing round the lake, it was found possible to provide a new and more substantial fence, reinforced concrete posts were thrown into the lake before they could be erected, others were deliberately smashed after erection. Because, with fences and gates gone, the Park could not be closed at dusk, and because of the persistent damage which was being done, police had to do special patrols there after nightfall . . . extra work with very little hope of results. And this destruction of the townspeople's property was not restricted to Wardown. A truly formidable list of damage in practically all the parks and recreation grounds was prepared at the end of the war. The Memorial Park, perhaps because of its location, seemed to be the only one to escape.

There were certain other responsibilities of the police which at the time were performed without publicity. They were responsible for keeping the Government informed of public reaction to specific events. To the credit of our people be it said that they never had to report any signs of unrest.

Nor will people in general know that some police had to be specially trained to deal with mad dogs. This was the result of an experience at Norwich. Some officers were trained in the use of special equipment for catching such dogs, and in the use of the humane killer.

*   *   *   *

To sum up, it may be said that all branches of the police acquitted themselves during the war with the greatest credit, while the high reputation of the force was upheld by those who went into the Services. Apart from two sergeants, all were constables. Fifteen obtained commissions, one rose to Lieut.-Colonel, and another to Major.

P.s. Tickner, P.c.'s Lewis and Hall, and Cadet Clerk Carter, gave their lives on active service.

Luton's Canopy

NOBODY mentioned smoke abatement campaigns when, in the early days of the war, Luton people were not only urged to make all the smoke they could one night, but were officially provided with the wherewithal.

Don't say you have forgotten those sawdust and tar blocks which you were invited to burn steadily from 11 p.m. to 1 a.m. ?

It was really rather fun. It was supposed to be an experiment in obscuring Luton from air observation but the result was never officially disclosed. Friendly planes were up that night to observe the effect and it could be gauged to some extent by the watchers on the Water-towers. It certainly created a fog but it took a long time to do it. There was to have been a second experiment on a later night but it was called off.

It was just as well this method of creating a smoke screen was abandoned. Sawdust and tar blocks were not an ideal fuel for a household grate. The quantity of soot made was colossal and there is no doubt that if there had been many of these nights there would have been an epidemic of chimney fires—and perhaps more serious ones—in the town.

This idea was superseded by the oil-burning canisters. They came along soon after the Coventry blitz and were planted in and all round the town. When the installation was complete it was estimated there were over 25,000 of them. They stood in rows along the pavement edge and along the grass verges of the country roads and lanes, only a few yards apart. Each had chimneys rising from a large flat looking reservoir, in which was oil to make the maximum amount of smoke. The story goes that it was soon found necessary to weight the bases heavily. Motorists driving in a raid, with dimmed side lights only, were apt to run into a smoking canister. One motorist upset a number of them like ninepins and in the twinkling of an eye the road was a sheet of flame.

The canisters were looked after by a Smoke Company of the Pioneer Corps. Never was there a dirtier job than theirs. Every night they stood by on the perimeter of whichever sector of the town the wind chose to come from, ready to light the canisters, and having lit them to keep watch and ward over them lest they should decide to flare rather than smoke. The following morning they had to be cleaned and replenished.

The smoke may have protected Luton from the Luftwaffe in those days because it certainly did the job more efficiently than the sawdust and tar blocks, but nothing could protect Luton houses against the smoke. A black oily deposit covered everything in the garden. Woe betide the housewife who had inadvertently left some laundry

Dallow Road was one of the many Luton streets where smoke screen generators were set up.

out at night. However, it was a small inconvenience to submit to by comparison with the protection the smoke gave to the town

The canisters disappeared in time, and mobile smoke machines arrived, equipped with tanks for oil, and apparatus for converting it into smoke and pumping it out as the machines moved along the windward side of the town. These mobile machines, with the canisters and with other smoke-producing devices, combined in a vital way to enable the B.L.A. to force a passage of the Rhine at comparatively low cost.

That, it will be agreed, was ample compensation for the inconvenience the early smoke experiments caused us.

Devil's Dew

WAR, in all its stark reality, came unheralded to Luton on a sunny afternoon at the end of August, 1940. There was no siren. Bombs rained down on the town. Within a few seconds 59 people were killed, 140 injured, many homes totally destroyed, and others so badly damaged that they could never again be made habitable. The A.R.P. services rose to the emergency in splendid manner. There was no panic—the people in general remained commendably calm.

By morning there were frantic inquiries from the North, where Luton Territorial units were combining training with defence duty. Was it true, they asked, that a thousand people had been killed, and most of the town laid waste? Of course it wasn't true. But, having regard to the way rumour had enlarged bad news, when no public statement of fact could be made, it was not surprising that men who had left their families here were worried.

To have had that number killed and injured, and so many homes destroyed, in a few seconds, was a hard blow. It was, fortunately, the hardest blow of its kind Luton was called upon to suffer, although subsequent incidents caused considerable loss of life.

* * * *

When Luton people were afterwards asked " Have you had many air raids ? " or " Has much damage been done in Luton ? ", or " Have you had many casualties ? ", and if they remembered the warnings about " careless talk," they could only reply non-committally, " Yes— and no."

Our total losses must be regarded as comparatively light when considered by the side of those suffered by some other towns of similar size and industrial importance. But while they were happening Luton was never identified officially. At one period it was " in the Midlands " ; at another, " in the Home Counties " ; and, in the closing stages, when planes did not come, but V-missiles did, we were merely " in Southern England."

Certainly our losses, grievous though they were, bore no relation to Luton's importance to the war effort as the foremost production centre in the Eastern Region. Its diversity of activity was as important for the enemy to destroy as it was for us to keep it going. In fact, some machines used here were of such prime importance that they had to be dispersed to lessen the risk of a total hold-up.

It is an odd fact that industry here suffered very little damage, when viewed against the background of nearly six years of war. It cannot be assumed that Luton was overlooked. The Luftwaffe photographs of some of our factories, found in Germany after VE-Day, effectively dispose of any such idea.

Vauxhall Motors, principal industrial sufferers in the big daylight raid of Friday, August 30th, 1940, quickly recovered. Percival Aircraft had a lucky escape when a parachute mine which lodged in the factory roof was safely removed, and when another exploded not far away. The Skefko works escaped with superficial damage when a big bomb blew up the L.M.S. main line close to one corner of the works. The V2 which extracted such a heavy casualty list in November, 1944, spent much of its force against a wall of Commer Cars, but work was resumed before the day was out.

*   *   *   *

There were, of course, many interruptions due to raid warnings, but these tended to get fewer and shorter. Workers, including women and girls, developed a stronger indifference to Luftwaffe threats, and stayed at their benches often until " immediate danger " was signalled by roof spotters.

In this they were fortified by the special raid warning which the Royal Observer Corps made it possible to circulate to factories where danger threatened. This was distinct from the public warning, and, not surprisingly, instances arose where tempers were frayed because workers received danger warnings not given to families at home.

The climax came when at mid-day on Saturday, September 5th, 1942, a bomb fell without warning in Midland Road and caused a number of casualties. Protests came from all quarters. The Emergency Committee took it up with the Minister of Home Security, urging that in an area such as Luton the factory and public warning systems should be linked. This specific result was not attained, but never again had Luton people cause to complain, except, ironically, that for some time sirens sounded so frequently as to be little short of a nuisance.

*   *   *   *

A remarkable feature of the first daylight raid was that in a large area of the town the bombs were unheard. When it was realised that, high in the sky, a bunch of raiders was dropping bombs on Luton as they were chased by the R.A.F., some people were foolhardy enough to climb points of vantage for a better view. They saw little except a column of smoke rising high into the sky. It obviously came from somewhere within the area of the Vauxhall Works. It suggested a serious fire. Actually the fire was of minor importance. Had it been all that happened there, a lot of suffering would have been saved.

On that afternoon, in a few seconds as it seemed, 194 bombs dropped in the town. They started at the Airport, hit the Vauxhall Works, the Corporation bus depot in Park Street, caused a line of devastation right through to Farley Hill, and still kept falling. Even Caddington and Whipsnade Zoo had some. Most of the major casualties occurred at the Vauxhall Works. Fortunately quite a number of the bombs fell in their cricket ground, and some that did not explode gave Bomb Disposal personnel considerable trouble afterwards.

A 1,000-kilo bomb hit the bus depot, killing one employee and injuring twelve. Most of the buses were out, but a double-decker finished suspended in the roof girders. A sunken petrol tank containing 2,000 gallons, was concertinaed. It was fortunate for the already stricken neighbourhood that, being only three parts full, it did not burst.

Many of the poorer homes in that part of the town became just heaps of rubble, and although some people had managed to get to Anderson or communal shelters, it was remarkable that the death roll was not higher. One man lost his wife and two children. When a public-house was destroyed, a woman and her grand-child lost their lives. The child's mother and her young baby were rescued after being buried a considerable time, as was another woman. The mother suffered considerable injury. Only part of one wall of the building remained, but on this three pictures hung undisturbed.

A six-years old boy ran into his grandmother's and told her the earth had opened and lifted him up. At the spot another boy was found dead. Can it be wondered at that the grandmother afterwards said she would in future believe in miracles?

Some almshouses were hit, but an old lady in the room which was struck escaped with shock, although found surrounded by debris. From a house which just collapsed when hit a woman was dug out, having escaped with an injured elbow and bruised shoulder. Death passed many people by that afternoon.

Quickly a relief fund was opened. It was felt by Alderman Burgoyne and others that, despite the very extensive statutory provision made for the help of raid sufferers, cases might arise which could be most speedily assisted from such a fund.

*   *   *   *

This raid, be it remembered, occurred on August 30th. Later a Canadian paper published a German High Command communique which stated—" A squadron of our bombers in daylight on August

A public house at the corner of Wellington Street and Windsor Street demolished in the August 30th raid in 1940. Pictures were left hanging on the wall.

ABOVE: *A Corporation bus was blown into the roof of the Transport Dept's. garage in Park Street.*

LEFT: *This woman and little boy had a miraculous escape in Farley Avenue on the same afternoon. A bomb burst as they were entering their Anderson shelter. They were blown into the shelter to safety . . . and the bomb left a huge crater.*

The parachute mine which fell in Park Street on September 22nd, 1940, caused extensive damage. Fortunately many people had taken shelter, with the result that the casualty list was small. Inset is the parachute on which the mine was suspended when it fell.

LEFT: *Fire Service vehicles parked outside their Park Street headquarters were wrecked in the September 1940 air raid.*

BELOW: *The adjoining Corporation bus depot suffered extensive damage at the same time.*

RIGHT: *Rescue workers searching for victims among the rubble after the Park Street incident.*

ABOVE: *The extraordinary thing about this incident, the picture of which was never released for Press publication during the war, was that when this house in Moor Street collapsed after a delayed-action high explosive bomb had gone off. each brick, though remaining whole, was neatly parted from its neighbour.*

BELOW: *When a bomb dropped in soft wet chalk at Limbury, it not only demolished this house, but covered other houses over a wide area with a layer of white slime, so that they looked like a snow scene.*

23rd, 1940, raided a plane parts factory in Luton, N.W. of London. The first machines started a huge fire, and following machines were thus guided to the target, which they completely destroyed."

Irrespective of the error in date, the huge fire was not at a factory concerned with planes, nor was it a huge fire. It was principally smoke from some oil barrels on the Vauxhall premises, well clear of buildings, and it gave the Fire Service very little trouble.

*   *   *   *

In the early hours of September 20th a solitary plane dropped a string of bombs which stretched from Wardown Park across Wardown Crescent and People's Park into Havelock Rise. A man who had been known to say that the chances against any particular house being hit were a million to one later rang up a friend and told him that the million to one chance had come off. The back of his house had been hit. The three occupants escaped injury, but in addition to the immediately obvious damage the whole of the house was found to have been so moved that it had to be demolished. One bomb landed in the back garden of a house on the other side of the road. Glass was broken, but children sleeping downstairs were uninjured.

*   *   *   *

Late on Sunday evening, September 22nd, the unfortunate bus depot got it again, for a parachute mine fell just in front of it. Shocked by the effects of the raid of August 30th, however, most people had profited by the warning and were in shelter. That is why the casualty list was so small, although damage to property by the terrific blast was tremendous. The mine caused a crater 38 feet across, about 12 feet deep, and only 30 or 40 feet from where the first bomb dropped. Park Street became a shambles, far worse than on the first occasion. Most of the deaths occurred in two adjoining houses which were destroyed. Fortunately many houses had been vacated, but about 100 people were rendered homeless, while lesser damage was done over a tremendous area. Shop windows at a great distance went to pieces, and had not been made good by the end of the war.

The parachute by which the mine was dropped was of somewhat loosely woven turquoise blue silk, and about 30 feet across. It held the mine by 20 or more white silk ropes of about three-quarters of an inch diameter.

Another 46 buses suffered damage, six employees were injured, the machine shop put out of action, the office and half a million tickets destroyed, and a quantity of stores lost. Only nineteen serviceable buses remained, because they happened to be out at the time. Nevertheless the undertaking continued in operation next day, with the help of buses on loan from other operators.

The mine also destroyed two vans belonging to the undertaking, as well as four ambulances, a mobile canteen, and three cars belonging to Civil Defence. Ready in case of a raid, they had been standing at an ambulance station in the forecourt of the depot !

An 83-years old cripple gave a fine example of the spirit of the people at that time. When the mine exploded he was in bed. The ceiling fell on him. He crawled out of the debris with only bruises, spent the night at a centre for those rendered homeless, and next morning said—" I shall have to go back, because I've got two chickens there. I haven't fed them yet."

Another parachute mine exploded in the air that night, causing no damage.

*   *   *   *

Here it may be said that there seemed to be a hoodoo on the bus undertaking about that time. Damaged buses were immediately put in the hands of bodybuilders for repair, and some were on the roads again within two or three weeks. Two which had to be sent to Ware, however, were totally destroyed by a direct hit on the repair workshops.

With the Park Street depot temporarily out of use, there was a move to a garage in Frederick Street, and within three weeks that also was damaged when a bomb fell in Old Bedford Road.

Following the parachute mine, the buses were dispersed every night for safety. Some stood under the trees in Wardown Park. This added enormously to maintenance problems, but it had to be done, and dispersal was continued until the end of the war in Europe.

In contrast, no damage to premises or buses was caused at the London Transport Board's garage in Park Street West, not far from the Corporation bus depot, nor to the Eastern National garage in Castle Street.

*   *   *   *

Before September was out another part of Luton had been hit. This was on Tuesday, the 24th, and it was the turn of the Dunstable Road district. Fortunately the casualties were limited to one killed and eight injured.

An invalid man was killed when an oil bomb fell on a house in Kenilworth Road. His wife, son, and others in the house had a remarkable escape, although some of them had to be treated for burns. A boarder who had been out to do some " spotting " was returning through the passage way to give warning that danger was imminent. The bomb blew him on to the lawn, and he afterwards said that if by any chance he had nine lives, he reckoned he lost one that night.

Another oil bomb fell through the roof of Bury Park Memorial Hall, causing a fire inside. London evacuees were billeted there. They must have thought Luton was not such a safe refuge after all. The only casualty was slight injury to a blind man.

Not far away, in Moor Street, there was a house into which the billeting authorities had put a family who arrived from London with no possessions, and only £6 between them. They had been there four days. A delayed action bomb hit their new home, exploded later and destroyed it. Some things from the house were found on top of one of the gasholders nearby.

Another caused a huge hole in the dividing wall between two houses. It was believed to have exploded, but for safety the occupant of one house wisely took his wife elsewhere for shelter. When he returned, very little was left of his home. He and his wife only had what they stood up in. The neighbouring family also escaped injury, but an alarm clock stopped, to record the time things happened.

A corporal who had his wife and two children in an Anderson shelter rescued a woman and four children from a damaged house. In the morning his two boys had a narrow escape from death. He had moved them from the back bedroom to the front. A time bomb wrecked the back of the house.

A furnishing firm which had come from Eastbourne had its frontages in Dunstable Road blown in—not the only trouble they were to experience in Luton ; but bombs which dropped near some works did only slight damage, and did not affect the plant.

*   *   *   *

That night Luton received two more parachute mines, one only damaging some cottages near the Airport. The other resulted in two George Medals being awarded for deeds of courage and fortitude. This second mine lodged in the factory roof at Percival Aircraft, Ltd. Security made it impossible to tell the story at the time. When the George Medal awards were announced, at a considerably later date, it simply said of Deputy Chief Constable—then Inspector—A. Sear that it was for " Bravery and devotion to duty in dangerous circumstances." Of Major J. C. Cunningham, D.S.O., security officer at the factory, it was said that he " carried out hazardous duties with gallantry."

The incident was certainly a hair-raising experience. Mr. Sear took charge as A.R.P. incident officer, and Major Cunningham had charge of a Home Guard platoon. The first task was to evacuate families up to a quarter of a mile or more from the scene.

Next came the problem of saving precious arms and ammunition, for the Home Guard was then none too well endowed. The platoon armoury was very close to the mine. With Mr. Foord, the works manager, Major Cunningham, Sgt. Parrott and Volunteer Kilby went into the armoury and carried out a number of rifles and two machine guns with ammunition. Previously, the same small party had removed to safety a number of aeroplanes which had been in danger of damage from falling debris.

A Naval expert, Lieut. Armitage, arrived next morning to direct the disposal of the mine. He was taken there by Major Cunningham and Sgt. Parrott, and a plan of action decided upon. Lieut. Armitage said that " with a bit of luck " he could render the mine harmless in a comparatively short time. It had two fuses, one magnetic in case the mine fell into water, and the other an ordinary contact fuse.

For twenty minutes Lieut. Armitage worked at the task, and then found that owing to the way the mine was wedged in the roof *it was impossible to remove the second fuse.*

He asked for volunteers to help him and Major Cunningham move the mine, and besides Mr. Sear he was joined by Sgt. Parrott, Sgt. H. A. Bradbury, Cpl. W. G. Hills, and Volunteers C. Lillywhite and Burnage, of the Home Guard, Police-Sgt.—now Inspector—Fryer, P.c. McKay, Commander Blinco, of the Special Constabulary, and Special Police-Sgt. Parks.

Carefully the mine was eased out of its position. Suddenly it slipped, tipped over, and fell nine feet on to the concrete floor of the factory.

In the years that have passed since that fateful moment, those few men have many times been asked what it felt like when they saw the mine slip and drop. Truth to tell, none of them realised what had happened. It was only after Lieut. Armitage had dropped down on to the floor and whipped out the second fuse to make the mine and its 8 cwts. of explosive harmless that they realised how close the scythe of the Great Reaper had come to them. It was not the hideous moment itself that made them sweat, but the aftermath of recollection that will remain with them for the rest of their days.

The only injury was slight one from debris, received by Major Cunningham when the mine fell.

*　　*　　*　　*

The following night some heavy bombs fell just outside the town. One made a crater 54 feet across and 15 feet deep, throwing chalk right across a main road.

It was a busy time for the Luftwaffe, for they were here again the subsequent night. Then they came their nearest to blowing up the Skefko works. A particularly heavy bomb dropped on the L.M.S. main line and blew up all the tracks, but did only slight damage to the corner of the works. Windows and doors of houses were wrecked over a radius of a quarter of a mile. There were no casualties, but many people had occasion to be grateful for their Anderson shelters. One woman said :—

" I am seventy next month, and it has been my greatest experience. It was dreadful, but after this experience I shall not feel the slightest bit nervous when in the shelter if such a thing happens again."

A family in a shelter only 20 yards from where the bomb dropped had tremendous damage done to their house, but when they returned they found ornaments on a shelf undisturbed, and the canary singing in its cage on the wall.

*　　*　　*　　*

The bomb which dropped in a field near a Stopsley brickyard at the beginning of October, 1940, had hardly worried anyone, but on the night of October 4th a snow scene was created by one which fell in a Limbury Road garden. It demolished one house, and cut another

Queueing for safety. As the sirens wailed for Luton's first daylight raid passers-by seek the shelter of the Alma Street tunnel.

Old Bedford Road completely blocked by debris, after a big bomb had been dropped on hat factories on October 15th, 1940. Ribbons draped lamp standards and telephone wires giving the appearance of a partly constructed spider's web.

This graphic picture was taken from the West Hill Road water to August, 1940. Flames and smoke can be seen gushing from burni which filled the evening

minutes after the first bombs had fallen on Luton on 30th
...uiners at Vauxhall Motors Ltd., the smoke forming a pall
south of the town.

Hoods and ribbons intermingle with the debris of wood, bricks and mortar in the crater where a big bomb fell in Old Bedford Road, on October 15th, 1940. Falling on a hat factory where employees were at work, this bomb caused thirteen deaths, and injuries to 35 other people.

practically in two. People who had been unable to get shelter, as the bomb fell almost on the sound of the siren, were smothered in wet chalk, which also gave the neighbourhood a snowstorm effect. From the wrecked house four adults and a child were able to crawl out after debris had been moved, and there was only one hospital case. In another house which was considerably damaged there were four children, evacuees from London. They were got out without difficulty, and did not seem at all frightened. A piece of the bomb which was salvaged showed that its diameter must have been at least 2 ft. 6 ins.

$$* \qquad * \qquad * \qquad *$$

The next incident in Luton might have had further bad consequences for Vauxhall Motors, but it was largely wasted effort, although it again shook up the Park Street district a bit. Actually it had an amusing aspect—when it could be looked upon from the safety of afterwards. Early on the morning of Sunday, October 6th, after a night of constant alerts, a low-flying plane dropped ten bombs there. Three were oil bombs. Three of the seven H. E. bombs failed to explode, possibly because they were dropped from such a low altitude, and were seen bouncing down a roadway to the canteen. One appeared to be chasing a fireman, who did his best to make good time. In the circumstances no-one would have had time to think of turning and running uphill. Total result was one slight casualty, the unexplodeds were quickly removed, and work went on as usual.

$$* \qquad * \qquad * \qquad *$$

Then came one of the most tragic incidents—one which caused the third highest death roll of all Luton's bomb experiences. Just before noon on Monday, October 15th, the sirens sounded again. Many people saw a lone raider circling over the town, and some saw a big bomb come down, causing a terrific eruption from some hat factories in Old Bedford Road. Thirteen people were killed and 35 injured. They were mostly women and girls. The majority were employees of W. O. Scales and Co., Ltd., but there were deaths also in the adjoining premises of Messrs. Gregory, and debris thrown across an open space into another factory which was badly damaged caused the death of a young married woman who had started work there only that morning.

On the other side of Messrs. Scales' premises was a former hat factory which was the headquarters from which the Luton Territorial Company of R.A.S.C. left for the war. They will not now find those headquarters, for, like the other premises mentioned, they had to be razed to the ground. Still in military occupation, they were only being used as stores, after being a military billet, which was fortunate.

The blast from the bomb was so great that part of a heavy blocking machine was blown from Messrs Scales' factory over housetops, landing in a back garden a considerable distance away. Sewing machines were scattered like chaff in the wind. Hoods and ribbons festooned the tall trees on the other side of Old Bedford Road, in New Bedford Road, and even in Lansdowne Road, giving them a bizarre

Christmas effect. The roof of the block of flats known as The Mount bore some grisly evidence of the disaster.

At Messrs Scales the young daughter of one of the principals was among the killed. The factory manager, Mr. J. J. Payne, was freed from debris, gravely injured, but told his rescuers, " Don't bother about me. See to the girls." In hospital he made an apparently remarkable recovery from his bodily injuries, but the shock may have been a contributory cause of his death later on—a death mourned particularly by those interested in many fields of sport.

The youngest victim in the factory, and the last to be recovered alive, was Tommy Walker, a village boy of 14. It was two and a half hours before he was got out, after being given morphia, but he kept singing to himself and talking to his rescuers, causing one of them to say, " If I had half as much courage I should feel satisfied with myself."

In addition to the buildings immediately involved, much damage was done over a wide area, North Street Methodist Church being one of the places which suffered.

Across the road from where the bomb fell, and not many yards away, hundreds of children at Old Bedford Road School sat in complete immunity in their shelters beneath the playground, where they had been taken by their teachers.

*   *   *   *

Nights which followed were frequently disturbed by sirens and by bombs falling just outside the town, but before October was out Luton had again received direct attention—with a different weapon. After some H.E.'s had dropped a little farther out, the Butterfield Green district had the doubtful distinction of receiving the first " breadbasket." " Like Blackpool illuminations " was one description of the fire bombs which were thrown out. They fell on open land, and burned, glowed and twinkled until Home Guards, wardens, and cottagers put them out. Even cottage children, no whit scared, turned up with shovels to help their fathers.

In the early hours of the following morning, however, another " breadbasket " threw about 150 fire bombs on to the town. They spread over an area from Highbury Road and Studley Road to Clarendon Road and Reginald Street. Most of the fires caused were quickly put out. Worst sufferers were Lye and Sons, whose premises seemed to get the centre of the bunch. Fire guards were quickly at work, and although about £1,000 damage was done, it was principally to stock.

Many of the fire bombs, however, fell on roads, in gardens, and on allotments, and some recovered intact bore the dates 1936 and 1937.

The following night three more " breadbaskets " were dropped outside the town. They only started grass fires, and although while these were burning some H.E. and oil bombs were dropped, they were also dropped in the right place, where they caused no damage or casualties.

The Dunstable Road district got it again on the evening of Monday, November 5th. About 15 H.E.'s and an oil bomb were dropped. Houses were destroyed, others damaged, but casualties were few. A girl of 18 was killed. Avondale Road suffered most. In Kenilworth Road a bomb dropped right in front of the house in which a man was killed when an oil bomb penetrated it on the previous occasion. Hazelbury Crescent, Beech Road and Oak Road suffered. Dunstable Road School was hit on one corner. There was some minor damage to the L.N.E.R. A fire was caused in the timber yard of Henry Brown and Sons (Timber) Ltd. Shop premises in Dunstable Road again suffered considerably. Bombs which fell in the roadway where Dunstable Road climbs Beech Hill caused great craters. One extended from kerb to kerb of this main road, and went right down to the sewers. This bomb caused damage, but no casualties. The glass of the clock at the Gas Works was blown out, but the clock was going next day.

The Odeon Cinema had a narrow escape, for several bombs fell within a short distance. The manager, having assured himself that the building was undamaged, had an ovation when he told the audience this, and the show went on. Practically no one left except Civil Defence personnel who went to report for duty. After the show, people from damaged houses nearby were accommodated for the night, and fortified with tea and biscuits.

*   *   *   *

On the night of November 15th more bombs were dropped—this time in the Turners Road and Crawley Green Road district. Two houses were demolished, and many badly damaged. An invalid man of 70 was killed when his house received a direct hit. On the mattress on which he was lying, he was blown through the window into the street. Four other people were injured, and there were some miraculous escapes of people who were buried in the ruins of their homes. One man counted himself very lucky. He was at the bus depot during the first daylight raid; he was there when the parachute mine fell; he was walking along a street on another occasion when bombs fell near. For the fourth time he escaped injury. From the wreckage of one house a canary, buried in its cage for eleven hours, was recovered alive, and soon began to sing.

The following night another " breadbasket " fell, and with about 150 incendiaries lit up the Sundon Road area, just on the edge of the town. Within ten minutes the district was in darkness again. What surprised the wardens most was the speed with which fire appliances arrived from both Luton and Dunstable. Some H. E.'s were also dropped, but fell in fields.

*   *   *   *

In these months Luton had been taking it, and showing a fine courage and ability to take it. Then, having had ample share of the bitterness of death, injury and destruction, it went for a long period without attack, but spent many dreary nights under threat, and watched from a distance the agony of London. Luton saw, and wondered. The red glow of the burning docks and humble Cockney homes, the vivid flashes and thunderous rumbling of bombs were terrible to contemplate. The bursting of anti-aircraft shells and the performances of searchlights added to the spectacle of symphony and noise. When the raiders found the Thames Estuary barrage increasing beyond their liking and began to swing in from the North, and return that way, the threat to Luton increased. Fortunately, bombs not dropped on London were generally jettisoned out in the open.

Who will ever forget the night the enemy burned a new word, " Coventration," into the mind ? From just after tea on November 14th, 1940, German bombers flew over Luton for hour after hour on their way to the Midland city of Coventry. Then they flew back— most of them. That was the kind of raid which the grace of God spared our own town.

Bombs, however, were not the only things which came down at that time. A Heinkel 111, one of seven brought down over England on the night of April 8th, 1941, crashed at Bendish. It was a complete wreck. The pilot was found dead in a wood. The other members of the crew were taken prisoner, one by 17-years old David Stedman, of the Home Guard, a Kings Walden employee of Vauxhall Motors, Ltd. Two nights later, returning from another Coventry raid, a Junkers 88 was brought down half a mile from the Heinkel. The crew of four had baled out over Harlington, Streatley, Putteridge and Breachwood Green. The pilot was taken prisoner in the vicinity of the wrecked machine. Another member of the crew was taken on the Hitchin Road and brought into Luton in a bus by the driver and an R.A.F. officer. Those who had been passengers in the bus had to walk, and probably thought the cause adequate. Others of the crew were picked up near Streatley.

*   *   *   *

Luton's bomb-free period was broken on Saturday, September 5th, 1942. Without warning a bomb fell about mid-day in Midland Road. Five were killed, 18 injured. Some houses were destroyed, others extensively damaged. The L.M.S. Goods Depot suffered to some extent, but a fraction of a split second's difference in the time the bomb was released might have put it right into the depot. Badly injured was a man on duty at the gate. He had previously had a narrow escape during the first Vauxhall raid. A man who came home to dinner found his house in ruins. He knew his daughter should be indoors, helped to find her dead body, and then, without a word, took off his coat and helped rescue parties in their work. Another woman who was killed was not identified for days. She had been on a visit to a brother, was walking to the station when the bomb fell, and was only identified when a telegram was later received asking why she had not returned.

94

A victim of the bomb which fell in Old Bedford Road is removed from the scene of devastation, while rescue workers search the debris for further casualties.

LEFT: *Hoods and materials were blasted into the tree tops after the Old Bedford Road catastrophe on October 15th, 1940.*

BELOW: *Frederick Street littered with debris and hat materials a few minutes after the bomb had fallen.*

Without warning one Saturday morning in September, 1942, a lone daylight raider, unperceived and at an immense height, dropped a bomb which fell on a house in Midland Road. There were casualties and in this picture rescue workers and others are seen searching for the missing.

On a bright November morning in 1944, a tremendous explosion rocked the town. Luton experienced its first and only V2 rocket. It fell in Biscot Road, between the despatch shop of Commer-Karrier's and the houses alongside. It killed 19 people, and injured 196.

Rescuers at work among the debris of the houses on the other side of Biscot Road. These pictures were taken within five minutes of the disaster.

A woman of 70, after treatment for shock, insisted on returning to sleep in her damaged home that night, " Hitler and all his bombs are not going to keep me from sleeping in my own bed," she said.

The Methodist Central Mission, so badly damaged by blast that later it had to be re-roofed, had the following notice outside next day—" Bombed, but the Pastor will conduct harvest services at 10.30, 2.30 and 6."

* * * *

Came another long interval, until on the night of October 21, 1943, a string of bombs was dropped across the Leagrave district. Ten people were injured, but only four were taken to hospital, three from one house. They had been buried half an hour. Over 400 houses were put in need of repair, and again the fine spirit of the people was made evident in the way those not affected took care of the less fortunate. Worst damage was done at the junction of Beechwood Road and Waller Avenue. One bomb fell right on the L.M.S. main line where it is on an embankment just south of Leagrave Station, and tore up all the tracks, but such a good repair job was done that trains were going through next day.

* * * *

For a time there was peace day and night, until the sirens began to wail for V-1's, otherwise Flying Bombs or Doodlebugs. Despite many warnings, however, only two of these fell in Luton, in the early hours of June 21st, 1944. One fell on allotments near Ashcroft Road and Sowerby Road, causing blast damage to a row of bungalows. A rest centre was opened, but many aged people refused to leave their homes, and at once set about making a very early cup of tea. The other fell on open land not far from Luton and Dunstable Hospital, which escaped completely although a number of houses had windows and doors blown in. Serious casualties were nil, and minor injuries few.

Another flying bomb made a terrific noise one Saturday night as it passed over the town. There was tension as people waited for something to happen, but the noise kept on and on. For some reason this one appeared to be out for a long distance record. It finished in the Northampton district.

* * * *

Luton, however, still had to take it. Like a bolt from the blue, a V2 caused part of the Biscot Road district to disappear just before 10 a.m. on November 6th, 1944. It landed in Biscot Road between the dispatch department of Commer-Karrier, Ltd., and adjoining houses, and shook the town. Houses nearest the scene disintegrated in a manner the like of which had never before been seen in Luton. They disappeared in a fine red dust, carried away across Wardown Park in the gentle breeze. The death roll of 19 was the second highest of any Luton incident. In addition 196 people were injured. Lucky it was for the workers at Commer-Karrier and the neighbouring works of George Kent, Ltd., that the rocket fell on the town side of the Commer building, and that the steel-strengthened walls took the strain of much of the colossal blast that would otherwise have swept this factory area. A newly-erected canteen on the upper floor of the dispatch building was wrecked. It had cost about £25,000, and had been open one week. Five minutes later and it would have been filled for the mid-morning break.

Although 1,524 houses were damaged, many of them seriously, no call was made on the rest centre which was opened immediately. Instead of having to provide sleeping accommodation that night, it was able to close down. This was a magnificent tribute to the spirit of the townsfolk in a terrible adversity, and to the courage and fortitude that became necessary ingredients of everyday life.

Hero of the day was Dr. H. O. O'Meara, whose house was completely demolished. It was surgery time, and patients were in the waiting room, but the only person needing hospital treatment was Mrs. O'Meara. Somehow Dr. O'Meara escaped, and, although badly shaken, took part in rescue work, attended the injured, and was afterwards a tower of strength at the Hospital. Later he was commended in the London Gazette.

At the time not a word of any V2 incident was allowed to pass the censor, and for days there were rumours that the incident was not due to enemy action but to a works explosion. There were even people who declared that they had seen notices posted to this effect, although there were no such notices. It can be said now that Luton was immediately visited by experts, who quickly satisfied themselves that Luton had had its V2.

*   *   *   *

Having had something of almost everything—H.E.'s, parachute mines, oil bombs, " breadbaskets," V1's and a V2, Luton was left alone for the few remaining months the war in Europe lasted. In all 107 people lost their lives, and close on 500 were injured. Four incidents, spread over four years, caused 99 of the deaths. What would have been the total if incidents had continued at the rate of the first few months is too grievous to contemplate. Luton had the protection of night fighters—some Defiants were stationed here for a period—and it had its smoke screen, but it had no heavy A.A. gun defence.

*   *   *   *

Tailpiece.—Nine hundred times the " Alert " sounded in Luton— that eerie wail that sent a cold tremor through many a heart ; 900 times they sounded " Raiders Passed," with nothing to distinguish the last time from any other.

Yet, although they sounded for the last time in Luton before the V-Days, there is a village not a hundred miles from Luton where, it is popularly stated, the " alert " has been on since 1941. In those days the local constable had to cycle through the village blowing his whistle in " short, sharp blasts " to give the warning, and then to cycle through the village again, giving a continuous blast to cancel the warning. One night in 1941, or so it is said, the officer received the warning and, true to instructions, mounted his cycle and, with his whistle between his lips, pedalled furiously through the village until his front wheel hit a big stone, with the result that he went over the handlebars into a wet and slimy ditch. His whistle disappeared into the mud, eluded diligent search, and, say the villagers, " We're still waiting for ' Raiders Passed ! ' "

The "IF . . ." Plan

INTO the archives of the Borough of Luton has gone the one great secret plan for a Luton at War. Only a few have seen it, but Lutonians, in common with every other community throughout the country, may count it as one of their major blessings that it was never necessary to put it in operation.

It might well have been called the " If— " Plan. *If*—. A small word of vast significance, for it loomed large in the thoughts of the leaders of town life in 1940, 1941 and even 1942. *If* Britain had been invaded, and *if* the spearhead of the enemy had approached Luton what was to happen ? The plan laid down the rules for Luton *in extremis* and here for the first time is the story of that plan.

* * * *

The preparation of the plan and its operation in its preliminary stages was the responsibility of the civil authorities. If invasion had in fact materialised, civil administration was to continue to be a matter for the civil authorities until the near approach of the enemy made military control essential. Even then, orders affecting the civil population were to be given as far as possible through civilian channels. It was understood that if there seemed likely to develop a state of panic beyond the control of the civil authorities, and if higher authorities ordered him to take over, or if the civil powers asked him to do so, the senior military representative, Col. A. J. Mander, O.B.E., would take complete control, but that absolute military control was to be relinquished as soon as it was considered safe to do so.

The essential thing was that in real emergency all civilian needs should be subordinated to military requirements in a co-ordinated effort to defend Luton " to the last man," without withdrawal. To this end all forms of activity had to be prepared to co-operate—those who had been trained for some form of special service, those who had to maintain the operation of the public utility services while they could be maintained, those responsible for keeping industry going while it was practicable and in the last resort for taking pre-arranged steps to deny its use to the enemy, and even those people who had no allotted duties, but were physically fit.

*   *   *   *

Planning was begun by the Town Council before the war. From the first day of war the whole of the local administration was temporarily vested in an Emergency Committee of three. When invasion threatened, their defence plans were inherited and developed by a still larger Invasion Committee. This Committee had to view their onerous responsibilities from two angles. They had to endeavour to assess the circumstances which might arise from an invasion which did not reach this particular locality, but which would have given them the additional responsibility of caring for thousands of people from coastal areas. They had to plan, also, so that everything would dovetail in with military requirements if and when the fighting did involve Luton.

The first essential was that the population should " Stand Firm." There were to be no homeless people wandering at large. They were to be directed to Rest Centres until they could be put into billets. And this billeting was to be done quickly, to make room in the Rest Centres for other homeless people as they came along.

There was a reason for directing that people should " Stand Firm." It was considered to be the lesser of two evils for them. It was realised that if they stayed in their homes they would inevitably be subjected to grave danger if fighting took place in the neighbourhood. On the other hand, if they tried to take to the roads, they would not only jeopardise the chances of successful resistance by impeding military movements, but would be subject to the risks of machine-gunning from the air, of bombing, of being run down by tanks, all of which had been the fate of a mass of refugees across the Channel. They would also be unlikely to find food or shelter even if they escaped these perils. The police had instructions to enforce the " Stand Firm " policy to the utmost practicable extent, even by the use of arms.

True, it was realised that circumstances might make some controlled dispersal of the people necessary, but where they were to go, and how they were to get there without using important roads, was all planned.

There were three people, however, who were expected to stay on under any circumstances . . . the Mayor, the Town Clerk, and the Chief Constable. Even if it meant falling into the hands of the enemy, these three were to stay, and they must continue to do the best they could for the people.

It had to be visualised that Luton might be cut off from all outside supplies, and have to exist on its own resources. The people would

102

not have starved . . . not immediately. Special stocks of food were stored about the town, to require minimum transport for distribution. They would have kept the people going for a little while. Then the "buffer depots," where were dispersed stocks of food not primarily intended for Luton, and which were to be put immediately under a close guard, would have been taken over. Food still on the hoof would have been driven into the town while it was still possible, and the people would have fed a little longer.

Sufficient food was in the town, even if no other supplies were obtainable, to last the population for at least six weeks, and there was power to requisition any other stocks which came to the knowledge of the authorities. It was not overlooked that rumour might start panic buying. The counter-measure was to close immediately such shops as were considered necessary, and to introduce a new rationing system.

With the enemy actually at the gates, all food, including any which could be salvaged from damaged buildings, was to be pooled and, in order to prevent the enemy from getting it in their control, it was to be shared out free among the people who were still alive. Emergency cooking and feeding stations were all in the plan.

Provision had to be made for the possible failure of water supplies in damaged parts of the town, with the consequent necessity of distributing water at fixed points for domestic use, and of delivering it to hospitals and bakeries. Then there would have been water police and water carriers. The domestic ration provisionally fixed at one gallon per head per day would have been insufficient for many things. There would have been no baths, not even in the regulation five inches.

Many things less vital than food and water had to be the subject of planning. Telegraph and telephone communication might have been interrupted by damage to cables. If so, there was telegraph equipment standing by outside Luton which could at once have been put into any one of three previously selected buildings. If the telephone exchange had been hit, local service would have ended, but certain priority lines would have functioned at once from another building especially equipped for this emergency. If that in turn had failed, then there were two places on the outskirts of the town where telephone engineers could have "cut-in" and re-established communications for official purposes. These were necessary precautions apart from the invasion threat. Any bomb dropped on Luton might have created that emergency.

Incidentally, the Post Office was charged with maintaining at least one daily delivery of letters and parcels . . . while there were any to deliver.

Adequate space was earmarked for burials. Bodies were to be clearly labelled for identification so that later, if desired, they could be disinterred for proper burial. Five mortuaries could have accommodated 600 bodies pending early burial to make room for more. Shrouds, etc., were stored ready at each.

Rather a grim picture of what might have been !

To facilitate the defence of Luton by improving fields of fire, it was planned deliberately to destroy some houses, and to evacuate people from others compulsorily. The scheme was no respecter of persons. Like other people, Ald. John Burgoyne, then Mayor and Chairman of the Invasion Committee, would have had to get out; his home was near important cross-roads. Like others similarly displaced, he would then have been billeted, if necessary.

How were the public to be told what was required of them? A local newspaper—even if only a duplicated quarto sheet—would have been published regularly by *The Luton News* up to the moment when enemy tanks broke into the town, and newsagents would have distributed it, but obviously in such extreme emergency the maximum publicity would have been needed for the orders of authority. Remember those official notice boards which appeared? They were rather suggestive of some specialised advertising, with their " nothing genuine unless it bears the facsimile signature of the Chief Constable." There were many of them about the town, and every precaution would have been taken to ensure that ill-disposed people were unable to utilise them. They would have been supplemented by a still larger number of official news distribution centres.

To make very important announcements to the people, the Mayor and the Chief Constable had authority to use a secret wireless transmitter not far outside the town. It looked nothing like what it was. Actually it was brought into use as one of the low-powered relay transmitters used by the B.B.C. during those times when, if reception was bad, listeners were advised to try certain unfamiliar wave-lengths, and so get better reception. There were a large number of such stations, so many that they were of no use to hostile aircraft as sign-posts. Actually neither the Mayor nor the Chief Constable would have left the town even for this purpose. An understudy, a local man with a local voice, was charged with the duty and responsibility of broadcasting any such announcements to the people of Luton. It was never necessary; the main thing was, the transmitter was there, if required.

If the worst came to the worst, it was expected that all the fit men in the Home Guard would be so fully occupied with fighting that some civilians would have to assist them in non-combatant roles by doing cooking, orderly room duties, etc., while civilians would also have had to undertake the disposal of both military and civilian casualties. With this in mind, routes to main and emergency hospitals were planned to avoid primary military roads to the utmost degree.

There were lots of odd little things which had to be remembered, such as the provision of lamps, oil, candles and torches for Civil Defence posts and depots, and having a paymaster available with money for those whose misfortunes left them without any for immediate needs, that is, of course, on the assumption that for a time at least money would continue to have had some use.

Car owners would have had a doleful time. It was their responsibility, if the enemy were at hand, to immobilise their vehicles if they were not earmarked for essential military purposes. Immobilisation of a kind which would have satisfied the law under other circumstances would not have done. The vehicles were to be driven to appointed dumps, and there the cylinder blocks were to be smashed. Where owners failed to do what was required, the police would have done the job. Even cycles were to be made useless.

At the same time all the petrol pumps in the town which were still in service would have been effectively sealed. There was only one exception which, under strong guard, was to remain in operation until the last minute to keep Home Guard transport supplied. The bulk storage depot in Leagrave Road was to have been blown up, but not until all the people in the neighbourhood had been cleared out and it was not expected that afterwards there would have been much left standing in that part of Leagrave Road. Stocks of fuel, oil and industrial spirit were also to have been denied the enemy.

The whole scheme of preparation hinged on two warnings. " Stand To " (the first) would have indicated possible danger, with the probability of considerable troop movements. " Action Stations " (the second) would have meant that danger was imminent.

*   *   *   *

Here, planned action was divided into four phases, according to the tactics adopted by the enemy. Phase A visualised a large-scale bombing attack as an invasion preliminary, and possible at any time after " Stand To," but unlikely after " Action Stations." Phase B presumed an invasion in progress, but the enemy still some distance away. Phase C, the most vital, assumed a battle taking place in the locality, or imminent, and would have required the town's full defence plan to be put into operation. Phase D was for when, the enemy having gained a temporary occupation of the neighbourhood, further armed resistance was useless, and all that remained was to do the best possible for the community, and to improvise services as a substitute for those which had broken down.

Nerve centre for all these and other preparations was Central Control, down under the Police Station, where there was ceaseless watching and listening. There was a duplicate control centre among the foundations of the Town Hall, and both had emergency lighting plant. If Central Control had been put out of action, however, it would have been immediately re-established elsewhere, right on the spot which was to be the military rendezvous if the gravest emergency had arisen. For this eventuality, lines of communication were already established. At " Action Stations," however, there would have been a joint H.Q. with the Military Commander.

So much for the civil preparations, some of which were known, many unknown, at the time. What of the preparations for armed resistance ? That was to be the great opportunity of the Home Guard, the primary reason for calling that body into existence.

Military defence had to be planned on the basis that, except for any small bodies of troops stationed in the town, the whole brunt of the fighting would fall on the two Luton battalions of the Home Guard, acting in close liaison with those of adjoining areas while contact could be maintained, but completely self-reliant if and when fighting reached close quarters and outside communications failed. Small parties of airborne invaders were expected, and everything was arranged to give them appropriate attention ; but it was the possibility of ground troops in combination with armoured vehicles that created the most serious outlook. It was realised that if these reached Luton, then, in the words of one member of the Invasion Committee, it would be " Hell let loose." Another summing up of the probable outlook was " just massacre."

The first object, therefore, was to keep the enemy as far away as possible, and to this end the rapid passing of information was bound to be important. Planned information channels were various. One of which little was heard, but which made it clear that our forbears knew something, was visual signalling by Aldis lamps. Even in daylight—it could not be practised in darkness—it was found that messages could be circulated fairly rapidly over a wide area, and that the vantage points from which these messages were flashed were almost invariably those selected by the Romans and Ancient Britons in their day.

Another thing of vital importance was to keep roads open for military traffic. If they were blocked or made unsafe by bombing, they had to be cleared or made safe. This was a task to which more importance was attached than saving civilian life and property.

As the area for which Luton was responsible stretched to Streatley, Hyde and Caddington, it was necessary to have an elastic scheme under which mobile reserves could have been rushed to threatened areas, of watching outposts which could fall back on strong points, of " Defended Localities " from which there was to be no withdrawal, and of an inner " Keep " which was to be held to the last man.

Barton Cutting would have been a nasty spot for enemy armour, so lined with fougasses were the sides. On other road approaches to the town there were hidden fougasses, so sited that they would have jumped the screening hedges at the critical moment.

The outer ring of road blocks was not expected to have much more than a delaying value, for tanks and other track vehicles are not restricted to the use of roads. As outposts they might have had their uses. Much more faith was placed on the inner ring and on the " Defended Localities." These were Stopsley, the Airport, Vauxhall Motors, the Castle Street—Windsor Street cross-roads, Kingsway,

Telephonists at Luton Central Control, which was housed in the Police Station.

The indicator board, which showed the location and strength of the various A.R.P. services in the town.

Skefko, Commer Cars and Kents, and Wardown Park. For these places the order was, " There will be no withdrawal. They will be defended to the last man."

If the enemy succeeded in getting through anywhere there was still the inner ring of tank stops, mostly under the railway bridges, where there was no avoiding route, but before these could be reached there were many other things which would have made passage very unpleasant for the enemy.

Whatever happened, it was laid down that " the enemy will be fought in every street in the town," with the object of holding at least the central " Keep." This included the Police Station, Post Office and Telephone Exchange, with the Town Hall to be held as long as possible. In view of the preparations made round about, the tank stop in George Street was calculated to be a very unpleasant spot. To get as close as this meant running the gauntlet of many unsuspected firing points, such as the parapeted flat roof of Messrs. Dickinson and Adams' garage in Bridge Street.

Ignoring any troops which might have been on the spot, the available fighting force consisted of something under 4,000 Home Guards. Not for nothing had they been trained in street fighting. Their range of weapons included rifles, light machine guns, Sten guns, spigot mortars, Northover Projectors, Smith guns, grenade-throwing rifles, Browning automatic rifles, Marlin guns and flame throwers, while after it ceased to be possible for Vauxhall to send any more tanks to the Army, any others that were or could be finished would have been handed over to the Home Guard, complete with 6-pdr. guns and ammunition.

Any prisoners who could be captured while it was still open warfare would have been passed on to cages elsewhere, so that the Home Guard were not bothered with their custody. It was planned, however, that if Luton should be cut off from other areas, safe local accommodation would be available for prisoners, and it was rumoured that the prisoners' cage would do equally well for any local Quislings or obstructionists who betrayed their true colours.

*   *   *   *

There you have the picture of what was planned for the defence of Luton. The necessity for such preparations was only a matter of conjecture when they began with the original A.R.P. training. The necessity remained uncertain during the period of the phoney war. Even Dunkirk was not a convincing proof. But what became known as the Battle of Britain, when the Luftwaffe was seeking to blast Britain out of the war, and when the outcome of the battle was still in the balance, brought invasion prospects very near. Those were care-laden days and nights for all who were charged with defending to the last their own particular part of the Homeland. Then the time did appear imminent when everything would be put to the supreme test.

Try-out exercises had been held. Everything went according to plan. But it was all based on theory, and theory and practice are often far removed when there is enemy interference. No one could foretell what would happen in grim reality. All that could be done was to prepare. So that no possible provision should be overlooked, the Invasion Committee conferences had been reinforced by the heads of all phases of activity expected to contribute to the common end. Each had to satisfy the Committee and the Military Commander that every emergency that could be envisaged had been provided for as far as was humanly practicable. The most momentous conference of all, having occupied all one Sunday morning, ended with these half-jocular words—" Well, we seem to have provided for everything . . . unless he comes at us from below."

Even with all preparations made, it could not but continue to be a period of great anxiety. It did not end with the defeat of the Luftwaffe in the Battle of Britain. It persisted while the coasts across the Channel were lined with invasion barges, and until it was clear that Hitler had turned his back on this country in favour of his disastrous adventure eastwards into Russia.

Then the sky definitely became brighter, although all the clouds did not roll away. Some still hung about while the Luftwaffe continued to rain death from the skies, and until D-Day had passed without precipitating a counter-invasion. The V 1's and V 2's created new problems, but invasion, airborne or otherwise, did not come. The end of the war in Europe did. The end of the World War did.

*   *   *   *

Then there was no more need for an Invasion Committee, which always seemed to be misnamed. It should have been the Anti-Invasion Committee. And there was nobody more profoundly thankful than the members of the Committee that the defence scheme never had to be put into operation, and that the people of Luton, though always standing firm, never had to move to " Action Stations."

The Home Guard

MAY, 1940, was a beautiful month in England. Spring had brought out its new finery ; the trees and meadows were fresh and green. Truly this land of ours was a wonderful country.

Yet there was tension in the air. The Swastika was sweeping through to the Channel ports. On May 14th, Mr. Anthony Eden broadcast his call.

It came in the 9 p.m. news. At 9.15 there was a queue at Luton

Police Station of men who had not waited for the broadcast to end. One was asked what impelled him to come . . . " Well," he said, " I've been thinking there ought to be something I could do. I'm too old for the Army ; other forms of the war effort seem too passive.

" Then," he added, " I heard Mr. Eden. It was as if he had opened the door to me personally and said—' Come right in—we'll be glad of your help.' So here I am."

That was the feeling of all who joined. It was largely inarticulate, but Nazism offended them, the country was being threatened. This was their chance.

Over a century ago, when the cliffs above Calais were dotted with the white tents of Napoleon's armies, the call had gone out and been answered. In the uncertainty of 1914 the call had gone out again and grey-clad figures of mature years and figures marched and counter-marched in the pleasant fields of Luton Hoo. They too were to be the ultimate defence of England's homes and families. In May, 1940, when the call went out again Local Defence Volunteers became overnight a million strong. Within a few days two millions had responded to the call to arms.

*   *   *   *

" To Arms " was perhaps a misnomer. The arms were not there yet the L.D.V. were not deterred. " Pikes, if necessary," said one politician. That was the spirit of the times.

Men flocked in, weapons dribbled in. Borrowed shotguns, antique carbines, revolvers that had done duty in 1914-18, German weapons " won " in the same period, these were some of the available arms. The fact that for some there was no ammunition seemed not to matter. The weapons were the outward sign of an inward determination. Ingenuity was not lacking. Home-made " cocktails " of paraffin and tar were mixed in J. W. bottles as anti-tank weapons. They inspired confidence, which was about all they could do.

In later days the Home Guard, as the L.D.V. were renamed, had many of the latest weapons ; but even without them the L.D.V. had the confidence of the nation. They were determined to fight on the beaches, in the streets and fields, on the hills if necessary. But they prayed silently for the arms and ammunition that seemed so long coming.

*   *   *   *

Mr. Eden was not worried so much by the possibility of a seaborne landing as by a repetition of enemy tactics which had proved so disastrous in Holland and Belgium—dropping troops by parachute behind the main defence lines to seize strategic points, and generally to disorganise things until reinforced.

Any such arrivals had immediately to be " contained "—to use an overworked term of the time—until real soldiers arrived, so Mr. Eden asked the old soldiers and others to be the eyes and ears of the Army, and to fight if need be. In Luton 60 enrolled the first night. Next day there was a procession to Dunstable Place ; the thousand mark was passed.

To enrol 1,000 volunteers in a day was eminently satisfactory. They had to be organised. An organisation took shape quickly. Mr. A. J. Mander, who served with the 5th Bedfords in the Palestine Campaign and, after the re-organisation of the Territorials, as a Company Commander in the same Battalion, was put in charge. Many of the volunteers had served with him. Many others had known him as their headmaster at school.

First intimation that things were moving was a summons at short notice to Beech Hill School, to hear what was required of the L.D.V., and to say what each could best do. The school hall could not contain all at one session. There were Monday and Tuesday meetings. All the notices had been addressed on the Sunday at Mr. Mander's own house, for a few volunteers had put in a bit of overtime in advance.

The meetings were crowded. Many at the Monday meeting only received notice when they got home from work. Some could hardly have stopped for tea. Mr. Mander, with a blackboard handy, put across a simple but grim story. These men, already sweating at their benches by day as never before, were ready for anything. Luton had to be guarded day and night. Whatever the reluctance of bone and sinew past their first youth, the job must be done, and done well. He explained that the town and outskirts had already been surveyed for defensive positions and look-out posts, divided into four areas, and a leader chosen for each.

As likely landing places in the surrounding countryside had to be patrolled at night, and watch kept on woodlands useful for daytime cover, it was facetiously suggested that because of their extensive and peculiar knowledge, and their ability to catch without being caught, poachers would make the most expert patrols. Alas, Luton lacked such experts.

The first patrols went out. Four hours on, four off, was the tour of duty. The moon was past the full, everything ideal for parachutists. The countryside lay dark and silent. But on Bradgers Hill, in the fields beyond Lewsey, on the windswept Downs above Skimpot, and in the high fields to the south, alert men kept vigil.

Silent, elderly figures, were most of them, with incongruous Army caps topping their working clothes. They dug out their winter mufflers and old overcoats, and made themselves armbands.

From the Water Towers at Hart Hill and Tennyson Road, watchers looked afield. From the south came the subdued rumble of guns ; the far horizon glowed from the water-front fires of Calais and Boulogne, over a hundred miles away. They studied the skies, these watchers, hour after hour, as their trouser-legs became sodden and the pre-dawn chill gripped their bones.

Night passed, the day came, dusk fell again. Other watchers came in their turn, and more of them, until night by night throughout that fateful summer Luton was ringed by its guardian L.D.V.

If the parachutes some saw floating in the air proved to be really cloud, if some patrol was apt to discover things which did not exist, they could be pardoned for erring on the side of over-caution. Of many such a one it was well said in a little history put out by one of the Companies after the Stand Down.—

" To the raw recruit, patrolling at night was an eerie experience. Many a guard commander has been awakened to investigate a star low in the heavens that appeared to the sentry to be a light signalling behind a hedge, and ' a blazing fire just beyond the sky-line,' that was in reality the rising moon.

" Sheep coughing at night sounded very human ; hedgehogs moving noisily through dead leaves ; bullfrogs croaking ; owls hooting ; electric cables sparking and fiercely crackling in the drizzle : all tended to fray the nerves of the inexperienced sentry. In addition, he had to listen to bombs falling on Luton, and to speculate on their nearness to his loved ones. "

The latter was no exaggeration. During the daylight watch from the Water Towers, one beautiful August afternoon, an L.D.V. saw bombs fall without warning and thought one was very near his home. He asked to be relieved so that he could go and investigate. Later he returned with the news that his house had been struck, his wife killed,

*   *   *   *

While day watchers and night patrols were doing what was required of them, there was much activity behind the scenes. First essentials were headquarters and headquarters staff. Dr. J. W. Bone promptly made headquarters available at 4, Dunstable Road. It offered a lot of rooms, cellars, some garden space, and a garage. All and more proved to be needed as time passed, but the original furniture was limited to a table and a chair—surely the minimum for dealing with 1,000 men ! Mr. Robert Durler, who was to prove a good friend in many ways, produced chairs, tables, and even a typewriter as if by magic. He even added furniture and lino for a small canteen near the kitchen.

The full-time paid staff authorised was one civilian administrator— also surely the minimum. Mr. Frank Facer filled this post. This was before the L.D.V. had become the Home Guard, and the Home Guard had become a regimental unit complete with officers from Lieutenant-Colonel downwards, including an Adjutant, a Commissioned Quartermaster, and even instructors from line regiments.

But the L.D.V. got to work without these frills, and there was a lot of work. Uniforms, arms, stores gradually came and had to be issued. Mr. A. N. C. Bennett did yeoman service as unpaid quartermaster, often seven days a week. When not quartermastering he concocted " cocktails " to give prospective bombers and others something with which to practise.

When rifles, American, did arrive, they could not just be handed out to men going on patrol. They came in cases which needed strong fatigue parties to handle them. They were smothered in mineral jelly. More fatigue parties took on the messy job of cleaning them for use. Then instructors from a unit stationed in the town gave some " old sweats " a brief refresher course, necessary even for them after the lapse of years. When the Canadian Ross also arrived, its bolt-action held puzzles for many an old soldier.

Defence positions had to be constructed, trenches dug. Tools, timber, wire, sandbags, etc., were drawn from headquarters by working parties who put them to good use. Road blocks had to be built. It was largely Saturday and Sunday work, with no union rate. Gardens were neglected.

Sunday mornings were particularly hectic, because most men were then available. Rifles for training were issued to squads still without them, and taken in again. Practice stores were drawn, and the non-explosives returned after practice, for use another day. And more working parties went out.

When the first patrols went out uniforms were still so scarce that it was a case of one man having a uniform and the other just an L.D.V. armlet to comply with international convention. Perhaps he remembered it should be sewn on. More probably he conveniently forgot. Observation posts were manned day and night. Day watches were difficult to organise, but there were always some who, to an extent masters of their own time, could hold the fort. Duties by day were often more pleasant than by night, but not always so. A lifetime of experience descended in a few moments on one party on the Tennyson Road Water Tower during that fateful afternoon in August, 1940.

It was a pleasant afternoon—blue sky above, peaceful homes below. Without warning came the sound of an explosion, and a burst of smoke from the Airport was visible. A second or so later, and there was a burst of smoke from the Vauxhall, with a pillar of smoke afterwards rising into the air ; this was but the beginning.

Above in the blue was a cluster of specks speeding across the town. The L.D.V., fascinated, watched stick after stick of bombs drop on unprotected Luton. Park Street, Strathmore Avenue, Baker Street— the next stick, one thought, was surely destined for the Tower. But the nearest fell 100 yards away ; the line of destruction continued through the Farley Hill district and on to Caddington and even Whipsnade Zoo.

The L.D.V. leader breathed a sigh of relief, sat down to write his report.

* * * *

Autumn saw the completion of various strong points on the approaches to Luton. The military sited many of them, not always to advantage, and a lot were afterwards superseded. They were mostly slit trenches and anti-tank obstacles. In theory they were to be delaying points for enemy spearheads. In practice they would have been by-passed, leaving isolated L.D.V. sections to be mopped up later, in blood and glory.

Nevertheless they had to be manned, with battle headquarters from which outposts could be maintained and patrols sent out. When sirens wailed these strong-points were manned, roads closed, traffic stopped, identity cards examined. At " Raiders Passed " they were abandoned, and " Home James " was the order. But when " Alerts " and " Raiders Passed " alternated all through a night, men began to wonder how long they must continue playing this apparently absurd form of " The Grand Old Duke of York." Fortunately it did not continue indefinitely.

It was just as well, for even night watches began to be a problem. In the early weeks there were plenty of men for rotas which cast an undue burden on no-one. But the seven-day week for factories, changing night shifts, etc., brought to headquarters a constant stream of messages such as " Father's got to work on Sunday and can you find someone else ? " Then lads in some of the older youth movements, who did messenger duty, had to hustle round the town. Somehow, however, the job that had to be done was done, not because anybody could give orders, but because of a general willingness to do what someone decided was necessary.

About this time the initials L.D.V. disappeared and the new name, The Home Guard, caught on. Supplementing the town organisation the big works formed their own Home Guard. The railways and bus undertakings did the same. The Post Office did the same, but for some queer reason that contingent was attached to Cambs. H.G., although it had to rely on Luton for the loan of extra rifles for Sunday drills.

Weapons and uniforms, as has been said, were scarce in the early days. The few Denim suits did not contribute to smartness. A man with a middle-age spread found that if his blouse was big enough the trousers had much useless length. A tall man, to whom trouser length mattered, would find his blouse go almost twice round. When every man got a uniform, jobbing tailors got a lot of jobs ; but, to begin with, Denims had to be passed from patrol to patrol, with no guarantee that men exchanging would be of a size. Wearing a uniform just shed by another was in any case not popular.

This phase passed. Denims were replaced by battle dress for all ; the clump of " ammunitions " became common, greatcoats, belts, gaiters, groundsheets, came along, and there was a general smartening up. Some " old sweats " revived an enthusiasm for " spit and polish," and were really annoyed when " dubbin only " became regulation.

Other changes took place. Patrolling and watching became interspersed with lectures, and classes for specialists. Transport, communication and intelligence sections developed. For H.Q. personnel there was the first T.E.W.T. (tactical exercise without troops). It lasted from Saturday to Monday, and included such diversions as an umpire ruling that the power station had been hit. This involved recourse to storm lanterns and flickering candles which were not the best things by which to read hurriedly written messages. Then he declared that the telephone exchange had been put out of action, so that runners had to be used.

But the umpires were the first to tire of this game.

*   *   *   *

The original thousand had grown considerably, and growing pains made the freeing of the Drill Hall by the military a welcome chance to move to quarters where the ammunition didn't have to be kept among the coal, and where some companies could also have adequate offices and stores. The L.D.V. having become the Home Guard, had also become part of the Army, although, as to the end, unpaid.

There came the introduction of a conscripted element, and the withdrawal of the option of resigning. Few, in fact, ever availed themselves of this option.

Naturally some of the originals, although still willing in spirit, fell by the way through age or infirmity as the years dragged on. Younger members were called to the Services. Strength had to be maintained, even increased. Therefore a conscripted element was probably unavoidable, but it is true to say that to the end the original volunteers were still the sound core of the force.

With military status came commissions for officers as a solution to the question of responsibility if the Home Guard had to do duty by the side of the Army. Mr. Mander became Lieutenant-Colonel in command of what was now the 4th Bedfordshire Battn. Home Guard, with Mr. J. W. Weedon, one of the original four leaders, as second-in-command, with the rank of Major. Mr. Facer, commissioned in the General List for the purpose, became Captain and Adjutant, and Capt. Connell came from the Hertfordshire Regiment to be Quarter-master.

Company commanders were :—" A," Major Colin Large. " B," Major F. G. Harmer, M.M. " C," Major J. H. Stephenson. " D," Major Russell Gregory. " E," Major J. H. Brett. Captains, lieutenants and second lieutenants became legion, with intelligence, weapon training, bombing, ammunition, transport, signals and other officers in addition to those doing duty with the companies. Maybe some didn't quite fill the bill. The justification for their selection was that posts had to be filled quickly, and without the benefit of later knowledge which might have modified the choice. Whatever the failings of some in other respects, all had a willingness to do things, which counted for much.

There were many things to be done as time went on. The watching days passed. Men still went on duty at night, but were trained to fight as well as to watch. Battle training became the order. Night exercises in open country were frequent. Joint exercises with neighbouring units were arranged, Luton sometimes providing the attackers, sometimes being the attacked. Street fighting was practised among

115

bombed buildings. Men of a mobile platoon had particularly strenuous Sunday mornings, and hurrying up and down a spot like Galley Hill convinced many that they were not as young as they thought.

*　　*　　*　　*

Soon the Battalion reached a strength of 4,000 or more. It was unwieldy. Other Battalions were having a similar experience, so what was probably the greatest change of all was ordered. Battalions were divided, and in Luton the 7th came into existence. One regrettable feature was that partition could not be made strictly on a company basis. Companies spreading across new boundary lines had to be divided, and men lost association with those with whom they had served from the beginning.

Concurrently a Beds. South Sector Command was created, and Lieut-Col. Mander, who had been awarded the O.B.E., returned to 4, Dunstable Road, as a red-tabbed Colonel in command of the Sector. He took with him Capt. E. Lintern, M.C., who had been responsible for Intelligence, to develop this work at Sector level. At Sector, Col. Mander was responsible not only for the two Luton battalions, but also for the one based on Dunstable. As Luton, to which East Hyde had been attached from the start, had had Caddington and Streatley added, and the Dunstable battalion also extended into the villages, Col. Mander had a pretty big area to cover. His Sector command also carried with it that of Town Commander in emergency.

Major Weedon went up to Lieut-Col. in command of the 4th Battalion, with Major Gregory as second-in-command. The 7th was placed under Lieut-Col. Brett, with Major Harmer as second-in-command. To give each battalion some continuity of internal administration, Capt. Facer went over to the 7th as Adjutant, Capt. Connell remaining with the 4th as Quartermaster. The new Adjutant of the 4th was Capt. W. Driscoll, whose rows of ribbons indicated much active service in many lands in an unbroken service with the Rifle Brigade from 1914. The 7th acquired as Quartermaster Capt. W. Brooker, who had had long service with the County Regiment, stayed until the Stand Down, then saw service in another capacity on the Continent, and, to the regret of many, died soon after his return to Luton on demobilisation.

Company Commanders became :—4th Battn. " A," Major K. J. Bennett; " B," Major W. Pottie; " C," Major A. N. C. Bennett; " D," Major W. Hartop; " E," Major Large. 7th Battn. :—" G," Major H. H. Cooke; " H," Major J. C. Cunningham, D.S.O.; " J," Major K. Smith; " K," Major J. H. Stephenson, (succeeded after his death by Major A. Godfrey); " L," Major Whitely, and, later, Major W. E. Hills.

The Drill Hall was H.Q. for both, but Quartermasters' stores, armouries, etc., had to be duplicated, and guns, transport, ambulances, etc., so absorbed space that thereafter company offices and stores were dotted about the town. In any case, there were better places to spend

RIGHT: *Some of the first to respond to Mr. Anthony Eden's broadcast appeal in May, 1940, for the Local Defence Volunteers. They are signing on at Luton Police Station.*

BELOW: *Mr. R. J. Verran, an ex-naval man and Mr. R. Gillingwater, Old Contemptible, on one of the first armed L.D.V. patrols, in May, 1940. The patrols covered the hills round Luton to watch for possible enemy parachute troops. At that time, most of the patrols, like Mr. Gillingwater, could not be provided with any other uniform than a cap.*

ABOVE: *Battle squad commanders receive their orders from a Platoon commander, at a demonstration given by "J" Company, 7th Battn. Bedfs. Home Guard at Luton Hoo.*

RIGHT: *As the battle platoon approaches an enemy strong point, reports are received on a field wireless.*

Twenty-one despatch riders of the 4th Bedfs. Battn. Home Guard line-up on their machines at headquarters during a Sunday morning parade.

ABOVE: *A realistic moment in bayonet practice by a works section of Luton Home Guard at their summer camp in 1942.*

BELOW: *Hand-grenade throwing was part of the training. The drill of "One-two-three-four-DUCK," is well-known to those who have handled live grenades on a range.*

BELOW: *Home Guards relaxing outside their bell-tent after a hard day's training.*

ABOVE: *A section of Luton Home Guard passing the saluting base outside Luton Town Hall after a church parade on Sunday, 23rd March, 1941, the national day of prayer. The salute was taken by the Mayor of Luton, Councillor John Burgoyne.*

RIGHT: *Lt. Col. A. J. Mander, Officer Commanding the 4th Battn., Beds. Home Guard, reading the lesson at a drumhead service on Wardown Sports Ground on Sunday, 26th May, 1952. On his right is Canon W. Davison, Vicar of Luton, who conducted the service.*

BELOW: *After the service the men were inspected by Lieut. General K. A. N. Anderson, then G.O.C.-in-C., Eastern Command.*

time than the Drill Hall, for the roof had not recovered from the effects of a bomb incident nearby, and when it rained hard there was a demand for buckets in the main hall.

Despite this it became the centre of great activity. New recruits had to be put through some training before being allotted to companies. They drilled out of doors when possible, in the Hall when they had to. Gun drill was often in progress on the lawn. Signallers could be seen on the roof, practising their portable wireless on others at distant points. In contrast, behind the Hall local fanciers maintained what was claimed to be the best Home Guard pigeon loft in the country. Even a band could be heard, and sometimes seen, at practice. People passing along Old Bedford Road had ample assurance of the long way the Home Guard had advanced.

*   *   *   *

Long before this, however, there had been a standardised issue of rifles to all. Northover Projectors had become almost playthings. The Smith Gun, a weapon never seen before the war, had come along, with other forms of sub-artillery.

One experiment with the Northovers deserves mention. Some tanks made a show visit to Luton. One of the largest, as a demonstration, pushed over the remains of some bombed premises in Park Street. The tank people heard what the Home Guard claimed they could do with Northovers. They were sceptical. They offered to let them have a go at one of the tanks. When the offer was accepted they thought again. Their tanks were nicely painted, they were to move on to another town for another show, and if by a fluke one lost its nice appearance it might be a bit unfortunate. They hedged— they offered to use a tank to tow a decrepit lorry as target. The offer was taken, Warden Hills fixed as the place.

The tanks towed the old lorry across the front of the Northovers. One bang, and the lorry was on fire. A fluke said the tank people ; they would put out the fire and do it again, but go faster, and then see what the Home Guard would say. They did. One bang, and the lorry was on fire again. Its wreckage stayed there for months.

The Spigot Mortar was supposed to be a mobile weapon for a similar purpose. It had to be assembled on the spot, and show teams could probably do this in the time allotted, but it came to be regarded as more suitable for emplacement work.

The Sten Gun, another wartime novelty, was issued so early that when the first arrived there were not even any printed details for the guidance of users. After the Sten came, much less was seen of the Tommy Gun, one of the early issues.

*   *   *   *

Even if the Drill Hall roof was not too reliable, the main hall at times made a very useful meeting place. There a high-ranking officer told the Home Guard on one occasion how few days home ammunition stocks would have lasted if Hitler had invaded in 1940 ; on another an

121

Admiral forecast exactly the island-hopping stages by which the Japanese would have to be driven out of the Pacific, the vast distances of which he well knew; and, perhaps best of all, a V.C. " Canal Buster " told how it was done. Dunstable men came to these talks.

*   *   *   *

There were combined exercises with the Army. Too often they resulted in large bodies of Home Guards being kept on their toes for long periods in areas which the Army never planned to enter, and during one particularly stormy week-end they realised the truth of the saying that " They also serve who only stand and wait."

In one exercise with the Army, they were called upon to save a vital place—the Vauxhall Works—from capture. Not all could have turned the tables at a critical time in the way Lieut-Col. Brett found possible—suddenly bringing some unsuspected Churchill tanks into the fray. It was understood that the Army took a very poor view of such tactics.

Night ops. in unfamiliar country also provided good training. So did daylight exercises when the " quarry " was supposed to be enemy paratroops dropped in some not too well defined area and given a chance to make themselves scarce before the hunt started. The success of some of the hunts was really creditable.

There was also a serious night hunt. Home Guards were out. Armed police were out. Some bombs arrived. They shook up Newlands Farm. Later it was understood that someone was collected not many miles away, but in another county, and never returned to the Fatherland.

*   *   *   *

On all big exercises, and on many other occasions, a fully-equipped medical unit attended. A number of doctors were Home Guards, and there were two motor ambulances.

When there was a long day out—and some Sundays tended to become very long—a gift mobile kitchen turned up at the right place with a ready-cooked meal. This obviated any recurrence of the " near catastrophe " of one very early night, when unfamiliarity with the tricks of a W.V.S. vehicle which brought sustenance nearly upset the dignity of the eminent lady in charge.

A works company whose work was not easily apparent, and Light A.A. troops complete with bow-and-arrow shoulder flashes, were later developments, and even a certain number of A.R.P. personnel had to be trained in the rudiments of war. It was assumed that circumstances might arise when, still in wardens' blues, they would slip on Home Guard armlets and be Home Guards temporarily.

*   *   *   *

Ultimately night patrols were also discontinued, and reliance placed on an inlying platoon which could function immediately from special quarters in Guildford Street. But some guard duties were still maintained, to the mystification of many. Why certain premises needed an armed guard by night, when they could be left at 6 a.m. just because it was 6 a.m. although perhaps still pitch dark, was one of the little things those who had to do this duty in turn were not expected to comprehend.

*　　　*　　　*　　　*

Such a big force could not expect to escape ceremonial parades. They started quite early on, with the commendable idea of showing the town what it was getting for nothing. Later it was natural that Gen. Sir Henry Jackson, Colonel of the Bedfs. and Herts Regt., should come to see its Luton and Dunstable offshoots. There was a fine parade at Wardown from the whole of the area, and the General afterwards stated in a Special Order :-

" The turnout of the men, their steadiness in the ranks, their handling of arms, and their marching past was beyond all praise, and shows that their discipline and pride in themselves and their units is of the highest order.

" I am proud to think that these battalions are an integral part of the Bedfordshire and Hertfordshire Regiment. The Home Guard are essentially a fighting force, and it is still probable that their training and fighting qualities will be put to the test. If so, I know all ranks will live up to the highest traditions of the Regiment. "

Less understandable elsewhere would be Luton's apparent ability regularly to secure the presence of the G.O.C.-in-C., Eastern Command, for the anniversary parades which became a feature. Gen. Sir K. A. N. Anderson came before he took the First Army to Tunisia. Gen. J. A. H. Gammell came before he went to Italy. No doubt Gen. Sir Alan Cunningham, of Abyssinia fame, would have come had another anniversary arrived before the Stand Down. The explanation, not broadcast in wartime, was that Eastern Command H.Q. at Luton Hoo came within the area of Luton Home Guard, and one much-used practice range was actually within the grounds of Luton Hoo.

Riddy Lane people also heard a lot of firing, and so did the people at Fancott, although the range there was sometimes closed to facilitate certain farming operations. Transport to ranges was provided. Other transport was marked down for commandeering in emergency.

But an Army still marches on its feet—sometimes—so the Home Guard had to do some hard marching. It may have been but a coincidence that, Home Guard premises being " dry," these marches often ended at some " non-sectarian meeting-house "—a term borrowed from one of the Companies—and that this often spurred feet inclined to lag.

Some marches were purely hardening marches. Others were to week-end camps before permanent camps were established closer home. Always all set out in fine style. Some finished in fine style. For those who suffered on the way the reason was generally the same—boots. But whatever the marching or weather discomforts, the camps were pretty popular. It was not all work and no play.

123

Towards the end there came into existence within the 4th Battalion a Special Company. There was the possibility, if not probability, that D-Day might induce some form of counter invasion. This Special Company, of which Major Gregory took command, was to fight on the Coast if needed. It had to be formed entirely of men physically fit for the job, and not employed on any high priority work. They familiarised themselves with what was to be their battleground, and when time proved they would not be needed as fighters, parties went there for a week at a time to give the local Home Guard a breather.

* * * *

No single story of the Home Guard in Luton can ever be complete. Even the story of a single company will always lend itself to additions, as one reminiscence prompts another. Nor is it possible to pay tribute to all who contributed to such success as was achieved, and which received such limited recognition.

The extent of this was the O.B.E. for Col. Mander fairly early on ; towards the close there was the M.B.E. for Lieut. W. W. Franklin, a Caddington original L.D.V. who was with the 4th Battalion until the partition, and eventually became a platoon commander in the 7th ; the B.E.M. for Pte. Samuel Gawley, one of the original "Chaul End Gang" : and the occasional issue of a good service certificate to someone not commissioned. There were only 800 awards at the close for the whole of the country, so perhaps Luton, with its 4,000 and more members was expected to be truly thankful for two.

* * * *

Nevertheless, those at the head of affairs locally who gave to the Home Guard practically every minute of their leisure and of business hours would have done much less effective work had it not been for those unpaid thousands who also gave the service which was within their individual capacity. The night vigils in the early months would have been impossible but for car drivers who turned out in the early hours to bring in the watchers so that they could get to work on time, and who rehearsed " action stations," each collecting his allotted men at the appointed street corner and trying to beat records to the rendezvous.

There could not have been such useful teams of dispatch riders but for an enthusiasm which prompted men to use their own machines, for it was nearly the end before some worse-for-wear W.D. machines came along. General transport at the start would have been non-existent but for voluntary provision, and many a non-member lorry driver drove on a Sunday morning as his contribution to the cause. Women relatives gave a lot of assistance in office work, and some made it their business to run the canteen (dry) and show how they could cook. Then there was that little team known of by few, who right to the end could be expected, within a minute or two of a siren sounding, to report " Post X manned." And Post X, at Chaul End, could not be classed as a place of comforts.

The Luton Home Guard Band leads the "Stand Down" parade past the saluting base outside Luton Town Hall after a service on Wardown Sports Ground, on Sunday, 3rd December, 1944.

ABOVE: *After the parade, the 7th Battn. gave hearty cheers for their C.O. outside the L.N.E.R. station.*

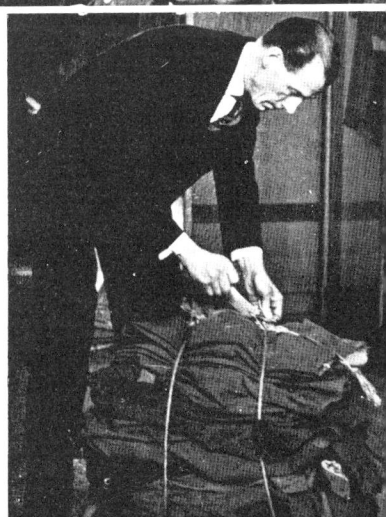

RIGHT: *Uniforms that are to be worn no more, are put to a useful purpose. Mr. A. J. Shreeve, chairman of Luton Rotary Club Community Service Committee labels the last bale to be sent to Holland for liberated workers.*

It says much for the fact that enthusiasm was not allowed to outrun discretion when it can be recorded that, despite the variety of weapons placed in sometimes unfamiliar hands during four and a half years of activity, there was only one tragic incident, and minor mishaps were practically unknown.

People of the Leagrave Road district, however, whatever their other war trials, can be thankful that one big bang provided for was never necessary. The petrol storage tanks were mined, and could have been sent sky high. Probably the man deputed to send them up was equally glad he never had to squeeze into a nearby pillbox for the purpose.

*   *   *   *

Having looked at things the Home Guard expected of men who had to be workers first, and unpaid soldiers as a side-line, mention must be made of other things they did which, while arising out of their soldierly activities, were really not part of the duties for which they volunteered. There were always men prepared to uphold the honour of platoon, company or Battalion in competitive events and, for those who won honours in these, in competitions open to a wider area. They were not easy—sometimes they involved very hard work, but they went into them with a zest more than once well rewarded.

It was to be expected that the comradeship engendered by being brought together in emergency would find expression in various ways. Sometimes, regrettably, it was in paying honour to one who had answered the last Roll Call. More often it found expression in sport or social activity. It will continue to do so, fostered by Old Comrades' Associations.

*   *   *   *

Looking back, those who served from May, 1940, will certainly regard as best the days before the " regimental " era clouded the spirit of adventure with which they answered Mr. Eden's call. The somewhat off-hand Stand Down was the least satisfactory feature.

There was a broadcast one night towards the end of 1944 which said a thank you to the Home Guard, and, in effect, told them they could no longer be regarded as useful or necessary.

Farewell parades were arranged, and some were actually held. Then came a countermanding order from above. The Home Guard had to go on being the Home Guard. VE-Day came, and VJ-Day. Other Services entered into the throes of demobilisation. The Home Guard alone continued in full strength—on paper.

Sans arms, sans equipment, sans premises, sans everything except uniform, they were not demobilised, they could not resign. They were held to the letter of their bond, and there still had to be nominal battalion headquarters to which could be sent almost daily those official effusions for which soldiers have a very expressive term.

This continued for more than a year. Apparently it took all that time to gather in all the arms and equipment of some battalions. At any rate, that was the nearest approach to a reason given in the House of Commons by the new War Minister, Mr. J. J. Lawson, when announcing on December 12, 1945, that from December 31 the Home Guard would be disbanded, and that from that time those who had been members could do as they pleased with such uniform and equipment as they had been allowed to retain.

> *" They folded their tents like the*
> *Arabs ; and silently stole away."*

They went to Blazes

" THERE it is.   Help yourself."
    Standing outside Redcross Street Fire Station and pointing to the blazing City of London, a London Fire Brigade officer gave this laconic reply to the leader of a party of firemen who had arrived from Luton.   The newcomers had reported how many pumps they had brought, and asked where their help was required.

So they helped themselves.

By then they were case-hardened.   They had been to many blitzed towns.   They had got beyond the " scared stiff " stage of some of their early experiences.   They had had a good initiation at Thames Haven and Purfleet among the blazing oil tanks.   They had learned that as " Andrew's Gang " from Luton they could be left to themselves by those whose hands were overfull already.

They had " nearly all the fun," they will tell you, while they were still the Luton Fire Brigade, if only part-timers, and before the Brigade lost its identity in the N.F.S.

Many of them had no idea of becoming firemen until Munich. Few could have foreseen that in a comparatively short time they would crowd in more active service than some soldiers saw throughout the war.

They undertook a job ; they did the job ; and that, they say, is all there was to it.

*   *   *   *

Mutual aid in emergency had been envisaged.   What was not expected was that it would be all give and no take, which was really very lucky for Luton, or that they would go the length and breadth of the country to give aid to others.

The so-called " fun " started with a call in the early hours of September 7th, 1940, when the Thames Haven oil wharves were ablaze. Five pumps and crews were called for.   Mr. Andrew sent four from

127

Luton and one from Dunstable. Mr. Whiting was in charge. They reported at Brentwood, and then went into the fray. That night Jerry was over again, the Purfleet oil depot got it, and pumps were sent from one job to the other. The job was not so much to put out the gasometer-like tanks that were already on fire as to put a water curtain round them and try to prevent the fire spreading.

With the raid still in progress, bombs dropping and machine-gun bullets flying, there was plenty of excuse for getting the breeze up. Some readily admit that it amounted almost to a gale for a time, and that they began to wonder whether, if they got away safely, they ought not to choose another hobby; but that feeling passed, as it so often does when aided by the feeling that a lot of other good fellows are sharing a common danger.

A relief party left Luton on the Sunday, with Mr. Philip Keens in charge, and they also found Purfleet a pretty lively spot that night.

About 5 a.m. there was a terrific explosion—whether through bombs coming down or tanks going up nobody knew. All they did know when debris stopped falling was that their first job was to extinguish their own engines. Everything seemed to be on fire.

A lot of good firemen were lost in that explosion. Happily there were no losses among the Luton contingent, although a roll call showed one man missing. He was missing for three hours. Then he was found mixed up in another roll call, believing himself the only Luton survivor.

That job finally ended on the Tuesday morning. Before it did so Mr. Keens had found himself in temporary command of a firefloat which was keeping the Luton engines supplied, but which later went down and left the engines waterless for a time.

He was not the only one who found himself in for an unexpected job. Mr. Bill Holliday became quite expert in filling petrol cans from a 50-gallon drum in order to keep the Luton engines running. Having filled them, he sat on them for safety. Others might have been covetous. No doubt he has some memories which should not appear in print.

Section-Officer A. S. Wright, an employee of the Davis Gas Stove Co., Ltd., later received the George Medal for his part in saving a badly-holed tank from destruction.

There was every justification for new hands to feel " scared stiff," as one of the party frankly admits he was. The roar of the flames drowned the noise of descending bombs. There was only the crash to intimate their arrival. A searchlight officer did give them a good tip. When the searchlight beams all met over a certain spot, he advised then was the time to duck. They ducked several times, usually under the pumps. Then they decided to give up ducking.

September 16th brought another call. When the party got the order to move off, there was no need to ask for directions. Thames Haven had had it again. This was plain enough.

Just beyond Enfield Jerry seemed very active overhead, so a halt was called and the men dismounted. A stick of bombs fell—one bomb on each side of the road where they were standing. It was unanimously agreed that it was just as safe to keep moving.

At Thames Haven they found that the job was entirely theirs. Silvertown and the Docks had also caught it badly—the other brigades had enough to do there. Luton men worked through the night, Southend took over during the day, and this went on for five nights.

In the daytime the Luton men were withdrawn to a convent at Brentwood for meals and rest. They slept in the crypt. When awakened for another meal before they went back to the job, they found their clothes dried, their socks mended. They never heard the nuns collect or return these things, but it was something that was appreciated.

It was only afterwards that they found that the nuns, each of whom took one fireman into the Chapel for prayers, had also sewn on to some part of his clothing a crucifix or other—call it a talisman, if you like.

Some of the men will remember the Thursday night at Thames Haven because of the rain. They found a damaged bungalow which had been abandoned by the manager of the oil wharves, and took possession. Three at a time, men went there for half an hour's rest. Some found firewood. They made a small fire. The windows were not curtained. Their small fire reflected on a window. A policeman took objection to this, although there were millions of gallons of oil burning close by.

*   *   *   *

In October a new phase of service developed—the relief of London firemen. Parties of 20 went to London for a fortnight at a time, and a similar number came from London to Luton for a rest. Of the many jobs provided by those visits to London, the one best remembered was a blaze at a Tooley Street wine and spirit warehouse. There they all got drunk—from the fumes.

Southampton called on December 1st, and off went Mr. Murch and party. They were given fires in residential areas. Water was scarce and, of course, it was low tide. They had to depend on mobile dams bringing water. The effect of one supply was pretty well lost before another arrived. And while this party was at Southampton, another set off for Bristol.

The Manchester blitz, which started on December 22nd, kept a party away over Christmas, although they only stood by in Leicester for the Leicester men who had gone on. They returned on Boxing Day, for a lull before another storm.

On December 29th the big fire blitz on the City of London started, and this was when, on arrival in Redcross Street, they were simply told to " help themselves." They finished up in City Road, where De La Rue's and other places were burning. Two things they have cause to remember—the very stout doors which, in the absence of fire-watchers, prevented quick approach to the seat of a fire, and the lack of arrangements to feed reinforcing firemen. They couple the latter with memories of 14 hours at Thames Haven with nothing to drink.

After this there was a lull until April 16th, when they did quite a good job at Maple's, Tottenham Court Road, and followed it with a week of fires at Tottenham and Edmonton.

* * * *

May meant Merseyside—sometimes Liverpool, sometimes Bootle. In the dock district sailors and dockers lent a ready hand. A sailor who attached himself to the Luton men told them he had made many wartime crossings of the Atlantic, but wouldn't have their job for all the tea in China, or words to that effect. They returned the compliment with an assurance that they had no desire to do him out of his job.

In Bootle they had a match factory blazing on one side of a narrow street, buildings burning on the other. Incendiaries were still coming down, mines were drifting earthwards. Somebody, apparently a civilian, sat on the coping of a high building, with a whistle in his mouth and his legs dangling, and blew the whistle every time a mine seemed to be drifting their way. When he blew they ducked. They never knew who he was. They summed him up as " exceedingly brave or crackers."

Down the middle of this narrow street, with blazing buildings on both sides and the raid still going on, came a little tot in search of her mother. Quite unharmed, she was handed over to a friendly policeman.

A Boots factory at Nottingham later kept them busy for two or three days. Then the policy of sending a brigade long distances, passing inactive brigades on the way, was discontinued, and it became routine to go part way and stand-in for a brigade which had gone forward.

* * * *

The Luton men may have had " their fun," or most of it. There was some to come at Norwich.

In the meantime they laid nine miles of water pipe in Luton, and stored 7,000,000 gallons of water in tanks varying from 5,000 to 450,000 gallons. With what was also stored at various factories, there were always about 12,000,000 gallons available, plus Wardown Lake, if the mains supply failed. So Luton benefited from the water shortage experiences which were common elsewhere, and the " Water Rats " later proved their worth away from Luton.

Norwich needed help from Luton several times, and here they made their first acquaintance with Mr. Malster, later to become their Divisional Commander.

There was a fire which needed a turntable long ladder. There was one at the fire station, but nobody to send for it. Mr. Malster went, drove it to the fire, erected it, got the hose up, and then, with a pump connected at the bottom, went up and directed the jet on to the fire. Truly a one-man episode. The M.B.E. later came his way.

On one of the Norwich visits the " Water Rats " took their own piping, and laid it during a raid. Column-Officer Egan will remember something about Norwich.

So will some remember Bury St. Edmunds. They were sent there from Norwich for a rest. They were there nine days. During those nine days they were in action at fires in Bury St. Edmunds itself, and also Lowestoft, Yarmouth, Ipswich, Diss, and other places. They wondered where the rest came in.

*   *   *   *

They had nothing very spectacular to do afterwards, home or away. But they might have been in it again. The East Coast was expected to get it hot as D-Day approached, so Luton firemen were among those who lived for a considerable time on the beaches. They saw flying bombs galore, but the expected heavy raids never came off. In fact, the firemen had only one useful job, although their engines were always on the jetties. The " hards " constructed for landing craft had to be washed clear after very high tide, otherwise the landing craft made trouble about it. The firemen became washerwomen for this occasion only.

*   *   *   *

At home they had little trouble from the flying bombs which came this way. Calls to villages on which they were supposed to have dropped were the worst nuisance, it so often being found that the flying bomb had actually landed well out in the fields. Messages were therefore specially checked before action was taken. This had one amusing result. Someone telephoned that one had fallen in his village. Asked whether he was sure it was in the village, he replied with some heat, " Yes, it's fallen on the — fire station."

The Offley bomb-lorry explosion was quite a different matter. Here the call was to " two lorries on fire," and the leading pump was only 500 yards away when the bomb-lorry went up. A few seconds later and the firemen, unless warned, would have been putting water on it. As it was, they got some of the injured away on their own vehicles before ambulances could arrive.

Divisional headquarters had a shaking when the rocket landed in Biscot Road, and some of the girls on the staff got cut about, but this did not prevent them turning the place into a first-aid station straight away.

*   *   *   *

What was the background which made possible all this service to others, while not leaving Luton unprotected ?

When the war started Luton had a Fire Brigade composed of a chief officer, second and third officers, a modest number of full-time firemen, and some Auxiliary Fire Service part-timers.

The addition of the latter was a precautionary move at the time of Munich. Recruiting was started; when fifty were enrolled they were put into training, and a start made on the next fifty. When the war started, from 150 to 200 were wholly or partly trained.

War was declared on a Sunday, but it had cast its shadows before. On the previous Thursday all part-timers were collected by lorry, and set to work unpacking stores, sandbagging, etc. On the Saturday Chief Officer Andrew induced a number to become full-timers.

There was only one real fire station—the Central Station in Church Street. Premises in Oxen Road, part of an old bleach works used as a store for fire-fighting equipment, at once became a combined store and training centre.

Appliances were dispersed. Some stood at Shaw and Kilburn's premises at Chaul End, others in the Biscot Road entrance to George Kent, Ltd. A boiler room at the Diamond Foundry became another station.

For the trailer pumps towing vehicles were commandeered or borrowed. Trade vans and private cars were acquired, and the firemen themselves made towing bars, and converted the bodies to trucks for carrying men and equipment.

When the first siren sounded at 7.26 a.m. on the Wednesday, and everybody unofficial had orders to stay put, all the fire appliances were manned, and one crew at each station for the first time spent a full hour in complete anti-gas clothing.

It was the first sound of war. They were prepared. For anything.

Then came the period already described as the " phoney war." The B.E.F. and the Germans watched one another across the Siegfried Line. They did not fight. Some of the hastily enrolled full-time firemen gave up. The part-timers maintained a wonderful enthusiasm.

The waiting period passed. Dunkirk passed. Air raids threatened.

The regulars, living around the Fire Station, were on call all the 24 hours. The A.F.S., having their own work to do as well, put in twelve on, twelve off.

When the first " yellow " warnings were received at night, all turned out. When this had happened many nights, and still the sirens had not sounded, the A.F.S. were put on a rota. All, that is, except the " key " men. They were usually on the telephone, and had a car with which they could quickly collect their men.

Women telephonists also reported on " yellows." Some were full-time, some part-time. The first to enrol was Mrs. Tom Murch, whose husband was then third officer, later succeeded Mr. Andrew as Chief Officer, and in N.F.S. days went on to higher responsibility.

Even before the war started some engines were put at the Vauxhall works, both because the works provided a big risk and because many part-time men were employed there and could make straight to their pumps if anything happened.

Men of the Auxiliary Fire Service march
ing along Manchester Street, after
special service at the Parish Church, f
Luton civil defence units, on Novembe
19th, 1939.

N.F.S. girls en route to Luton Tow
Football ground on August 29th, 194?
when Luton civil defence units wer
inspected by Wing Commander E.
Hodsoll, Inspector General of A.R.P., an
the Regional Commissioner, Sir Wr
Spens.

ABOVE: *Recruits to the Auxiliary Fire Service, which later became part of the National Fire Service, are shown the inner workings of a fire extinguisher.*

RIGHT: *A lesson in escape drill.*

RIGHT: *A girl worker from a Luton store is shown the correct method of tackling an incendiary bomb with a stirrup pump.*

BELOW: *On the roof of a building, the learners watch a demonstration.*

This dramatic picture shows the scene which met the eyes of Luton firemen in the early hours of September 7th, 1940. The Thames Haven oil wharves had caught fire during an air raid, and five pumps and their crews were called for from Luton and Dunstable. PHOTO: *Planet News, Ltd.*

This foresight paid when, during the first daylight raid on Luton, the works suffered pretty badly. When the raid started the men at the Central Station were just being paid, it being a Friday. Off they went, and Mr. Butler, the officer responsible for paying out, still doesn't know how he managed to lock up the unpaid money. But he was told afterwards that he did.

The column of smoke rising from the works suggested that the firemen were in for a big and long job. Actually there was more smoke than fire. It came from a dump of oil barrels clear of buildings, and if the works had escaped with this fire damage only, many would have been much happier.

In fact, throughout the whole of the war such bombing as the town suffered caused little in the way of fires. But bombs dropped so thickly in that first daylight raid that from then onwards it was considered advisable to disperse the fire appliances still more. From that time when sirens sounded, they dispersed to " action stations."

From the Central station they went to the Bridge Street car park, to Langley Street, and to the back of the Children's Hospital. Oxen Road dispersed to North Street and to the Old Bedford Road gateway of the Larches. From the Diamond Foundry some went to Brown's Timber Yard and to a garage in Castle Street. Kent's sent to the Open Air Pool in Bath Road and to the British Legion Club, Marsh Road. Shaw and Kilburn station spread to a garage near Kingsway and to Electrolux.

Subsequently the West End Garage, at the foot of Beech Hill, became available, offered much more accommodation than was possible at Chaul End, and became a combined fire and ambulance station.

Kent's was left when the local authority opened a combined fire and rescue station in Alder Crescent.

This was the layout when the Fire Brigade became part of the N.F.S. in 1941. Afterwards fire stations in Park Street and Brantwood Road, planned in 1940, were opened.

Peak strength after nationalisation was between 150 and 200 full-time men ; a part-time personnel of about 400 ; some 30 to 40 full-time women ; the same number of part-time women ; and some boy messengers, who were given their own instructional headquarters in Old Bedford Road. Some of the women, primarily " back room girls," became extremely handy with certain of the lighter fire appliances, as they more than once demonstrated in competitions.

It fell to them chiefly to direct men and appliances to fires in an area which stretched into four counties, but were sometimes with the men who on occasion went much farther afield. As despatch riders they convoyed reinforcing appliances. Some actually followed the Fire Force to the scene of action. Norwich provided one notable illustration. With reinforcements called from Luton went mobile kitchens. These, with the exception of the driver, were manned entirely by women, if such a term is permissible, and they worked at

Norwich through three days and nights of raids.

Some were also intimately concerned with preparations for D-Day. Thirty volunteered for special service, chiefly on the coast, to take charge of equipment and stores. They were sworn to secrecy . . . they maintained secrecy. Divisional Officer Malster afterwards said, " Notwithstanding that women are often said to be chatterboxes and unable to keep a secret, it is to their credit that they did not disclose their whereabouts, nor did they at any time give away anything which might have assisted the enemy."

*   *   *   *

After the nationalisation of the Fire Service the women's section became a separate branch, various ranks were introduced, and its first leader was Group Officer D. Lester. Training was as comprehensive as in any other service, but if work was hard at times and hours long, there was relatively little wastage of personnel, maybe because physical training and sport were considered highly important. Where squad drill was concerned, Luton girls were the envy of those in many other areas. Because of their smartness they were chosen on several occasions during the war years to take part in a march past in London, and on some of these occasions they were inspected by members of the Royal Family.

*   *   *   *

For N.F.S. purposes the country was divided into regions ; each region into fire areas ; and each fire area into divisions, each with a strength of about 100 pumps. Luton was made the headquarters of a division covering about 570 square miles, and Mr. Cartwright, Chief Officer of Coventry Brigade, came as Divisional Commander. In time he went to take charge of a training college at Cambridge, and was succeeded by Mr. W. J. Malster, M.B.E., ultimately commander of a sub-area based on Luton.

*   *   *   *

This, then, is the story of the Luton N.F.S. who locally always had the backing of the Works Private Fire Brigades. Like all other Civil Defence units, its ranks were filled with men and women from all walks of life. The work was often hard and grinding, sometimes dangerous, at other times monotonous. Pay and conditions were perhaps not commensurate with the risks which had to be taken at times, but that was a common experience in many fields of war service, and there were few complaints.

The men who went through the fire together developed that keenness of perception which became a characteristic of Commando troops. Their common experience developed a comradeship which will long continue.

*   *   *   *

Peaceful afterthought : A Luton Fire Service Benevolent Fund was inaugurated in February, 1941. The money came from weekly subscriptions, donations, and the profits of social activities. Members

RIGHT: *Members of the Auxiliary Fire Service (later the National Fire Service) load fire-damaged ribbons on to a cart after an incendiary raid had caused an outbreak at Lye's, New Bedford Road.*

BELOW: *Fire forces battling with burning oil drums, which had caught fire at Vauxhall Motors, Ltd., after Luton's first air raid on August 30th, 1940.*

ABOVE: *The National Fire Service had a difficult task when an American lorry carrying bombs blew up between Lilley and Offley, in January, 1945.*

BELOW: *Luton firemen went to Norwich when the city was blitzed and helped to fight fires which lasted many hours.*

PHOTO: *Eastern Daily Press, Norwich.*

requiring assistance during the war years as the result of injury or other causes were helped. With the end of the war, and a very considerable depletion in the number of those remaining in the Fire Service, a balance of £1,025 14s. 1d., with thanks for past services rendered to members, was sent to Luton and Dunstable Hospital to found a bed.

Tribute to the Few

AUGUST, 1940, was the prelude to crisis. The English scene was an unforgettable picture, but the thoughts of Englishmen were grim and their hearts were steeled against the stark realism of the times.

Over Kent and Sussex and the English Channel there was blue, often cloudless, sky. The eye could hardly pierce the dazzling heights. Day by day during that fateful month the air was filled with a faint subdued hum. Miles above the earth tiny specks—many of them —were coming in formation from that dim low coastline, barely discernible through the haze, that was the coast of France. But other tiny specks—though not so many—were speeding south to meet them.

As they came closer to each other, they moved into a new atmospheric area. Vapour trails began to form. At first they stretched out like long straight tails. Then, as the formations met, the trails swept round in mammoth arcs and the watchers miles below knew that battle had been joined.

There were many—so many—advancing north, and few—so few—to stop them.

Yet they were stopped. The Few were writing in the skies the story of the Battle of Britain, writing it with their Spitfires and Hurricanes in fantastic whorls of vapour, writing it in the pinpoints of red and the long vertical smoke trails from blazing Nazi bombers that crashed harmlessly in the sea and in the Kentish countryside ; yet writing it not in ephemeral vapour only on the tablets of the sky, but indelibly on Britain's scroll of glory.

The Englishman is not demonstrative and does not wear his heart on his sleeve. Yet the emotions of the story, as it unfolded day by day, stirred his heart. These few—these very few had fought and won the battle for him, for his home and for his children. " Never in the field of human conflict was so much owed by so many to so few." What could he do for them, in return for what they had done for him ? What did they need most ?

He knew the answer—Spitfires, and more Spitfires.

ABOVE: *A competition for a doll, at Luton Home Guard Headquarters, brings in cash for the Luton Spitfire Fund.*

LEFT: *Mr. L. Connell raised £78 for the Fund at an auction sale.*

BELOW: *Luton High School girls present a cheque for the fund to Mr. R. A. Glenister, editor of "The Luton News," and associated newspapers.*

So the common man set himself to the task.

*   *   *   *

In Luton, as in other towns and villages throughout the country at that time, a Spitfire Fund was started. *The Luton News* took it in hand. £5,000 was needed to name and give a Spitfire to " The Few," but within five months, not one but two Spitfires had been proudly named from Luton.

The Fund was largely—very largely—the small man's effort. True, big firms gave big donations, but it was the " widow's mites " that really built up the Fund and reached the £10,000 that Luton raised.

How was it done ? In local life there are conventional ways of raising money. Collections, matinees, dances, whist drives, bring-and-buy sales, these are the usual channels through which the pocket is touched and lightened, but here there was something different. Luton was not content with the accepted methods only. The small man, his wife and his children, in the full flush of human ingenuity and enterprise, went deeper and deeper into the unorthodox.

It would take too long to list the individual schemes that swelled the total. The hat went round in the shelters after every " All clear." Children, who always love dressing up, gave back-garden concerts— admission one penny, threepence to grown-ups. Small boys built up their model railways and made their friends pay a penny to come in and watch. Threepence entitled the friends to work the trains. Every public house had its empty bottle that had to be filled. Every household catalogued its fines for questionable table manners. More bad language cost more money than ever before. Farthings ?—one never imagined that so many of these insignificant coins existed.

Someone held an auction sale of gifts, and others followed. These were not jumble sales of goods that were only lumber and that the owners willingly got rid of. They were genuine gifts and real personal sacrifices. To the 1946 victim of austerity, living in urgent need of all those things he would like to buy but may not and cannot, these sales would have been treasure houses, At one sale one could buy a piano that came from a very humble home and had been well cared for, a nearly new refrigerator (electric), a pedigree puppy, a cask of good honest 1940 beer, roller skates, " budgies," antique silver, a fat Michaelmas goose, a new pre-war overcoat, a £2 gold piece, and a wedding ring. These and other personal possessions in great variety, goods that have long since disappeared from the shops, made prices that were high by 1940 standards. Buyers did not mind what they paid. It was a good cause. But by 1946 standards they were dirt cheap.

This spontaneous effort of Mr. and Mrs. Luton and their family showed how grateful we were to the heroes of the R.A.F. The Fund paid for two Spitfires. They were officially named " Luton I " and " Luton II." Luton never saw them but Luton men in the services did. They saw them on operations against the enemy, and Luton was grimly satisfied.

Man (and Woman)-Power

MEN and women of Luton went to war in the factories just as surely as did those who went into the Services. Toil and sweat were their portion. Long hours they laboured amid the high pitched whine of the machines. Hard jobs, unfamiliar jobs, monotonous jobs, the sameness of which seemed to reach forward unceasingly into an infinite future.

Often spending the whole shift in a perpetual blackout; hearing above the shrill note of their machines the eerie wail of the siren followed by the deep throbbing overtone of enemy bombers; staying at their work because the job had to go on; thinking and then repressing dread thoughts, not of their own peril but of the dangers besetting their own homes and families; so, throughout day and night, the weeks, the months, the six long years of war, they made their great contribution to ultimate victory.

*   *   *   *

Unlike August, 1914, it was not a free-for-all war which began in September, 1939. Men not already in the Services, the Territorials or the newly-enlisted Militia, had to wait the call. Because of this the factories which had to back the fighting forces with material were not so denuded of skilled men as they might have been. Some, even, of those who had gone as Territorials in the first days, were after a time returned temporarily to their former jobs when a bigger and bigger output of material was of far more vital consequence than the loss of a few men from the Services.

To ensure that production of munitions of war was maintained at the highest possible level, many occupations were classed as " reserved," and men above the reservation age fixed for their particular trade were automatically exempt, for the time being, from call-up under the National Service Acts. The combination of these factors, prevented any marked labour shortage showing itself in the early days of the war.

*   *   *   *

Dunkirk altered all that. The B.E.F. lost practically all its equipment in France. Thousands of Luton-made Bedfords and Commers had to be abandoned over there. Even if they were left in such a state as to be of little, if any, value to the enemy, they had to be replaced. In practically every way the Army had to be re-equipped, and had to have many things not normally made in Luton, but which Luton could and did make.

Some of the things wanted, of course, were right up Luton's everyday street. Others, except for the changes inevitable with the years, were not far removed from things produced in vast quantities for the previous war. Perhaps it was fortunate for the supply authorities that

144

some of the principal firms had considerably increased their productive capacity in the years immediately preceding the beginning of the war, had built up the necessary labour force for this increased production, and in 1939, therefore, were able to speed up quickly on the immediate requirements of the Services.

So much was wanted after Dunkirk, however, that it was quickly obvious that there was not sufficient skilled labour to undertake all the work that would normally be done by skilled operatives. Other labour was being made available through the various registrations for employment, and also by " concentrating " some industries not regarded as essential to the war effort. It was mainly unskilled in so far as modern engineering was concerned, but it was also in the main of a very adaptable type.

To begin with it was chiefly men—but quite early on there were many women volunteers too—who were brought into the war effort from other and less essential occupations. Blockmakers, for example, quickly adapted themselves to woodwork for aeroplanes. Some of the older women from the hat trade, perhaps because of, and not in spite of, their age, were found to be far more valuable as capable and conscientious storekeepers than they could have been on machines.

But the machines had to be manned (or womanned) and as the Services had prior claim on the younger age groups of men, the only thing to do was to turn every available woman on to the production of war material. In time over 22,000 Luton women were registered for this purpose. Not all, even though liable to register, were liable to direction, but the great part women did play locally in the war effort is made evident by official records showing that 20,000 industrial vacancies which occurred in Luton alone were filled by women. Some, of course, were placed more than once, but so were men, yet the number of jobs to which men were compulsorily directed only totalled 10,000.

This disparity may seem startling. It has to be read in conjunction with the fact that 23,000 men registered under the National Service Acts, although not all were called up. Many were in vital occupations which precluded this. But it does show that women played an extremely important part in Luton's war production. Some of them from 1941, and the remainder from 1942, had practically no say in what they would do and where they would do it until the end of 1945— an impact of war on their lives which we shall do well to remember. They thoroughly earned the tribute paid to them by Mr. H. L. Marsden, manager of Luton Employment Exchange through the war years, who, in this capacity, was concerned perhaps more than anyone with getting people out of their normal occupations and into others which the circumstances of the time made far more important. Looking back over the war years just before he left for a Regional appointment in the latter part of 1945, he said :—

" The women workers of Luton have undoubtedly performed a

marvellous job. I pay tribute to them, and particularly the married women, who had to look after their homes in addition to working in the factories. They were a big factor in winning the war."

*   *   *   *

From what sources was extra manpower obtained? Some of it turned to war work without being asked. There were some who realised there was only a speculative future in their customary occupation because of limitation of supplies for the businesses in which they were engaged, and were, moreover, anxious to play a more active part in the war effort. Some, rejected for active service, yet still wanting to be in the fight, decided that the only way was to be a sort of man behind the man behind the gun, and help to keep him supplied. But the sum total was still only a trickle compared with the number which was quickly needed.

When the seven-day week was accompanied by night shifts, still fewer men were available by day, and something much more drastic had to be done than just collect a few here and there from shops, offices, the distributive trades generally, and any others who would come along.

To get.big numbers, and quickly, what more natural than to turn to the hat industry, the next largest collective employer to engineering? The hat industry had already lost a lot of workers, but it still had some thousands, chiefly women. So the hat trade was told it was a luxury trade, very useful to the town and country in peacetime, but of much less importance in time of war.

There was quite a stir when the trade was told that it was " voluntarily " to release 25 per cent. of its remaining women, and that the 25 per cent. must be made up of the very best for the work to which they would be put. The trade perforce had to agree to release them, in batches spread over three months. To have refused would not have made much difference. Official cuts in supply of materials were already making a good many of the women superfluous, and in any case registration of women for direction into industry was not far off. It is to the credit of the 25 per cent. that they did not make much fuss about it. They certainly gained in one way by this early transfer. They could elect to go to the factory of their choice, either because of its convenience from a travel point of view or because it would enable them to work with people they knew. Later it became a case of being directed to the factory which, wanting extra labour, was turning out what happened to be No. 1 priorities at the particular moment.

*   *   *   *

When registration of women for industry came along, the net was spread still wider. More women were taken from offices, from shops, from domestic service, and the hat trade did not escape because of its previous surrender. Women not normally following any occupation were not exempt. Married women, unless they had children under fourteen, were expected to turn out and work, as some had always done from necessity. Where married women with young children wanted to lend a hand it was considered necessary to free them from responsibility for their children during working hours, by a day nursery scheme which, whatever its value in increasing the labour supply, was certainly expensive.

It had to be accepted that all these things were necessary, even to the squeezing out of some newly-introduced clothing firms, so that their labour resources could be freed for other work. Chiefly uniform clothing contractors, they were directed to places where labour for engineering was not in such demand or could not be fully utilised. Sometimes the places into which they proposed moving were blitzed before they could enter into occupation. That was their misfortune. They had to leave Luton. Some smaller firms producing civilian clothing were allowed to continue here, apparently on the assumption that they would ultimately be a useful addition to the variety of the town's peacetime occupations.

To stop leakages, control of engagement orders made it obligatory on everyone between certain ages who was seeking new employment to do so through the Employment Exchange, and for every employer to fill vacancies through the same channel. The net result, therefore, was that, by the end of 1941, practically all workers were subject to direction to work where they were most needed. Then, in December of that year, the National Service Act (No. 2) for the first time in our history rendered single women liable to conscription for the Women's Services.

*   *   *   *

It was one thing to make all this untrained labour available for factories engaged on war work, and quite another to ensure that it was utilised to the fullest advantage, adaptable as much of it was. An unskilled worker, man or woman, could not just take on where the skilled worker had left off. This was where the technical inspectorate branch of the District Man Power Office came into the picture.

There had been a Labour Supply Committee in existence for some time, and while it was common knowledge that certain well-known local people like Mr. P. W. Currant and Mr. T. H. Knight had a good deal to do with the Man Power Office, it was never a publicised work. Fewer knew that in the background was Mr. R. Dymond, a predecessor of Mr. Marsden, who had gained a very intimate knowledge of industrial Luton when Luton was one of the few bright industrial spots in the somewhat gloomy years following the previous war. Then Mr. Dymond was also concerned with putting people into new jobs, but for peaceful purposes, and they were generally people who had come from afar in search of the promised land. This time, after being away a few years in an area where he had greater responsibilities, he was sent to Luton again for a somewhat different purpose. He still had to do with getting people into new jobs, but they were home people who had to be pulled out of other jobs first.

The technical inspectorate working under the Man Power Office was composed of men all skilled in their own particular trades. They had to encourage the simplification of factory processes—in other words, de-skilling operations to bring them within the capacity of the new labour. At the same time some training classes were organised. The Technical College did particularly good work in this connection, and in some small workshops elsewhere quite a number of people were enabled to make advance acquaintance with the type of job on which they were going to work, without delaying production in the major factories while they were gaining this knowledge.

Having access to all the war factories, which for security purposes were closed to all except the operatives, and being able to study the varying methods of each, the technical inspectorate were not only able to suggest to executives how simplification could be secured, but they could often arrange for an interchange of production ideas between factories. This was essentially a war-time feature. It certainly could not have been brought about under pre-war conditions.

They had the closest contacts with the trade union side and the employer's side of industries and a good deal of confidence was placed in them by both. Whatever process was involved, there was no attempt at secrecy. Everybody seemed willing to co-operate in this exchange of views. Maybe this co-operation of all parties was one reason why, even when the feeling that everyone must do his utmost because the country was " in a jam " had worn a bit thin, there was no major labour disturbance in Luton throughout the whole of the war years. The introduction of Works Advisory Committees, on which both sides were represented, also led to a closer understanding, and undoubtedly was another contributory factor in smooth running.

Had " shadow factories " been built in the district all sorts of additional problems would have risen. The local demand for labour would have been accentuated, with the prospect of a " redundant labour " problem when such factories were no longer needed. One problem alone would have been how to house the extra workers. Luton was too full already for a " closed town " policy to have had much practical value. This was adopted, however, in the neighbouring town of Letchworth, which had to import a lot of workers. The effect was that when it was " closed " no newcomers were permitted to get accommodation there unless they had come to engage in some essential war work. In Luton compulsory billeting powers sufficed, for comparatively little labour had to be imported. If we include all the workers who came in daily from surrounding villages, and those who came, as for years they had done, from London, Luton proved almost self-sufficient.

Such labour as had to be imported was principally female. It was largely rendered necessary by the extremely monotonous jobs some of them had to do. They made, or assembled, something which was

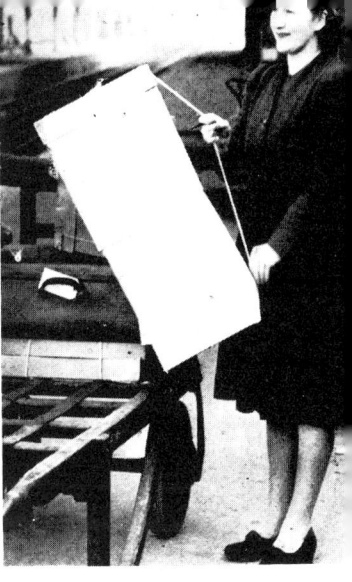

One of Luton's women bus drivers stands beside the producer unit on a Corporation bus adapted to run on producer gas.

The hats must go through . . . and a woman porter at Luton station plays her part in seeing that they do.

When is a football ground not a football ground? These women workers give the answer as they make camouflage netting on the stands at Luton Town football ground.

ABOVE: *Luton's postgirls cheerily took the place of the postmen during the war, and continued into peace time.*

RIGHT: *While her father went on to work of National importance, a Leagrave girl and her friend took over his window-cleaning business.*

Had it not been for the women street cleaners, Luton would have become a very untidy place in the war years.

ABOVE: *Luton girls registering for National Service at the Employment Exchange.*

BELOW: *Another registration . . . this time for fire watching, in October, 1942.*

Women played an important part in gathering the harvest in the war years. Here, members of the W.L.A. stack straw as it comes from the threshing machine.

Women engineers marching through George Street, in the procession to Luton Town football ground in June, 1942, when nearly 10,000 people assembled for Luton's observance of United Nations Day.

going to be just part of something else. They did exactly the same little job all day long, day after day, week after week, month after month. They had not the stimulus of seeing the complete article grow under their hands. Often they did not even know what use was to be made of what they were handling. No wonder some of these workers fell by the way, and had to be replaced.

*   *   *   *

But if not much labour was brought to Luton, some had to be drafted away, still further reducing the number of skilled workers. To bring " shadow factories " and other new centres of production into activity in other parts of the country, there had to be a nucleus of skilled men around which the labour supply of a factory could be built up. Those who were to operate the factories had no skilled men going spare. Luton had to release some, and rely on a general move-up of those who had attained varying degrees of skill.

Men had also to be drafted away for such urgent jobs as Mulberry, Fido and Pluto. The endeavour was to make them feel that these jobs depended on them personally. It was the same when men who at some time had worked in shipyards had to be returned to their old occupations. They had left the yards in the lean years, being too enterprising to hang about with little prospect of regular work, and some had found pretty good jobs in Luton. Ships, however, were going down at an alarming rate, and only shipbuilders could build new ships. Some men went back from Luton knowing they would lose substantially in their pay packet, but it was a time of crisis, and they went.

Time came when men of the type of those who returned to the shipyards were badly needed in Luton. The production of the Churchill tank, with its weight and the use of armour plate, created tasks for which they would have been eminently suitable. They could not be withdrawn from the shipyards. The job had to be done by the people on the spot. It meant that, right down the scale, everybody had to tackle a heavier job than before. Men who had been concerned with the heaviest lorries had to be switched to the tank shops. Those who had been on lighter vehicles had to take on the heavier ones, and so on right down to the point where women could be effectively employed on jobs which even under wartime conditions had continued to be done exclusively by men. The result showed how well this stepping-up worked out.

There were times when interchange of labour between factories had to be arranged. Maybe one was finishing a contract, and would be some time tooling up for new production, while another was over-loaded with work which for some reason had become a first priority. It was always the endeavour to plan any such transfer well in advance, but even if the transfers were of short duration, it cannot be said that they were very popular. Sometimes it was also necessary to send workers away to acquire experience of a new type of work later to be undertaken in their own factories, as, for instance, when Percivals were about to change over from Oxfords to Mosquitos. This kind of transfer was much more popular.

*   *   *   *

It might be thought that with the wide range of war material which was produced in Luton, and which is described elsewhere, and with losing skilled men to other centres, Luton had quite enough on its hands. The willing horse, however, is always expected to pull a bit more weight, and Luton had to be the willing horse when misfortune overtook some other towns. There were urgent things which could not wait until damaged factories were put right. Some of the work transferred to Luton simply meant just a bit extra to do. Some involved very special work of a type not normally done in Luton, and gave an initial headache to those asked to take it on. It was done, and well done : proof that Luton still has engineering craftsmen to whom nothing comes amiss.

Naturally among the many thousands working day after day in the factories, and many of them not from choice, time disclosed a very few who could not be rated 100 per cent. Sometimes drastic action had to be taken to convince them that they must pull their weight, but the number of cases that reached the Courts was very few, and they only reached that stage when the Works Advisory Committee had found that persuasion and warning alike were useless. The number was really extremely small when it is remembered that something like 22,000 people employed by nearly 200 firms had no free voice in where they should work or what they should do. Similarly there were only a few people who had to be brought before the Courts because they had failed to take the jobs found for them.

*   *   *   *

While the constitution and functions of the District Man Power Office changed considerably as the years went by, it can be said that the responsibilities of the office largely fell on three people, Mr. Currant, Mr. Knight and Mr. Dymond. Mr. Currant had a job which started early, and finished earlier than those allotted to the others of the trio. He was the deferment officer who, when bloc reservation ceased, and individual employers had to apply for the retention of individual employees, had to decide whether or not the work on which that employee was engaged was of an importance which justified the Services being denied one potential recruit.

Mr. Knight, as District Technical Officer, and Mr. Dymond, as Labour Supply Officer, found that with VE-Day their tasks did not end, but changed somewhat in character. They ceased to be so much concerned with labour for industry. The call-up policy was altered and men born before July 1st, 1915, were no longer wanted for the Armed Forces. Nevertheless unless there were exceptional circumstances, those who were younger must still do their tour of duty . . . duration still unstated. There was provision, however, for deferment for apprentices to skilled trades provided they had reached a serious stage of training, and these deferments became a matter for the Man Power Board to decide.

The Resettlement Grants Board was also to all intents and purposes, the Man Power Board. As such, the Board had to deal with applications for grants from men who were in business on their own account before being called up, and wished to resume in business of a similar kind. They also had to deal with applications from disabled men in cases where the Rehabilitation Officer considered that, having regard to the nature of the disability, to start a man in business would be the best form of resettlement.

*   *   *   *

Much has been said about the men and women full-timers in the factories, but they were not Luton's only war workers. There were also the women part-timers, who were the subject of a special recruitment campaign. To find out what they could usefully do, they were not asked to present themselves at a somewhat depressing-looking Employment Exchange, but at a special and attractively-furnished interviewing centre which was opened in Upper George Street. Here they had the sympathetic ear of officers specially selected for their understanding of the problems which would be submitted to them. Some women could only work in the mornings, others only in the afternoons. It was not practicable for all factories to fit in such workers, but some found that these part-timers could be paired up quite usefully.

There were also " Sunday morning squads "—bank clerks and others—who went to some smaller workshop, got into overalls, and were quickly trained into some operation which, while it did not involve a lot of skill, still had to be done by someone.

Many others, quite outside the munition works, felt the impact of war in relation to their daily work. There were those people who had to work beyond their expected years to try to keep businesses together for younger men who would otherwise have been lightening their burdens. There were others who had to work longer and harder because no extra help could be obtained. There were the wives who did their best to carry on their serving husband's jobs.

Some of these married women were among those who did such good service as postwomen, not an enviable job even in summer if the day was wet, and still less so in the blackout of winter. " Women more or less carried the Post Office during the war years," says an official at Luton Head Post Office, " and their work cannot be spoken of too highly." The maximum number of women employed in connection with the Luton Postal service during the war was 340. Of the normal staff responsible for sorting, telegraphic and counter duty the war left only four males out of 57, while of the outdoor staff only 40 remained out of a peacetime total of 126. No wonder there was plenty of work for women, and not only for those regularly seen de-

155

livering the post during all weathers. Women did all sorts of things, inside the Post Office and out. Most of the bright red vans were ultimately driven by women. They drove very efficiently and reliably during the blackout. Through periods of bad weather there was very little absenteeism, and most of these temporary drivers qualified for " Safety First " awards. Even with all their help, however, the Christmas rush could not have been handled without the aid of batches of senior schoolchildren.

*   *   *   *

There were the women who drove and the women who conducted buses. Without them our public transport could not have operated so uninterruptedly. Some of the women drivers could ultimately give points to their men colleagues in gear-changing, and the way they handled double-deckers in particular was beyond praise. The conductresses had to carry on under conditions of overcrowding which became such an accepted feature that it came almost as a shock to the travelling public when in the latter part of 1945 they were forcibly reminded that it was only a wartime relaxation, and that from then onwards the number of passengers who would be permitted to stand at even peak hours would be considerably reduced, and that during certain hours no standing at all would be allowed. Conductresses were the first women to appear on buses. Six pioneers began in July, 1940. Subsequently some hundreds were engaged. For women drivers a training school was inaugurated in September, 1941, by Mr. C. S. A. Wickens, Luton Corporation Transport manager, but the number of women drivers always remained comparatively small. The chief reason was that early shifts, irregular hours, and some other conditions of the job made it an impossible one for some married women. As with the conductresses, so with the women drivers ; they worked the same shifts as the men, often starting before 6 a.m., and having to walk to work into the bargain.

One woman driver's record was particularly noteworthy. Until her first day of training in 1941 she had never sat behind a wheel, yet it took her only four weeks to become proficient, and later she drove every type of bus in public service.

*   *   *   *

Some women had jobs which were not merely unattractive, but definitely unpleasant. Who could have foreseen before' 1939 that the time would come when Luton would be glad to engage women to work as street cleaners, or to join forces with the dustmen ? Yet it became necessary within a year of the start of the war to ask women to engage in this unglamorous work. Some members of the Town Council were against engaging women for such jobs, but they had to sink their prejudice, and Luton was one of the first authorities to take this step. Twenty were employed as street cleaners. Fortunately for them, there was once a man named Macadam who left us a legacy of hard roads ! Four women learned to drive refuse vehicles. Forty

156

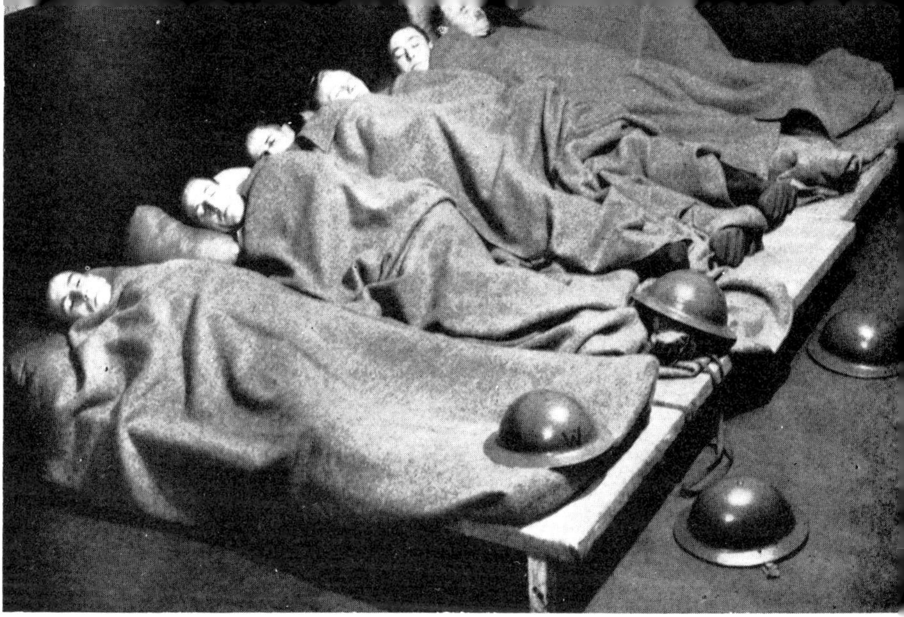

ABOVE: *"Good night . . . sweet dreams" . . . they hope! Some of Luton's fire watchers bed down and trust no warning will disturb them.*

BELOW: *Girls directed into industry in Luton found a home from home at Luton Crescent Club. This picture was taken at the official opening. Sir Walter Citrine, General Secretary of the T.U.C., is seen second from the left.*

Luton bank officials responded to the call for volunteers as spare time engineers, and, in white coats instead of black jackets, made a useful contribution to the war effort.

The rhythm of the assembly line urged the war-worker on to greater efforts . . . and great efforts were made at Vauxhall Motors, Ltd., where this picture was taken of Army trucks under construction. PHOTO: Vauxhall Motors.

went round with the dustmen or worked at the salvage disposal depot sorting paper and rags. Originally they all worked a 47½-hour week, the same as the men, but later they were allowed Saturday mornings off to do their shopping. They were provided with protective clothing for their uninviting tasks, worked conscientiously, and, strangely enough, seemed to enjoy their work while the need was there. Real war jobs, these, but not jobs for which medals were awarded !

*   *   *   *

The women who had to leave their home districts and come to work in Luton factories were the subject of a special welfare scheme. All these transferred workers were met at the station on arrival, and directed to suitable billets. This was a matter not without its difficulties, but it is true to say that the majority of these new arrivals settled down well in their new surroundings, and many made lasting friendships. Maybe the outstanding example of the way a stranger can settle down in a new home was provided by one instance in which the billeted war worker eventually married her landlady's son. As shortage of coupons seemed likely to be a stumbling block to wedding attire, the mother-in-law-to-be rose to the occasion and gave up some of her own coupons so that her erstwhile lodger could look her best on her wedding day.

To many of these women war workers, some of whom came from as far afield as Scotland, Wales and Ireland, the Crescent Club proved a real boon. Sometimes new arrivals were able to get sleeping accommodation there if suitable billets were not immediately available.

*   *   *   *

While so many of the women of Luton, and particularly the married women, were contributing materially towards maintaining the output of the factories and keeping going some of those public services which are such an essential part of the life of the community, many of the younger women chose a different field of effort. They went out into the countryside to give the farmers a helping hand in maintaining our vital food supplies. Over 300 girls from Luton enrolled in the Women's Land Army, and even after the war was over about half of them were still serving, for the need for home food production had not lessened in the slightest with the end of hostilities. Although to most of them land work was entirely different from anything they had done before, many were eminently successful in their new jobs. They lived in special hostels, went out daily to engage in such seasonal tasks as threshing, potato lifting, hoeing, haymaking, harvesting ; when there was not a definite seasonal job, they joined in the ordinary work of the farm. Some became forewomen or gang leaders ; some became supervisors in charge of hostels.

A Luton girl who joined the W.L.A. as early as 1939 was one of the volunteers who received 6-year armlets from the Queen in November, 1945. She had specialised in dairy work, and when in March, 1945, she was promoted to Milk Recording, she was one of the first girls to be employed in Bedfordshire on this official work. Luton also produced three of the outstanding women tractor drivers in the county. One won many local contests, and gained distinction in the first Tractor Driving Proficiency Test ever held in the county. There were others who specialised in greenhouse work at Luton Hoo or in some nursery. The Luton Hoo Estate, in fact, was a training ground for many raw recruits under a Ministry of Agriculture scheme, and also employed a number of Land Girls throughout the war.

Luton was well represented by Land Army veterans who, early in 1946, were inspected at Bedford by H.R.H. Princess Elizabeth on her first official visit to the county.

Fuel, Power and Transport

"LOWEST summer prices," as a dull season bait to fill the coal cellar against the rigours of forthcoming winter, was a slogan which was forgotten during the war years. War, in fact, gave even some courageous people the shivers, because sometimes they had not the fuel for necessary warmth. Sometimes, also, the Clerk of the Weather took an impish delight in upsetting the calculations of those Government officials who decided they could prophesy a period of the year when it would be so warm that central heating in non-domestic premises could be dispensed with. The official ban having been imposed, along would come a cold spell. Then, as output dropped because people were cold, and as low office temperatures caused administrative staffs to go sick, the ban had to be lifted.

Fuel of all sorts was a vital necessity for the war industries. It was also essential for the homes of the people if they were to keep fit to play their part in industry or any other form of war activity. Fuel was the subject of restrictions from the beginning of the war. Even in the early days it was a very complex problem. Later, what with falling production, rising consumption, and merchants' transport and labour difficulties, it became a problem which provided many headaches for those responsible for planning its control.

Coal, gas and electricity, for heat, light and power, all had to be considered as inter-related. It was obviously of no use to control one variety of fuel if control was countered by increased consumption of an alternative. Petrol had to be brought into review in relation to transport and power. Even such a humble commodity as paraffin could not be ignored, so that people entirely dependent on it for cooking, heat, and light should have their supplies guaranteed, even if people who used it for other purposes had to go short.

Preparations to control the distribution and consumption of solid fuel, gas and electricity had been made even before the start of the war. To give local effect to a Statutory Order which came into operation immediately the war started Mr. Fred Oliver, the Borough Engineer, was appointed Fuel Overseer, and a Fuel Advisory Committee was appointed. Original members were two representatives of the Luton coal merchants, a Co-operative Society representative, the Borough Electrical Engineer, and the Engineer and Manager of Luton Gas Company.

Under the Statutory Order all premises except industrial premises using over 100 tons a year were assessed on a standard year's consumption prior to September, 1939. This figure, expressed in quantities for each quarter of the year, was to be the basis of a percentage " allocation." Like some articles of food, it was not to be a " ration," but " if available." In experience it was not always available when wanted.

Registration with a merchant was necessary, and if anybody's merchant had incomplete records on which to base an assessment, then it was up to the Fuel Overseer to fix an assessment and notify the consumer. Small households normally buying small quantities from street hawkers were exempt from registration. They were left free to buy not more than 1 cwt. at a time from any merchant throughout the year, always assuming the street hawker was still making his round.

Gas and electricity provided so many early obstacles to control that they were eliminated from the Order in January, 1940. Coal distribution was based on restricting customers to a given quantity in a stated period, which varied from one month to three months, and in certain cases to even longer periods. To protect the consumer from inflated prices there was a Maximum Retail Prices Order, but this did not prevent price schedules being subject to frequent official increases, attributed to rising cost of production, transport, etc.

Until June, 1942, the Mines Department was responsible for overall fuel control. Then this department became the Ministry of Fuel and Power, which consolidated most of the previous Orders. When fall in coal production, and rise in consumption for war purposes, brought real rationing into prospect, the Fuel Overseer had to be provided with information relating to coal, gas, electricity, and paraffin consumption in all non-industrial premises. The position received very considerable attention in Parliament, together with a report from Sir William Beveridge on the most effective means of rationing all fuel. In the end the House decided against rationing owing to the many difficulties involved in making a scheme which would be equitable, comprehensive and simple to administer. It was hoped that by variations of the existing Order, plus the House Coal Scheme, it would be possible to get through the remainder of the war without rationing.

The House Coal Scheme, voluntarily agreed to by the merchants, was based on co-ordinated deliveries to save time, petrol and manpower, and all coal arriving at any depot being available to all merchants working from that depot. A customer might favour certain " nuts " or " brights," but had to take what came.

To economise fuel there were regulations restricting the heating of greenhouses, illuminated advertising was prohibited, as was the lighting of shop windows purely for the display of goods, and the not always bearable ban on central heating in specific periods was introduced.

These arrangements held good, without absolute rationing during the rest of the war, and even afterwards. They resulted in a reasonable distribution. It cannot be said that everybody was satisfied. Sometimes, owing to traffic dislocation, the coal did not even arrive in Luton, so the merchants could not distribute it to time. The merchants themselves were short of vehicles and men. Unlike those who dealt in foodstuffs, they did not have to cope with a demand which was fairly constant throughout the year. The demand on them rose sharply at times when weather conditions were the greatest handicap to distribution. Even customers who could build up enough stock during the warmer months to carry them through to December began to join the crowd of those wanting service when the weather was bad.

January and February were always the worst periods. In those months not only a cold spell but the resultant sickness in households all tended to increase the already heavy burden on the merchants at a time when they might also be shorter-staffed than usual through illness. Under the circumstances which prevailed, therefore, the best that could be done was done to maintain an equitable distribution, even to making Sunday deliveries and getting Service volunteers with Service vehicles to lend a hand at one particularly critical week-end. The Fuel Overseer always had power to alleviate any specially needy case.

There are many Luton consumers, however, who will recall the latter years of the war as years when it had to be " cash with order " for coal, and even then they had to wait with what patience they could for the coal which never seemed to be coming, no matter how loudly they complained. If, by good fortune, they received a token delivery, they had to go on wondering if and when the balance would ever be delivered.

Had this state of things ceased at the end of the war—and people could not be blamed for expecting it would—they would probably have shrugged their shoulders at memories of inconvenience and regarded it as something inevitable during war. But the end of the war did not end their coal problems, and during the winter of 1945-46 there were complaints about the impossibility of getting coal and of a growing number of households being absolutely without anything for a fire. The fact was that the coal just did not come into Luton in anything like adequate quantity, and the merchants could not deliver coal they themselves did not receive.

*   *   *   *

The war contributions of Luton Gas Company had many ramifications, many of them probably little realised by the people who turned on their gas fire or gas cooker. It was not only gas and coke which mattered. They certainly mattered very much. The by-products of gas manufacture were also of first importance. They were so important, in fact, that the Select Committee on National Expenditure, in a report on " Fuel and Power," issued during the 1942-43 session of Parliament, recommended that where possible gas should be used in preference to electricity because of the resultant by-products.

The Gas Company had three major responsibilities during the war years. They had to meet a greatly increased demand by munition works for gas and coke. They had to cope with an increasing domestic demand, caused by a rising population, while at the same time keeping careful watch to ensure that neither in industrial establishments nor the home was there any waste consumption. They had to deliver by-products in the greatest possible quantity.

At the Government's request, a plant for washing benzol and toluol from the gas was installed early in the war. The benzol was needed for high value aviation spirit, the toluol for the manufacture of explosives. This extraction from the gas was not without some distribution drawbacks. Things seemed to happen in the service pipes, and a special apparatus for clearing them was kept fairly busy. Any consumers who experienced a little difficulty at times can therefore regard their temporary disadvantage as an indirect contribution to the war effort.

Tar went from the Luton Gasworks to Dunstable Tar Distillery, and in part came back to Luton in a new form as Tar Oil 200—a pitch/creosote mixture which as a heating substitute for imported oil was an important saving of shipping space during the height of the U-boat campaign. Refined tar went for the construction and maintenance of aerodrome runways. From the lighter components of the tar were produced special oil for hydrogenation for aviation spirit, benzol, xylol (a solvent used in the manufacture of paints and varnishes) toluol, and naphtha as a solvent for rubber and special paints.

War conditions also required the production of the maximum amount of tar acids, for use in the manufacture of synthetic resins for the plastics industry and in varnishes for the aircraft industry ; from the Gas Company's by-products also came pyridine for drugs, including the famous M. and B. 693, and for many other wartime uses. Many valuable drugs and chemicals could not have been made available but for a tar base.

So much for the by-products. To make the gas from which they resulted, and in the quantity which was in demand, the gasworks had to carry a greatly increased load with supplies of coal irregular in delivery and very often poor in quality, and with a depleted operating staff. Sometimes unavoidable delays in plant repairs, due to shortage of material and manpower in the contracting industries, also hampered output.

To economise coal the Ministry of Fuel and Power directed that a maximum amount of carburetted water gas should be made. C.W.G., as it is known, is made by passing steam and oil over red-hot coke and it is mixed in with ordinary gas without loss of calorific value. To this end additional plant was installed. While this increased the amount of gas available, it also decreased the amount of coke available for sale. In normal times carburetted water gas plants are only brought into operation to meet peak loads, but this plant had to be used continuously in conjunction with the coal carbonising plant.

There were other factors which caused private consumers to go short of coke. Not only was it in greater industrial demand, but a number of military camps and hospitals also had to be supplied from Luton.

There was always the possibility that production and distribution might suffer by enemy action. But this could not be permitted to stop the work of some essential factories where gas was needed for various metallurgical operations, irrespective of its use for heating or canteen cooking. Because of this the Company was provided with a confidential list of factories which must be kept operating at all costs, and there was an emergency plan for keeping them supplied even though the gasworks was put out of action. This was part of a regional scheme to meet such an emergency. In some places preparations went to the length of installing special burner equipment to enable plant to be kept in operation at sub-normal gas pressure.

This was only one phase of the Gas Company's preparations. Others were put in hand even before the declaration of war. Shelters were built for the protection of the Company's personnel. Stocks of pipes and repair tools were considerably increased, and dispersed. Facilities for isolating individual distribution mains were put in hand, and stand-by squads to deal with damage to the distribution system were organised to cover the 24 hours of the day. Repair gangs were issued with special identity cards so that there should be no delay in moving quickly over the area. Practices were carried out to ensure that there was effective organisation to deal quickly with fractured mains, services, etc., and following the experience of some other places in the earliest air raids additional equipment was obtained.

That these preparations were really necessary is shown by the fact that during the period when Luton was getting attention from the Luftwaffe the repair gangs were called out to deal with 15 fractured mains and 159 broken and damaged services.

The blackout caused its own problems. To blackout the retorts and coke ovens was no easy task, but it was done. It had to be done if production was to be carried on right up to the imminent danger signal, and great credit is due to many of the gas workers for carrying on even when bombing planes were right overhead. Camouflage played a large part in the protection of the works.

Over 100 skilled employees of the Gas Company went to the armed forces, which meant that the rest of the production, distribution and office staffs had often to carry on under very adverse circumstances.

*   *   *   *

It might be regarded as presumptuous for Luton to claim that it taught London something, but an experience of the Luton Electricity Undertaking in January, 1945, was a pointer for London early in 1946.

The highest pre-war maximum demand experienced by the Luton undertaking was one day in December, 1938, when it reached 45,800 kw. In January, 1945, despite savings effected as a result of the Fuel Economy campaign, it touched 61,500 kw. Something had to be done to reduce it. Instead of cutting out consumers entirely for a short time, as was done in London, a pre-arranged plan was put into operation. At a crucial moment there would be a quick call to some of the big industrial consumers to shed part of their load in a manner which would affect production and labour to the minimum extent for the very short period necessary to tide over the peak demand. This plan brought immediate co-operation. A year later the same policy was adopted by the Central Electricity Board for other areas.

Maximum demand, however, was no guide to the way the output of the station was increasing. Maximum demand is a temporary phase of a winter morning, when lights continue in general use after the industrial load has come on, and when, maybe, many electric fires are also in use. The real guide to output is to be found in the total units distributed year by year. The Luton undertaking's total for 1938 was 126,672,104 units. For 1944 it was 232,367,995 units, despite a considerably lower consumption by domestic and commercial users as distinct from industrial plants. This increase of almost 100 per cent. came not because of an increase in the peak load but principally from the greatly increased night load. In other words, a high level of demand continued over a greater period of the 24 hours of the day.

Having reached this maximum in 1944, there was a falling off of war production in the district and a consequent drop in output, although domestic and commercial use was again approaching the 1942 figure, with the result that the 1945 total was 220,000,000 units.

Even in 1938 the generating station, sub-stations, cables and overhead lines were becoming overloaded, and some modernisation schemes were imminent. The most urgent of these were carried out in the war years. In a new switch house, commenced in 1940, 36 new 6,600-volt switch units were installed. A complete changeover of the station switchgear was also made, involving the removal or modification of 45 switch units. Despite the heavy load, all this was done without interfering with the continuous supply to war industries. In addition, in 1944 automatic boiler control was installed for the two largest boilers, with a resultant increase in generating efficiency.

The most important development, however, was the provision of a new grid tapping station at Sundon. Early in 1939 the Electricity Commissioners had approved the purchase by the Town Council of 192 acres of land at Sundon. The Council regarded it as an ideal site for a generating station which, in the years to come, would supersede the existing station in St. Mary's Road which has many disadvantages. Whether that scheme will ever materialise is still in the lap of the gods, although it is pretty certain that there will have to be a new generating station somewhere in this area. For the moment the grid tapping station has to serve.

This 33,000-volt transmission centre, designed and built under the supervision of the undertaking's engineers, came into full commercial operation in December, 1944. It was one of the developments of which nothing could be said at the time. It involved new primary sub-stations at Chaul End and Dunstable; an oil-filled 33,000-volt cable for the triple route between Sundon and Chaul End; and a double-circuit 33,000-volt steel tower line, beginning and ending in an oil-filled cable, between Sundon and Dunstable. This development scheme cost £297,000.

Because of the national shortage of materials and labour, all developments in domestic and similar electrification were banned quite early in the war, and restrictions placed on extensions of supply and connection of new appliances. Ruling factors were, necessity for the war effort, or grave hardship if approval was withheld, and hundreds of applications for new supplies had to be refused. Rural development also had to be discontinued unless food production was concerned, a saving clause which enabled many farms to be connected.

Although the average price obtained for supplies was below the national average, the output was such that from March, 1942, it was possible to make a rebate to consumers. During the war a total of £223,532 was returned in this way, but when an increase in operating costs, and particularly cost of coal, began to be felt, this rebate was gradually reduced, and eventually discontinued during the year ended March 31st, 1945. At March 31st, 1939, the undertaking obtained its coal at 23s. 4½d. a ton; at March 31st, 1945, the figure was 42s. 4½d. a ton, while the quality had so deteriorated that the effective price was quite 100 per cent. above pre-war.

*   *   *   *

Goods transport by road came under restrictions from the beginning of the war. Preparations for this had been made during the 1938 crisis by registering all transport in functional groups, butchers, grocers, greengrocers, drapers, furniture dealers, road hauliers, and so on, each group appointing its own organiser.

ABOVE: *With the rationing of petrol and paraffin, the "Pool" lorry became a familiar sight in the town.*

RIGHT: *The benzol extraction plant at the Luton Gas Company's works which was introduced during the war.*

GAS
INLET

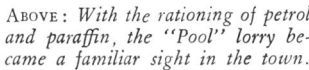

Part of the grid tapping station at Sundon, completed in the autumn of 1944. It helped to ensure an adequate electrical supply throughout the Luton area.

When the war started, therefore, the Ministry of Transport, which became the Ministry of War Transport and continued as such well into 1946, had some information on which to proceed. Petrol restriction came into force at once, and it could be based on the calculated normal consumption of each functional group. The petrol ration of so many one-gallon units was based on the unladen weight of each vehicle, with a supplementary ration where necessary. The bulk ration for each group was drawn by the group organiser, and by him allotted to the group members.

In Luton there were forty such groups, the original issue of coupons was made weekly, then fortnightly, and later monthly. Up to July, 1942, "A" licences had to be renewed as in peacetime. After that period they were renewed automatically, without payment, a practice which continued into 1946. Then the petrol ration became a matter for individual application. Users were free to continue through the group arrangements if they pleased, but this had to be a matter of mutual arrangement. The coupon validity was further extended at the same time to two months, and a new type of coupon came into use. No longer had its validity to be the subject of hand-stamping—the coupons were issued ready printed.

Up to April, 1943, haulage contractors were free to operate over any distance. From that date the Government took over many big concerns, made them controlled undertakings, and registered their vehicles as war transport for all long-distance haulage—that is, over 60 road miles.

The 1942 restriction of retail deliveries, the pooling of some, and the abolition of many had a direct effect on the whole community. From then onwards people had to carry home their groceries, their fish, their parcels from the draper's, in fact, practically everything they bought. True, the butchers could do a certain amount of delivery, but only once a week by bicycle. Greengrocers could still deliver such things as potatoes in bulk. Apart from these, shop transport was practically limited to bulky goods like furniture. Even for that transport was pooled, so it did not follow that anything bought from a particular firm was delivered by that firm's van. As a result, goods emerging from a van often presented some queer anomalies.

From June, 1945, traders regained their freedom to deliver their own goods, but it was a freedom more apparent than real. They had not the vans, or the manpower, to take advantage of this relaxation. People had to go on carrying their parcels, and the traders were saved a lot of expense.

Bread and milk, two necessities of every household, could always be delivered, but were the subject of special restrictions. The baker was allowed to call only three times a week, but, there was never (until 1946) any rationing of bread, and there was also no requirement to register with a particular baker. Anybody who ran short between the deliveries of their own particular baker was free to get more from any baker just by fetching it. For milk, however, there was a rationing which varied seasonally, and it was necessary to register. No longer could six or seven milkmen deliver in the same street. Except where a producer delivered a special grade milk, two was the maximum, and this only because the Co-operative Society had so many thousands of registrations, covering every street in the town, that they were held to be entitled to continue delivering everywhere. All the other suppliers had to confine themselves to their allotted zone. It was an arrangement which did not give complete public satisfaction, but it undoubtedly eliminated much waste of transport.

It was not to be assumed, however, that any system of transport control would please everybody. Certainly people could not be expected to like the position which developed in regard to heavy transport when the petrol and rubber supplies were at the worst. The Government was then able to decide whether goods should go by road or rail, and to force everything they thought fit on to the railways, despite the abnormal war loads the railways were already carrying, and irrespective of the time taken on the journey, or the cost.

It may not be true, but it is rumoured, that from one Luton factory with private sidings from the L.M.S. a consignment was sent to another Luton factory with L.N.E.R. sidings. To move those goods from one Luton factory to another involved a rail journey of about 60 miles, there being no physical connection between the two systems in Luton. How long it took . . . well, it is not wise to inquire.

*   *   *   *

Like other places, Luton lost its Green Line coach service to London two days before the war started. This was the outcome of an arrangement that in the event of war all these coaches should be withdrawn for conversion into ambulances, to enable London hospital patients to be evacuated. These coaches had given direct access to the West End shopping centres and Victoria, and their withdrawal, together with the disappearance of all coach trips to seaside holiday resorts, accentuated the rail travel difficulties of the war years.

That was the war's first effect on public road transport in Luton. The next resulted from the bombing of Luton from August, 1940. Bomb damage reduced Luton Corporation Transport's fleet from 64 to 21. Fortunately the Eastern National, London Transport, and Birch Bros. escaped any damage locally, 27 buses were obtained by the Corporation on loan to help tide over the position, the service did not fail for a single day throughout the war, and gradually the fleet was built up to 72.

From November, 1942, drastic restrictions were imposed on all undertakings. There was a 9 p.m. curfew, after which no bus was permitted to start an outward journey. All Sunday morning services were suspended. It was November, 1944, before 10 p.m. was substituted for 9 p.m., and September, 1945, before there was even a partial resumption of Sunday morning services. From the early part of 1946 further resumptions were permissible, and the Eastern National did manage to extend the Dallow Road service to 10.30 p.m. But the general experience was that, although employees were returning from the Services, the women who had carried on so wonderfully well during the war were leaving at an even faster rate, and a new labour shortage delayed further development of services.

Replacement difficulties during the war meant that vehicles had to last 50 per cent. longer than usual, and only Luton's lead in staggering factory hours made a reasonably adequate town service possible under the conditions which existed.

There was a promise that from the spring of 1946 things would be better, and people had to be content with the hope that the promise would be fulfilled, as it has in fact been.

*   *   *   *

The private car user was one of the first to feel the effect of wartime restrictions. The Petroleum Board came into operation on September 4th, 1939, motorists ceased to be able to buy their pet brand, and had to be content with " pool " spirit. Rationing started within about three weeks. The amount allowed varied with the h.p. of a car, and was assumed to allow about 200 miles of travel a month, although the 20 h.p. car was the limit for which the ration provided. A good many motorists did not think 50 miles a week justified keeping a car licensed and insured. They laid up their cars for a long wartime sleep and not until 1945 did they appear again on the road.

In June, 1940, with the threat of invasion, the majority of filling stations were closed, and the pumps sealed. Luton was allowed to retain one on each of the five main entrances to the town. Those who operated these five did so under a scheme where they were entitled to a first charge on the revenue for handling the petrol, and the balance was shared by those who had been compulsorily deprived of business.

Owing to the seriousness of the petrol and rubber position the basic ration for private users ceased entirely in July, 1942, although a little extra grace was allowed for motor-cyclists. It was not restored until June, 1945. Where cars were used for business purposes petrol was available even when there was no ration for private use, but the specific purpose for which it was required had to be stated, and if anyone was caught using it for other than the stated purpose, or even on a route that was not the shortest available, well, that was just too bad. There was, of course, plenty of questioning as to why so-and-so always seemed to have petrol when another person was denied an allowance, but it had to be believed that it was allowed for good reason. Service personnel on leave from overseas could always obtain petrol, even when there was no basic ration, a minor anomaly being that if they came from the Orkneys they were from overseas, but from Northern Ireland they were not.

So, as the war progressed, the number of cars and buses on the roads began to diminish. Not until 1945 did they begin to return.

Weapons of War

"GIVE us the tools, and we will finish the job."

This was one of the historic appeals of the war, uttered on an historic day. Broadcasting on February 9th, 1941, the day the " Lend—Lease " Bill passed the United States House of Representatives, Mr. Winston Churchill read part of a letter he had received from President Roosevelt introducing his opponent in the late presidential election. He ended his broadcast :—

" What is the answer that I shall give, in your name, to this great man, the thrice-chosen head of a nation of a hundred and thirty millions ? Here is the answer I will give to President Roosevelt : Put your confidence in us. Give us your faith and your blessing and, under Providence, all will be well. We shall not fail or falter ; we shall not weaken or tire. Neither the sudden shock of battle, nor the long-drawn trials of vigilance and exertion will wear us down. Give us the tools, and we will finish the job."

*   *   *   *

Long before this, however, Luton factories, in common with others throughout the country, were turning out those " tools," or weapons of war. Production was in crescendo, and the town was rapidly on the way to becoming one of Britain's huge arsenals.

But the weapons of war were not merely arms and ammunition. Some were of a kind which might be expected to emanate from Luton. Others were strange, extraordinary things, only conceived by the mind of man spurred on by the exigencies of the war. Many Luton factories in time had to turn out things vastly different from those on which they were normally engaged. They tooled up for the new jobs, and got going. Men and women went into the factories in increasing numbers. Out came an ever-increasing flow of the things which mattered in those critical times.

They ranged from Churchill tanks to ships' bells which called men of the Royal Navy to " action stations." They included highly scientific apparatus for application in fields never before explored, as well as such things as shells, mines, grenades, rockets and fuzes which were impressive only in the fact that of some the output reached millions. Depth charges went from Luton to put an end to U-boats, food reached our troops in tight corners only because it could be delivered from the air in special containers made here. Mosquitos took the air from one Luton factory. From a neighbouring factory Sabres, one of the war's outstanding successes in aero-engines, sent other planes hurtling through the air. The safety of many a man who had to take to his parachute depended on the strength and reliability of tapes woven in Luton, while " tapes " of another kind, woven in the same factory, were the indication of many an award or promotion.

Photographic film, chemicals, and even concentrated foods, were also among the many Luton products which all played their part in winning the war.

*   *   *   *

To see Luton industry at war one may be excused for turning first to Vauxhall Motors, Ltd., for there the labour force grew to 12,000, and there the Churchill Tank—Luton's biggest war baby—was born. It did not begin as the Churchill Tank. It began merely as an engine, or, to be strictly accurate, as lines on the drawing board of an engine-to-be. The vehicle for which it was intended was being developed elsewhere, and was to be heavier than anything which had preceded it. Vauxhall were asked to put an absolutely new engine on the drawing board, overcome material and production problems, and deliver within a minimum time. Conditions were that it must be a petrol engine, develop 350 h.p., and fit into a prescribed space. They did the job, although the space limits into which they had to tuck the engine involved a return to side valves, which they had abandoned nearly twenty years before. The first engine was giving satisfaction on the test bed in 89 days. It could be felt that the job was done.

Actually it was only begun. Having designed an engine to fit into a tank, Vauxhall were asked to return to their drawing boards and design a tank to fit round their engine. It was to be of a size and weight hitherto unknown, and it was wanted in production within a year. That was in July, 1940, just after Dunkirk. It involved designing, building prototypes, establishing sources of supply for themselves and other firms, planning production operations, building a new factory, and teaching other firms to do what they themselves were still learning. The only guide was a vehicle which had hardly run.

Tracks, petrol feed at queer angles of tilt, clutches—these were only some of the things presenting knotty problems as incidental to keeping production going here and at ten subsidiary centres. Machining of wheels alone had to be spread over 60 machine shops. If some part failed to stand up to much mileage, tanks still had to roll out while the cause was being proved and remedied. The main thing was that, when a tank of this sort was badly needed, it was got into production within the stipulated time. Its early faults aroused criticism, which often found voice only after those faults had been remedied. The argument of the higher powers was that in times which were so critical the value of the mobility of a tank which ran only a few miles might be incalculable.

The criticisms were to be expected, but the reliability of the Churchill was steadily developed until 100 miles " trouble free " became 1,000 miles, a stage at which long-distance troubles of a different kind tended to develop. These were also overcome, and distance records continued to go up and up. Rushed out in a very short experimental period as a defensive weapon, it became a very successful offensive weapon. Its weight of armour was increased. Its original two-pounder, once described as "a peashooter on an elephant," but the only high-velocity anti-tank gun then available, gave place to higher fire power. In North Africa, in Italy, and again after D-Day, the Churchill proved invaluable. It brought to Luton H.M. the King, who himself drove one, Mr. Winston Churchill, and many other notabilities, to obtain visual evidence of its potentialities. In North Africa it was the first tank to knock out a Tiger. In Italy Churchills were used in a decisive smash-through which did much to shorten that campaign. On the European Front a Churchill was the first to knock out a Panther. It proved that heavy German armour was not invincible.

Canadians were so proud of the Churchills that they decorated them with the Maple Leaf. Armoured R.E. Companies used them for carrying demolition charges. The flame-throwing Crocodiles were Churchills, and so were many of the tanks which flailed the land mines out of the ground. Before the war in Europe ended the Vauxhall employees had reason to be proud of their handiwork in what was for them quite a new field of engineering. Altogether 5,247 Churchills were delivered, and of the earlier models 2,911 went through the works again to be stripped, rebuilt, and brought up-to-date.

Early 1942 brought a rush job of a different kind. A gun-carriage was required for a new type of quickfirer then pouring into this country by the thousand. A mounting was designed, made and approved within seven weeks. Manufacture was spread over other firms. Vauxhall made the first 100 mountings to give the job a start, then provided all the jigs and fixtures for rapid production by other firms, and did all the sheet metal work. The gunner's seat, which took under three minutes to make, would have taken 18 man-hours to shape by hand.

Trucks, of course, were right up Vauxhall's street. About a third of those supplied to the Forces by British manufacturers were Bedfords. The first contract took seven days to plan, seven days to execute. The first convoy left Luton on September 23rd, 1939. Throughout the war the production of trucks for the Services averaged about 1,000 a week, and by VE-Day 209,096 had been delivered, plus many thousands of other vehicles for authorised civilian use. The Service vehicles were used for all sorts of purposes—A.A. gun tractors, "Queen Mary's," light armoured vehicles, fire tenders, troop carriers, water tankers, street washers, and even mobile dental surgeries.

To enable the Services to get the best use out of them, drivers were supplied with simply-written handbooks, a practice other manufacturers were recommended by the War Office to follow. Some were translated into other languages. The most famous was one *For B.F.'s.* Unofficial, illustrated by a *Punch* artist, and described as an "unexpurgated" edition, it was very popular with the men in the Forces, to whom 200,000 copies were given. It was reprinted in

America, Canada and Australia. This was only one way in which the troops were helped. Service engineers from the works, experts in trucks and tanks, lived and worked with the troops in all parts of the world. The Forces, however, seemed to eat up spares. Because of this, they had to be supplied with spares worth £18,450,000.

As side-lines, over 5,000,000 Jerrican pressings, 250,000 rounds of 2-pounder ammunition, and just over four million Venturi tubes for rockets were made. Thousands of special jigs and dies for other factories were made. Prototypes of decoy aircraft were produced. Jobs were undertaken for other firms who had bottlenecks, including work on disc harrows, bomb cases, magnets, hand-grenades, concrete mixers, machine guns, plane parts, and even snow-ploughs and gas ovens.

All these things were done for needs which were known. Some very interesting things were done for expected needs which did not materialise. One was a three-quarter track vehicle with steerable front wheels, so adaptable that it could tow a Bofors, 17-pounder, or 25-pounder, and carry crew and ammunition. There was no available engine of adequate power. To cut out the delay which producing a new engine would involve, and which would have meant the Army carrying another range of spares, the problem was solved by V-coupling two Bedford engines at the gearbox. Pilot vehicles had won high praise when the collapse of Germany made them unnecessary.

The " Kangaroo " was another which did not get beyond the prototype stage. A Ministry of Supply idea for the D-Day transfer of supplies from ship to shore, the driver was perched up 10 feet, and the engine was 7 feet from the ground, so that the vehicle could plunge into several feet of water without the driver, or engine, being drowned. The idea was abandoned in favour of " waterproofing " ordinary vehicles. In this direction very successful experiments had been carried out in the lake in Wardown Park. Eventually special ramps were built there so that drivers could practise taking the water as they would from a landing craft, and a special unit of R.E.M.E. took over the waterproofing.

Another unused novelty was the Vauxhall Resilient Wheel, which was to keep traffic moving without rubber tyres. The rubber position never became so bad as to bring it into use, but, ready for large scale production, it was there if required.

* * * *

Even in pre-war times the engineering products of Hayward-Tyler & Co., Ltd., Crawley Green Road, had a world-wide reputation. Some were of a specialised type for which there is always a need, war or no war. Where they were capable of helping the war effort, their production was intensified. Others had to be pushed into the background, so that existing or additional shops could be turned over to something of more vital need.

The early days of the war, therefore, saw the Company making steam engines for Admiralty barges. This was not unusual work. It was something quite different later on when, under a sub-contract, Archdale milling machines were made for the Ministry of Supply (Machine Control). This involved accurate work of quite a new type, but well within the Company's capacity.

Soda water machinery was an important field of activity which had to be suspended for the time being, except for spares of the greatest urgency. It gave place to gun parts and breech mechanisms for the Admiralty. A quarter of a million Oerlikon and automatic gun parts and breech mechanisms were supplied.

To help Vauxhall Motors, Ltd., keep Churchill tanks rolling out, 710,000 parts or sub-assemblies were supplied, and at one time Hayward-Tylers were the only people machining turrets for Churchills, and casting and supplying engine sumps, which throughout the war were made in cast iron instead of the more usual aluminium.

The heavy pump shop continued to produce pumps for oil tankers, and many other standard lines of pumping machinery for the equipment of war factories, military camps, and other war installations. Pumps were also supplied for Pluto, the petrol pipe line from Britain to France. At the other end of the scale a small pump for the No. 7 Predictor was so designed that it could be tooled up for batch production, and 1,750 units were supplied. In the submersible department 70 complete sets of submersible salvage equipment, each with its own mobile power supply unit, were turned out. Submersible borehole pumps went from this Luton works to help restore the water supply in freed territories. Others were used at home in blitz areas, for which they were peculiarly suitable, the whole of the unit being underground and not susceptible to aerial attack. Water circulating centrifugal pumps were also supplied for T.L. craft, while a vast amount of other work was undertaken in the form of sub-contracts.

As was the case so generally, unskilled labour had to be utilised to help maintain production, and for the first time in the history of the Company, women were employed in their works. In time, because labour was so scarce in Luton, steps had to be taken to enable even women who were tied to their homes to lend a hand, and the result was an outworking centre at Harpenden, where very valuable work was done until June, 1945. All this new labour had to be very dependent on old craftsmen of the kind Hayward-Tylers have produced. Typical examples are Mr. George Peck and Mr. A. Brown, who during the war received presentations to mark 60 unbroken years with the Company, and who, it being wartime, still carried on.

In quite another way the Company made what can be regarded as a major contribution to the war effort. In July, 1942, Mr. H. Weston Howard, who had become Chairman and General Manager following the death of Mr. Francis W. Howard in October, 1941, went at the invitation of the Rt. Hon. Oliver Lyttelton, Minister of Production, to become chairman of the Eastern Regional Board and Regional

Controller, Ministry of Supply, Cambridge. It was a full-time job until 1945, when he relinquished the appointment of Regional Controller, although continuing in a part-time capacity as chairman of the Eastern Regional Board for Industry.

*　　　*　　　*　　　*

Naval craft ploughing through dirty weather, torpedo men firing their tin fish, aircraft pilots watching their instruments, A.A. gunners laying their guns, men operating Fido to clear aerodromes of fog, factory workers elsewhere processing some vital part—all these and many other people engaged in the most mechanised of wars relied wholly or in part on some piece of equipment produced by the Luton works of George Kent, Ltd., which has always been regarded as the Luton home of instrument makers.

It was a very different war for Kent's, when compared with 1914-18. Then they had to halt all their usual work on meters for fluids of all kinds—air, gas, steam, oil, acids, etc., and concentrate on fuses. They built a special works at Chaul End for the dangerous job of filling the fuses they made. All this involved a rapid expansion of premises and labour, and a correspondingly difficult change-back after 1918.

In the intervening years the war machine as a whole became so mechanised and technical that Kent's instruments were in normal use, directly in the Services, and indirectly by other firms that supplied the weapons.

One outstanding result was that, working for four years by day and night shifts which averaged 55 hours a week each, an output equivalent to three times the best pre-war year was obtained with the same factory space, although many of the things they were called upon to produce were foreign to their normal output.

A typical example of the part played in war production by one of their standard instruments was provided by the Multelec pyrometer. Some 4,000 were made, mostly for the Ministry of Aircraft Production. They were used for exact control of temperature, so vital in the heat treatment of many aero engine parts, shell casings, and so on.

The work involved by this one production alone can be imagined when it is mentioned that each instrument had 2,000 parts. Design and assembly were so planned, however, that most of the operations could be performed by girls with little or no previous engineering experience. At one period of particular pressure, day and night shifts operated on this particular job seven days a week for five months.

Another standard product used to a very large extent was the Kent Clear View Screen, a disc of polished glass rotated at high speed by an electric motor, and fitted in the bridge structure of all types of warships, from battleships to M.T.B.'s and R.A.F. rescue launches. Providing clear vision in all weathers by throwing off rain, snow or spray, some 3,000 were supplied after September, 1939, for navigational and fire control purposes.

Long experience in the manufacture of water, oil, and petrol meters facilitated the development of a meter suitable for measuring the supply of fuel to aircraft engines. It proved of great value in training pilots in fuel economy, and in helping to reduce casualties due to petrol exhaustion. When put into full production for the Ministry of Aircraft Production the average output was 1,000 a month. Other petrol meters were supplied for use with Fido.

Special equipment made for the Admiralty included fire control instruments for major naval vessels, and some 5,000 gyro compass repeaters. These electrically operated compass dials, fixed in various parts of the ships repeat step by step the main gyro compass readings as an aid to gunnery and searchlight control, and for navigational purposes. Kent's also produced instruments for torpedo firing control—mechanical calculators converting visual observation into exact settings, and taking into account the speed and direction of the ship firing the torpedo and also that of the enemy target. Valve assemblies for torpedo propelling gear, steering equipment for light warships, and the Helmsman's Indicator, an anti-submarine protection device, were other jobs for the Admiralty.

Ministry of Supply contracts called for a quarter of a million steering gears for wheel and track vehicles ; for four million shell fuses, mostly of the type used with anti-aircraft shells and rockets, and also for large quantities of 25-pounder percussion fuses for use in the invasion of Europe. The Fuse Shop was manned almost entirely by women, and a peak effort of some 32,000 complete, fuses a week was reached.

Another precision instrument made for the same Ministry was the Boulange Chronograph, used for testing the accuracy of projectiles and guns of all calibres from 3 in. up to 16 in., by recording electrical impulses as the projectiles pass through screens.

The anti-aircraft predictor owed much to Luton. George Kent, Ltd., was one of the four or five parent firms or heads of component-making groups, and assembled and tested complete predictors, as well as manufacturing components and sub-assemblies in much greater number, for complete assembly elsewhere. Of one of the principal components, the torque amplifier—a high precision driving mechanism of which a pair went into each predictor, over 6,000 pairs were made in Luton, all requirements of this particular assembly being met by Kent's and one other firm.

Big figures of small things which emerged from the Biscot Road works were :— a million and a quarter cannon shells for aircraft ; twenty million fuse components, in addition to the complete fuses already mentioned ; seven million sleeves for incendiary bullets ; half a million chemical shell bursters—just part of our available reply had the enemy used poison gas ; 10,000 special valves for controlling the flow of cooling liquid to Aircraft engines.

Odd jobs included knuckle attachments for the folding wings of Fleet Air Arm aircraft ; special toothed chains for coal-cutting machines ; and a great quantity of small machined components and

M

non-ferrous castings required by other manufacturers.

In addition to all these outputs from the main works, the Hibbert Street factory turned out quantities of the small electric motors used in wireless sets, searchlight driving mechanisms, radiolocation, and other instruments. This factory also made large numbers of DC/AC convertors for Army Signals, small generators, phasing motors, dynamo control motors, small transformers for wireless transmitters, and some 20,000 of the dynamo exploders used by the R.E.'s to fire demolition charges.

The long working hours could not have been maintained without a good canteen service. This continued all round the clock, with main meals at midday and midnight, and breakfasts, teas, and other refreshments at other times. As many as 200,000 teas were served in one month.

The number of men and women employed rose to 3,000, and from the works 428 men and 26 women joined the Services.

*   *   *   *

The Davis Gas Stove Company, Ltd., made a quick change-over to almost 100 per cent. war production. The normal products of Diamond Foundry practically disappeared from the market. Only large-scale cooking units went out—for hospitals, bomber stations, ordnance factories, British Restaurants, evacuation centres, and so on.

In contrast to 1914-18, when many millions of hand grenades were turned out, only a mere 50,000 were called for this time, despite the fact that the continuous moulding equipment, regarded as the largest in the light-casting industry in the south of England, put the company in a specially favourable position to undertake such work. But the demands of war, like other things, change with the times, and if there were no colossal quantities of such grenades to be made in Dallow Road, plenty of other jobs ran into huge figures.

Over 750,000 25-pounder shells were turned out under one of the earliest contracts. This was a job which finished long before the end of the war, because the tremendous output throughout the country was proving far more than adequate ; over 3,350,000 shell-cases—25-pounder, 3.7 and 4.7 A.A. shells—were re-formed by a plant capable of handling 80,000 cases a week, although never used to capacity ; 780,000 special ammunition boxes were made for the carriage of both shells and cases ; 1,400,000 special plugs to protect the 25-pounders in transit were made.

Other production jobs were 27,000 29-pounder shells ; 318,000 3 in. mortar bombs ; 100,000 4.2 mortar bombs ; 600,000 land mines ; 10,000 anti-tank grenades ; and 1,700,000 2 in. h.e. mortar bombs, each of which involved many operations.

If none of these jobs presented any particularly novel feature, others did. As casting specialists, the company was called upon to produce vehicle track links. It was a new process for them, but in a building erected for the purpose 3,500,000 were produced, and much satisfaction was felt with the result. Very little trouble was experienced with the links they made, and they were regarded as equal to those produced by firms having long experience of this class of work.

One of the most important and highly secret jobs was what the employees knew as " W.O.49." This involved equipping an almost entirely new shop with specialised machinery for making 5 in. U.P. tails for special rockets fired from batteries, and similar to the 3 in. projectiles used against enemy aircraft. They were used with great success from barges in the landings in Sicily, Italy and Normandy.

Other activities resulted in 6,690 insulated containers being supplied for the transport of hot food to the troops, and 32,000 6 ft. long containers for dropping by parachute to airborne troops and for other purposes, including dropping food supplies in liberated countries. This, of course, was a long remove from the days when the company, with its associated companies, made all the castings for the Northover Projector, and also 652,000 Smith Gun projectiles, because of Hitler's expected invasion.

Plus wholly completed jobs, machined parts and pressings for motor vehicles reached 106,000 ; castings for sea smoke flares 121,000 ; castings and pressings of marine parts 772,000 ; pressings for radio equipment 37,000 ; parts for barrage balloon equipment 37,000 ; parachute container pressings 514,000 ; tank motor parts, 32,000 ; and reel lanyard bomb release equipment for aircraft, 11,000.

Numerous other parts were manufactured, making a grand total of twenty million assemblies, and also twenty million reasons why people could not have the new " Regulos " or other things they thought they wanted.

*　　　*　　　*　　　*

If gas cookers had to go by the board, so also had vacuum cleaners, refrigerators and other domestic appliances. Electrolux, Ltd., had far more important work on hand. Their factory in Oakley Road supplied a large proportion of the Royal Navy's depth charges, and mine charge cases were also made. With over half a million to their credit, Electrolux was one of the largest producers in the country. The technical department did much important development work in connection with both mines and depth charges.

Although Luton received a fair number of German bombs, the enemy was repaid a thousandfold. Over a million high explosive and incendiary bombs destined for Germany flowed out of the Electrolux factory. They were of all weights up to a thousand pounds, and to help the R.A.F. drop them to most advantage they were accompanied by 40,000 target markers and flares for Pathfinders.

In addition over 300,000 bomb tails were made, and 12,000 special containers for the airborne forces. Other orders included more than a quarter of a million ammunition boxes, including special insulated types for desert warfare ; more than 100,000 insulated containers for the transport of food ; and 3,000 tons of bridging material, while the

Edgware factory assembled nearly two million Jerricans.

Perhaps the most secret of the company's activities was the treatment of shells to make them immune from the effect of corrosive gases. They treated over a million shells in this way. The company continued to make some refrigerators—special types for trawlers and M.T.B.'s. The Army and R.A.F. also took a number.

* * * *

Millions of ball, roller and thrust bearings were made in Luton by the Skefko Ball Bearing Co., Ltd., to further the war effort. They might be, and were, put to novel uses, but to the workers producing them it was a job which could offer very little variation . . . always in front of them rings, cages, balls, rollers . . . the very ones that might have been in front of them months before and might still seem to be in front of them in months to come.

Four thousand men and women carried on this monotonous job. Work tickets conveyed nothing to them as to the uses to which the bearings they so carefully made or assembled would be put as a contribution to winning the war. They did not know whether particular bearings would help the tanks to keep rolling from El Alamein to Tunisia, to win the Battle of Britain or the Battle of the Atlantic, or to contribute to the successful final assault on Germany. To learn these and many other things they had to wait until after the war.

Even the technical experts were not always more informed. When a snag occurred in the development of something in which Skefko bearings were incorporated, then they were called in to join with the designers in puzzling out a way to overcome the snag. If vibration, or the intrusion of a speck of desert sand, tended to reduce the accuracy of some delicate instrument, again there was a job for the technicians. But although thousands of bearings were used in Radar, and they were also used in connection with Fido and Pluto, even to the technical experts these names had no significance at the time. It was quite impossible for the men and women at the machines and the benches, on inspection, or doing anything to ensure that the bearings used for those new purposes were of the highest degree of accuracy, to have the stimulus of knowing in what direction their monotonous work was a contribution to the making of war history.

Perhaps they sometimes wondered why, after all their patient and careful work, large numbers of bearings were scrapped. The story of Asdic was another that could not be told at the time. Asdic was the name of an apparatus installed on the bridge of every escort ship. Its utility depended on a motor alternator revolving 7,000 times a minute for the whole of the 3,000 miles crossing of the Atlantic. A slight variation in the speed of the alternator, and a U-boat might remain undetected. On test an alternator might run perfectly for hours, and then disclose a slight variation in speed. The cause had to be tracked down. It might take hours. It might be traced to an error of one-ten-thousandth of an inch in the bearings. To produce

100 bearings of the accuracy demanded by Asdic might mean scrapping 1,000 bearings, but it had to be done, to ensure the safety of our merchant ships. Now the women, who for five years watched the indicator of a testing machine, or carried on visual inspection under the unceasing glare of powerful lights, understand why some of the bearings they handled had afterwards to be scrapped.

Once, however, they did see what their work meant to the R.A.F. In 1944 a Bristol " Hercules " engine, cut away to show clearly where Skefko bearings were used in it, was installed in the canteen. It helped very much to convince the employees of the importance of the work they were doing. On another occasion the Army brought along a tank for demonstration. But of necessity such demonstrations could be few, and for the greater part of the war years the workers just had to go on making bearings...bearings...more bearings. That was their job. It was the job of other people to see that they were put to the best use. Whether they went into aero-engines, tanks, gun mountings, predictors, radar, Asdic, or, farther back, into the vast variety of ingenious machines used to turn out anything and everything required for the effort, was outside their ken.

Even in wartime there were all sorts of " other purposes " for Skefko bearings, and one of these " other purposes " is the subject of a very human story. One wet morning, after a night blitz on London, a grimy dispatch rider dashed into the main hall. He said, " Morning ! Got a bearing like this one ? It's for an excavator. The people were still alive down below when I left." He got his bearing.

If anybody elsewhere needed any convincing of the importance of the ball bearing industry in time of war, it was most strikingly demonstrated after a disastrous raid by the R.A.F. on the principal German ball-bearing plant at Schweinfurt. There was reason to believe that, the Schweinfurt plant having been wrecked, the Germans would at once endeavour to ensure the maintenance of these vital supplies from Sweden. To forestall this, Mr. W. Siberg, joint managing director of the Skefko, was one of two experts who dashed off to Sweden. The urgency of the journey was such that they made the direct 800-mile crossing of the North Sea and Skagerrak in two unarmed Mosquitos. The bomb-bays of the Mosquitos were hurriedly converted for the purpose. There was no room even for a chair. A pilot's seat was nailed to the floor, a lap strap added to prevent the semi-recumbent passenger being thrown about too much, and off they set. The journey was a success both in initiating a new form of air transport and in its purpose. Afterwards many Very Important Personages travelled in bomb-bays.

Annotated German maps found after the end of the war in Europe clearly showed that the Luftwaffe were fully alive to the importance of the Skefko factory at Luton. Fortunately they could not do what was done to the Schweinfurt factory. They did no more than once slightly damage the extreme end of the buildings. Inside, some manufacturing operations were carried on in bomb-proof bays, many more were not, and those four thousand men and women went on producing bearings...bearings...more bearings, just as they did the year before, and would still do in the following year, while right across the factory roofs stretched a dummy road, complete with dummy trees designed to cast un-dummy shadows on the dummy road.

To mark the final Victory celebration on June 8th, 1946, the company paid employees a Victory bonus of £10,000, including in the distribution all who had worked for three consecutive years before VJ-Day, even if they had subsequently left the company's employ.

*   *   *   *

Of the many Commer and Karrier vehicles which left Luton for the Services during the war years, the most unorthodox was the one which became an armoured reconnaissance car. Running about Luton, the chassis looked extraordinary. Engine and radiator were at the rear, and because of this it was difficult at first to realise whether they were going or coming. Having the power unit at the rear was not original, of course. Years ago a small vehicle was marketed which had nothing under the bonnet; but that was for ordinary road use. This reconnaissance car had to be capable of going practically everywhere, even up a gradient of one in two, and combining with this a decent speed on good going, although the total weight was in the neighbourhood of seven tons. The welded hull accommodated a crew of three, and the traversing turret of bullet-proof steel housed a 15 mm. shell-firing gun and a 7.92 mm. machine gun as well as a wireless transmitter. It was, however, but one of a wide range of Service vehicles which went out from the Biscot Road factory. They ranged from 15 cwt. load carriers to 3-tonners, and also " Queen Mary " tractors and gun tractors. They found their way to practically all the fighting fronts, and to these they were followed by experts from the works to ensure that under field conditions they gave the best possible service. One of these experts will not soon forget a journey right across Central Africa by flying boat, which took him over vast areas of country where the only sea below was a sea of tree tops.

*   *   *   *

PF.388 was a Mosquito with a history. For 36 consecutive nights it delivered 4,000 lb. bombs on Berlin, as one unit in a striking force of Bomber Command. Previously attached to a different squadron, it built up a record of over 100 sorties in comparatively short time. The two officers who formed its crew flew together all over Germany, and together made 20 trips to Berlin, up to that time a record for any Bomber Command crew. PF.388, and many others like it, took shape in the hands of the workers at Percival Aircraft, Ltd.

Percivals also built thousands of Proctors, used for wireless and navigation training in the R.A.F. and Fleet Air Arm, and over 1,000 twin-engined Oxfords for advanced flying training, as well as repairing more than 1,000 aircraft, many of them in remote parts of the country.

When war became imminent, the Percival Vega Gull was chosen by the Air Ministry for conversion into a Service training machine, and became the Proctor I. Specially modified for the Fleet Air Arm, it was the Proctor II. When much heavier Marconi radio equipment for bomber aircraft came into use, it was found possible to instal this in the Proctor III, although it was still only a single-engined light aircraft. Experience with these three Proctor types led to the design of a special model for wireless and navigational instruction, flying qualities, maintenance and servicing, and the comfort of the crew, all being taken into consideration in this Proctor IV. The thousands of Proctors turned out operated at all Signal Schools within the United Kingdom, also in Australia, South Africa, India, Ceylon and Trinidad, and they had to be capable of maintaining a steady training programme even if conditions were sometimes adverse. Many Proctors had over 2,500 flying hours to their credit, and they also had the lowest accident rate per 1,000 flying hours of any comparable aircraft used by the R.A.F. As a four-seater communication and observation plane it was used by the three Services, notable occasions being the Dieppe Raid and D-Day operations, as well as by the Americans and by Marshal Tito's Balkan Air Force Staff.

When twin-engined Oxfords were in demand for advanced bomber flying-training and for teaming up air crews, well over a thousand were turned out at a production rate even faster than stipulated by the Air Ministry's schedule. It was once demonstrated that the Oxford could also rapidly become an air ambulance. A Fortress landed at an R.A.F. emergency landing ground, with two of the crew badly wounded. The air ambulance could not take off from its own airfield owing to bad weather. Two R.A.F. officers hastily converted an Oxford, flew through the bad weather, and had the wounded men in hospital all inside 30 minutes, and in time for blood transfusion to save their lives.

With the training programme so well advanced that more attention could be concentrated on combat machines, Percivals were asked to turn over to production of the Mosquito B Mark XVI—the fastest bomber in the world. It meant new jigging, new tooling, but the company produced the first in the time allotted, which was considered an achievement meriting congratulations from the Air Ministry. Luton-built Mosquitos thereafter played an important part in the devastation which descended on Germany and German-occupied territories.

Work was dispersed, as a precaution against a major disaster of the kind which nearly happened when a parachute mine lodged in the roof of the main factory. It was a wise precaution, but did not make production any the easier.

During the war years a third of the employees were women. They learned a new job. They did a good job.

The war being over, Percivals scored another winner by being the first British firm to export civil aircraft.

* * * *

Vital parts of Mosquitos came into being in other Luton factories. Normally manufacturers of high speed paper folding machines, the Cundall Folding Machine Company, Ltd., of Hitchin Road, found themselves almost wholly engaged on aircraft parts before the war was very old. Over 1,000 Oxfords were fitted with landing gear assembly made by them, and then the compression legs and retractable rear wheel used on the Mosquito almost monopolised their activities. They made over 3,000 sets of these for De Havillands, originators of the Mosquito, and up to VE-Day 98 per cent. of the capacity was absorbed by aircraft work.

De Havillands, incidentally, had one of their dispersed factories in Luton. They occupied a substantial part of the fine factory built a few years ago by Paul Walser, Ltd., and there fashion hats gave way to Mosquito parts.

* * * *

" Rush jobs ? They were all rush jobs." This was a summing-up of the war-time experience of the Adamant Engineering Co., Ltd., Dallow Road. Not one of the big firms from the point of view of number of employees, Adamant normally made a patent steering gear which was fitted to anything from the 12 h.p. family runabout to the double-decker bus. They went on making the steering gear, but it went into armoured and reconnaissance cars, into tank carriers. But they took on all sorts of other jobs. One rush call was for 2,500 Blacker Bombard spigot mortars, to help make good the Army's losses at Dunkirk and in Greece. They turned out some thousands of P.I.A.T.'s, the anti-tank weapon. They made sparking plug testers, for which they were the sole contractors to the Air Ministry. It was not unusual to get an urgent order for a lorry load of small parts vitally needed at some military depot. It is true the number of employees doubled, but they were largely war-trained reinforcements to make good in part the loss of skilled employees who went into the Services. Production never stopped ; until April, 1945, it went on night and day. An output three times greater than peacetime was secured, although the proportion of skilled labour available was much reduced. It was said that whenever a Government department had an awkward engineering job to be done the slogan was, " Send it to Adamant."

* * * *

Early in 1940, E. W. Hudson & Co., Ltd., Latimer Road, Luton, and the associated Hudson's Foundry Co., Ltd., were asked to produce machined parts and castings for motor torpedo boats and gunboats which were to be mass-produced at yards all round the coast. The result was that over 1,000 tons of gunmetal, manganese bronze, and aluminium castings were produced by the foundry section, and

ABOVE: *A section of the machine shop at Luton Technical College where many war-time engineers were trained.*

RIGHT: *H. M. The King, clad in white overalls over his Field Marshal's uniform, inspecting the turret of a Churchill tank when he visited Vauxhall Motors.* PHOTO: *Vauxhall Motors, Ltd.*

BELOW: *Churchill and a Churchill. Cigar in mouth, Britain's war-time Prime Minister strides past a tank named after him, during his visit to the Vauxhall works in 1941.* PHOTO: *Vauxhall Motors, Ltd.*

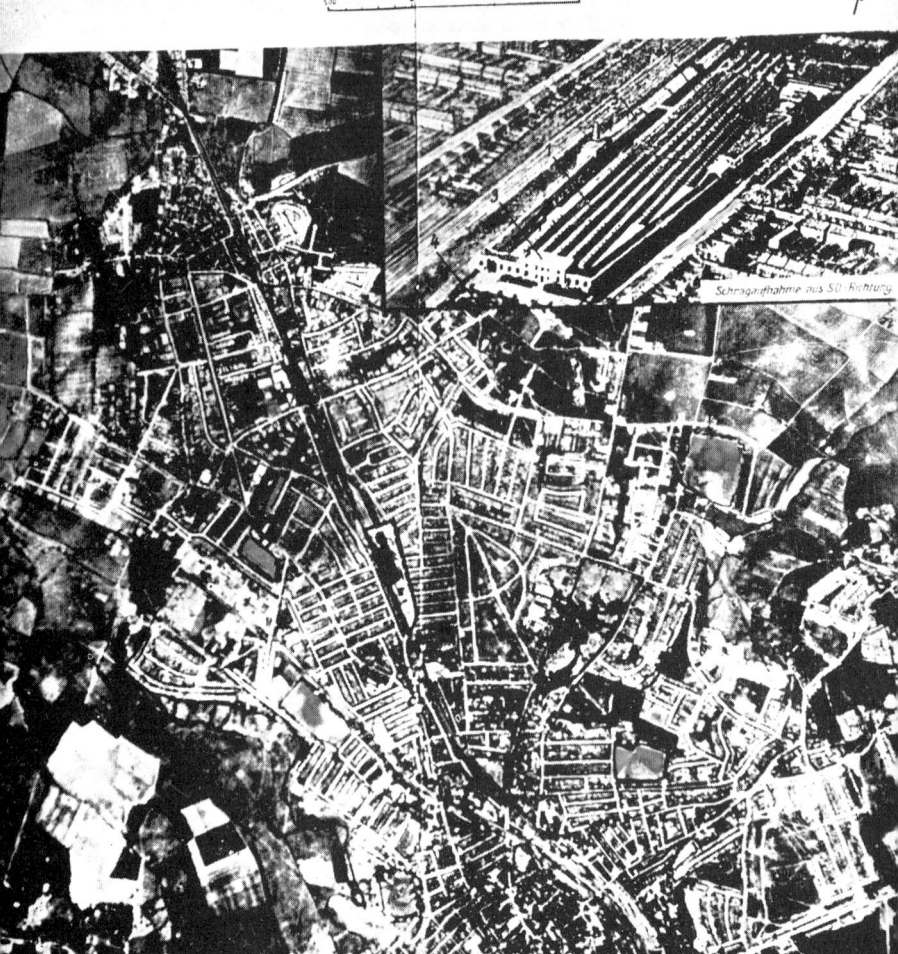

Luton

Kugellagerfabrik Skefco

Länge (westl. Greenw.): 0° 26′ 00″ Breite: 51° 53′ 30″
Mißweisung: — 10° 39′ (Mitte 1940) Zielhöhe über NN 120 m

Maßstab etwa 1 : 22 700

Genst 5 Abt. Oktober 1940

Karte: 1:100 000

GB E 29

Schrägaufnahme aus SO-Richtung

Issued to the Luftwaffe in October, 1940, this captured German map showed the
Skefko Ball Bearing works in Leagrave Road as the objective. The factory is
outlined in black in the centre of the map, and an oblique aerial view is seen
inset top right. Why the works were not subjected to an attack is a matter of
conjecture, but the only damage done to Skefko was a month earlier when a
particularly heavy bomb dropped on the L.M.S. railway running past the factory.
The tracks were blown up but only a corner of the works damaged.

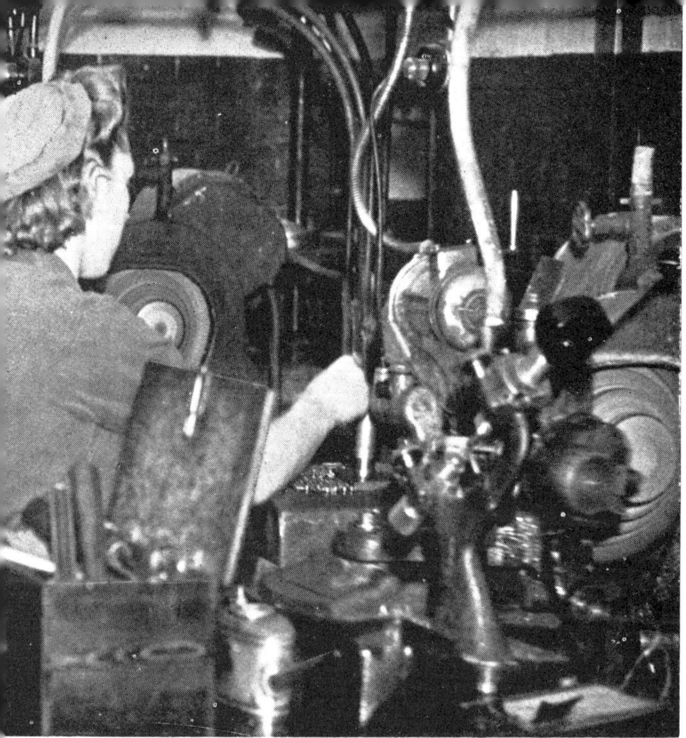

Ball bearings essential to the running of war machines of all descriptions were produced by the million at the Skefko Ball Bearing works.

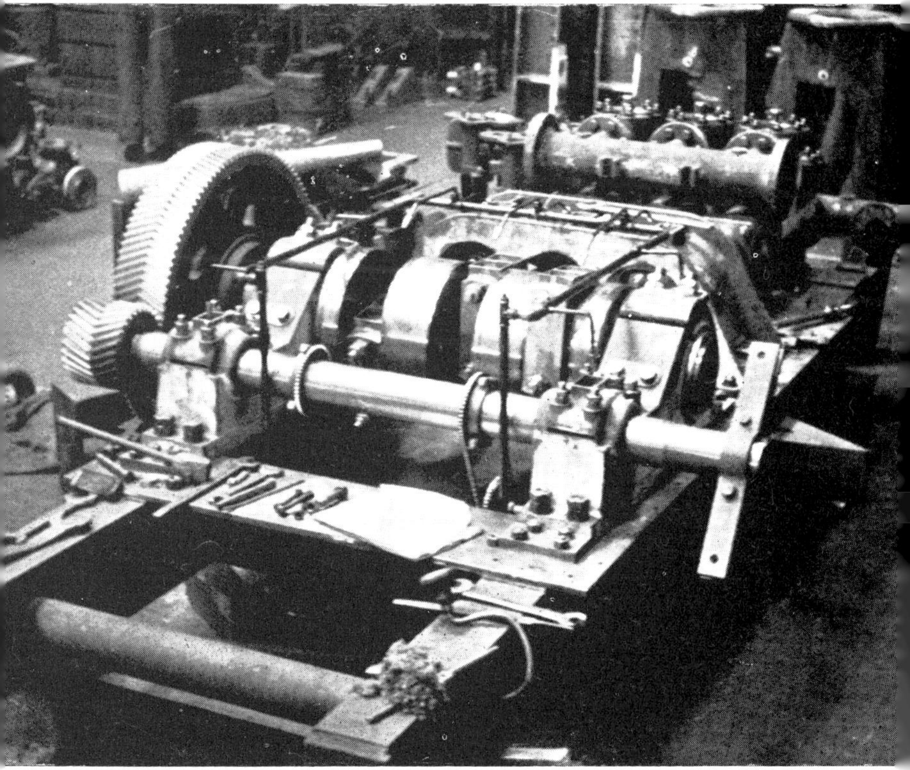

This pump for "Pluto" . . . the pipe line which supplied fuel to the Allied forces invading the Continent . . . was produced by Messrs. Hayward-Tyler and Co. The picture shows a pump under construction.

A section of the aircraft fuel meter
assembly and test shop at Messrs. George
Kent, Ltd. Meters were produced for all
types of R.A.F. aircraft.
PHOTO: W. H. COX

Two G.I.'s loading a "newspaper bomb"
on to a truck. Millions of copies of special
propaganda newspapers were dropped
over Germany and occupied territory
during the war years. They were printed
by Home Counties Newspapers Ltd., and
packed by Gibbs, Bamforth and Co.
(Luton) Ltd., at The Leagrave Press.

machined by the engineering section. A wide range of parts was called for, such as propellor shaft sleeve bearings, bulkhead bearings, water circulating pumps, gun pump drives and 1,000 h.p. reduction gearboxes, these all being fitted and tested at the works before delivery. Deck fittings included bollards, fairleads, aerial masts, stem headplates, etc., while jobs in other fields were tank gearboxes, tank bridging equipment, fittings for the Mulberry Harbour, steel moulds for rubber manufacture, Diesel engine parts and refrigerator parts. As this kind of work monopolised the activities of the two companies until the war was over, orders for the things in which they normally specialise had to wait. The result was that they were able to enter on the post-war era with large orders on hand for hatters' machinery, stainless steel dyeing machinery, mechanical stokers, etc.

*   *   *   *

Brown and Green, Ltd., normally make laundry machinery one of their principal specialities at Chaul End. Even during the war years they were able to continue this activity to a limited extent, for their machines accompanied the Forces in all parts of the world. But they also did much secret experimental work, and their foundry and machine shops made very substantial contributions to the war effort.

First call was for 3 in. h.e. mortar bombs. To avoid delays otherwise inevitable they designed and made special-purpose machines for the job, and had the bomb at a high level of production by March, 1940. When the supply of steel forgings for the bomb became inadequate, their foundry made the body of the bomb in cast iron, and by the time this size was discontinued they had produced over a million.

In the meantime they had laid out a special department for shrapnel mines—a complicated mechanism with a substantial cast iron body and a very large number of components. Full production was reached in three months, and 300,000 were made.

While this job was running a 4.2 in. mortar bomb was called for. Plant was re-designed, extra machines obtained, and a production of about 4,000 a week secured.

Another new type of work came along—machining steel forgings to become the base of a range-finding smoke mortar bomb, on which they had done all the experimental work. Here production exceeded 4,000 a week.

Production of catapult and rocket firing equipment led to other jobs, and because the company produced so many specialised machines to speed up their own output they found themselves pressed by Ministry departments into another quite new field of business—that of machine tool makers for other companies on munition contracts. Out of this came a real headache. They were asked to design and make a machine which was quite out of their field. It involved using heavier castings and doing bigger machining operations than those with which they were familiar ; but they tackled the task successfully, and so relieved what threatened to be a serious bottleneck in the machining of tank turret rings in particular.

While they were doing all these things, their laundry machines went on working—among other places at Gibraltar, in the only laundry in the world using salt water. To-day they are at work in Stalingrad.

*   *   *   *

In some 7,000 ships at sea " Action Stations," the call which makes every Navy man " jump to it," was sounded on bells cast by the Alliance Foundry Company, Ltd., Icknield Road. At the other end of the scale they produced for the Admiralty 3,750 cast iron sinkers, weighing from 1 cwt. to 2 tons each. During the war period they turned out 9,780 tons of grey iron, semi-steel, alloyed cast iron, and non-ferrous castings.

For the Admiralty also the company turned out 23,750 naval fittings—ventilators, bollards, fairleads, and engine water strainers for M.T.B.'s. The Army and R.A.F. also relied on the Alliance Foundry for a number of things, including 121,500 parts for radiolocation and searchlights, 23,000 mortar bomb fuse castings and 5,000 parachute counterweights. Many tons of castings were supplied for the " Mulberry " harbour, fire fighting equipment, tanks, armoured cars, barrage balloon and target winches, and jigs and tools for aircraft production.

The work was done by a labour force diluted with 30 per cent. of women, who worked as floor moulders, coremakers, electric truck drivers, pattern shop assistants, turners, fitters and painters.

*   *   *   *

The smoke screen which was such an important factor in the brilliant episode of El Alamein was made possible by the workers at Frickers' Metal Co., Ltd., Portland Road. Later the workers were officially shown how it was done. Similar apparatus to that used at El Alamein was taken to the factory, a smoke screen put up, and the workers invited to walk through it. They did, without any harmful results. That was but one war use for the zinc oxide and other zinc products of the company. The Government took practically 100 per cent. of the output ; a small balance went to paint manufacturers, although perhaps not of the grade they obtained in pre-war days. Then rubber tyre, linoleum and paint producers were some of the largest consumers   Zinc oxide from Luton went into all sorts of other unexpected articles—boot polish, cosmetics, shaving soap among them, but many of these products had to do without it during the war years.

*   *   *   *

Hydrogen peroxide, especially in a high-volume form, had important new uses during the war, and B. Laporte, Ltd., of Kingsway, did a lot of experimental work in this direction. Holding a commanding position as hydrogen peroxide producers before the war, the company also manufactures, directly or through subsidiaries, a wide variety of chemicals. For all there was an accentuated wartime demand, and in new or adapted plants the company manufactured chemical products not previously made in this country.

An outstanding development, to ensure an adequate supply of an essential raw material for the Luton works, was in connection with a barytes mine in high, remote and rough country in Westmorland. It involved building local offices, cottages for workers, and ropeways five miles long so that the dressed barytes could be conveyed to rail-head. Another barytes mine is now being developed in Cumberland.

Another development was the installation of a large sulphuric acid plant in 1941. This has continued in full operation, and gradually the company or one of its subsidiaries will absorb its full output. The company also added to its range of fine chemicals required for essential purposes during the war, and has found a peacetime market for them.

Titanium oxide, produced at Luton by National Titanium Pigments, Ltd., the company's largest subsidiary ; the edible phosphates of Associated Phosphate Manufacturers, Ltd., another wholly-owned subsidiary, and the bottled hydrogen peroxide of Genoxide, Ltd., also a Laporte subsidiary, were all in considerable demand during the six years of war, and the unexpected war uses of other things produced at Kingsway was well demonstrated by the company's display at an industrial exhibition held in Luton just after the end of the war.

*   *   *   *

Another manufacturer of hydrogen peroxide was Alcock (Peroxide) Ltd., Chaul End. It was well known that over a period of years the Germans had spent millions in erecting huge hydrogen peroxide plants. It was also known that, whereas hydrogen peroxide is usually marketed in 10 and 20 volume strength, German factories were producing it in 350-400 volume strength, with an explosive power 30 per cent. greater than gunpowder. What was not known was the purpose to which they intended to apply it. That only became apparent when the flying bombs and rockets began to arrive. Fortunately before this new form of aerial attack had been fully developed, the war was in its closing stages.

The question arose, " Could these new weapons be countered by producing similar peroxide in this country." The answer of Alcock was " Yes." As early as 1937 they were aware that the high volume peroxide was available in Germany, and were satisfied that they could produce it in their existing plant if necessary. After bombing of this country had started in 1940 the company went further into the matter, and in early 1941 put before the Government the possible potentialities of high volume peroxide for retaliatory purposes. Apparently little or nothing was known in this country at that time of the possibilities of peroxide as a war weapon, but Alcocks did not wait. They went ahead, and in February, 1941, were producing a 95 per cent.

peroxide. This, they believe, was the first production on a commercial scale in the British Empire.

In quite another field Alcocks were producing something which helped to ease soap rationing. This was sodium metasilicate. The basic raw materials are soda from Cheshire and fine silica sand from the Leighton Buzzard district. They are chemically combined at a temperature above the melting point of the sand, and ultimately result in a white crystalline product now largely used by laundries as a " detergent," and also in a number of proprietary cleaning compounds.

*   *   *   *

One of Luton's smaller factories made a most interesting contribution to the variety of new weapons used in the war. It played a major part in the development of the rocket, which became such a valuable anti-aircraft weapon, and later, in a larger version, such a war-winning weapon. Like so many other war jobs, it was far removed from the normal work of the company responsible, Parkinson and Cowan, (Gas Meters), Ltd.

From small beginnings at the Frederick Street factory which they took over for this specific purpose they reached maximum output by the spring of 1941, and provided experience and plans for other rocket factories in various parts of England and Scotland.

Developed to supply a much-needed requirement in the defensive days, all branches of the Services came to appreciate its worth. The wrecks of many tanks, ships and planes as, long before D-Day, rocket-firing Typhoons carried the war far behind the enemy lines, gave the Hun a foretaste of British striking power.

It was one of the major success of the rapid advance from Normandy to the Rhine, and saved many lives by the havoc it caused in destroying enemy convoys, dumps, and troop concentrations. Some of the workers may have guessed the object of the labours, but only one or two at the head of things could have appreciated its full worth to the Allied cause.

Bangalore torpedos, fired from tanks for the demolition of wire, tank barriers and other obstacles ; flame floats ; sea markers ; parachute flares ; these were other things which followed in quick succession, ready for the explosive and other charges to be inserted elsewhere, and although the Frederick Street factory had only about 200 workers, the ideas born there had a result out of all proportion to the number of people concerned.

*   *   *   *

When R.A.F. reconnaissance planes were obtaining and recording priceless information by camera, when other things were being recorded by gun camera, when X-Ray photographs were taken for scientific or beneficent purposes, few of the camera operators were probably aware that for success they were dependent in the first instance on the employees of the British Gelatine Company, Ltd., New Bedford Road. This company had always specialised in photographic gelatine, although other branches of the trade apply it to its ultimate use, and throughout the war 90 per cent. of the output at New Bedford Road was photographic. The Ministry of Aircraft Production was the one most interested, but the Admiralty and the Directorate of Medical Supplies also placed contracts. Most of the 10 per cent. balance went for the manufacture of medical supplies for the Forces overseas, mainly to combat malaria. A very small amount was left to go into the preparation of certain foodstuffs. Other things were more important than table jellies ! The staff fell by 15 per cent., but overtime and extra mechanisation made this loss good, and output was in fact increased by one-third.

* * * *

From Leagrave to the Middle East is a long journey, especially in wartime, but men and products from one firm met there, during the Desert campaign. The men were former employees of Chas. J. Ell & Sons, Victoria Well Works, and they saw water pumps sent from Leagrave to help them chase the enemy out of North Africa. It was one of the triumphs of the little firms of Britain in helping to make victory possible.

When the war started the firm had 70 men sinking wells and erecting pumps in what had been a peaceful countryside. As men went into the Services the number remaining was gradually reduced to 20. Those who went could not be replaced, and outside work had to be discontinued. On the premises, however, they got busy on machines to help the Army by wringing water from an unfriendly soil. A couple of thousand drive-tube wells were the first result. Then followed deep bore-hole pumps, fitted with 24 h.p. Diesel engines, and delivering 6,000 gallons an hour from a depth of 300 ft. They were followed by smaller sets to deliver 2,000 gallons an hour from the same depth, and by plant for 300 gallons an hour.

A former employee wrote : " I saw one of our pumps trundling along, and thought it good to see a bit of Luton here."

Providing these pumps, of course, ran much along peacetime lines, but one job was a great departure from normal. For the famous Sabre engine the firm produced a test bed—it filled the shed in which it was built.

* * * *

It may surprise many people to be told that $10\frac{1}{2}$ million yards of tape woven in Luton helped to win the war. It was not, however, the red tape beloved of officialdom, although a lot of it was coloured.

Three and a quarter million yards, one inch wide, made of real silk, and tested to a breaking strength of 280 lbs., were used as the periphery tape of parachutes. This was but one of the things done by Lye and Sons, Ltd., and the associated company R. Westly & Co., Ltd. Over 1,250,000 yards of tape in various widths were also made for the manufacture of the pack and the attachment of the parachute, while another 3,000,000 yards were produced in various colours.

N

Of the two companies, Westly & Co., as ribbon weavers, dyers and finishers, undertook the greater part of this work. They also produced thousands of yards of chevrons for N.C.O.'s, and worsted tapes for Naval uniforms, thousands of yards of fuse tape, webbing for gaiters and equipment, and ribbons for Service women's outfits, particularly the A.T.S. Some of this had to be specially treated to stand climatic changes without deteriorating.

Tapes and kindred products ranged from an inch to 14 inches in width, and one speciality was elastic webbing for surgical purposes, while elastic braid was made for a number of service requirements. All this was done despite the fact that under a concentration scheme the company had to find room for three other ribbon firms.

Lye & Sons, on their side, also undertook a lot of very important work, particularly in their felt department. Among other things it proved how important a part felt washers can play. They were made for secret instruments used in some of the most spectacular bombing performances of the war, and they were told by letter that their work had helped indirectly in such notable events as the bombing of the *Tirpitz* and the Eder Dam.

One particularly unexpected job fell to these firms. Thousands of yards of expensive silk used for parachutes and balloons, salvaged after a destructive fire elsewhere, arrived in truckloads for cleaning and rehabilitation. It was sodden, partly burned, damaged by chemicals and in other ways. It was dealt with, and after re-test was found still fit for use. They were informed that their work had resulted in the saving of thousands of pounds.

They themselves had one fire, caused when a " breadbasket " burst practically overhead, but it was mainly stock that suffered, damage to buildings being slight.

Lye's, were affected by concentration, having to take three other firms, and in addition to provide considerable storage space for the Ministry of Supply, while a third associated company, Automobile Engineers (Luton), Ltd., was almost completely taken over by the Army for a tank training school.

*   *   *   *

If less Luton felt went into Luton hats during wartime, it was partly because it was helping to win the war as a substitute for rubber. There was an urgent necessity in 1942 for a serviceable substitute, most of the world's rubber supply then being in enemy hands. S. Hubbard, Ltd., of Regent Street, were responsible for the application of specially treated felt to many new purposes. It involved a tremendous amount of experimental work. The result was a mechanical felt utilised by the aircraft, engineering, electrical and marine industries for many purposes for which rubber had been regarded as the only possible material. After treatment which rendered it flexible and rubber-like, this felt offered reasonable resistance to water, sea water, dilute acids, and exceptional climatic conditions. It was also found possible to make felt resistant to high octane fuels and hydraulic fluids. It could be adapted for upholstery, to give the same comfort as sponge-rubber seatings. It could be made into solid tyres for small trucks. As an incidental result of Luton felt going to war, " Mechofelt " was but one of several words added to our language.

*   *   *   *

From producing ribbons and felts for hats, the Chaul End Works of Blundell Brothers (Luton), Ltd., underwent a complete wartime transformation. Originally built in the 1914-18 war as a filling factory, they went back to war. The existing machinery was cleared out and stored. Other plant was gathered from all over the country, workers were trained into new jobs, and from small beginnings there was developed an output of thousands of much-needed parts for tanks, armoured vehicles and planes. Some of the tools for the job were made on the job, and then duplicated for other firms.

*   *   *   *

Barclay Stuart (Plastics), Ltd., of Brunswick Street, developed during the war out of the Barclay Stuart Engineering Works, Ltd., and were responsible for adding to Luton's already varied industries the production of plastic goods by the compression moulding of thermosetting powders. These thermosetting resins, especially of the phenoplastic type, have always been known to make very good electrical insulators, so the biggest field of application during the war was components for electrical apparatus. The range turned out at Brunswick Street required about 100 different types of moulding tools. The greater part of the output was used for wireless sets, mostly on aircraft, as components for wireless transmitters, ammeters, volt meters and cabinets for electric clocks. In the general electrical field a big quantity of terminals for switchgear was also supplied.

*   *   *   *

Ash for sleighs for the Russian front, oak for " Mulberry," and silver spruce for Mosquitos—these were some of the purposes for which timber went from the stock of Henry Brown & Sons (Timber), Ltd., Bute Mills, Luton. At the start of the war they held a big stock of imported timbers, mostly from Russia, Finland and Sweden, and to a lesser extent from Canada. At once there was a day and night demand for timber for air raid shelters and the like, and for other urgent demands. This was happening all over the country, and before long there was only timber from Canada and the United States to rely upon. As a result, the most familiar timbers became silver spruce, Douglas fir, cedar, Western hemlock and balsam from the Pacific Coast, and spruce from the Atlantic maritime provinces.

Early on the company were appointed wharfingers to the Ministry of Supply (Timber Control), and on their behalf handled over 5,000 standards of Canadian and American softwoods, much of which went to meet the requirements of the R.A.F. Silver spruce, one of the most expensive woods, figured largely in the manufacture of

Mosquitos, and Horsa gliders took a large quantity of timber from the company's yards.

Naturally the English timber department grew as the imported department diminished, and some 21,000 trees, including both hardwood and softwood, were cut up. This was a great ship-saving factor, for it represented about three-quarters of a million cubic feet. Some of the trees were really remarkable specimens and, laid aside for special purposes, were admired by people from all over the country. To cut up these trees new machines were installed, and large orders executed including 30,000 railway sleepers and crossings, 50,000 telegraph arms, 30,000 cubic feet of railway wagon scantlings, 15,000 cubic feet of railway keywood, and 12,000 pit props.

Normal activities in the joinery and case department soon came to an end, but equally soon 8,000 shelter bunks were on their way to London, while urgent orders were received from various Ministries for packing cases of every kind. Over 100,000 were made, while 20,000 special ration pack boxes were rushed through just before the North African landings. One local order was for 60,000 crates for packing clay pigeon targets, involving well over two million lineal feet of timber. Bomb crates and large cases for packing valuable machinery had to be made. The Far Eastern War created a demand for special packing. Valuable car spares such as engines, radiators, etc., each had to be packed in a separate case, and over 10,000 of these were sent from Luton.

Labour ? Of course it was a problem, as with all Luton firms in those times. But Brown's had a substantial core of veterans who could have considered themselves past retiring age but, feeling they had a part to play, kept on. Some were well over 70, and had been with the company over 50 years. As in the 1914-18 war, also, women gave very valuable help.

*   *   *   *

Planes in the air, tanks in the North African Desert, submarines under the sea—that was the range of uses of work done by J. Simpson & Son, Ltd., Moreton Works, Round Green. They did much experimental work for Bristol, Blackburn and De Havilland aircraft, which were still on the secret list. They did many special jobs which gave life to tanks in the North African Desert when this was badly needed. They lent a hand in the development of radiolocation, and made scientific instruments for a variety of purposes.

*   *   *   *

From hatters' machinery and, to a lesser degree, garage equipment, to a big volume of components for Bailey Bridges was the war conversion of the activities of F. H. Eve, Ltd., Dunstable Road. They also produced equipment to facilitate the rapid erection and overhaul of aero-engines and the powerful marine engines used in motor torpedo boats.

Like other firms, the Luton Motor Company, Ltd., of Beech Hill, and its associate, Motor Bodies, Ltd., had to undertake unusual tasks. They did early experimental work for the exterior and interior panelling of special Radar (Baby Maggie) trailer cabins, completed six prototype cabins, and made, panelled and finished 644 doors for others. They made 43,500 parts for Horsa Gliders, thousands of small parts for Spitfires, Mosquitos and other planes, machine assembly stands for aircraft work, 15,000 parts for the P.I.A.T. anti-tank gun, and undertook a long run of machining jobs on tank transporter parts. As a contrast they also did many " one off " experimental jobs, built ambulance bodies for Luton Corporation and repaired blitzed buses.

*   *   *   *

Sometimes war industry was directed to a beneficent end. Witness the fact that over 200,000 four-ounce tins of cocoa went in a single year from a Luton factory, through the Red Cross, to our prisoners of war. Those whose misguided zeal led them to deface Luton walls with " Open the Second Front Now," should ponder over the fact that, nearly a year before D-Day, production began in the same Luton factory of vitaminised chocolate for the children of countries, the liberation of which was already being planned. It contained vitamins A, B^1, C, and D, and incorporated Creta Praeparata to combat rickets. It had been found that chocolate retained the vitamin content extremely well, and provided a health-giving food in a small space. Of this vitaminised chocolate some 410 tons were prepared, representing about 8,000,000 two-ounce bars. Its production, and that of the thousands of tins of cocoa for our men who were prisoners, was part of the wartime activities of the English and Scottish Joint C.W.S. Chocolate Factory, Dallow Road. This and other work was not done without difficulties. Quite early on machines had to be dismantled and re-erected elsewhere in the factory because the Admiralty and the Ministry of Supply wanted storage space for spares for motor torpedo boats, tanks, jeeps and other war material. Then, with the concentration of the chocolate industry in May, 1942, the productive staff dropped by 50 per cent. inside a fortnight. As far as possible this was made good by part-timers, often married women who averaged 26 hours a week. Even so, production figures could not have been maintained but for the co-operation of the remaining men. Unable to work at night because of their depleted numbers, they agreed to put in a 56-hour week to keep things going. As a result the War Department got 1,620 tons of cocoa, as a sort of Lend-lease in reverse the U.S. Forces had 116 tons, and the rest went to the Food Ministry. At the end of the war cocoa production was back to 100 per cent., but chocolate production was still only 43 per cent. of normal.

*   *   *   *

The combined staffs of Home Counties Newspapers, Ltd., (*The Luton News*) and Gibbs, Bamforth & Co., (Luton), Ltd., produced for the Propaganda Department of the Foreign Office the first " Daily

Airborne Newspaper " in the world. Started a month before D-Day, the order quickly rose to over a million copies a day, including Sundays and holidays, for over 15 months.

The newspapers were packed into leaflet bombs each 6 ft. high and 14 in. in diameter. 10,000 to a bomb. The bombs exploded 1,000 ft. from the ground, and scattered the newspapers over an area of two miles.

Over 26,000 of these bombs were despatched from Luton and their contents came into the hands of the German troops defending the West Wall. From these newspapers the enemy learned the truth of the battle front positions, and of the R.A.F. destruction in the Fatherland. Thousands of Germans are known to have surrendered to the Allies after receiving these papers.

This " paper war " conducted from *The Luton News* played an important part in General Eisenhower's invasion plans. The same presses also produced French news sheets for liberated France, and *Shaef*, the official newspaper of General Eisenhower, giving instructions in five languages to the Germans, displaced persons, and allied prisoners.

Other leaflets with a total figure of 1,500,000,000 units were printed and despatched from Luton and Leagrave, as well as high priority work for the War Office, Post Office and Ministry of Supply. All the pictures and maps used in the newspapers and leaflets were made in the Photo-Engraving department of Home Counties Newspapers, Ltd.

*　　*　　*　　*

Because much has been written about the more unusual jobs undertaken by Luton industry at war, it is none the less recognised that much other work which had to be undertaken, although lacking in novelty, was of added importance in wartime. For instance, L. Weekes (Luton), Ltd., electrical engineers, of Wingate Road, say they just went on with their ordinary work. That can best be interpreted in the light of the fact that for years before the war one of the principal buyers of some of their specialised equipment was the Admiralty—a connection which dates back to the time before they outgrew their original home in Langley Street.

Between them and newcomers like the Britannia Engineering Works, who produced sheet metal work in quantity at North Street, and Piece Parts and Assemblies, Ltd., who at one place or another turned out huge quantities of small components and assemblies, all sorts and sizes of factories were playing their part, if only as sub-contractors. From the works of G. F. Farr, Collingdon Street, and the Borough Engineering Works, Leagrave Road, a lot of material went elsewhere, to be used among other things in submarines, motor torpedo boats, etc. In time there was hardly a workshop, however small, that was not contributing in some way to maintain the production of war material.

Parts of hat factories rendered surplus by the quota, even if the whole factory was not vacated under concentration, became engineering works, sometimes run by their original owners, sometimes by firms which only came into existence because of the needs of the moment, or, as in the case of what had been one of the finest showrooms in the trade, as a dispersed unit of a big concern elsewhere. Garages, with no cars to serve, no petrol to sell, no spares to be obtained, were yet hives of activity. Few capable mechanics were left to them, but for such men as were available so much other and more urgent work was on hand that anyone hoping to get car repairs done needed almost inexhaustible patience.

*   *   *   *

Production could not be developed to its peak, however, with just a wave of the hand, even if the necessary labour force had been available at the start. It was inevitable that some of the better-known firms should have been overloaded with work in the early days, to the apparent neglect of smaller units the productive capacity of which was still unproved. But it was realised that these smaller units must be utilised to the fullest advantage, when it was clear what they could best do. To this end the Regional Office of the Ministry of Supply established a Clearing Office at Gordon Chambers. Its function was to utilise local knowledge in an endeavour to get local capacity used to its fullest extent. The local knowledge was supplied by a committee which, although changing in personnel from time to time, was composed of producers, executives, and workers. Was one firm overloaded with work of a particular kind? Did another local firm have suitable plant which, not for the time being fully occupied, could take some of the overload? It was the business of the Clearing Office to bring such firms together, and then leave them to make mutually satisfactory arrangements. In time the Clearing Office built up a pretty good picture of what was being done in Luton, where it was being done, and where anything else which had to be done could be done.

*   *   *   *

And so, as the war developed, Luton factories and Luton men and women concentrated on their jobs. Such as have been mentioned by name were a few only of hundreds in and around Luton. To list them all, to describe the magnificent work they all did would make a book thicker than the whole of this volume. And if most of them have gone unrecorded it does not mean that their part in the industrial effort was less important than those described here. All had one inflexible purpose—final victory, and whether work was carried on in mammoth steel and concrete buildings or back rooms and garden sheds, it was due to these factories, big and small, and to the men and women who manned them, no less than to the fighting man, that the great objective was finally reached.

The Staple Trade

LUTON'S hat industry survived six years of war, and the aftermath of war. It is only a shadow of its former self, but the foundations are there on which to build anew.

The town had to battle to keep it at all. It nearly lost for ever what is still regarded as its staple industry, even though before the war engineering in its various phases had outstripped it as an employing medium.

Other towns are engineering towns. Other towns are hat manufacturing towns. But no other hatting centre is quite comparable. Luton founded its industry on straw. Through the years it adapted itself to almost every usable material. It has never relied entirely on felts, beyond the use of which some hatting centres have never ranged.

The trade put up with the suspension of imports of materials, with the transfer of the bulk of the workers to other industries, with a production quota which severely restricted output, with the closing of some businesses for the duration because their principals were in the Services, and with moving to smaller premises so that their own could be used for something concerned with the war, but the trade did not realise how difficult it was going to be to recover them when the war really did end.

When it was suggested that what remained of this definitely Luton industry should be uprooted and replanted in sterile soil on the North-East coast, or in Scotland, they really did kick. Other hatting centres, seeing the possible precursor of a similar threat to their continued existence where they also were located, joined forces with Luton in a unity of action never before known in the trade.

Leading people in other local industries, anxious that the future well-being of the town as a whole should not be prejudiced, joined in. Support came from far and near. The issue at stake aroused wide interest, so much so that the daily Press took notice, and also came down heavily on the side of Luton.

When Whitehall tried to evade the issue, a town's meeting produced very plain speaking. Whitehall eventually found it politic to climb down—not very gracefully—on the pretext that there never had been any proposal to uproot the industry.

The peculiar thing was that Whitehall did not discover that Luton was making much ado about nothing until a widely-representative deputation had actually invaded the sacred portals of the Board of Trade, although it had been known for days that a deputation was coming, and why.

Why it should have been necessary to wait until then to tell the deputation, all busy men, that their journey really wasn't necessary, when a shilling telegram would have saved waste of time and money, is beyond ken outside a Government department. It can only be assumed that someone high up had given someone else a last-minute tip that there was a red light ahead.

*   *   *   *

To appreciate the position which had been reached it is necessary to recall war's impact on the hat industry from the beginning. War came in a year full of promise. Six " flying salesmen " had put hats in the news by doing their Manchester journey by air. It was a good season for straws. After long negotiations the Hat Manufacturers' Federation and the Millinery Distributors' Association had arrived at a reciprocal agreement framed to end some of the evils which had marred the trade. Steps had been taken to establish a millinery trade school at the Technical College. There appeared to be a good time ahead.

War clouds early caused some London firms to look for accommodation elsewhere. Hat firms were among them, and available Luton premises became in demand. War was declared. Trade stopped suddenly. Workers had to stand off, but before long they were all back, or the women were. Many male workers were lost by mobilisation of the Territorials and by enrolment in the Militia. Otherwise it was " business as usual," while possible.

This was not for long. Within a few months there were restrictions on import of materials. Import licences were necessary, and even when obtained, hoods, capelines and other goods for processing were limited to one-third, on a sterling basis, of those imported in the year immediately preceding the war, and to 20 per cent. if of Swiss origin.

But worse was to come, and without the necessity of regulations. Practically all Luton's sources of materials became involved in the world war. No more hoods for the cheaper end of the trade could come from Italy, no velours from Austria. At war with nobody, Switzerland became encircled by Axis forces, so there could be no more Swiss braids and fancies. Exotics were practically limited to stocks already here. Goods on the way from the Far East went down at sea, or were held up in non-British ships which fled into port and dare not come out again.

It was said that home manufacturers could supply all material requirements, but some firms who had relied on foreign hoods in particular were not optimistic, and, in any case, hood manufacturers were not allowed to maintain even their pre-war output.

One result, as in the 1914-18 war, was to give a new value to materials the popularity of which had waned, to some which had long before become definitely unsaleable, and to remnants of past seasons. It would be interesting to know how much per piece was ultimately obtained for some old braid which, still in its original bales, had no better value in 1940 than to be used in the blast wall of a factory.

In their haste to realise while the going was good, and particularly when hat production was limited by quota, some firms made these old braids into baskets, shopping bags, etc. The time came when they wished they still had these braids for hats ; but there always seemed to be small parcels of something forthcoming from the merchants, and for exotics in particular more was paid per hood than they had fetched per dozen before the war.

Long before the shortage of materials became acute, however, the trade, having lost many of its men to the Services and its women to other industries, was called upon to release 25 per cent. of the women who remained. Dunkirk, and all that it involved, meant that the Army had to be re-equipped almost entirely, and there were not enough men in the war factories to do it. The authorities looked for other sources of labour. They said the hat industry was a luxury, could surrender a lot of its younger women, and must depend on those too old for transfer to munition works to keep the trade going until better times dawned.

" Why Luton only ? " was the immediate question. " Were other hatting centres to get an unfair advantage over Luton, where 2,400 women had already gone from hat factories into war work ? " The effect of the official answer was that Luton need not worry about other places—they would be dealt with in the general scheme of things.

Agreement was therefore reached in March, 1941, on the " voluntary " release of the 25 per cent. To avoid trade dislocation, it was spread over three months—5 per cent. in April, 10 per cent. in May, and 10 per cent. in June. About 1,500 women were affected, and employers themselves had the thankless job of selecting those for release. The immediate experience of some was that the whole 25 per cent. wanted to go at once, regardless of the effect on their employers' business. Naturally there were some who didn't see why they should go before others, but in the main the release seemed to be carried out satisfactorily, to the Ministry of Labour and the employers, at any rate. Subsequent tribute of a trade representative to the Ministry officials who negotiated the release was—" They have enabled Luton to take its medicine with as much sugar-coating round the pill as possible."

But that there was a bit of the " big stick " behind the request for a " voluntary " release of these women was shown when employers received an official hint that if they did not submit satisfactory lists of those to be released, someone would come and get them, and that an unkindly eye would fall on lists which consisted too largely of older women. Manufacturers apparently knew one another's failings. To prevent poaching, they resolved that, excepting people who had not worked in the trade in the preceding six months, no person should be engaged without consulting that person's last employer.

It has to be remembered that this was before compulsory registration of women for the Services or industry. That was to come, with other and more drastic steps to get women in particular out of the hat industry.

A straw in the wind had been a statement by the Chancellor that women would have to make a hat do for another year. The retort was that, however much a woman suffered otherwise, she would have a new hat if she felt so inclined. Official steps were therefore taken to ensure that she did not find a new hat so readily obtainable.

In November, 1941, a Board of Trade Order imposed a 30 per cent. limit on the use of felt hoods for the home trade. The effect was worse than appeared on the surface, for the " basic year " on which the 30 per cent. was to be calculated was one in which hood supplies had already been restricted.

In June, 1942, the hood ration for the ensuing six months was further cut to 10 per cent., with no obligation on the hood manufacturer to apportion supplies on that basis. Dyers had to confine themselves to lighter shades to economise dyestuffs. Carton manufacturers had their own trouble, having been largely dependent on Dutch board in pre-war days.

Simultaneously with the additional cut in hoods, coupons for linings were suspended, and the Board of Trade took a lot of convincing that linings were essential to hats, that the necessary material already existed in quantity, was unsuitable for any other use and that its release could not affect the yarn position.

The Board struck in another way in November, 1942, and started the tremendous controversy over the retention or otherwise by Luton of what remained of the industry. They issued the Headwear Directions Order, 1942—two printed pages, plus six pages of Explanatory Note which explained practically nothing. All that was clear was that, no matter of what hats were made, there was to be a cut to 30 per cent. " in value " of the 1941 turnover. As to other implications, not even officials of the section of the Board responsible for putting the Directions into operation could give authoritative answers to questions, and the position was not helped by the fact that this section of the Board was in process of moving back to London from its seaside retreat. If any official had authority to give a definite answer, which is not common in the Civil Service, he never seemed to be available.

Did the restrictions apply at the manufacturing or selling end ? What was to be the effect on the many phases of the industry which could not be so categorised ? After a time a ruling was applied that it would apply at the manufacturing end, and only indirectly on other branches. On other questions officials would not commit themselves. All one could be sure about was that output for the period October 8th to January 31st, covering roughly four months and partly retrospective, was to be cut to 10 per cent. in value of 1941 figures.

The Directions, of course, made form-filling more fashionable than popular. To be entitled to produce even the 10 per cent. manufacturers had to register. If they preferred to be unregistered producers, their limit was to be £85 for the period to November 30th, and £50 in each of the succeeding two months. To register involved answering questions and supplying much detailed information. What the Board required to know was :—

Do you manufacture headwear (manufacture includes trimming, repairing or remodelling) on your own behalf, on a commission basis for another firm, or for the public ?

Do you manufacture partly on your own behalf and partly on commission ? State the percentage of your business which consists of manufacture on your own behalf.

Give selling value, excluding purchase tax, of headwear supplied to any person " including Government departments and export," during the year ended December 31st, 1941—(a) Felt hat hoods, capelines, manchons and grey bodies (sold as such). (b) Straw shapes or other hat shapes sold as such and not included in (a). (c) Men's or boys' wool felt hats or fur felt hats or straw hats. (d) Men's or boys' caps. (e) Women's or girls' hats, trimmed or untrimmed. (f) Infants' bonnets or other infants' headwear. (g) Any other headwear (give description).

The Explanatory Note stated that the chief reason for the restrictions was the need to transfer labour to more important work, and that the amount of production still permitted should suffice for those who required headgear for protection against cold and wet, or for industrial purposes, and to provide employment for the small amount of workers not suitable for transfer.

It also indicated that concentration and transfer of the remaining production to some area where labour was in less demand would follow, and it was the projected transfer which raised a storm

The South of England Hat Manufacturers' Federation and the Luton Hat Manufacturers' Association were only two of many trade bodies asking for a clear interpretation of all the Directions involved. The British Hat Manufacturers' Federation, acting for Northern interests, the Direct Hat Manufacturers' Association, whose members trade direct with the retail, the Millinery Distributors' Association, on behalf of wholesale houses, and trade bodies less directly affected, all had questions to which they wanted clear answers. A combined deputation to the Board was planned, with a preliminary conference in London so that an agreed case could be stated.

By the time the Northerners came South they were full of home troubles which threatened to obscure the main issue. They had heard that the greater part of their labour was to be withdrawn. They found they were being hit no harder than the South, and particularly Luton, which, having released so many workers voluntarily at an earlier stage, was faced with a demand for many more.

The deputation went to the Board. An early reply on some points was promised, and some clarifications and modifications did in fact follow. So far, so good. It did not seem so good when through the Employment Exchange Luton employers received a warning that whether production at all would be allowed to continue in the town was

The Mayor of Luton, Ald. John Burgoyne, addressing a meeting at the Odeon Cinema, in 1942, called to protest against the proposal to move the hat trade from Luton. Council members and officials, and prominent members of local industrial concerns were on the platform.

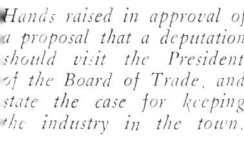

Hands raised in approval of a proposal that a deputation should visit the President of the Board of Trade, and state the case for keeping the industry in the town.

ABOVE: *Talking it over. Some of the members of the deputation to the Board of Trade, on the platform at Luton Station before their departure. Facing the camera from the left are Ald. John Burgoyne, then Mayor, Mr. H. E. Brightman, and Mr. V. M. Sunman. The Town Clerk, Mr. W. H. Robinson, is on the right.*

BELOW: *Representatives of the Town Council, hat manufacturers, hat workers, and other Luton industries photographed on the platform.*

dependent on certain things, and that unless in regard to labour they acted on certain approved lines they might have cause to regret it.

This revived the threat of transfer, which would have thrown old people adrift. For thousands of people it would have meant there would be no local employment after the war, although the hat industry was Luton's saving grace when its heavier industries were having a lean time after the 1914-18 war.

Despite the changes the trade had undergone through the years, it was said, a steady total of about 12,000 insured workers were employed in normal times. This total had already been reduced to about a third, even including those who had followed blitzed hat firms from London. Some could only be outworkers; others could only be factory workers because of the elastic hours of the hat trade; still others were already rejects from heavier industries.

In some factories there was not a male or female within the age limits which rendered them liable for the Services or for industrial transfer.

Under such circumstances, it was asked, how could taking the remnants of the industry away from Luton help the war effort? What was to be the outlook for these, to say nothing of those who had gone into the Services, or those who, having transferred to munitions, must ultimately become redundant in that capacity? How could employers honour their obligations to those returning from the Services?

The Board of Trade kept silence.

Luton Town Council took up the matter, at a meeting which made local history. In a Council Chamber where the public gallery was filled with employers and workers, the Council listened to those who could speak with authority. Sir Thomas Keens, Chairman of the County Council, spoke for the South of England Federation; Mr. Horace Brightman for the Hat Manufacturers' Association; Mr. J. S. Llywarch for the Chamber of Commerce; Mr. E. K. Hickman for the Chamber of Trade; Mr. T. W. Sweby for the Trades Council; Mrs. Barton as one employed in the industry.

It was suggested that not Mr. Dalton, but Sir Thomas Barlow, who held the wartime post of Director of Civilian Clothing, was responsible. Sir Thomas Keens, in fact, said he had challenged the other Sir Thomas to say whether it was possible for the Luton hat trade to give up any considerable proportion of the remaining workers, and whether it was necessary for the war effort—a challenge to which he could get no word of reply.

The Council devoted nearly three hours to the matter before touching their normal business, and some of its members spoke plainly. Councillor W. G. Roberts, who became Mayor in 1945, used these words—" It is not merely a question of shifting part of an industry. It is a question of tearing the heart out of Luton." It was said that transfer would leave the centre of the town a dead spot. Alderman John Burgoyne, the then Mayor, said he at first regarded the proposal as " a fantastic sort of idea," but had been convinced that it must be taken seriously.

So seriously, indeed, were the Council impressed that they appointed a special committee to take all possible steps to ensure the retention of the hat industry in Luton, even to petitioning the King if necessary.

All sorts of associations, trade and political, held meetings to consider how to help. The County Council decided to send a separate memorial to the Board, and to appoint members to a deputation. Dunstable promised 100 per cent. support; Mr. E. L. Burgin, then Luton's M.P., enlisted the support of the M.P. for Bedford. Small shopkeepers expressed their concern at the possible loss of what their spokesman described as " the fairy godmother of the retail trade." Hatters' engineers joined in, saying that unless any new centre was equipped with new machinery, which was impossible, the trade would be at a standstill, for transfer of plant from Luton would mean a minimum of six months' work for 100 millwrights, even if they were available.

Rising feeling caused Councillor Roberts to make this strong statement to the special committee of the Town Council—" I issue this warning. The temper of the people is rising. Unless some concession is made we shall have to be very careful that things don't get beyond our control."

A Town's meeting, called at barely 24 hours' notice, packed the Odeon, and cheers and prolonged applause encouraged speaker after speaker who attacked " Whitehall Dictatorship." Sir Charles Bartlett's term for the scheme was " preposterous." There were suggestions that it was " really part of a plot." It was said that Luton " would fight to the last ditch, and had every justification for fighting." Mr. Burgin declared that no one Minister would be allowed to enforce a step of such gravity, and that if the deputation did not succeed he would raise the matter on the floor of the House and, if need be, go to the Prime Minister himself.

Well, the deputation went. It was very widely representative. The prepared case took two hours to state, and was heard not only by Mr. Dalton, but by representatives of several other Ministries. Then Mr. Dalton gave an answer which astonished everybody. His answer, embodied in a statement issued by the Board the same afternoon, ought for ever to be preserved as a classic of the way a Government department can abandon an untenable position. It said :—

" Mr. Dalton expressed his surprise at the widespread and circumstantial reports of the alleged proposal, which in fact had never been made by the Board of Trade.

" He said the Board of Trade had never contemplated uprooting the hat industry from Luton, and that the anxiety, therefore, had been caused by a misunderstanding of the real position, and by the rapid growth of rumour for which there was no foundation."

If Mr. Dalton has felt it worth while to keep a copy of that answer, he should attach it to a copy of the " Explanatory Note," underlining these words :—

"*Discussions will be opened as soon as possible for concentrating the remaining production and transferring it as far as possible from areas of great labour scarcity to areas where labour supply is not so difficult.*"

That, according to Mr. Dalton, was rumour !

So the battle was won for Luton, and not only for Luton, Other hatting centres were also freed from threat of transfer, for no more was heard of it. Luton settled down to a less-disturbed Christmas than had seemed probable, and the Council placed on record appreciation of all the support the trade had received, and particularly that from sources outside the trade.

Memory is proverbially short, so it may be well to place on record the names of those who went from this district to Whitehall to champion the cause of Luton.

Trade delegates were :—South of England Hat Manufacturers' Federation, Mr. G. E. Morris (*president*), Sir Thomas Keens (*general secretary*) and Mr. C. H. Smee ; Luton Hat Manufacturers' Association, Mr. H. E. Brightman (*chairman*), and Mr. H. J. Darby (*vice-chairman*) ; London Millinery Manufacturers' Association, Mr. D. Ashton (*chairman*) ; Direct Hat Manufacturers' Association, Mr. John Collett (*chairman*), and Mr. Vincent Sunman (*vice-chairman*) ; Millinery Distributors' Association, Mr. T. W. Caves (*secretary*) ; Luton Hat Makers' Association, Mr. Cyril Clark (*chairman*) ; Luton Hat Workers' representative, Mrs. Barton.

Supporting them were Alderman J. Burgoyne, as Mayor, Aldermen A. E. Ansell and W. F. Mullett, Councillors A. W. Gregory and W. G. Roberts, with the Town Clerk, Deputy Town Clerk and Borough Treasurer. County Council support included not only Sir Thomas Keens, the chairman, but also Mr. Frank Kenworthy, a former Mayor of Dunstable in respect of Dunstable interests, Mr. Ben Hartop, chairman of Luton R.D.C., Mr. Harry White, of Bedford, district organiser of the Transport and General Workers' Union, and himself a former hat operative, and the Clerk. Sir Charles Bartlett, managing director of Vauxhall Motors, Ltd., represented Luton's heavier industries, and Mr. T. W. Sweby, the Luton and Dunstable Trades Council.

Looking back, this question presents itself. Why was the native, old-established hat industry threatened with transfer, and not some of the non-hat firms which had lately sought refuge in Luton and had so shown that they could settle wherever they could find factory space ? Why were they not told to look elsewhere instead of increasing the local demand for labour ? Or was that too simple for the official mind ?

There remained the question of concentration. A very few firms did get together on the lines officially indicated as likely to meet with approval, but it was not nearly as simple as suggested. The outcome

o

was another conference at the Board of Trade, and one that surprised delegates in quite another way. They found it possible to get straight " Yes " and " No " answers to questions. It was announced that there would be no compulsory concentration, although freedom to continue operating independently would still be dependent on surrendering all labour suitable for other purposes.

So the hat trade continued to make the best of things as they were. In addition to turning out what hats it could for the home trade, and doing a bit of export trade when it could be done, it hatted or capped Wrens, Waafs, and the girls of the A.T.S. Many a soldier from this country, and from India, had reason to be grateful in the Burma jungle for the tropical hats and helmets which arrived from Luton ; and many a Naval or Marine officer, donning his best shoregoing cap, put on one from the same source. This takes into no account the millions of battle-dress caps which were made, which are not a normal part of Luton's trade, and which were largely made by firms who found it convenient to come here for the purpose.

*   *   *   *

Two very different things will show how hard pressed manufacturers were for materials when things were at their worst. No longer was there any excuse for working late at night to get away the last possible hat to a clamouring buyer who had lacked confidence to order well in advance. The five-day week became general. When Easter closing came it was considered abnormal. Even this paled into insignificance when at Whitsun, 1943, many firms closed for a week, and some even for a fortnight. The significance of this will present itself only to those who recall that for many firms June was the end of the financial year, and that normally Whitsun marked the height of the rush in their factories. The effort was to get out every possible hat for the summer trade, and to carry forward the minimum of made and unmade stock. The problem of Whitsun, 1943, was not to reduce stocks, but to hold on to some materials, and particularly felts, to ensure having something on which to work later.

The other striking, and less savoury, illustration, was the emergence of the " Dustbin Hat." It did not actually come from the dustbin, but that should normally have been its fate. Old hats, originally made of good quality fur hoods, fetched an almost unbelievable price. They were put through some cleaning process, refurbished, and sold again to people who didn't know they were buying someone else's cast-offs. The only two good points about this enterprise was that it did not last, and that none of the Luton firms of old standing participated.

Gradually things began to improve as small increases in quota were permitted. The chief snag was that the supply of materials did not keep pace. Hoods were still restricted at the source, and the import of materials was still banned. There came a time when the public was led to believe that a large quantity of hats was coming on the market.

Manufacturers were not responsible for this belief; they could only do their best.

When a further increase in production was authorised in 1945, there were complaints even in Parliament about the " fantastic prices " of some retail shops. Hat manufacturers immediately disclaimed responsibility, and set about devising a scheme to ensure that good hats reached the public at a reasonable price. It was agreed, even by Mr. Dalton, that a " utility " hat for women was out of the question, so by agreement between manufacturers, the Board of Trade and the Price Regulation Committee, steps were taken to put one-star and two-star wool felts on the market. Three-quarters of the wool felt output were to be attractive one-star hats selling in the shops at not more than a guinea. The balance was to be made up of two-star hats, to retail at not more than 25s. Only furs, fabrics and straws were to be outside this scheme.

*　　　*　　　*　　　*

From then onwards the hat industry, having weathered its storms, can be said to have started moving towards better days. Its experiences, however, show why hats were about the only article of wear for which it was unnecessary to surrender coupons. Limitation on buying had been enforced by limiting the number of hats which could be bought.

The quota was gradually increased, and from the end of 1945 it was abolished. Manufacturers started 1946 free to make and sell all they could, but it was a freedom more apparent than real. There was still control farther back, based on the fact that there were fewer hood manufacturers than hat manufacturers to control. However, odd lots of braid continued to appear from somewhere to supplement the available hoods, and from the latter part of January, 1946, import of raw materials became permissible, in theory, without regard to pre-war standards—on conditions. Those from Switzerland had to be used wholly for the shipping trade; from other specified sources, two-thirds. China was one of the permissible sources, Japan was not. Having regard to what so many Luton men went through at the hands of the Japanese, it cannot be imagined that Japanese straws and woven hoods will ever be very acceptable in future.

" Export ! " was the call, but efforts to comply only too often resulted in more form-filling and lengthy correspondence which got nobody anywhere. Maybe even this will sort itself out in time. At any rate, Luton still has a hat industry, it is on the up-grade again, and later on may even make plastic hats. Or so we are told.

Fifteen Million Pounds

WHEN "Thanksgiving Week" ended in November, 1945, War savings in Luton since January, 1940, had reached the total of £15,255,321.

A very nice nest-egg, you may say, but it isn't quite as big as it sounds. The reason? In every special "Week" there were big investments by the banks, insurance companies, etc., and although they do business in the town, their investments cannot be regarded as the money of the "ordinary people."

All the same, "ordinary people" had a big finger in the Fifteen Million Pie for, with the exception of that "Thanksgiving Week," about half the total in each special "Week" came from traders and small savers.

When to that is added the thousands put into war savings every week by small savers, and for the collection of which group secretaries were so largely responsible, the "ordinary people's" share of the nest-egg must be pretty good.

·Added to this is the deferred value of those "tax credits," which, we are told, will not be realisable until all the shops again have all the goods we want, so that money represented by these credits can be spent without forcing up prices still more. Then it may even be a useful stimulus to industry.

The big stepping stones towards the fifteen millions were :—

1941—War Weapons Week (jointly with Luton Rural District and Dunstable). Target, £1,000,000. Result, £1,420,423.

1942—Warship Week. Target, £1,000,000. Result, £1,421,714.

1943—Wings for Victory Week. Target, £1,425,000. Result, £1,442,299.

1944—Salute the Soldier Week. Target, £1,500,000. Result, £1,522,635.

1945 — Thanksgiving Week. Target, £1,000,000. Result, £1,084,757.

*   *   *   *

The money didn't just fall into the bag. It took a lot of campaigning, the introduction of the competitive spirit at home, and the stimulus of challenges thrown out to, or accepted from other towns. At times there had to be even an approach to the spectacular.

Luton had had a Savings Committee since 1917, and even in the year preceding the start of World War II there was quite a number of Savings Associations, whose members were putting away something like £150,000 a year. The new war was not many days old before the Savings Committee was enlarged into a Savings Council, and made as representative as possible of every phase of life and industry in the town.

The days of austerity were, at that time, still a long way ahead. All spending was not suspect. In fact, Alderman John Burgoyne told the inaugural meeting of the Savings Council—" Saving can be just as big an evil as spending if pushed to foolish extremes. How to strike the balance between wise spending and wise saving is what we have to determine and try to get across to the people."

Plans for a National Savings Week early in 1940 were soon maturing, with the establishment of 200 savings groups a practicable aim. The theme for the first special " week " was—" Only a few can do a lot, but most of us can do something." The aim was to encourage the many who could " do something " to do something a little better.

National Savings Week actually produced £25,058, which was above expectations. Only once before had £20,000 been exceeded in a single week, and that was in the previous March. No doubt employees of Vauxhall Motors, Ltd., could easily give the reason for a record week that March. The £25,058, however, was only a preliminary canter. The time was to come when Luton could be regarded as falling from grace if normal weekly savings fell to anywhere near £25,000.

By July, 1940, savings groups numbered nearly 250, and the schools were doing particularly well. Street groups had still to come into existence, but a move to establish them had been initiated. Luton had already reached second place in the Eastern Region and before long it was possible to report 410 savings groups, putting Luton over 100 ahead of any other town. Of 250 street groups aimed at, 134 were formed in four weeks. Immediately the aim became 500 groups By the time the war was a year old there were 510. Then it was asked, Why not 500 street groups, alone ?

Luton was then averaging £100,000 a month in current savings, and was far ahead of any other town in the Region. Before the end of October that year it was possible to say that Luton had saved a million since January 1st. We were not far into 1941 before the cry was " Why not 1,000 groups ? "

*   *   *   *

Then came the first of the really big ventures—" War Weapons " Week. Luton, Dunstable, and Luton Rural District banded together in a first effort to raise a million in a week. It was regarded as a tremendous effort even in combination. Sir Nevile Henderson, British Ambassador in Berlin until the war began, came to Luton to inaugurate the effort. He said—" National savings mean the saving of the nation. Better to pour your money out like water if it is going to save one drop of English blood."

That Sunday saw the first of those big parades which were thereafter to be a feature of all the special wartime weeks. The total rose and rose. The result showed that for the combined districts it was not really such a bold objective after all. People did not merely put up the million—they added nearly another half million to be on the safe side. They set a standard for the future. The total was more than enough for two large destroyers. It covered a third but smaller one. There were high hopes that they would bear names of local significance. The Lords of the Admiralty eventually decreed otherwise. Then one local speaker went so far as to suggest that the money had been obtained under false pretences. Be that as it may, the Royal Navy never included H.M.S. Luton, H.M.S. Dunstable or H.M.S. Whipsnade.

*   *   *   *

After this, " Million " weeks became an annual feature of the savings campaign, but they were only the highlights of the years. The real saving was done week by week. The Savings Council were always alert to ideas for maintaining enthusiasm between the " Million " week of one year and that of the next, and the suggestion of a Town League eventually developed into an Industrial League, to give wider scope to the inter-departmental competitions already running in some of the larger works, and to bring others into the fold.

*   *   *   *

A knight, attended by a herald and page, created a stir in 1942 by riding into Luton on his trusty steed and throwing down the gauntlet at the foot of the Mayor. He introduced a new note into the savings campaign. He brought a bold challenge that Watford would beat Luton in " Warship Week." For Watford it was claimed that there was no audacity in the challenge ; that it was merely perspicacity, and that the men and women of Watford would dig deep into their pockets and bring out a weight of metal that would crush Luton.

" Luton braggarts," said the challengers, " need not think we shall fight with kid gauntlets. We shall not spare them from receiving the full weight of our mailed fists. If they think to overcome us with knavish tricks we are equal to them. We, too, realise that all is fair in love and Warship Week."

The gauntlet was hung from the Town Hall balcony, and the knight was told to return to Watford and there proclaim that there would be only one winner, and that not Watford.

Some time later bold pirates, complete with skull and crossbones nailed to the mast, set sail from Luton by lorry for Watford, to give the challengers opportunity to withdraw. It was rumoured that they also aimed at capturing " Miss Watford "—maybe this was one of the knavish tricks expected of Luton—but from coyness or wisdom the lady evaded this honour.

Perky messages passed between the two towns on the opening day. Luton, with a target of £1,000,000, got off with a flying start. The young King Peter of Yugoslavia was the centre of tremendous interest when he came on the Sunday and took the salute at a great parade which for the first time in Luton included representative of the Allied Nations. The Americans had yet to arrive, but there were Czechs, Poles, Yugoslavs, Norwegians, Dutch, Free French and

ABOVE: *Sir Nevile Henderson,
pre-war British Ambassador in
Berlin, and Mr. Maurice Healy,
K.C., visited Luton to inaugurate
Luton, Dunstable and district War
Weapons Week in March,* 1941.

BELOW: *A section of the large
crowd in George Street who heard
the Mayor, Councillor John Burgoyne, announce that* 1941 *War
Weapons Week had raised*
£1,385,000.

LEFT: *King Peter of Yugoslavia outside Luton Town Hall, at the Warship Week parade march past in March, 1942.*

BELOW: *Admiral Sir Lionel Halsey inspecting Sea Cadets on Wardown Sports Ground.*

LEFT: *One of Luton's own "Battle of Britain" heroes, Wing Commander Christopher Currant, D.S.O., D.F.C., opened the town's "Wings for Victory" week in May, 1943. He is seen with Alderman John Burgoyne, then Mayor, and the Wings Week "Queen," Dilys Evans.*

ABOVE: *Straw boaters for victory. The fact that the late Dr. Leslie Burgin, then Member for Luton, and Ald. John Burgoyne were wearing boaters when they came out to make the final announcement showed that Luton had achieved its "Wings" target*

RIGHT: *The salute at the Sunday parade in "Wings" week was taken by Colonel Milton Turner, United States Acting Air Attache in London, representing Mr. John Winant, the American Ambassador. He is seen speaking after the parade.*

Belgians in the parade. It also included women munition workers in the distinctive overalls of their particular factories, to indicate the part they were playing in the productive capacity of the nation.

As the week progressed there were dark rumours that Watford was really after two millions, but at the end of the week Watford was well and truly beaten. The figures were :—Luton, £1,421,724. Watford, £1,203,040. Watford was generous with congratulations. Luton replied that the challenge had been a wonderful spur.

As a sequel to the " Week," Luton " adopted " *H.M.S. Ceres*, for which *H.M.S. Diadem* was later substituted. A considerable time elapsed, however, before this substitution could be announced. No mention could be made of the fact that *Ceres*, a veteran of the 1914-18 war, had been retired. The enemy had to be allowed to assume that the gallant old lady was still a useful unit of the British Fleet. Another long period elapsed before a small party from *Diadem* could visit Luton to present a plaque, and even that involved silence, so that the enemy should not be told that temporarily *Diadem* was not at sea. It was not until December, 1945, that the Captain could bring a large party to sample the hospitality of Luton, to say " Thank you " for £250 which had been sent for the benefit of the ship's complement, and to tell something of *Diadem's* part in the war at sea. Later still, a small official party from Luton paid a visit to *Diadem*.

*   *   *   *

After " Warship Week " the savings campaign pursued its steady, normal course until the time came for another Million Week. Then Luton savings became a matter of Transatlantic importance, and a straw boater attained a new significance.

" Wings for Victory " Week could not be made the subject of a challenge to the Luton on the other side of the Atlantic, so the English Luton challenged New Bedford, Massachusetts, to a savings battle, and set its own target at £1,425,000, or £15 per head of the total population. New Bedford accepted the challenge. So much interest was aroused that the Ministry of Information and the American Embassy arranged for daily totals to be exchanged. They were displayed side by side at the Luton indicator, and did much to stimulate interest, particularly in the early days, when Luton led. Another new departure was the selection of a " Wings " Queen.

There was no need to look outside for an opener for Wings Week. There was an obvious No. 1 choice in Wing-Commander Christopher Currant, D.S.O., D.F.C. and Bar, one of those who in the Battle of Britain inspired Mr. Winston Churchill to make his historic pronouncement—" Never in the field of human conflict has so much been owed by so many to so few."

Wing-Commander Currant told a vast crowd at the opening ceremony that they had the chance of a lifetime to do a bit to help crush the foulest tyranny that ever befel the world. It had been his honour to live and fight with comrades who had gladly made the

Great Sacrifice with gallant courage and selflessness. All wanted victory and freedom; but, as " The Few " had fought, so all in their own way would have to fight, by being ready to sacrifice their most treasured possessions, luxuries, comforts, above all even lives. There were now, he said, hundreds and thousands of lads who had done, were doing, and would do when opportunity offered, bigger and better things than he had been lucky enough to do. " Let us be worthy of them, and worthy of victory."

Before and after his speech three planes gave a wonderful flying display over the town, coming down almost to the roof tops of George Street and the Town Hall, where the British and American flags were flying.

On the Sunday there was another great parade, in which the Air Services were naturally given pride of place. It included, for the first time, a contingent from the American Army Air Force, of which subsequently we were to see so much, in and over Luton. Fortresses flew over Luton during the parade, and the salute was taken by Col. Milton Turner, an Air Attache from the American Embassy.

During the week Lord Halifax sent a very encouraging message from America. Mr. Henry Morgenthau, junr., Secretary of the U.S. Treasury, cabled from Washington congratulating Luton on originating such a friendly competition with New Bedford.

For a few days Luton kept ahead of New Bedford. It had to acknowledge defeat in the end, but it had again beaten its own target and that was what primarily mattered. This is where a straw boater took on a new significance. When Alderman Burgoyne came out of the Town Hall to announce the figure as far as it was known on the Saturday night, he did not need to tell the crowd the target had been passed. He wore a straw hat, as did other members of his party. The crowd cheered him on sight. Had he been wearing a black hat, they would have known that he was mourning a Luton which, for the first time, had let him down.

The final figure was £1,442,299. New Bedford put up £1,833,829. There £569,218 had been added on the last day, and that saved the Stars and Stripes. They would still have been beaten had the terms of the challenge not been modified in the closing stages. There was at the time no bond issue in which the big firms and industrial undertakings of New Bedford could invest. Therefore it was agreed that it should be an " all in " contest, and whereas the whole of the Luton total was made up of " money on the drum," New Bedford was allowed to include promises of big investments to be made when there was a suitable issue.

How much the small savers through the groups helped towards beating the target can be gathered from the fact that their own target was £38,000; their result, £110,341 5s. 3d.

Papers received here during and after the campaign showed that if nothing else had come out of the challenge, Luton secured tre-

LEFT: *"Miss Luton of 1943"—Miss Dilys Evans—sticks a savings stamp on one of three bomb cases which were on exhibition in the town during "Wings for Victory" Week in May, 1943. The bombs were later filled and dropped on Germany.*

BELOW: *Making a tour of Luton works, "Miss Luton" stops to chat to the finalists of the Beauty contest at the Davis.*

LEFT: *One of the many bright ideas of the Publicity Committee of Luton's "Salute the Soldier" week in 1944 was this poster at the top of the Town Hall tower . . . standing out against the drab camouflage background.*

RIGHT: *A "Naval man" takes a peep through the sight of an Army gun at an exhibition of weapons during Luton's "Salute the Soldier" week.*

BELOW: *Baseball was an unusual game to see on Luton Town Football Ground in the "Salute the Soldier" week. There was a good crowd to watch the Brooklyn Dodgers and the St. Louis Cardinals in their "battle."*

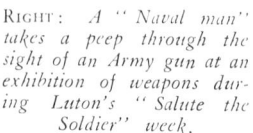

ABOVE: "Miss Luton of 1944"—Mrs. Nellie Robinson battled with a giant straw hat measuring seven feet across, when the Mayor, Councillor J. Burgoyne, announced that Luton had smashed its "Salute the Soldier" target of £1,500,000.

LEFT: The indicator at the Town Hall showed how Luton had beaten both the target and the figure for the Savings Week of 1943.

BELOW: Part of the large crowd which formed a solid mass in front of the indicator to hear the speeches after the "Salute the Soldier" procession.

RIGHT: *A view of one of the aisles at the Luton Industries Exhibition, at the Winter Assembly Hall, held in connection with Luton's Thanksgiving Week in November, 1945.*

BELOW: *The Rt. Hon. Arthur Greenwood (nearest camera), Lord Privy Seal, inaugurated Luton's Thanksgiving Week in November 1945, appealing for £1,000,000 in savings. At the microphone is the Mayor of Luton, Councillor W. G. Roberts, with the Town Clerk, Mr. W. H. Robinson, and the Deputy Mayor, Councillor H. C. Lawrence.*

mendous publicity in news, pictures and even cartoons on the other side of the Atlantic, and many friendly messages were exchanged between people who otherwise would have had no point of contact.

* * * *

The Navy and the Air Force having had their Weeks, it was the turn of the Army in 1944. Plans for " Salute the Soldier " Week were actually being made when plans for the Army's greatest adventure—the landing in Normandy—were being completed. It was therefore fitting that the target should be higher than anything so far achieved. It was fixed at a £1,500,000. Again, and despite the first effects of P.A.Y.E., Luton did it, and again added a few thousands for luck. This was just a month before D-Day.

The opener was General Sir Kenneth Anderson, who had led the First Army in the Tunisian Campaign, and had returned and temporarily resumed his former appointment as G.O.C.-in-C., Eastern Command. He cheered a big crowd by telling them that unlike four years earlier, when it was hard to see what the end of the war was going to be, complete victory could now be seen as the only possible end. He was wisely cautious, however, when he said the Germans knew they had earned all that was coming to them, so would not readily give in, and people must not be disappointed if the end of the war did not come by the end of the year.

Instead of a " Queen," there was a " Miss Luton," the young wife of a prisoner in Germany. Again the Sunday was made the occasion of a grand parade, and first place was given to over 300 veterans from overseas. It was Luton's first opportunity to welcome home some of the men who had helped to clear the enemy out of North Africa, made possible the landings in Sicily and Italy, and opened the Mediterranean again to our ships. All along the route these veterans were loudly cheered. One great contrast in this procession is worth recalling. There were Churchill tanks. There were also G.S. waggons that might well have seen service in 1914-18, drawn by smartly-groomed horses—they were a reminder that even in this mechanised age the Army has not entirely deserted the horse for horse-power.

Field Marshal Sir Cyril Deverell, who took the salute, was in prophetic mood. He recalled the grim and difficult times of Dunkirk, Greece, Libya, Hong Kong, Crete, and other setbacks. Now, he said, we were all set to stage a great come-back. The Army would receive tremendous support from the Navy and R.A.F. ; but it was the Army which would go in and deliver the knock-out, and soldiers away fighting had the right to expect the utmost backing from those who had not been called up.

Later it was said that Luton had never been known to set its heart on anything and fall short. The result of the Week was £1,522,733. Again it was an occasion for straw hats. They were worn easily by the men, but " Miss Luton " was nearly lost under a 7 ft. straw hat

P

made some years earlier for exhibition purposes. She made a gallant struggle to wear it. Then, decorated with the black and amber of the County Regiment, it was hoisted on to the indicator, before which there were two symbolic figures—one of a soldier in the full dress of the original 16th Foot, the other a typical infantryman in battle dress.

$$*\qquad*\qquad*\qquad*$$

In " Salute the Soldier " Week the street groups did it again. Asked for £150,000, they produced £217,282. And people still kept on saving afterwards, without any special stimulus. There came a time early in 1945 when their normal weekly savings reached £50,450.

$$*\qquad*\qquad*\qquad*$$

The last great effort was " Thanksgiving Week." The war in Europe had ended, Japan had given in. All sorts of celebrations had been held. There came the inevitable reaction.

For various reasons " Thanksgiving Week " was deferred until late in the year. It was not a good time. Bad weather and dark nights told against the work of the street group collectors. The wage-earning peak had passed. Big investors were not so promising. There was a feeling that Saving for Reconstruction had not the appeal of earlier causes. For the first time a target was fixed which did not equal the result of the previous effort. It was reduced to the round million. There was no " Queen " no " Miss Luton." There was no big Sunday parade—the substitute was a not very well attended Thanksgiving Service at the Indicator. The one outstanding visitor was the Lord Privy Seal, Mr. Arthur Greenwood, who came as opener.

Otherwise the week proceeded as usual and, as usual, Luton did what it set out to do ; but it took a big effort on the last day to make the total £1,080,757, and so take Luton's War Savings past the Fifteen Millions mark.

$$*\qquad*\qquad*\qquad*$$

Of the many who contributed to this total achievement, but one received official recognition. Mr. W. A. F. Hearne, honorary secretary of Luton Savings Council from July, 1940, until business took him away to Northampton towards the end of 1944, received the M.B.E. in the 1942 Birthday Honours.

$$*\qquad*\qquad*\qquad*$$

No review of the war savings effort in Luton would be complete without reference to what the schools did. In the early war years school groups were the chief savings groups. There were groups with membership figures of 1,099 ; 691 ; 618 and 542. It was obvious that they were handling more than the children's own money. Peak membership in any one half-year was 11,746. It naturally decreased as street and works groups sprang up.

Schoolchildren, however, saved in other ways than through their school groups. A check-up throughout the schools, and covering those of every category, showed that through these groups, the Post

Office, the Trustee Savings Bank, or the Co-operative Society, 95 per cent. of the children were saving through one channel or another. Some schools reported 100 per cent. savers.

In the big weeks they were very active, and returns made public showed that some schools, as distinct from groups, had totals of over £3,000, £2,000 and £1,000. The £500 total for a school was fairly common, and the achievements of some infants' schools in passing the £500 mark was particularly praiseworthy. Best effort of any school in one half year was £4,339.

Up to September, 1945, £214,537 had gone into National Savings through the schools. In " Thanksgiving Week " they added another £10,000, and they still go on saving.

The Christian Spirit

IN the years before the war, a frequent topic of discussion in public and private was the influence of the churches on the problems of everyday life. Much was written and said on the subject. It was pointed out that congregations at Sunday services were diminishing, or at best it was becoming increasingly difficult to maintain them, and that there were few young people coming in to church life to interest themselves in the work.

To the superficial observer all was not well with the churches. Were they facing up to the responsibility of the age ? If, as it appeared, they were unable to hold their own in the face of the other interests that jostled for a place in family and social life, what would the future hold for them ?

The prospect was disturbing. Thirty, forty years ago the church or the chapel was the centre of social life. It spread its wings over the family, and indeed the community, but, by the fourth decade of the twentieth century, the development of entertainment as an industry in its broadest sense had widened social life and provided an easy temporary escape from the problems and anxieties that crowded thicker and faster on the human race. The tempo was fast. There was little time for reflective thought, and, too often, the instinctive call of conscience had sunk to a mere whisper.

The war brought to the churches supreme difficulties but also a supreme opportunity. The difficulties were material only. The churches' worst enemy was the black-out. Church-going, it cannot be gainsaid, was more popular with the middle-aged and the old than with the young, and the older folk, or the great majority of them, did not care to venture out after dark unless it was absolutely necessary.

Then there was the difficulty, the impossibility in some cases, of completely blacking out places of worship. Afternoon services had to be substituted for evening services. Change is not always welcome or convenient, and church attendances suffered. The withdrawal of Sunday morning transport was also a particular handicap in Luton, where so many of the churches, sited in what were once populous districts, but now almost entirely given over to business, draw their still faithful congregations from areas at a distance.

Many churches lost valuable officers and members through the call of the Services—although Luton did not suffer so much in this way as some places. The town's many war industries, Home Guard, Civil Defence and Firewatch duties, not forgetting the many who had to carry on with their war work on Sundays, interfered greatly with attendances, though the influx of evacuees and some war workers offset this to a certain extent.

A great blow to some of the churches was the loss of their premises by military requisitioning. This caused curtailment of many activities, the suspension of others, and they were unable to put into operation ·projects that would have had a social value or could have helped the many Service personnel who at various times were stationed in the town or made a habit of visiting it. In almost every case halls were requisitioned, and churches possessed of basements had them taken over for A.R.P. shelters or first-aid posts.

But it is not the object of this record to enlarge upon the difficulties that beset the churches during these six years. Rather should stress be laid on the magnificent way in which they rose to their great opportunity.

The outbreak of war had a sobering effect on the nation. The churches sensed the road they must travel. They saw that the fundamental principles of the Christian life, and the freedom of the spirit of man were the heart and roots of the impending struggle. They saw, dimly stirring in the souls of their people, the deep ingrained philosophy that they had always felt they could not have taught for two thousand years in vain.

Then in the thunder of the German advance, in the holocaust of Dunkirk, in the blood and toil and tears and sweat of 1940, they saw the vision of their great purpose. Their pathway lay through the hearts of men, to steel them against fear and adversity, to sharpen the sword of their courage, and to clothe them in the full armour of God.

*　　　*　　　*　　　*

To some extent, perhaps, the difficulties of the churches were a blessing in disguise. They spurred those who remained to greater efforts to keep things going. At any rate, sceptics who might have thought that a second big war in twenty-one years was going to mean the end of something they had declared for years to be dead or dying were confounded. The churches of Luton carried on, maybe with lesser activities in some directions, but still with vitality enough to launch out into new avenues.

Foremost in everyone's thoughts was, naturally, the idea of helping those who had gone to serve their country in uniform, and many ways presented themselves. They were remembered in the services, they were written to, and parcels and other gifts were sent to them. Thousands of messages must have passed to and fro, and expressions of gratitude came from far and wide.

There was also a keen desire to meet the social and recreational needs of the men and women stationed here. One of the leading ventures was the provision, by the clergy and members of Luton Parish Church, of a rest house and social centre, at a roomy old house in Church Street.

The idea originated with the Rev. G. B. Gerrish, then a curate at the Parish Church and afterwards a Chaplain to the Forces. With the ready consent and backing of the Vicar, he formed a small committee consisting of himself, Mr. Cyril Hyder, Mr. A. C. Fellingham, and Mr. Jim Wing, and they got the necessary workers together and carried on. At first Mr. Gerrish acted as Warden, assisted by the Rev. R. K. Miller, and later he was succeeded by Mr. Hyder.

St. Mary's House, as it was known, came into being in January, 1940, when it was declared open by Miss Elsie Green and dedicated by the Vicar, who acted as its President, and its good work was carried on until after the end of the war with Germany. It was the first canteen for the Forces to be opened in Luton, and thousands of men and women found pleasure in its welcoming atmosphere. They particularly appreciated the lounge, with its brightly glowing fire on cold days, and the " quiet room," where they could gain some of the peace not always to be found where Service people foregather.

Another centre for quietness and reflection was the little chapel tucked away at the top of the building. Evening prayers were always said there, and there were services, too, the most notable being held at the Christmas when Mr. Gerrish was on leave. Then the place was full.

On the whole, though, the workers at St. Mary's House found that the call upon them was mainly for material things. Games, reading and writing facilities and refreshments entered into the scheme of things. Christmas was naturally marked in a special way. Both on Christmas Day and Boxing Day tea was free for all, and annually an order was placed for a thousand mince pies.

One difficulty a good many Service men experienced while stationed in Luton was in finding accommodation for the wife or " best girl " whenever she wanted to pay a visit. This led to the establishment of a room at St. Mary's House which became known as " the creche." Wives, families and sweethearts could be taken there, instead of walking about the streets. This, and all the other activities at St.

Mary's House, were thoroughly appreciated by the Service men. Their thanks were expressed personally to the workers, and in letters which came after they had left Luton.

The Free Churches, gravely handicapped by the requisitioning of premises, were not behindhand in their desire to do something for serving folk, but it was only those in the central part of the town that could really be looked to for action, because it was there the uniformed visitors were mostly to be found.

Chapel Street Methodist Church, not having the use of its school buildings, extended a special invitation to troops to attend concerts given after the Sunday evening services, but the response was so small that the concerts were discontinued after one season.

Beech Hill Methodist Church started a club, but it was only sparsely patronised, probably owing to the fact that it was not centrally situated.

The Salvation Army adapted the old Bridge Inn in Bute Street into a Red Shield Club for troops. Being opposite one of the largest buildings in the town in military occupation, it was most conveniently situated.

Union Church was in a more fortunate position than some. It did manage to retain its Lecture Hall, and carried on a regular Sunday evening social for the Forces, with musicians from the district offering entertainment and the ladies of the church providing refreshments. Usually the minister, the Rev. E. B. Keeble, conducted a short epilogue, and this and the friendliness shown were so highly appreciated that letters of gratitude were received from soldiers who had moved to all parts of the world. This good work was carried on for five winters, and it was only when the need was obviously diminishing that it was discontinued.

Union Church, incidentally, had very good basement facilities for shelter, and these were much sought after by people in the neighbourhood at the height of the enemy attacks. When less attention was concentrated on Luton, and it was thought that the bombers were only passing over to a more distant target, the desire to seek shelter out of the home became less.

While catering for the safety of the shelterers, the church also had some thought for the comfort of the families—from grannies to little children—temporarily in their care. The shelterers themselves subscribed the cost of heating, the church held services for them, and members of the choir went down to sing to them.

*　　*　　*　　*

While many of the churches could do nothing on their own premises, their members were not idle. The town's voluntary canteens were very largely supported by workers from the churches. The latter also provided helpers for all kinds of flag days and house-to-house collections which had their origin in some war emergency.

During the blitz times, when evacuation was at its height, the

RIGHT: *There was free tea for the troops who attended the opening ceremony of the Red Shield Club in Bute Street, Luton, in February, 1940. This was one of the many Salvation Army Welfare centres which sprang up all over the country.*

BELOW: *A typical evening scene in the lounge of St. Mary's House, Church Street, which was run as a canteen and rest house for the Services. On the right is the Rev. G. B. Gerrish.*

ABOVE: *Led by the Vicar of Luton, Canon W. Davison, a procession of clergy and ministers of all denominations paraded with sandwich boards during Luton's Religion and Life Week, in June, 1942.*

BELOW: *10,000 spectators packed Luton Town Football Ground, together with 3,000 people who had marched through the town in procession for a United Nations Day Service on 14th June, 1942.*

LEFT: *Canon W. Davison, Vicar of Luton, with the Rev. W. H. Sansom, of King Street Congregational Church conducting an open air service on Wardown Sports Ground, on June 13th, 1943.*

BELOW: *"This magnificent crowd—one of the finest I have seen here yet in my seven years in Luton," said Mr. Sansom, to which the Vicar rejoined, "John Wesley would have rejoiced could he have seen this crowd to-night." 3,000 Lutonians from many churches in the town attended this service.*

The scene inside Luton Parish Church on Sunday, September 3rd, 1944 ... the National Day of Prayer ... when the Archbishop of Canterbury, the late Dr. William Temple was preaching The service, which included singing by Luton Choral Society and the B.B.C. Singers, was broadcast on the National programme.

churches were again able to render valuable aid. People arriving hungry, tired and dispirited were catered for in the matter of temporary accommodation, and found fresh friendships in the life of the churches. Quite a number of church members also did a wonderful job of work in helping to clothe and house evacuees and, in a number of instances, in showing them a different standard of life from what they had known before.

The Baptist churches coped with a big influx of evacuees received voluntarily through the West Ham Central Mission. Baptist homes were circularised and asked for volunteers, so that when the visitors arrived it was already known exactly who would receive who.

All the Sunday Schools were considerably increased for a time by evacuees, and even now there is contact with some of the children who grew up in the homes of Luton people and joined various youth organisations. This was only a temporary growth, however, for Sunday School work was badly affected by the war. The tendency for children not to go increased, beginning with the daylight sirens, which naturally led to parents wishing to keep their little ones under their own roof. On the other hand, some of the older-established youth organisations showed definite growth. The Boys' Brigade offered a notable example. The Battalion more than doubled its membership, and the few remaining officers did a noble job in holding these young people during such difficult days.

Financially it may be said the churches of Luton did not suffer because of the war. Wages were high, and people were wonderfully generous. Christ Church was able to invest £252 of church funds in support of Warship Week in 1942, and earlier in the war had installed a new organ, although, as the Rev. G. B. Carlisle, who was then Vicar of the parish, said at the annual parochial church meeting in 1941, some might think this was tempting fortune !

*   *   *   *

One of the greatest signs of vitality shown by the churches during the war years was the emergence of the Religion and Life Movement, in which an unprecedented measure of unity was achieved. Its activities were held up for a time by war conditions, but on June 14th, 1942, Luton saw the opening of the Religion and Life week, marked by scenes of wonderful enthusiasm and the visits of many notable people. It was a week during which, to use the words of the Vicar, Luton people had an opportunity of knowing all that was meant by the impact of the Christian religion upon the social, educational, civic and industrial life of the community.

Virtually every section of industry, every form of social welfare, and every phase of religion was enlisted to ensure success. This success was abundant and religion in Luton was proved to be neither dead nor moribund. Over 5,000 people attended the inaugural service on the Town Football Ground on the Sunday evening, and on weeknights, crowds ranging from 1,500 to 2,000 were attracted to the meetings at Chapel Street Methodist Church.

Highwater mark was reached when the Bishop of Lichfield and the Rev. Donald Soper spoke on " The World of Nations." A quarter of an hour before the meeting began the Chapel Street church was filled with 2,000 people, and an overflow meeting at King Street Congregational Church for another 600 had to be improvised.

As was said at the time, the Week was only a beginning. Commissions dealing with the home and social work, industry, education, and evangelism were set up, and the Crescent Club, which has done and is doing such good work for girls, was the direct child of the Home Commission. The Rev. H. E. Frankham, then on the staff of the Parish Church, was the first secretary of the Club, which was established in a large house in Crescent Road formerly run as a private hotel.

Thousands of pounds were raised to secure the premises and to get the Club in running order, and it was typical of the spirit of co-operation which prevailed between ourselves and the U.S.A. at the time that a notable contribution came from friends on the other side of the Atlantic. The Ministry of Labour and the big works also proved most helpful, and hundreds of girls who came into Luton during the war years to help the industrial effort had very good reason to be thankful for the social and recreational facilities of the Club, and for the friendships it enabled them to form.

An advisory bureau on marriage difficulties was another outcome of the work that followed the Week, and in wartime, with its hasty marriages, its separations and infidelity, the bureau had many knotty problems to tackle.

Out of the Industrial Commission, following long conferences at the Skefko Works with leaders of industry, came works chaplains, whose work has been spoken of as highly encouraging.

The Educational Commission provided courses in religious training for both day school and Sunday School teachers, and the Evangelistic Commission did a good deal of work in the way of open air services at Wardown and also in arranging brains trusts and conferences.

Handsome tribute was paid by the B.B.C. to the vigour of the Religion and Life Movement in Luton when it asked the Council of the movement to inaugurate a series of inter-denominational services to be broadcast in the General Forces programme, other services of a similar character following from Leicester, Bristol, Leeds and other centres. The broadcast took place on the morning of Sunday, April 16th, 1944, and all denominations were represented at the service. The King Street minister, the Rev. W. H. Sansom, read the Lesson, and the address was given by the Rev. Wilfred Wade, of Beech Hill Methodist Church.

Services at the Parish Church are always marked by a dignity and an excellence in music and singing that cannot fail to be noted by the visitor, and the world in general had opportunity of taking in this point on more than one occasion, for this was not the first time the Parish Church had been " on the air." It was estimated that more than six million people participated in a service broadcast in the Home Service in July, 1944. The congregation included a large number of Service men and women, and the Vicar officiated and preached.

Most notable of all broadcasts from St. Mary's, however, was that on the first Sunday in September, 1944, when Dr. William Temple, revered Archbishop of Canterbury, led the nation in its Day of Prayer. It was possible by that time for the church's fine peal of bells to be heard heralding the service, and the service gained additional distinction by the fact that the singing was led by the church choir, Luton Choral Society, and the B.B.C. Singers, under the conductorship of Mr. Leslie Woodgate, with Dr. Thalben-Ball at the organ.

*   *   *   *

Firewatching may have been one reason for people being absent from church or from their duties in connection with churches, but firewatching also took people to church. The Parish Church, with its rich historical associations, its many interesting architectural features, one of the few buildings, indeed, to which the Lutonian can point with any sense of pride, naturally loomed large in protective measures taken to guard against damage, either from high explosive bombs or incendiaries. From 1941 to 1944 the church was never left and it was a tribute to the affection in which the old building was held that all the many people who watched over its safety in those fateful years were volunteers. The clergy, in the midst of their many other duties, were ready to play their part. As early as 1937 they had been trained as Wardens, etc., and in 1938 they underwent a refresher course. They also helped in the distribution of gas masks.

Fortunately there was never any great call on their services although the Parish Church did not escape scathless, and many others had windows and roofs damaged. Park Town Methodist Church was the most seriously affected, and had to be closed for some time, while the Methodist Central Hall, after a daylight bomb which fell in Midland Road, had to be re-roofed. Considerable damage was also caused by an oil bomb which penetrated the roof of the Bury Park Congregational Memorial Hall in September, 1940, causing a fire inside the building. North Street Methodist Church suffered when another daylight raider destroyed factories in Old Bedford Road. Oak Road and Bailey Hill Methodist Churches also had their quota of damage, and the Rev. H. Goldstone Edwards, of St. Margaret's, lost his home when a rocket fell in Biscot Road in November, 1944.

*   *   *   *

The Rev. G. B. Gerrish has been mentioned as becoming a Chaplain to the Forces. Another to go was the Rev. N. Goodwin Burndred, who had charge of the Methodist Churches at Church Street, Round Green, and Stopsley. He went to France in January, 1940, and, attached to a Clearing Station, experienced " Dante's Inferno "—his description of Dunkirk. The Casualty Clearing Station with which he was working was the last to leave Dunkirk, and he had many narrow escapes, coming safely through between 70 and 80 raids.

Of the clergy and ministers who remained here, several undertook chaplaincy work. During the war years Canon Davison was, and still is, chaplain to the Church of England troops in Luton. He was also chaplain for about two years to the R.A.F. at the airport, and acted in a similar capacity to the Home Guard until the Stand Down. Further, he was, in conjunction with the Rev. E. Allan Roberts, chaplain to the A.T.C. all through the war, and for five of the war years was chairman of the Luton and Dunstable Hospital, work which he took up definitely as war work.

Regularly there were parades of uniformed men to the churches and chapels ; the A.T.C. attended in force one church a month, and the Home Guard on frequent occasions. Members of the Forces were also regularly to be found at services they were not called to attend, and it was not unusual to see a Salvation Army band parading through the streets with a man in khaki, navy blue or Air Force blue taking part as an instrumentalist. There were also parades to churches other than St. Mary's for members of the Forces, and Luton clergy and ministers took part in services at Luton Hoo, both when it was a hospital for officers and after it became Eastern Command Headquarters.

Contact was maintained with the military to obtain lists of men who might be visited, and there were also " Padre's Hours," at which the men could shoot questions at whoever was conducting the proceedings, an opportunity of which they freely availed themselves.

In an educational series put on by the Army Welfare Department music courses were included, and at least one Luton church organist took part, giving piano evenings, with duets and talks.

The presence of Service people in the district led to one innovation. For the first time in the history of the Parish Church a midnight Communion Service was held on Christmas Eve, 1944. It was specially arranged at the request of Service members, and the congregation included a goodly number of them, and also a number of Americans. The experiment was repeated in 1945, but time alone will show whether it is to become a permanent feature of the Christmas Services.

*　　　*　　　*　　　*

These are the known facts of the churches' contribution to the war effort in Luton, but the thoughtful will read much between the lines.

Unobtrusively, and often at the expense of physical well-being, the clergy and ministers of the town, supported by countless men and women of high Christian principle, devoted themselves through six years of war to work for others that will never be recorded except in the Great Book.

Scarcely a home in Luton during those years but was visited at some time by sorrow, anxiety and distress of a personal and intimate kind. In the dark hours of the black-out, when spirits were at their lowest ebb, friends came and brought comfort and solace to stricken homes, loneliness was dispelled, and courage re-born. This was a service performed not as a duty, but because of an instinctive consideration for others. It was a great work, a necessary work. The war could not have been won had not the high ideals and spiritual well-being of our people here, as throughout the nation at large, been so consistently maintained.

6,000 Women

WHILE the Services and the war factories made big calls on thousands of Luton women, there were many other war responsibilities which women were best fitted to shoulder, and which they carried well in a voluntary capacity.

By far the largest group was the Luton W.V.S. The Women's Voluntary Services came into being primarily to provide a second line of Civil Defence as and when regular Civil Defence was depleted by other war demands. While waiting the call to serve in this capacity they managed to do a thousand and one other jobs nobody else found time to do. Working in close collaboration with the local authorities, they saw to such things as the provision of comforts for the troops and shelter for the homeless. They assisted with evacuation, clothing and welfare schemes, transport and clerical work, salvage and savings collections. In doing these things they displayed a team spirit with which women had not before been credited.

The Luton Centre came into being early in 1940, following a meeting addressed by Lady Reading, chairman of the national organisation. Lady Keens was appointed Centre Organiser, and did valuable preliminary work with Mrs. P. Stanbridge, who later became Joint Centre Organiser. Membership grew rapidly, and within a few months 3,000 Luton women had enrolled. In February, 1942, Mrs. R. O. Andrews, who had been head of the Leagrave and Limbury branch, became Centre Organiser, and continued in this capacity to the end of the war. From 1943, Mrs. Bart Milner acted as Deputy Centre Organiser.

In this period membership reached a peak of 6,319. Of these, 400 were Rest Centre personnel, 4,000 belonged to the Housewives' Service, and the rest were canteen workers, knitters, work party members, or carried out the many other duties allotted to them. Central offices were in Gordon Street, and parallel activities were carried on at two sub-branches. These were Leagrave and Limbury, under Mrs. Turner and Mrs. Hyde, and Dunstable Road West, under Mrs. Clews and Mrs. Coombs.

*   *   *   *

Surveying W.V.S. activities in connection with A.R.P. during the war years, one has to bear in mind Luton's comparative luck in the matter of air raids. Although after a few bad months Luton had considerable immunity, the emergency organisation for the feeding, clothing, and general welfare of bombed-out people was always " on its toes," and on occasions which put it to the test it worked smoothly and well.

Continuous practice at the twelve first-line Rest Centres made members familiar with the geography of these places under black-out conditions, and steps were taken to ensure that all stores, covering feeding, heating and sleeping equipment, were available at a moment's notice. Mrs. J. C. Venniker was in charge of all Rest Centres.

One factor which was of immense value in equipping members to face emergency was a scheme which provided basic training in cookery, home nursing and first aid, with qualifying tests for every intending wearer of the W.V.S. badge.

The Housewives' Service, which covered every street in Luton, gave opportunity to lend a helping hand to the busy housewife who was tied to her home by family responsibilities, but the most important work was done by mobile teams ; these rendered invaluable assistance after raid incidents. They visited bomb-damaged houses, gave a hand in getting things cleared up and the home life started again, and sometimes did all the clearing up for the woman of the house. They assisted those rendered homeless, and in many ways gave that human touch of sympathy so essential in circumstances of tragedy and distress. The provision of clothing for bombed-out people, who often lost everything except what they were wearing, was in charge of Mrs. Bart Milner.

The W.V.S. Clothing Exchange was another valuable activity. Started early in 1941, when the clothing shortage was beginning to make itself felt, it proved a godsend to mothers of growing children. The depot in Melson Street was organised by Mrs. R. Hickman, who had the help of a staff of eight. It opened two afternoons a week, it helped not only Luton people but many from surrounding districts, and by the end of 1945 the depot had an index of well over 1,000 people to whom it had proved of great benefit.

*   *   *   *

Figures from the books of the W.V.S. Wool Depot are proof of the great contribution this department made to the war effort. From May, 1941, to December, 1945, 32,391 garments were knitted for the Navy Army, and R.A.F. personnel, 1,282 for the Red Cross and 1,450 for

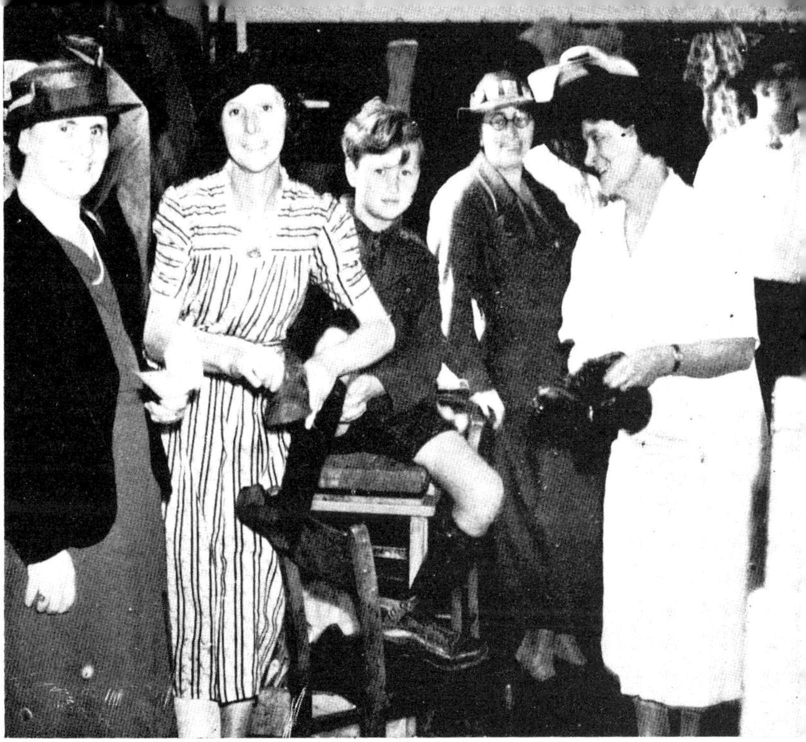

ABOVE: *A young evacuee is fitted with a new pair of shoes at the Waller Street centre.*

BELOW: *Luton women interested in a demonstration of emergency feeding, held in Wardown Park, in June, 1941. Steam for heating was supplied from a traction engine.*

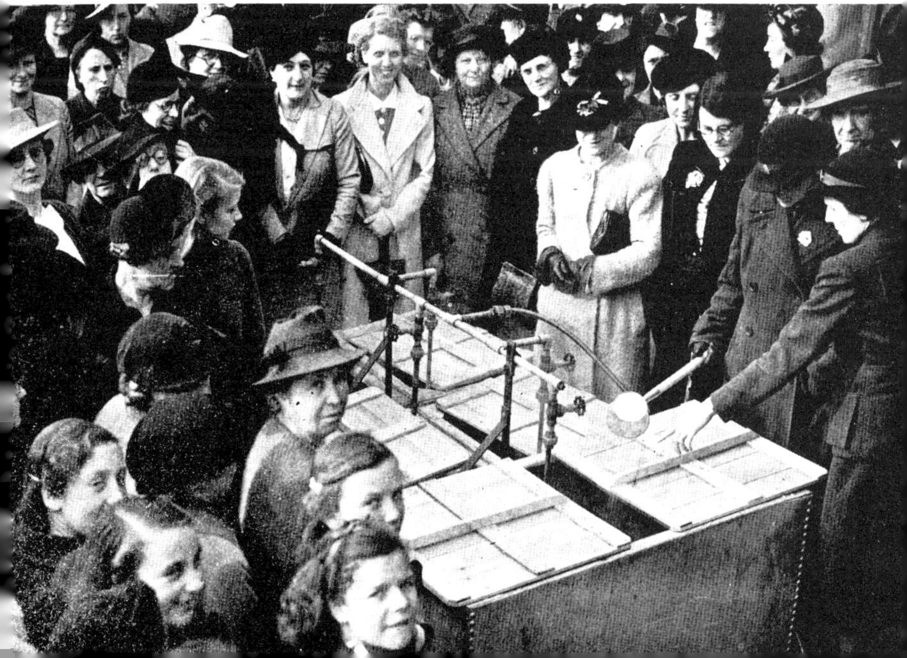

A member of the A.F.S. receives a hot meal from a woman helper at the Waller Street canteen, which catered for the town's A.R.P. services.

Lady Keens serves a cup of tea to Mr. Northam L. Griggs, special representative of the American Red Cross, from the Luton W.V.S. mobile canteen.

ABOVE: *The Luton W.V.S. wool depot, where workers issued wool to knitters, and received and packed garments made for members of the Services. At the telephone is Miss Cumberland, who was in charge.*

BELOW: *Nimble fingers make do and mend at the W.V.S. workroom at Waller Street Methodist Church.*

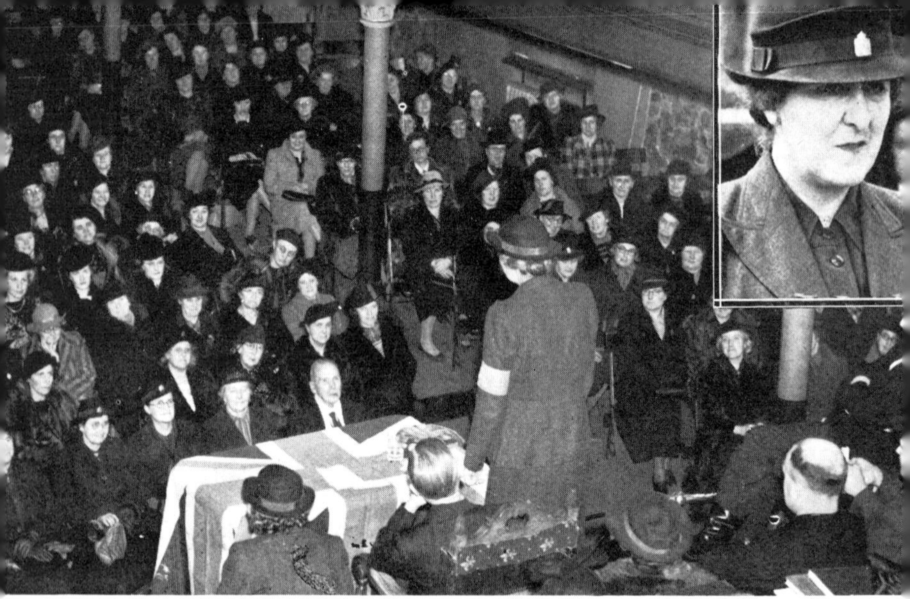

The Dowager Marchioness of Reading (also inset), National Chairman of the W.V.S., addressing Luton W.V.S. workers at the Central Mission in February, 1942.

Christmas cheer for the kiddies at a Luton W.V.S. party.

overseas relief of children, a total of 35,123 garments in all. Over 10,000 lbs. of wool were issued to knitters, and to these figures must be added a further 4,000 garments knitted by work parties at Gordon Street and the sub-branches.

Local war canteens owed their efficiency in great part to W.V.S. workers. The Civil Defence canteen in Waller Street, run so successfully and for so long by Lady Keens, was staffed by voluntary helpers, while the W.V.S. also supplied staff for the British Restaurant in New Town Street, and provided a rota of 80 helpers for the American Red Cross Club in George Street.

The Food Emergency Van Service was also operated by the W.V.S. Hot meals prepared at the British Restaurant were taken out daily to men working on isolated constructional jobs, and to other workers without canteen facilities.

Another transport job was efficiently done by the Voluntary Car Service Pool, of which Miss Read was in charge. There were 30 members, and this Service proved its worth after air incidents in moving homeless people and their belongings, and in answering constant calls from local hospitals.

Another task undertaken by the W.V.S. was keeping an " accommodation register " to facilitate the billeting of Service personnel sent here for special purposes, and also for factory workers and evacuees. Credit for its smooth working is due to Mrs. Thripp and Mrs. Eaton.

No account of W.V.S. activity would be complete, however, without reference to the part they played in recruiting for the Women's Land Army, the visits they paid to old age pensioners, the bandage work they carried out in our hospitals, and the help given to the Blood Transfusion Scheme in looking up lapsed donors. In addition, the W.V.S. Savings Group handled over £25,000 during the war years, and by various efforts raised the whole of the Campaign Funds—a total of more than £5,000—for Luton's Savings Weeks.

Health Services

ONE September morning in 1939 Luton's Medical Officer of Health, Dr. Fred Grundy, seated in his office in the Town Hall, placed a file in his out-basket and started to make notes.

It was the end of one era and the beginning of another.

The story in the file was of the general progress that had been made in Luton's health services ; there were the blue-prints, if such an unmedical term can be pardoned, of future plans. The fact that the file was in the out-basket indicated that these plans were to undergo a radical change.

So Dr. Grundy made his notes. First things were about to come first.

About the same time, at his office in the Luton and Dunstable Hospital, secretary R. E. Lingard was holding a serious conference with the Matron, Miss Redman.

There was still the smell of new paint about this modern streamlined hospital, with the sunny outlook and green approaches, and it had been open for only six months. Now there were new responsibilities to be added to its teething troubles.

Both Borough Council and voluntary organisations had a share in a significant task—ensuring the health of a community during a war of unknown length, against a threat of unknown dimensions, in conditions calculated to undermine the resistance of the population to disease, while dealing with a substantial quota of service and civilian casualties. They had to accept as a *fait accompli* a population swollen by evacuation and the influx of industrial employees.

It was true that all departments of public life had added responsibilities in war. But the successful functioning of industry, supply and communication pre-supposes an efficient medical service; it is a factor which is common to the planning of each. Just as a military commander assumes a proper medical arrangement in his operational planning, so all the facets of civil defence take for granted that the health organisation is 100 per cent efficient.

And in the wards, not only at Luton's premier hospital, but in the smaller institutions, they made ready . . . just in case. Dr. Grundy called his conferences . . . and made his notes. He made so many, and led his department at the Town Hall into such a state of organisation that for five days he remained shut in his office, perfecting the technique of Luton's health defensive.

One difficulty was that of co-ordination, and we shall appreciate it better if we examine the " set-up."

*   *   *   *

Certain medical services in Luton were the responsibility of the Bedfordshire County Council—they included public assistance and tuberculosis arrangements—but the greater part of the health provision devolved on the Town Council, who took under its wing extensive maternity and child welfare schemes, nurseries and laboratory facilities. In addition to the Luton and Dunstable Hospital, there was a Children's Hospital run on similar voluntary lines.

We have said this was the end of an era in health development. In fact, when Luton switched from peace to war, the plans which were left on the stocks were part of an enlightened growth and advancement which had been proceeding since the middle thirties.

The town's arrangements were on the crest of a wave when war broke out, and were well fitted to take the transition in their stride. A policy of zealous application to necessity had given Luton a health service comparable with the best in the country.

The end of an era ? Yes, but if plans had to be shelved, progress was made in other directions. The graph maintained the upward curve, and we propose to show not only how, but why.

*   *   *   *

For the first three years of war, Luton Corporation's Public Health Department deliberately concentrated on maintaining services, and adopted a policy of consolidation, while placing priority on civil defence. Only after that period did the department begin seriously to plan for the future.

The file which we left in Dr. Grundy's out-basket had the outline of a new health centre, a larger maternity centre, and better hospital facilities. The energies which would have been expended on these things had to be directed to other channels.

As the Public Health Department was not able to build, it concentrated during the last two years of the war, when defence matters no longer required 100 per cent. attention, on laying down the basis of a future policy by developing health education both for children and adults. The resultant scheme was something considerably in advance of anything else in the country.

The important thing was that the Department recognised that this was not a time in which advances could be made requiring bricks and mortar.

What could be done was to develop those services not dependent upon building, and to put the Department in the most advantageous position, by the collection of facts, to build on the best plan as soon as it was possible to do so.

Further, war propaganda made the public receptive to new ideas. The Department seized the opportunity created by the readiness of the man in the street to co-operate, to push quietly ahead with a number of campaigns and at the same time to watch current tendencies for evidence of an increase in the incidence of diseases.

Laboratory arrangements were steadily improved, there was a successful crusade in the cause of immunisation, a Health Education Week offered new opportunities for capturing the imagination of the public, and youth in particular ; nurseries were built, health centres expanded, and the evacuees from London and the East and South coasts were invited to share the benefits enjoyed by their new neighbours.

*   *   *   *

One of the first to be open to Luton's new population was the Department's maternity scheme, which had been improved consistently since 1936.

The Maternity Hospital was an up-to-date building dating from the start of Luton's medical renaissance—it had been opened in 1936—

247

but with the evacuee public and a Luton growing from natural causes, it was hardly expansive enough to cope with the first war-time winter. In 1940, the Grove Road extension of the county-controlled St. Mary's Hospital was opened, and the Borough Council succeeded in negotiating its use as an Emergency Maternity Unit.

In the dying days of the war a further extension was added at Chaul End, in a building originally intended as a war-time nursery.

Institutional confinement had become much more accepted in Luton immediately prior to the war. In 1936 only one birth in 10 took place outside the home, and municipal midwifery was non-existent; in 1940 half the births were institutional, while no birth was notified by a private midwife. There was a similar trend throughout the country as a whole, but it was more marked in Luton because the Corporation had anticipated it by providing the facilities.

The Department's scheme for training midwives went on throughout the war.

The second wave of evacuees in 1940 again set the experts thinking. The Luftwaffe brought fresh terror to the East End in mass raids, and low-flying enemy aircraft bombed and machine-gunned the coastal belt daily. The expectant mother, rushed from these surroundings to safety, needed sympathetic treatment and understanding. Routine billeting was no answer for a woman whose admission to the maternity wards was probable within a short time of her arrival, and on November 19th, 1940, a hostel for evacuees who were expectant mothers was opened at 48, Napier Road.

Ten women were received there each week. They arrived by coach, and the scheme worked happily from its inception.

Progressing hand in hand with the maternity services had been the Health Centre scheme. Two of these centres were in operation throughout the war. One, at Dallow Road, was used principally as a clinic in co-operation with the schools, with some maternity and child welfare work thrown in as a secondary issue. At Beechwood Road the reverse was the order of things. They were well-appointed buildings, and represented the start from which war-time progress was made.

Premises were hurriedly requisitioned in widely separated districts for use as temporary infant welfare centres as the work increased, and at the same time, came the demand for children's nurseries.

*　　　*　　　*　　　*

The real story of the nurseries is that they were not an unmixed blessing. To begin with, they were essentially a war development in which the Department had little experience. But they were a national departure, and Luton toed the line. The town's contribution to the war effort did involve a high percentage of female labour, and on the face of it, day nurseries were a definite requirement.

So six of them were built on sites which were widely distributed.

Four were brick structures, modern in design, and two were " pre-fabs."

Although considerable pressure was brought to bear by the Ministry of Health, Luton successfully resisted the attempt to provide temporary and pre-fabricated nurseries in many other parts of the town. With the exception of the first two in London Road and Manor Road, where the urgency of the situation demanded something temporary, the Council, with an eye on the post-war possibilities, provided structures of a permanent character. Labour was at a premium ; it could not be wasted.

In siting, the Nurseries were placed with an eye to possible future Health Centres and Clinic needs, and the existence of these four ready-made buildings may mean that certain clinical requirements of Luton's post-war policy will be completed five years earlier than would have been the case.

Were the war-time nurseries a success ? In their limited sphere, they achieved what they set out to do, but it is doubtful whether they justified the outlay. They were, as has been said, essentially a war-time feature, and the Health authorities were not anxious to encourage their retention. They were costly—£3,000 apiece was the charge for their erection—and it cost £150 a year to maintain each child at a nursery.

Considering the cost, staff, amount of labour which had to be diverted to build them, the number of children which they received, and the relatively small number of women they released for war work, it is doubtful whether they were in themselves a material contribution to the war effort. But they did provide the Corporation with some excellent sites for future Health development.

*　　　*　　　*　　　*

In the meantime, what was happening to the birth rate in this town which made such elaborate arrangements for babies arriving ?

It did some remarkable things, and finally earned Luton the title of a boom town for babies !

It sank to 13.83 in 1941, the lowest figure since 1933, but thereafter climbed steadily until in 1944 the birth-rate was 22.7, the highest since 1920.

Why did this happen ? The story behind statistics is often simple, and in this case, the rise in the birth rate was due probably to the spate of early marriages which the town experienced during the war. These reached their peak in 1941-42, and the babies from these marriages began to arrive in 1944. Answer, then, is that there was not so much an increase in the size of families but rather an increase in the marriage rate ; he who searched for bachelors in Luton in 1943 searched hard.

We have said that the Department campaigned. Generally it campaigned for prevention rather than cure, and this was true particularly of the Health Education Week which was organised in 1943. The main aim was to support the Government's anti-V.D. campaign, and in conjunction with the County Council, public meetings, film shows, lectures, exhibitions and conferences were held.

Most productive of results was a conference to which teachers were invited. The outcome was a plan for a system of long-term health teaching in the schools on human biology and sex education. An agreed policy was formulated and a year later, in September, 1944, a whole-time biologist was attached to the Health Department, to complete arrangements for biology teaching in the schools. A health education theatre was opened in Napier Road, and a system of adult education worked out.

*   *   *   *

Luton led the field again in the drive against diphtheria, for efforts to popularise immunisation had been made long before the Ministry of Health policy was formulated. Results had not been startling; even in 1939 only 112 children of indeterminate ages were immunised, and in 1940 the number was only 204.

Prevention rather than cure . . . the war years laid children open to more treacherous conditions, and 1941 became the anti-diphtheria year. In those 12 months, 7,838 children were immunised.

The first indication that the drive had paid a dividend was in 1942, when Dr. Grundy was able to tell the Corporation that diphtheria had reached a new low level, with only one fatality in the borough—a child who had not been immunised. A diagnosis had been established in 18 cases, but only one had been in a person immunised. During the year, 2,874 more children were immunised.

The diphtheria incidence was even lower in 1943 ; 16 civilian cases were notified, and there was only one civilian death—a person not immunised.

And in 1944 there was not a single death in Luton due to diphtheria. The only two reported cases recovered. That was Luton's war-time diphtheria story.

*   *   *   *

Still, the watchers kept watch, for diphtheria was not the only complaint to be feared in war. If mothers and teachers watched in the homes and schools, the wardens of health were out at night just as much as the wardens of the air raid precautions.

Frankly, the Department was worried. It is, for a conscientious department, a disturbing thing to have to accept a breeding ground for disease as an integral part of your defence scheme. The source of the worry was—the tunnel shelters.

The story goes back to 1940. The sirens wailed nightly and London burned in the south, the red of her wounds reflected in the night sky. The angry glow on the horizon was a testament to her suffering. Hitler had promised blitzkreig, and this was it.

Underneath Luton four tunnel shelters had been built, and as the blitz intensified, these were used as dormitories.

The health of Luton's shelter population was a constant source of

RIGHT: *Dr. J. W. Bone, president of the Luton and Dunstable Hospital showing the Mayor of Luton, Councillor John Burgoyne, part of the new laboratory opened at the Hospital in January, 1942.*

BELOW: *Some of the seventy-five children evacuated with the Alexandra Orthopaedic Hospital to Stockwood, Luton, bask in the sun on the lawn in front of the house.*

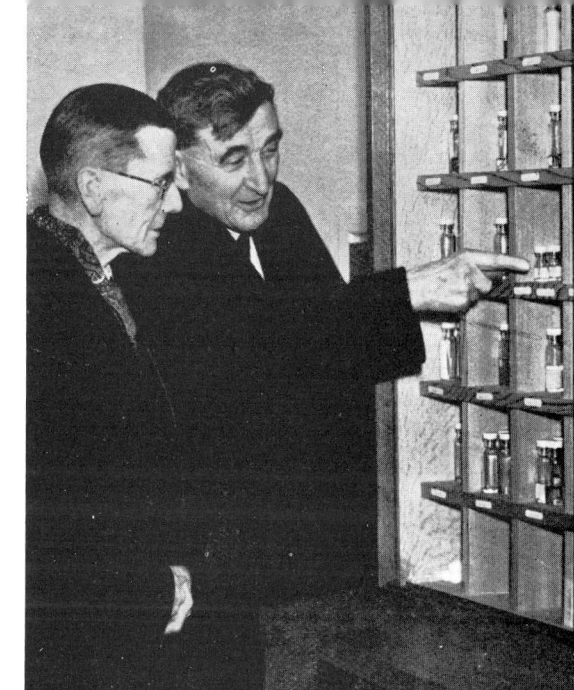

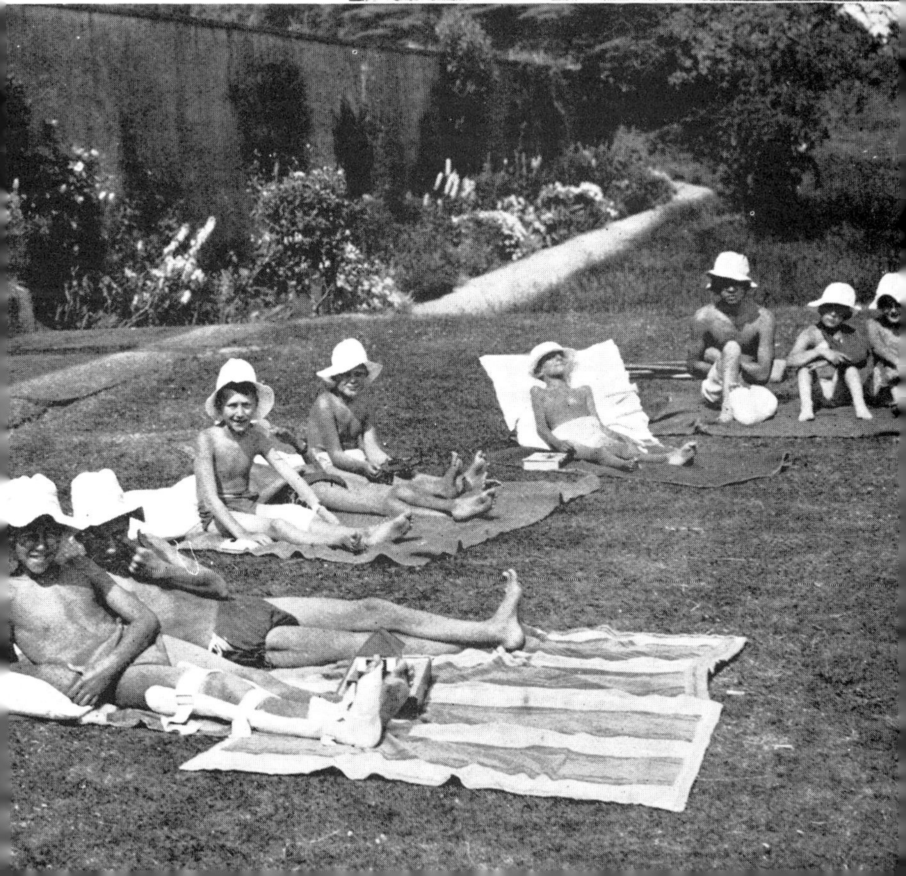

ABOVE: *A bombed-out Luton fami[ly] whose home was left roofless and u[n]inhabitable by a raider, slept [the] nights in one of Luton's pub[lic] shelters.*

LEFT: *Luton's tunnel shelter f[or] had their Christmas brighten[ed by] the Salvation Army, who provi[ded] decorations and held a party for [the] children.*

To enable Luton mothers of young children to carry out war work, day nurseries were opened in various parts of the town.

LEFT: *Children looking at picture books at the Linden Road Day Nursery.*

BELOW: *Toddlers play in the sand while their nurses look on.*

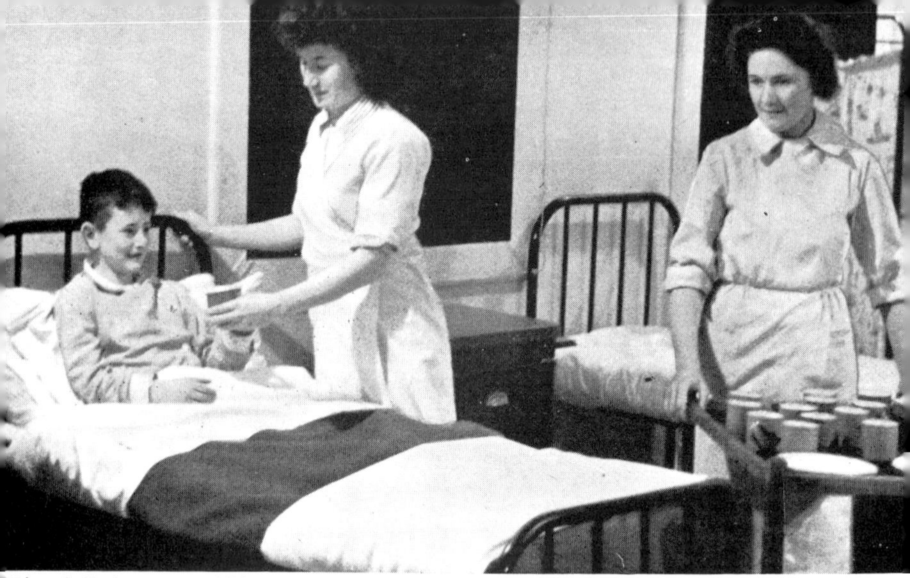

When half the Luton Children's Hospital had to be closed in February 1944 owing to an acute shortage of domestic and nursing staff, a number of Luton war workers, of whom these ladies are two, volunteered and carried out domestic duties there in their spare time.

H.R.H. The Duchess of Kent chats with Sister M. M. Hopkins, Assistant Matron of Luton and Dunstable Hospital, when she inspected members of the hospital's nursing staff, who with other units of the women's services, formed a guard of honour, during the Duchess's visit in April 194

concern, and at the same time provided one of the freaks of the war.

Tackling the job from a factual angle, the Department computed that there were 1,277 people sleeping in the tunnel shelters on October 2nd, 1940, and that 404 were under school age. Most of the children came from poorer class homes, and there was no immediate evidence that they were suffering. However, a panel kept watch, and in January, 1941, a survey of the child population was conducted.

Anxiety was relieved when this revealed little to indicate ill-effects, and the story remained unaltered until the end of " shelter-sleeping." The degree to which infectious disease could be attributed to contact in the shelters remained negligible.

Indeed, infectious disease in Luton never reached the heights expected. Vigilance did not relax, and an Emergency Committee remained in office to keep an eye on unusual tendencies, but war ailments and war diseases left Luton alone.

In common with the rest of the country, Luton experienced an increase in tuberculosis during the early years of the war. A similar experience had occurred in 1914-1918, but this time the peak was not accentuated to the same extent, due probably to a wiser nutrition policy on the part of the Government.

Luton did not suffer severely from the increased incidence of scabies which occasioned alarm in some parts of the country, but the Department opened a cleansing station at Bury Park Memorial Hall, at which some cases were treated, and through which whole communities passed when it was considered that there was a risk of infection.

*   *   *   *

Why was it that Luton escaped war infections ? First, it must be remembered that Luton shared this comparative immunity with the nation as a whole. It is largely a matter of conjecture, but the more ordered habits of the people probably had something to do with it. Whatever other effects the black-out had on our lives, at least it was one of the primary causes of getting people to bed early. It kept children at home and advanced their bed-time to an hour which would be considered unusual in days of improved transport and street lighting. During the war many people were schooled into the frame of mind which accepted 9.30 p.m. as a late hour to be out.

People tended to move about less, herded together less in public places, and diminished the risk of contagion. There is evidence, too, that the Government's nutrition policy increased resistance to infectious disease.

During the last two years of the war, however, there was a general medical impression in Luton that the vitality of the adult population was falling off. It was difficult to place a finger on the cause, but the impression was that the ordinary cold, for example, seemed to take longer to shake off, and to hold the victim in its grip for an indeterminate number of days.

It is not beyond the scope of this review to discuss to what extent

Governmental policy in the calling up of men and women affected the vitality and resistance of those left behind.

Local medical opinion, taking Luton as a typical industrial section, questioned whether mobilisation and the call-up had not gone too far. It had placed an immense strain on civilian social services, and especially medical services, and had reduced the capacity of the ordinary family to withstand crises that would have been unimportant in peace time.

The amount of time lost by women workers on health grounds, by male workers to look after sick wives, and by both to take care of children was an example. There were two instances of the strain in local organisation.

Anticipating that the demand for home help in cases of sickness and confinement would exceed the supply, the Council prepared an excellent scheme on paper. But home helps were not forthcoming. The St. John Ambulance Brigade, the W.V.S. and V.A.D. were among those answering the Mayor's request for an emergency force in case an epidemic broke out. But they had to tell the Council that they hardly knew how to meet their own commitments.

The fact, brutally and frankly, is that had there been a serious epidemic of influenza during the last two winters of the war, it is difficult to see how the authorities would have coped with it. It is a fact to be faced, and one which few people realised at the time.

Another example of the shortage was at the Maternity Hospital, where accommodation, too, was restricted. In the last two winters of the war, premature births presented a dilemma. Mothers could not be retained because of the limited number of beds and the shortage of staff, and on the other hand they could not be sent home to what nurses knew would be inadequate heating and unsuitable domestic conditions.

But providence was on the side of the people, and whatever retrograde tendencies may have been evident to the medical mind in the later stages, the town came through largely unscathed and the Health Department never had to face the expected crisis.

*   *   *   *

If the air-raids threw a heavy responsibility on the municipal health services, what effect had they on the Hospitals ?

So far we have taken no account of the part played within the framework of the health organisation by the voluntary institutions, whose sisters and nurses were on call night and day to deal with the casualties whenever the enemy struck.

It was a difficult time for Luton and Dunstable Hospital. In February, 1939, Queen Mary had opened this fine modern building on the Dunstable Road. It was a tribute in bricks and mortar to the progress which the voluntary hospitals had made since 1872, when Luton's first cottage hospital opened with three beds !

The new hospital had 170 beds, and a further 44 were provided under a government scheme.

The hospital's war-time record is an impressive one; not only was it called on to deal with local patients; it was a valuable auxiliary as well for London, from where casualties were evacuated. From Luton's raids, 271 casualties were admitted, many of them severely injured.

Many people walking in Luton to-day owe their lives to the skill of the staff of Luton's hospital, and to brilliant surgery often performed under arduous conditions. The staff was under a constant strain, and shortage of nurses was aggravated by the fact that the hospital was serving a growing area.

During the war, between 70 and 90 beds were reserved for service and civilian casualties under the Emergency Medical Service scheme. The fact that they were not always utilised does not mean that the pressure was appreciably less; the planning to meet the contingency had to be there.

The hospital attended to 4,530 service patients, and these figures pale into insignificance beside the civilian returns. The number of in-patients treated was nearly 23,000, while over 127,000 out-patients came on to the Hospital's books during the same period. The total out-patient attendances were 332,134 and the in-patients and out-patients served under the Emergency Medical Service Scheme amounted to 6,393 and 10,413 respectively.

It was an inspiring performance. But figures and charts do not tell the story of heart-aches and battles for life that were the routine of the war-time hospital; they do not tell of the exhaustion and mental fatigue suffered by a nursing and medical staff taxed to its limit.

$$* \qquad * \qquad * \qquad *$$

The Hospital's biggest success of the war was the production of penicillin in workable quantities.

This episode came at the end of the war-time story, in the spring of 1944, but it is worth telling at this stage, for it put the Hospital on the national map. Once again Luton was first in the field.

It was the first time in the history of voluntary hospitals in Britain that penicillin had been produced for civilian patients. The drug had been very much in the news, but so far its use for civilian purposes had been restricted.

March, 1944, was the month in which it was produced for the first time in Luton, and since then thousands of civilians have benefited from the Hospital's enterprise.

In early 1943 the Hospital was handicapped by the scarcity of penicillin, and it was decided to try to produce it locally. Months of research produced no result. There were searches for mouldy green cheeses, among other things, to see if the mould could be found, but the results were always nil.

Not disheartened, the Hospital persevered. Then, in March, 1944,

R

Mr. H. Alison Blundell, a member of the Board, succeeded in obtaining a small culture of the mould. This was merely the start of the work.

Night after night Mr. Blundell and Dr. Seiler, the hospital's pathologist, worked in the pathological laboratories. It was an anxious time, and there were many disappointments. But at last success was announced.

The staff of the Hospital will remember the first occasion on which their penicillin was used. A patient was suffering from a disease of the hand which had resisted all known treatment and which was, to all intents and purposes, incurable.

In April penicillin treatment was started, and the patient responded ; at the end of a week's treatment the infection was gone. This was the first of a long chain of successful applications of penicillin made within the walls of the Hospital itself. The equipment to produce it was elaborate and the technique complicated. Yet soon after its initial production, enough was being manufactured for 25 local treatments a day.

*   *   *   *

This is near the end of the story. For the rest it is not all the romance of laboratory research, but the story of realities, which at the time were grim enough.

Turn back the clock to 1939. The work of the hospital had already increased by 72 per cent., and people were saying " The Hospital is too small."

In 1940, casualties started to insinuate themselves into the routine cases in the wards ; the hospital was administering to the needs of a six-figure population. It was a time for action.

In the winter of 1941, when nurses worked with the distant thunder of the London barrage in their ears, the first plans were formulated for an extension to the Hospital. At this time as many as 94 beds were vacant, under the control of the Ministry of Health. It was a relief when the extension was opened in October the same year.

To take some of the pressure, the Hospital called on auxiliary accommodation, and Emergency Medical Service patients were directed to Ashridge, Arlesey, Friern Barnet and Hill End.

Reserve base was Luton Grammar School. In 1941 a scheme was announced for it to be converted into a reserve hospital in the event of Luton and Dunstable Hospital being damaged, but fortunately, the necessity for this scheme to be put into operation never arose.

A further extension, this time to the casualty department, was opened in 1943 at a cost of £800, and in April of the same year, the Hospital was visited by the Duchess of Kent.

Staff difficulties became more and more acute in the later years of the war, and assumed serious proportions in 1944.

When, in the summer of that year, the first Allied forces were storming Normandy's beaches, and the toll of the V-bombs mounted on the home front, there were signs that the staff shortage might make it

RIGHT: *A nurse answers questions at an exhibition at the Electricity Showrooms during Luton's Health Education Week in September, 1943.*

BELOW: *Luton's Medical Officer of Health, Dr. Fred Grundy, (right) taking part in a recorded discussion on the town's health services for a broadcast in the B.B.C.'s European Service in March, 1945. He is standing in front of a graph illustrating Luton's increased birthrate . . . the rising line can be seen above his companion's left shoulder.*

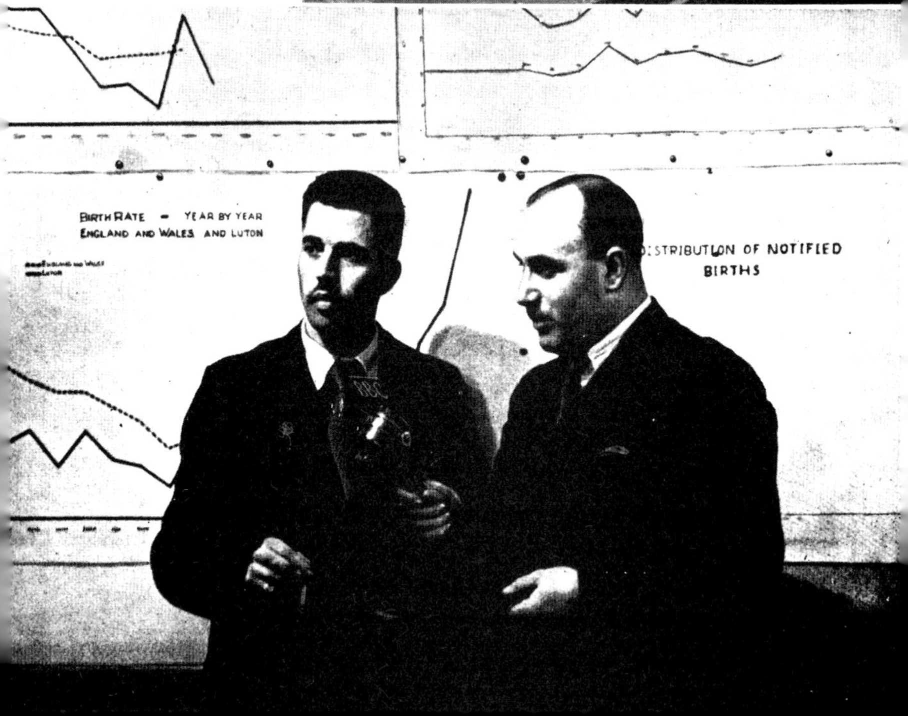

BIRTH RATE — YEAR BY YEAR
ENGLAND AND WALES AND LUTON

DISTRIBUTION OF NOTIFIED BIRTHS

difficult to meet a major crisis. In the following spring, when the Canadians and the British were going down through the Reichswald, the Hospital was coping with even more patients than before. When Montgomery was carrying the battle across the Rhine a few weeks after, the nursing position was being described as " acute."

Not until June, 1945, was a staff improvement reported, and by that time other Hospital news took priority. There were rumours of a changed constitution, of a merger with the Children's Hospital, of a doubled capacity when building was possible again.

*   *   *   *

That was no part of the war story ; the Hospital had done its job, and written some notable additions to the history of voluntary medicine. Big things had been done, but to conclude this miniature hospital saga, here are two of the smaller stories . . . two of the human pictures which illustrate the inner greatness of a country at war.

In September, 1941, an effort was being made to raise £1,000. One day in that month, three small children, rather shy, but determined, were ushered into the Secretary's office.

They waited, and then the eldest stepped forward. His little hand clutched an envelope, which he thrust towards Mr. Lingard.

The secretary opened it, and inside was a note :—

" Please accept this small effort. We have had a little concert and collected from a few friends. Enclosed 5s. K. Churcher, V. Churcher, A. Pearson."

The three children had given a concert in their front room to an admiring audience of relatives and friends. And the complete proceeds of this command performance had been given to the Hospital—and the sum, was in fact, the first amount to be credited to the new fund.

The second of the stories concerns the staff itself. In the rush and pressure that was war-time hospital work, the nurses could still spare time to think of the welfare of those who were in uniform and facing terrible dangers on active service. It is a story not without its tragedy, and not without its happy ending.

In 1940, the nurses decided to " adopt " the submarine *Undaunted*. Adopting it meant sending, originally, the gift of a few books. These the nurses obtained by saving amongst themselves. Gradually the gifts grew—it was no longer only books, but harmonicas and gramophone records. They sent their cigarettes, and they sent Christmas presents.

They formed pen friendships with the men of the *Undaunted*, and many were the letters exchanged between the crew and the nurses of the Luton and Dunstable Hospital.

Then, quite suddenly, in 1941, the correspondence stopped The *Undaunted* was missing. The nurses never saw their friends of the submarine . . .

They decided to try again. This time they adopted one of the sister submarines—the *Unbending*. Again they sent gifts of books, and again they collected, through their social club, to send Christmas boxes. And more pen friendships were formed.

In July, 1945, seven members of the crew spent a 48 hours leave at the Hospital as guests of the staff, and were given a royal time. They were welcomed by the Mayor, Alderman Lady Keens, and highlight of the visit was a dance held in their honour. They presented the matron, sisters and nurses with a silver fruit basket, and a replica of the submarine's " Jolly Roger " flown from the periscope whenever it entered harbour after making a " kill."

In the nurses' home, there is a replica of the submarine's crest.

Perhaps some of the crew of the *Unbending* will see this. If they do, this incident is recalled in the hope that it will provoke reminiscences of a happy association, and for seven of their members at least, memories of a leave spent at Luton, with their friends the nurses at the Hospital.

*   *   *   *

At Luton Children's Hospital, the first rush of evacuation was felt at a time when the staff was busy converting one of the wards into a first aid post, in preparation for the possibility of heavy casualties.

In 1940 an influx of bombed-out children caused a problem. At the same time, Luton had its own taste of air-raids, and the Hospital suffered some structural damage. However, it carried on, and when the real crisis came in 1944, it was not from the air.

In common with other institutions it was feeling a staff shortage. The handicap became so serious that eventually the position was reached where nurses were doing domestic work. The position worsened and one ward containing 26 of the 56 beds had to be closed.

Then there came a demonstration of the spirit of mutual help which was so often manifest during the war. Workers, their energies taxed by a heavy day at the factory, might justly have claimed that they were already making their best possible gift to the war effort, but they volunteered to work for the children during their off duty.

Rangers and guides came forward, and the principal industrial concerns of the district provided teams of helpers. Twenty employees from Electrolux were early volunteers, and Vauxhall Motors started an organisation to promote regular help. Soon the ranks of applicants to help had swollen to such an extent that a meeting had to be arranged at the Town Hall to fix a rota !

St. Mary's Hospital, under the aegis of the County Council, was another institution which suffered both from shortage of staff and accommodation. Luton Area Guardians Committee was responsible for the direct administration of both the institution and the hospital, in Dunstable Road. The days of the institution pictured in the crusades of Dickens had gone, but the new Master, Mr. J. A. Green, came in 1941 to find a legacy of accommodation rendered inadequate by war demands.

In 1940 Hitler's planes started their machine-gunning and mining attacks on the East Coast . . . the low-lying Essex beaches facing the North Sea, were no longer a playground for the young. Crippled children of Clacton were evacuated to St. Mary's.

The story of St. Mary's is briefly one of more patients than beds, and appeals for more nurses. In 1943, for example, there was reached a situation where six nurses were attending to 123 cases. The accommodation situation was eased when in December, 1944, a wing of the old Bute Hospital was taken over.

Not all the Hospitals in Luton during the war were local organisations. To St. Margaret's, formerly the New Bedford Road Casual Wards, came the Home and Hospital for Jewish Incurables.

The inmates of the home had been refugees since the first air-raid sirens. They evacuated from Tottenham to Essex in the early days—providentially, for their home was badly damaged by bombs. Then, their new home in Essex was damaged by an explosion.

They arrived in St. Margaret's, bringing about 60 patients, and later a further 40 were accommodated at the request of the Middlesex County Council.

Another refugee hospital was the Queen Alexandra Orthopaedic, from Swanley, Kent, which evacuated to Stockwood. Swanley was a railway junction, destined to see most of the Battle of Britain. Moreover the tentacles of greater London spread towards it and close by the chimneys of industrial Kent belched their smoke into the Thames skies. It was a legitimate target, and on the road to even better targets. It was also no place for a Children's Hospital.

To Stockwood, home of the Crawleys for 500 years, came the children of the Alexandra Hospital. They played on the smooth, green lawns, and the house echoed to their laughter. Few of them will forget their first Christmas at Luton . . .

*   *   *   *

A far cry, perhaps, from Luton's planned health campaign, from a record of municipal achievement to a little child playing in the summer sun on Stockwood's lawns . . . a far cry, perhaps, from a chemist working hard into the night to produce life-saving penicillin, to three little children shyly handing 5s. to the hospital secretary.

But it is not, perhaps, an inappropriate note on which to end Luton's war-time health story, for the children of those days will be citizens of the town which will see the Public Health Department's plans brought to fruition, and the vision of a bigger Hospital realised.

For the Hospital which made the penicillin found that it progressed not in spite of, but because of, the war.

And in the Town Hall, a file has come back into Dr. Grundy's in-basket.

The Stream of Life

THE transfusion of blood to fortify the vitality of the human body is a comparatively modern development of surgery.

In the public mind it is still believed widely, but quite erroneously, to be a " last resort " to which recourse is taken when a patient is *in extremis*. That is not so now. It is a valuable aid to surgical science and its use is so widespread that it has become a commonplace treatment in all cases where the natural resistance of the human constitution can be—not necessarily must be—strengthened.

By experience, too, it has been found that the donation of a pint of blood by a normal healthy human being leaves no ill effects ; so responsive is the natural function that the deficit soon disappears.

The Red Cross started their Blood Transfusion Service as early as 1921, but the imminence of war in 1938 and early 1939 demanded a lightning expansion of the facilities.

The fruits of this have been the saving of countless lives. Men, women and children, hundreds, nay, thousands of them, are alive to-day only because this great national service was at hand when it was needed.

The Emergency Blood Transfusion Service began to operate in Luton early in 1939, when preliminary tests were made of volunteers. When war started Luton became one of twelve centres where a depot was established, and one of four intended to serve London and the Home Counties in a national emergency.

The emergency came, and blood given by Luton people helped to save the lives of hundreds injured in air raids. It had been collected at regular intervals from the numerous donors and stored in special cooling chambers at St. Mary's Hospital. This was Luton's Blood Bank.

During the war the Luton depot, of which Dr. J. Shone was director, collected over 170,000 bottles of blood from volunteers in this area, and all demands for civilian air raid casualties in London and the Home Counties, and for the vast needs of the Navy, Army and R.A.F. in all theatres of war, were met. Blood was also provided for the Merchant Navy, U.S. Forces, for Malta, and for the Chinese, Belgian and Dutch Red Cross Organisations.

Local donors came from all walks of life. They were mainly factory workers. Nearly every Luton factory had its own panel, and periodically had " blood drives " for new donors. Quite a number of the donors were housewives.

The week before D-day saw the peak in the number of donors offering their blood. Good attendances were maintained throughout the early months of the invasion, so inspiring were the events of the time.

RIGHT: *A section of the blood bank at the old Luton Bute Hospital, later known as St. Mary's Hospital, where blood was preserved in specially built cooling chambers, ready to be sent out at a moment's notice.*

BELOW: *The way it was done. The donor's arm is bound up and from a punctured vein, blood is withdrawn into a specially sealed bottle.*

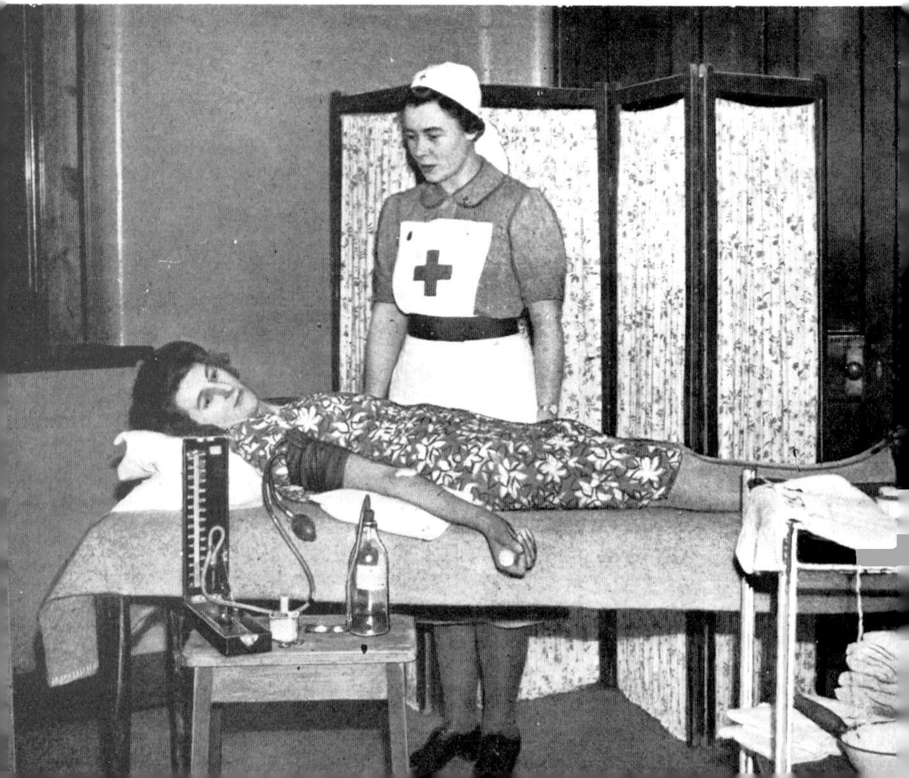

Some interesting figures of the work of the Depot during that period can be given. In May, 1944, 2,485 new donors were enrolled, 5,002 were called upon, and 4,859 responded. In June another 2,005 donors were enrolled, 8,007 were called upon, and 6,741 responded. In July, although new donors had increased, the need proved to be not so great for the Normandy casualties were far fewer than had been anticipated. New donors totalled 2,937, 7,821 were called upon, and 6,392 responded.

In the three months of June, July and August, 1944, 1,700, 1,800, and 1,600 bottles of whole blood (liquid blood) were sent from the Luton depot to meet war needs.

There was much enthusiasm among donors in the Luton area. Many a person was seen proudly exhibiting the small blue and gold card recording the dates on which blood had been given. For every ten occasions the donor received a special certificate, and although no person could give more often than once in three months, a sort of competition developed among many as to who could put up a record.

Blood transfusion has long since proved its worth. Although for the last seven years it has been essentially a wartime service, the need for its continuance exists in peace as in war.

The donors of 1939-1946, unlike members of other war organisations are not standing down. They are still at hand and the stream of life is in their keeping.

War Against Waste

OLD iron caused more bad tempers in Luton than anything else concerned with the salvage campaign.

It was not the old iron for which the itinerant collector formerly shouted, when he also wanted rags, bones, and bottles. It was the iron garden fences and the front garden gates from thousands of Luton homes. People were not asked whether they would like to surrender them. It was announced that they would be taken, unless they had definite artistic or historical value, which would have to be substantiated, and that a very modest value would be allowed,—if the owners claimed it. Whether claimed or not, it was nothing like the probable cost of reinstatement.

The average Luton fences and gates had no claim to art or history. They disappeared. The immediate result was to give a pretty forlorn appearance to many a hitherto neat frontage. The householder's willingness to stand the loss might have been greater but for a considerable doubt as to whether the sacrifice was really necessary. He heard of dumps of this old iron accumulating for months, for no apparent use or reason. He heard that after the metal had been collected it proved unsuitable. No wonder he asked whether his fences and gates were a real contribution to the war effort.

He was told that the old iron in the dumps was not the same old iron all the time—that it was going to the foundries as well as coming to the dumps. He still doubted the truth of this, and looking at neighbours' fences and gates which remained because they were wooden, had a feeling that he had been hardly used.

Where people could afford it, and could get it done, there was considerable activity in getting brick walls and wooden gates erected, so what was gained in one material was lost in others. For the majority, however, this kind of replacement was impracticable.

In Luton, there are two main objections to the open garden. One is that people in general are rather conservative. Their gardens always have been enclosed and they always must be enclosed, otherwise, they feel, they are robbed of their privacy. The other reason, a much more cogent one, is that a few people are no respecters of unprotected gardens. What happened was a peculiar form of vandalism. Not only were flower beds trampled down, but shrubs were stolen or torn to pieces, and saplings were broken and irretrievably damaged. There was no rhyme or reason for it.

But it was not only the individual householder who suffered at the hands of hooligans after the fences and gates went. Immediately it ceased to be possible to close the parks and recreation grounds at dusk a wave of wanton destruction began. Further reference is made to this elsewhere, but it will cost the ratepayers as a whole thousands of pounds if these pleasure grounds and open spaces are ever to recover their pre-war beauty.

Those are some of the things about the salvage campaign which have left unpleasant memories. It is an ironical comment that some old iron abandoned in Pope's Meadow by the Army even before the fence-grabbing started remained there for years, although for a long time Luton was the headquarters of the Army Salvage Training School. That old iron remained until it ceased to be worth salvaging. It may still be there.

*   *   *   *

Happily other aspects of the salvage campaign were free from any such repercussions. They can be regarded as an asset to the war effort, with no debit.

The Luton News was the first in the town to organise a waste paper collection scheme. The first entry in the books was three-halfpence paid for a small parcel on October 5th, 1939, The following day, 10d. was paid for waste paper, and thereafter the scheme grew like a snowball. By May, 1940, *The Luton News* scheme had been adopted

ABOVE: *Any old iron? Luton children enter into the spirit of Luton's Salvage Week in 1941.*

LEFT: *Part of a week's accumulation of waste paper at Luton Corporation Depot.*

BELOW: *Mrs. Day, of Kennington Road, receives yet another saucepan to add to the pile of aluminium in her front garden.*

LEFT: *Food waste collected from bins in the streets of the town, being fed into the boiler at Luton Corporation depot.*

BELOW: *The finished "meal" . . . fit for a pig.*

by practically every provincial newspaper in the country, and thousands of tons from newspaper offices alone were finding their way back to the mills.

One of the features of *The Luton News* scheme was a weekly collection from the schools. A van went round, the bundles brought to the school by the children were weighed, cash was paid on the spot, and the money went to some special school fund. A league table was published, and the enthusiasm of the children was tremendous. The record of collection goes to Maidenhall Junior Boys' School, who collected over 23 tons while the league was in operation. The league aggregate from the schools of Luton was over 114 tons, and this takes no account of the quantity afterwards collected by the schools and handled by the Cleansing Department's Salvage Collection Scheme.

The most comprehensive contribution in Luton to the general salvage campaign was made through the Public Cleansing Department. When the Government launched the salvage campaign in November, 1939, the Town Council acted at once. Facilities for collection and disposal were provided at the Cleansing Depot in Windmill Road, an advertising campaign was started, and early in 1940 a leaflet was distributed to every house urging people to prepare a weekly parcel for the dustman. They were asked to save every scrap of waste paper, and also rags, bones, bottles, jars, and anything in the way of of scrap metal.

By the time a Defence Regulation made it obligatory on local authorities to salvage waste paper, Luton's voluntary scheme was well under way, and in the three months to June, 1940, salvage collected totalled 280 tons, worth £1,122. It was a good beginning, but nothing to what was to follow.

To increase recovery of waste, the Town Council varied a long-standing policy to enable certain classes of waste to be collected from trade premises without charge.

At the meeting where this decision was made, the Director of Cleansing, Mr. John Stephen, reported that he had initiated another move, destined to put Luton right into the forefront as a pioneer salvage authority. This was the special collection of kitchen waste which could be prepared for feeding pigs and poultry, and so supplement or take the place of imported feeding stuffs. To begin with, collection was only possible in certain parts of the town. In these areas each house received a card to hang in the kitchen, as a reminder of the need to save the food waste, and as a guide to what was useful and what was not. If, as town dwellers, they were not certain, they learned from the card that pigs and poultry did not appreciate rhubarb leaves, tea leaves, coffee grounds, or orange peel, but that there were a lot of kitchen odds and ends they would like. Collection was combined with the usual collection of house refuse.

Happenings of 1940 and 1941 made it difficult to extend the salvage effort. Manpower was short; transport was short. Many of the employees were key A.R.P. personnel, and had a lot extra to do when there was bombing. A mortuary for civilian dead had to be established and maintained. It had a heavy duty in the first big raid of August 30th, 1940 The department was responsible for a lot of other jobs in connection with Civil Defence. The winter brought a heavy snowfall.

It became clear that the regular collection of food waste would become increasingly difficult, and to obviate people having to keep it for unduly long periods in their homes, the communal bin system was adopted. Then the whole town was covered ; 1,000 bins were provided.

Out of this expansion came the installation of a concentrator plant, to process the waste and provide a ready-cooked food for pigs and poultry. The livestock liked it, and it found a ready market, so much so that Luton began to import the raw waste. In addition to the direct collection of a small amount from the villages, food waste was received from the local authorities of Dunstable, Leighton Buzzard, Harpenden, St. Albans and Welwyn Garden City, and from the Service and prisoners-of-war camps in Bedfordshire and Hertfordshire. At the end of the war 250 tons a month were being collected in the town, and 140 tons received from these outside sources. By evaporation about a third of the weight was lost in the concentrator plant, but there remained about 260 tons a month for sale to farmers and poultry keepers.

Some other figures are enlightening. During the period of the war the Cleansing Department collected and returned to industry 17,199 tons of essential raw materials, of the value of £76,011. Food waste totalled 10,522 tons, value £41,248. Waste paper took second place with 4,793 tons, £27,025. Scrap metals were third, 1,240 tons, £2,092. The scrap metals must not be associated with those fences and gates, with the removal of which the Cleansing Department had no concern.

The total weight was roughly equivalent to a whole year's collection of household and trade refuse. The value was equivalent to £12,880 a year, or a 4d. rate. At £76,000 the total was only about £8,000 less than the net cost of running the Public Cleansing Department for the last three years of the war.

As a sideline, help was given with the occasional book drives, which had a threefold object—to get books for the Services, for blitzed libraries, and for salvage. These campaigns brought from the shelves books which had probably never been read for decades, and just over 360,000 were of no better value than to go for salvage ; but 2,605 were picked out for blitzed libraries, and 26,661 were of a type it was felt the Services would appreciate.

The Army Salvage Training School, during its three years at Luton, made good use of the Windmill Road depot as a practical instructional centre. Mr. Stephen lectured to officers and men on municipal

ABOVE: *Sign of the times . . . 1. Luton Parish Church was denuded of its iron railing when the call for scrap iron was made . . . but somehow the gateway was left behind.*

BELOW: *Sign of the times . . . 2. The war years increased hooliganism in Luton's public parks. Taken in Kingsway Recreation Ground this picture of a shelter shows broken windows, woodwork ripped away, and tiles smashed on the roof.*

salvage, and from time to time there were distinguished visitors to inspect the methods of handling, sorting and grading salvage. They included Field-Marshal Lord Milne, General Sir Walter Venning, Quartermaster-General; Major-General Buckley, Director of Economy, War Office; and Brig.-General Badcock, Director of Salvage, War Office.

From 1942, at the request of the Ministry of Supply, and having got the Luton Salvage Campaign well established, Mr. Stephen was lent to the Ministry's Salvage Department, and was Deputy Assistant Director of Salvage and Recovery until recalled in April, 1945. He still acts for the Ministry as honorary district salvage adviser for Bedfordshire and Hertfordshire.

*   *   *   *

It has been noted that it was around the collection of waste paper that the salvage campaign originated. The war created new uses for paper and cardboard. Many sources of raw materials for the paper industry were cut off. Dutch board went off the market until early 1946. Waste had to be utilised. Old newspapers largely went back to newsprint mills, although only a limited proportion could be incorporated with new material. Rough waste was just as important. Sent back to the mills, it emerged again in quick time in new forms. As board, it largely superseded metal when made into containers for the transit of certain types of munitions. As coarse paper, it had many war uses.

It was easy to collect in the early stages. When newspapers were reduced in size and restricted in numbers, when many magazines came down to diminutive size or disappeared altogether, when papers magazines, and books, once read, were sent to menfolk overseas, when traders were no longer permitted to wrap their goods, quantity collection of waste became far less easy.

Most of the waste paper passed through the hands of Messrs. Mitchell and Outen for transfer to the mills, and they handled 10,290 tons. It is clear that this salvage activity saved a considerable amount of shipping—and dollars. But even that figure was not the complete total. A considerable quantity of used newsprint went by rail direct to the mills, and there were consignments of printed waste so secret that lorries came from the mills to fetch it, and a special escort had to accompany the waste to the mills to ensure that no bundle was opened on the journey.

*   *   *   *

Supplementing the salvage campaign Luton was covered by the Container Recovery Service, a co-operative effort by manufacturers to collect from retailers cartons, tins, wooden boxes, drums, sacks, and any packing material good for further service. Luton made its fair contribution to the six years' total of two hundred millions for the whole country.

The Fruits of the Earth

IN 1940 and early 1941 the food situation in Britain began to look rather grim, and the Englishman was faced not only with the necessity of tightening his belt, but with the prospect of pulling it in even further in the future.

There were no early potatoes coming from the Channel Islands or sources farther away. Tomatoes did not come from warmer climes. Spanish and Egyptian onions were off the market. Cauliflowers could not be brought from the Continent. We had no bananas, and for these there was no home-produced substitute. Other things for the table were cut off, for ships were going down at the rate of one a day, and those that stayed afloat had more vital cargoes to carry. So, lest we should go shorter than need be, people had to set to and dig.

Some of the diggers, of course, were old hands, cultivators of long-established allotment fields. But they were few, whereas wartime diggers became legion. At the peak period they were estimated to number 5,000.

They dug, and did other related work, in about 60 allotment areas often in the most unlikely quarters. They dug up corner sites which had not been built upon. They dug up patches of ground so cluttered with rubbish that it seemed almost hopeless to try and bring it back into cultivation. Old bedsteads, bicycle remnants, rusty parts of antiquated prams, and so on, came up with the forks. Never was there such a clearance.

It was recognised that the nearer a plot was to a man's home the more attention it would receive, as the minimum of time would be wasted in getting to it, and there was scarcely a part of the town which did not have some plots handy.

Individual plots were often larger than the recommended ten poles, so that part could be devoted to vegetables suitable for winter storage. A cup materialised to stimulate interest in winter greens particularly, as these were of special value at a time when so little else could be got from the ground.

Many plotholders were more enthusiastic than expert, but as the plots were in groups there was usually somebody handy who had the knowledge and, what was more important, was willing to share it.

Lectures, films, brains trusts also helped, and as time went on even those who had been novices could exhibit their produce at the shows held annually, with more than reasonable hope of winning awards.

And those shows ! Well, village folk know what their annual show meant in the years when they were at the height of their popularity. The allotment holders' shows eventually bid fair to rival the glory of those old village shows.

Allotment associations increased to seven, and were linked in a

S

ABOVE: *Week-end volunteers putting sheaves into stooks on one of Luton Corporation's farms.*

LEFT: *Cabbages among the flowers, in Luton Parish Churchyard.*

BELOW: *Four air raid wardens were the founders of the first Luton pig club, and are seen admiring their proteges in the piggery near Wardown Crescent.*

RIGHT: *Girls of Surrey Street School, Luton, hoeing and watering the crops on the allotment, which was their contribution to "Digging for Victory."*

BELOW: *The result of their efforts. The produce on view at the Harvest Festival, in the school.*

Above: *Mr. C. H. Middleton, the famous broadcaster, congratulated the people of Luton on their great efforts when he opened the Ministry of Agriculture's exhibition at Wardown in August, 1945.*

Left: *Exhibits at a produce show arranged by the Dallow Road and district allotment holders.*

Below: *A smart detachment of Land Girls parade round the arena at Wardown Sports Ground on Farm Sunday in June, 1943.*

Federation. The various Association shows not only stimulated the production of good quality vegetables, which was their primary aim, but also raised considerable sums of money for the Red Cross Agriculture Fund and for local charitable causes.

They were generous people, those plotholders. They put the pick of their plots into the shows. They generally ended with all the exhibits being sold for charity, and more than one prize-winner bought another man's non-prizewinning exhibits—all could not be winners— for the good of the cause.

Meanwhile home gardens were not neglected. There were fewer flowers and more vegetables. The latter sometimes monopolised even front gardens ; but this does not mean that a few flowers in the corner were frowned upon.

Did not the late and great Mr. C. H. Middleton, who more than once visited Luton in connection with " Dig for Victory " weeks, always advise that in seeking the useful one should not wholly ignore that which was beautiful, and that even to grow more vegetables one should not uproot all the roses ?

          *   *   *   *

While allotment holders were busy on their plots, and home gardeners on their patches, some of the larger factories started allotment fields for their employees. Thirty schools had allotments or large gardens, and the Parks Committee practised what they preached by doing similar things, but on a larger scale.

On 30 sites they cultivated about 500 acres which had not been producing food crops. There was a large area at the Airport, and another at the Chalton site for the new Electricity Works.

Smaller areas were scattered about the town. All were open and there was no provision for storing the necessary machinery, which had to be driven miles to and fro. Skilled agricultural labour was practically unobtainable, and crops produced probably cost far more than they would have done under other conditions. Nevertheless they were grown without loss to the town.

Off this land came wheat enough for about 1,400,000 loaves of bread. 12,860 cwts. of additional vegetables, and considerable quantities of barley, rye, oats, and cattle food.

At the same time, through getting the allotment holders organised, the Committee was able to arrange for the distribution of fertilisers and seed at specially favourable prices, and, from Wardown, etc., to supply a lot of hardened-off young stuff ready for planting on the allotments.

          *   *   *   *

Extra food production was helped in the town in other ways. They had nothing to do with digging, but they justify mention here. Pig clubs were started, and although they did not become very numerous, those who had a stake in one found themselves well provided when in due time a pig went to a bacon factory. The factory kept part and returned part for clubbers to share.

But, if pigs did not become numerous, back-garden poultry did. Many people who found it difficult, and sometimes impossible to get eggs through normal channels, decided to become poultry keepers. Neighbours often benefited by registering for eggs with the amateur poultry keeper. They passed over their food scraps, and got a more regular egg supply than they would have done through the shops. It all helped the food supply.

*　　　*　　　*　　　*

While all these efforts at increased production were going on in the town, the countryside was not ignored. People were encouraged to go to farm camps and lend the farmers a hand in harvest or other busy seasons ; some went to help lift the potato crop ; some even know now what it means to help lift sugar beet.

" Dig for Victory " was the slogan of the times. The result through six years of war was staggering. The allotments alone in Luton, provided vegetables for sixteen million meals, according to the statistics and report prepared by Mr. R. J. English, Luton's Director of Parks.

" Dig for Victory " in Luton was much stimulated by Mr. English's help. It was intended as a personal encouragement to the individual to fend for himself and grow, as far as possible, his own needs. In fact it became synonymous with every aspect of food production, and nothing was of more value in offsetting war shortages and keeping the kitchen well supplied.

Whatever the monetary value of these homegrown vegetables, they had a far greater indirect value. They maintained the vigorous health of the individual not only by their own nutritive properties but by the benefit they brought through exercise and an open air occupation to many a stale or jaded worker. They were in a large measure the regenerating agent for industry.

Rationing and Prices

THE story of rationing is the story of the retailer, and the story of the consumer. We can leave out of it for the moment the unapproachable and often unpredictable Government departments responsible. The retailer was their instrument, and he got the kicks from the consumer. Both were harassed in mind and exhausted in body. The retailer tried to cope with crowds of disappointed shoppers, hopeful shoppers, bullying shoppers, wheedling shoppers, legally-minded shoppers, sinister shoppers, what-have-you-under-the-counter shoppers, and those wolves in sheeps' clothing, Government inspectors disguised as shoppers.

He tried all the time to keep tabs on the latest rationing regulations, and writhed as " registrations " and " directions " abstracted from his employment, one by one, his well-trained, experienced, and always helpful assistants whose successors, more often than not, were inefficient and sometimes irresponsible. Some seemed only too regrettably unaware that however long the war might last, courtesy and helpfulness need never be included among the things " in short supply."

The consumer, the housewife charged with feeding the family and clothing the children, found her responsibilities and difficulties growing steadily as the years of war went by. Here is the view of one of them who, in addition to bringing up some small children, also went out to work :

The war, she maintains, could never have been won without the scheming and planning of the British housewife to get the best possible value out of the rations. Yet the housewife was probably the only " war worker " who had no official recognition of her services, which, at times, taxed her patience and ingenuity almost to the breaking point. Apart from the problems which faced her within the home, there were the added troubles of shopping under great difficulties. When queueing was at its worst, and because the things which were wanted were at their scarcest, it was a heartbreaking and tiring task . . . one which took three or four times as long as before the war. This, plus doing war work to make good the absence of a man in the Forces, usually meant early to rise and late to bed, with the home tasks squeezed in between work and shopping.

And to this particular housewife, as probably to many others, it came as a shock to find that the worst period of rationing seemed to be when one really expected things to become a bit better, the world war having ended. Meals, if adequate, had been no more. Their sufficiency for young and growing people, she had always thought was open to question, and their value was not increased by their monotony. Having learned kitchen economy in the hard school of experience, however, and having hoped for some easing of her burdens, the housewife saw this hope fade, and submitted to the imposition of more cuts, and talk of still more, because after the liberation of Europe all the food that could be spared was not enough to feed Europe's hungry mouths.

*　　　*　　　*　　　*

Rationing had no prophet to honour ; few people had any concrete idea of what it would be like after the first three years. It has not gone without its historians, and they have not been tardy in pointing out errors in the system.

Nobody will pretend that everything attempted by authority was a complete success. The lessons were too often learned at the expense of the consumer and the man behind the counter.

Rationing was a necessary evil. Any cross-section of life in Luton would show that it succeeded largely because there was, from the first day of the war, an acceptance of the fact that this was 1917 again ; there was another war afoot in which a priority target for the enemy would be the larder of the ordinary housewife. But there was this fundamental exception—this time we knew more, and rationing started almost with the first sirens of 1939. As a result, there was no outstanding shortage of food in Luton.

Some commodities were occasionally difficult to secure. Transport difficulties started a small bread scare in January, 1940, and many bakers still remember the sudden outbreak of panic buying which took place, as the impression gained credence that there was a serious shortage. For once many Luton shoppers were fooled by rumour.

Policy in higher quarters was not free from blame for the periodic difficulties which arose in the supply of unrationed foodstuffs to Luton. At no time did it seem that the problem of ensuring a fair supply of these foods had been solved to satisfaction. Account did not appear to have been taken of Luton's inflated population. Luton retailers will tell you that supplies of unrationed foods never followed the people that moved into the town to an adequate degree. As a result proper allocations could not be made. Shopkeepers were supplied in many cases on a datum basis, that is, according to quantities bought in 1939, which meant that subsequent movements of the population were not considered.

*   *   *   *

Generally, Luton's position as regards rationed commodities compared favourably with other districts. The prompt introduction of food control in 1939 was on the whole welcomed by the retailer. Control meant legislation, it meant restrictions, it meant officialdom. It meant many unpleasant things, all of which spelled headache for the man serving you in the little shop on the corner.

But it also meant something else. It meant that his supplies of rationed commodities to meet his registered customers' allowances became the responsibility of the Ministry of Food, and for that he was thankful. The little man was freed from the task of searching anywhere and everywhere for someone who could and would supply ; it limited the purchases of those with more time on their hands and more money in their pockets than others less fortunately placed. So far as rationed goods were concerned, it stopped shop-crawling and unequal distribution.

*   *   *   *

The retailer may have grumbled about rationing, but that was not his biggest headache. That came from the spasmodic and uncertain appearance on his shelves of the unrationed goods. It is when one draws a comparison between the easy way in which rationed items were obtained from the shops, and the muddle which frequently attended other commodities, that the value and success of rationing became clear. Often the problem of obtaining equitable distribution of other foodstuffs to complete the family shopping list assumed nightmarish proportions.

Action was inevitable, and a nation-wide demand for the Ministry of Food to regulate the provision of non-rationed goods in short supply resulted in the introduction of the points rationing scheme. This was delayed until November 17th, 1941, and by that time most of the larger establishments in Luton had instituted schemes of their own to ensure a fair share-out.

After retailer and consumer had mastered the routine of points rationing, the benefits of the scheme were evident. But this did not end the retailers' troubles. Certain branded foods such as canned salmon and canned meats, were very popular, and to secure these goods on points customers started to go from shop to shop. The problem of the retailer was this. If he sold these goods to all and sundry, his registered customers stood a poor chance. If he reserved goods for them, it was against the expressed desire of the Ministry of Food that the public should get points food anywhere. Eventually, the Minister ruled that it was in order for retailers to reserve goods on points for registered customers.

With the points rationing system came the points banking system. Under this scheme the retailer's bank opened for him a points account, which he worked in all respects as if it were a current account in pounds shillings and pence.

*　　　*　　　*　　　*

One of the earliest phenomena of control was the institution of meat distribution centres.

The scheme was introduced in November, 1939, and was put into operation for the first time during the second week of January, 1940, when all private slaughtering ceased.

From that date, livestock were taken over by the Ministry of Food through collecting centres. The wholesalers were permitted to form a body called the W.M.S.A. (Wholesale Meat Supply Association), and this distributed the meat on behalf of the Ministry.

Luton was one of the local centres selected for the grading of cattle ; from the slaughter-houses the meat went to the distribution centre in Crescent Road, from where the butchers were provided with their requirements.

The ration to the public varied from time to time but even during the worst shortage the butcher was able to provide his customer with a bigger ration than at the time of the gravest shortage in the previous war, when prices were higher.

*　　　*　　　*　　　*

The unrationed wares of the fishmonger were more than ever in demand in Luton to eke out the ration, and a system operated to ensure that inland towns received their fair share of the catch. As a result of a zoning scheme, Luton's fish generally came from Fleetwood, although a few retailers received fish from Grimsby, through an inland wholesaler at Hitchin.

The zoning system, however, had one great drawback, a drawback which accentuated queueing. In pre-war times Luton's fish arrived early in the morning, and was on sale from the time shoppers began to get about. Under the zoning delivery it often did not arrive until mid-day. Shops did not open until they had the fish, and then the pavements were already being blocked by queues. And the kinds of fish! Many a housewife has banned for ever from her household menus the name of salted cod. For this inoffensive fish familiarity bred the utmost distaste. At one period also catfish had risen so much in the social scale that it lay unashamedly on the fishmonger's slab.

*   *   *   *

The arrangements made for meat rationing, points, and canned foods, however, were simple compared with the problems which arose when milk rationing was introduced in October, 1941.

A complicated business from the start, it involved a complete record of the constitution of every family, as the quantity of milk was regulated according to the number of children, adolescents, and adults in each home. Then the price was dependant on the economic conditions of the home. Free milk was provided where the financial position was acute, cheap milk was supplied for children under five, while full price was charged for the remainder.

Special allowances were allocated for medical cases and some classes of workers were also regarded as priority consumers.

The remainder of the milk went to non-priority customers—that is people not in the special classes already enumerated, and as the amount to be supplied to priority classes varied considerably at differing periods, it followed that non-priority consumers found their allocation fluctuating frequently.

A number of farmers were allotted to each dairyman, and where the supply allocated was insufficient to meet demands, as in the case of the larger distributors, the deficit was made up from big creameries at a great distance, and transported by road and rail, with price margins severely controlled.

Not only did the authorised allocation vary, the yield from the farms varied with the seasons, and this meant an occasional surplus after the dairyman had effected normal delivery. The retailer could never regard the position as reliable and the system, necessary though it was, involved an elaborate recording system, throwing considerable strain on milk producers.

Later, in order to economise in labour, petrol, tyres and vehicles, a scheme of block distribution was introduced, and with the exception of the Co-operative Society the customers of all the Luton dairymen were placed in a common pool. They were then re-allocated to each dairyman within a limited compass, so that instead of travelling all over the town to deliver to his clients, the dairyman was given the same number of customers within the radius of a few streets. Registrations were frozen, and only in exceptional circumstances were customers allowed to re-register.

When the block distribution system worked hand in hand with the rationing system proper, a tremendous amount of labour was involved, and in the transitional stages there was some confusion. Rationalisation of delivery started early in 1943, and for a few days some householders found they had insufficient milk, or even none. Others found they had too much.

Ultimately the scheme settled down to organised working, and although it was never perfect owing to the high level of administration required, it was a step towards economy, and contributed to the sharing of the milk resources on an equitable basis.

*   *   *   *

Bread was unrationed until 1946, but Luton bakers were confronted with a peculiar situation almost immediately on the outbreak of war. The first influx of evacuees created a demand which it was impossible to meet with immediate labour and materials. There was, of course, no transfer of these from the home area. It meant, too, long hours for the master and the operatives.

Local bakers found the call-up of the men for the services affected delivery rather than production, and getting the bread to the customer was the chief worry. Three-day delivery, though it brought a saving in rubber and petrol, was not the complete answer.

Bread became darker as the war went on. It was found necessary to increase the extraction milled from the wheats, which, to the man in the street, simply meant that darker coloured flour was used. With less choice of wheats, the flour varied considerably, and the baker had continually to alter his process to produce a satisfactory loaf.

Luton bakers were well prepared against the emergency which would have arisen had the yeast supply failed. They were generally instructed in the use of barms, and arrangements were made to store considerable quantities of yeast with the local brewers. Facilities would have been available to manufacture a considerable quantity at the breweries had the need arisen ; the arrangements included the installation of special water tanks.

A mutual aid scheme was devised by the bakers, and an outline issued to all concerned, but happily it was never found necessary to bring this plan into effect. The scheme was co-ordinated with other areas in Eastern Region.

While Luton bakers had their difficulties, they were all surmountable, but there remained the human element with which to contend. The manufacture of bread was one thing which could not be postponed from day to day ; it had to be continuous despite staff shortage.

Yet the bread supply never failed. The bakers could echo the sentiment of a London theatre and claim that they never closed. Production rose, and in most cases output was doubled compared with pre-war figures. It was almost impossible to assess public demand, whether upwards or downwards—but the bread supply never failed.

*   *   *   *

Luton had certain advantages when it came to the supply of fruit and vegetables. Situate in an agricultural surround, it was favoured to an extent which was never true of the larger industrial towns of the North and Midlands, and when items were scarce, it was generally attributable to climatic conditions. Of course, there were the inevitable disappearances—oranges, lemons, grape-fruit, bananas, etc. ; but the district was usually fortunate in the supply of the home-grown article.

Rationing of foodstuffs brought with it barter on a small scale, and the inevitable black market. The country districts were a favourite prey for the mobile black marketeer ; rural food inspectors could not check up on every pound of grain threshed, or every egg laid.

During the Christmas period, chickens which could be bought at 7s. 6d. before the war were fetching 35s. ; a goose might easily cost £3. It was said that one could go to certain farms in some areas and buy all the milk, butter, and eggs one required . . . at a price. But there was little evidence of organised black marketing, except in poultry-stealing, which was worked on planned lines.

*   *   *   *

Rationing has so far been reviewed in relation to necessities. There were, however, other retailers, whose goods, if not claiming the same priority as food, were in demand by an extremely high percentage of the population.

Behind his counter, the Luton tobacconist soon found that his stock of cigarettes was not going to meet the call. The first real signs of a shortage occurred in December, 1940, but it would be more accurate to say that what actually occurred was a big increase in consumption. This increase, which started in September that year, was consequent upon the great expansion of night-work and the nervous tension of air-raid vigils, and was one of the first signs of war strain.

Subsidiary causes of the shortage were the reduction of bonded stocks, and the dislocation or diversion of distribution through bombing and moving populations. Another was labour reduction.

When the air-raids slackened in 1941, this first deficiency ceased, and there were no real difficulties in Luton shops until June, 1944. In that month, at the time of the Normandy invasion and the onset of V-warfare, tobacconists found that cuts had to be made in the civilian supply owing to labour difficulties, and absence of materials. A further cut was made in September, 1944, and the result was a heavy and false demand.

The curtailing in 1945, of " duty-free " cigarettes for troops abroad

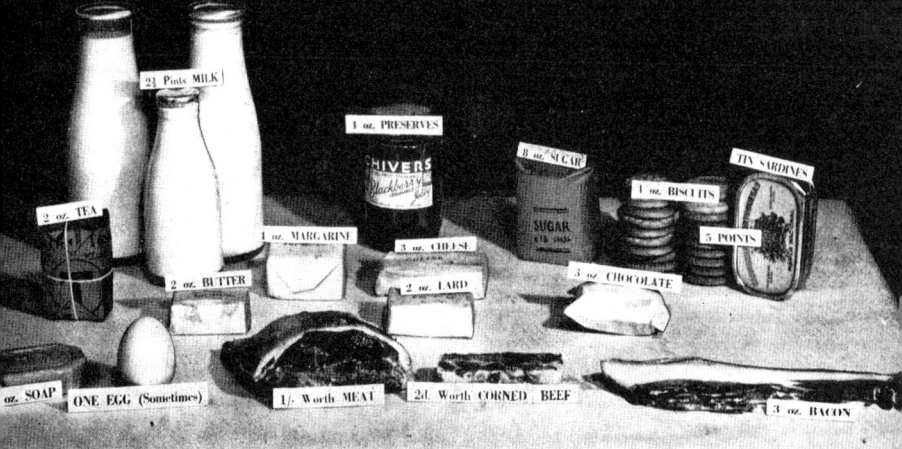

Labels in image: 2½ Pints MILK · 4 oz. PRESERVES · CHIVERS Blackberry Jelly · 8 oz. SUGAR · TIN SARDINES · 2 oz. TEA · 1 oz. MARGARINE · 3 oz. CHEESE · 1 oz. BISCUITS · 5 POINTS · SUGAR · 2 oz. BUTTER · 2 oz. LARD · 3 oz. CHOCOLATE · oz. SOAP · ONE EGG (Sometimes) · 1/- Worth MEAT · 2d. Worth CORNED BEEF · 3 oz. BACON

ABOVE : *Food rationing . . . the housewife's headache! This picture of a week's ration for one person at the end of the War speaks for itself.*

RIGHT: *No this . . . and no that. How often this was seen on the doors of Luton's shops, during the War and after.*

BELOW: *The worst has happened!*

TURKISH · EGYPTIAN VIRGINIA

THIS IS FACT NOT FICTION

NOTICE NO CIGARETTES NO TOBACCO *Positively*

NO TOBACCO

NO CIGARETTES

CLOSED BEER SHORTAGE

PUBLIC BAR

ABOVE: *The food storage depot between Luton and Dunstable, where reserve stocks for the area were held.*

RIGHT: *"Almost as good as mother's" . . some youngsters tuck in to a square meal at Luton's British Restaurant, in New Town Street.*

BELOW: *Drawing contentedly through their straws, these Luton schoolchildren drink their daily one-third of a pint of milk.*

Qu ues, queues, queues . . . Luton housewives, in common with those all over the country, became queue conscious during the shortages brought about by the war. Here cakes were the attraction.

Ration books became a housewives' headache . . . the first pains came with the queue to obtain them.

Victory is ours: it is March, 1946, and there is peace on earth if not plenty. Bananas make a welcome re-appearance after an absence of six years . . . but only for the 18's and under, and then there were the queues, queues, queues.

caused a slight improvement, but this was soon nullified through the requirements of returned demobilised men and women.

Tobacco manufacturers have been, and still are, selling more goods than ever before in the history of tobacco, but have yet fully to meet the greatly increased demand, and this with prices higher than ever before.

*   *   *   *

Luton's licensed houses never experienced the acute beer shortage of the war of 1914-1918, and there was generally enough beer to satisfy customers. Here again a favourable comparison with other towns of similar size can be made ; the opinion of many connected with the trade was that Luton, where houses rarely had to close because they were sold out, was one of the most favoured towns in the kingdom from the point of view of beer supplies.

The war years saw Luton provided with an output which exceeded by hundreds of thousands of barrels the pre-war figure.

To achieve this, the sale of heavier gravity beers was discontinued, and J. W. Green, Ltd., the local brewers, concentrated on two beers representing a penny increase on what was previously the cheapest gravity beer. This meant that materials formerly used for brewing the heavier gravity beers were available for increasing the output of the new beers, which were a light bitter and a mild at the same price. The Brewery plant was therefore kept at maximum output, which would have been impossible with a more varied range. An extension to the brewery made just prior to the outbreak of hostilities was capable of adding 1,000 extra barrels a week to production.

The result was that although retailers on isolated occasions had to admit an inability to cope with demand, there was nothing like the all-round deficiency existing in the bars of other districts.

Luton-brewed beers were very popular with the Americans, who came from all parts to obtain supplies. Characteristic ruses adopted to persuade the company to increase individual quotas included the story that a certain unit, having brought down a large number of enemy planes, qualified for extra supplies !

When the Battle of the Atlantic was at its height, beer was considered so important to the Americans that supplies of their native malt and hops were shipped to England for delivery to Luton, so that the quota for their forces could be maintained without interfering with the materials allocated for the production of Luton's own beer.

*   *   *   *

Other items, considered to be luxuries, became subject to an entirely new impost in the form of a Purchase Tax. It was intended to be not only a revenue-producing tax, but a deterrent to spending on non-essentials and an encouragement to saving. Goods were graded for this tax according to their degree of necessity. Some commodities carried no tax at all. Others, such as jewellery, furs, and cosmetics, were subject to as much as 100 per cent. tax. As a deterrent to spending, however, the tax was to some extent ineffective. So much money was in circulation that on the sales of many classes of goods appealing particularly to the less thrifty it had no limiting effect. Footwear was a case in point. Cosmetics, too, kept up their sales, even though the prices rocketed, even though the goods were sometimes of unknown origin and doubtful quality. Even the 100 per cent. tax could not persuade girls educated to lipsticks to forego these adornments.

Regularly the price tabs of cigarette cases, pipes, and leather goods, were altered; regularly the retailer watched the reluctant figure rise higher, but he never saw the demand decrease. Ornaments and handbags were constantly required; coupons were not needed for their sale, and they made good presents at a time when coupons made gifts difficult to choose. All types of gramophone records, heavily taxed, had an eager public. The spending power of the purchaser seemed competent to cope, according to his or her particular weakness, with the rise in prices in these markets. An effect particularly noticeable was the tremendous boost given to the secondhand market. Many owners cashed in nicely on things which in pre-war days they had regarded as practically unwanted junk.

*   *   *   *

Legislation confronting the retailer of clothes was hardly less impressive than that affecting the grocer, the butcher, and the milkman. Clothes rationing was the Government's present to the nation at Whitsun, 1941.

The austerity restrictions imposed on suits and shirts probably accounted for the lack of popularity of men's utility clothing. For example, the single-breasted style became universal; there were only eight pockets for the whole three-piece suit, and even the number of buttons came within a prescribed margin. Trousers were shorn of turn-ups although, singularly enough, they were still permitted on ladies' slacks. Tunic shirts had to be single cuff only, and regulation lengths were imposed with geometric precision. Socks dwindled in length. These rules came into force almost immediately, and were baffling to the retailer who had not previously regarded his merchandise as such an elaborate and complicated piece of machinery. And everything, except hats, was on coupons.

When restrictions were removed, the quality became quite good, but towards the end of the war, a government claim of over 80 per cent. of cloth and garments led to a temporary shortage. The basic reason for this latest development was the demand for suits for ex-servicemen.

The retailer of footwear found that utility shoes for men, were popular to an extent never reached by those for women. The reason is not hard to seek; they were of an austerity pattern, and female technique is to regard the shoe as something more than a machine for walking. A wedge heel, for example, is held to double the attraction. Such artistic adventures in footwear have more often than not been

T

out of stock, since they are not manufactured under utility grades, and this, logically or otherwise, added to their value in the assessment of Luton ladies.

When it came to clothing, the ladies were more tolerant. After the first sighs had been offered up, they accepted the situation very well. Fashion quite failed to thwart feminine intuition where a bargain was concerned, and it was necessary always to remember that the non-utility product was subject to heavy purchase tax, although frequently equalled by the utility product.

When this word utility first reached a new public, women's and children's outer garments were unattractive, and often poor both in quality and style, but they improved considerably as time went on.

Popular wartime lines were ladies' and children's gloves and hose. Most glove lines were well made and were at a reasonable figure, compared with non-utility articles bearing $33\frac{1}{3}$ per cent. purchase tax or, if trimmed with fur, 100 per cent. tax. The hose were good value for the price, but of course, the range of colours was not so all-embracing as in the halcyon days when shopping was really shopping. But the public was practical about it, and utility hose never remained on the counter very long—or under it either, for that matter. Retailers found growing difficulty in meeting the heavy demand for fully fashioned hose.

Corsets became a subject to be discussed with due solemnity in the House, and the technical complaint was expressed that there was a lack of support in articles which had to be made without steel. And so the Board of Trade deliberated, and manufacturers in due course became acquainted with an order to prepare better and stronger corsets, especially for larger figures.

The clothing coupon system had many peculiarities and some anomalies. It also had a curious flexibility. Any one could buy anything, provided the appropriate number of coupons were surrendered. There was no question as to whether or not one already had a sufficiency of what it was proposed to buy. The coupons were primarily for the use of the individual, but in the family they could be pooled. They could not be offered loose over the counter, but could be cut out and sent loose through the post on a mail order. Women who didn't mind what they spent on clothes found that there were ways and means of disposing of part-worn clothes in a manner that helped them to get something new. Where the law stepped in, however, was where new goods were sold without the surrender of coupons, and where the coupons were bought and sold. In proved cases heavy fines and penalties were imposed ; nevertheless the racket continued. There were stories of deals in coupons at prices which varied with the district. Other things supposed to be done in the black market were to sell lengths of material at double price and no coupons, or for double coupons and no money. But it was always a risky deal.

The problem of children's clothing became acute almost immediately coupons became necessary. After a time an extra allotment of 20 was given for children who had reached a certain age or stage of growth, but even these were quite insufficient when children were growing visibly. The extra eased the situation, but there still had to be handing down within families, each child being merely the temporary lessee of clothes which another had outgrown. Where children, on admission to a new type of school, required a special outfit, somebody else had to go short of coupons : many a young man who carefully stored away his civilian clothes when he went into the Services found when he returned after a period of years that a younger brother had " inherited " them.

Another very sore point with the housewife was that although household furnishings, linen, towelling, etc., were all on coupons, there were no special coupons for these things. Where the inevitable wear and tear of the war years necessitated renewals, somebody in the family had to go short of clothing coupons, or there could be no new towels, bed-linen, or whatever might be needed.

*   *   *   *

Setting up home was a serious business in war-time. Luton had about 1,200 empty houses in 1939, but it was not long before accommodation was at a premium, and later, renting a house became practically impossible. Property prices soared. By 1945, a pre-war £600 house would fetch £1,000, if offered with the magic words, " Vacant Possession," while in a better residential district a house for which £1,000 would have been taken in earlier times would fetch over £2,000. In a number of cases better class houses costing £1,600 or so pre-war fetched nearer £4,000 at auction.

As far as furniture was concerned, the man in the shop, doing his best to help, was only too painfully conscious of the fact that he could not do very much. Furniture was obviously going to be one of the biggest sufferers in a world where raw materials were at a premium and the war effort claimed labour and stocks.

In 1943, in order to make the best possible use of timber available, and to ensure a reasonable price, utility furniture came on to the market Generally, an official permit was necessary to buy it.

It was sold against units, and those eligible for these units were bombed-out people and newly-married couples. The quality on the whole was good, the retailer did not hesitate to advise his customers, and usually he could recommend it. Sixty units were the stipulated supply, but only 30 were valid at a time because of the long waiting list which every retailer had for furniture. And yet, as the man in the shop knew, as he showed you what he had for sale, those 30 units just furnished one room. And the remaining 30 could not be used until a further six months had elapsed.

Second-hand and antique furniture prices shot up into the clouds. As far as the former was concerned a control order fixed maximum

291

prices for types of furniture, and these governed the shops and the auction marts, but bargains between private buyers and sellers remained uncontrolled. In the result a second-hand three-piece Chesterfield suite worth pre-war about £20, might easily fetch £70 or £80. Carpets, part worn, of a new pre-war price of £10 to £15, commanded £60 to £70 and many other items of furniture were quite unobtainable.

But if you had been lucky enough to buy some furniture, your next problem was to get it home. The family who furnished one or two rooms—it is too much to say they furnished a house—had their furniture delivered to the door on the pool scheme.

This idea of pooled delivery was not confined to furniture dealers. The objective saving in labour and transport and such vital materials as petrol and rubber was achieved through the co-operation of all the firms taking part, and the first scheme in March, 1942, covered 36 different businesses supplying furniture, drapery, musical instruments and hardware.

When the scheme was extended to include butchers, retail delivery within the borough by motor vehicles ceased. Five vehicles were available to deliver outside Luton once a week, and deliveries inside the borough by cycle and hand were made on the basis of once per house per week.

The pooled delivery scheme was symbolic of the whole of the attitude of Luton retailers towards the war. True, there were grumbles, and often they were justified ; true, there were mistakes made—how many of the customers would have been foolproof in similar circumstances ? Many of the mistakes were the result of the system, in any case.

But generally, the retailer accepted an organisation of rationing which he knew aimed at ultimate fairness and a solution of the distribution of available resources. Because he accepted it, and because he knew his own responsibility, whether he was a manager in a big store, or the man in the shop on the corner, the rationing system worked in Luton, and worked as well as it did anywhere.

*　　　*　　　*　　　*

There are two other aspects of rationing which ought to go on the record, one general, one affecting Luton in particular.

That which affected Luton was not perhaps so much the rationing itself as getting the rations. So many women were at work in the big factories, and the shops closed so much earlier, that an agitation arose about the impossibility of their doing their necessary shopping and also going to work, and it was urged that this was having a prejudicial effect on output, and causing absenteeism. The matter was taken up officially, a special committee appointed to investigate the need for some special arrangements, and in due course the traders arranged to co-operate by keeping open late one night a week particularly for factory women. This scheme was in fact put into operation in the very early days of 1942. It was not a success. The shops were open for the service only of women factory workers. The extent to which this facility was utilised did not justify the shop assistants' time, the lighting involved, or anything else. After a trial it was abandoned. The women had been given their chance. The agitation was never renewed. There were not even any protests that the experiment was not continued.

The other aspect of rationing was one that affected Luton only as it affected every other place. Those who had the time, and the money, could economise on their rations by going out to meals, which, unlike what happened in the latter part of the 1914-18 war, did not involve the surrender of coupons. Sometimes, when wives had insisted on their menfolk getting meals out, the men got their own back by describing the wonderful meals they got in their particular canteen, for perhaps 1s. or 1s. 2d. Perhaps the stories had some sub-stratum of truth in the early days of the war; but, like Army cooks, there are canteen cooks and canteen cooks, and of some canteen meals towards the end of the war the teller of tales had to be able to tell a convincing fairy story if he hoped to be believed. But where canteen meals were really, or only reasonably, good, and where more than one member of a family could utilise such a canteen, then the family had an undoubted advantage over another which had to make the week's rations last the week.

Wastage of food was quite properly made a criminal offence, but proceedings in court were rare compared with those which arose out of selling articles of clothing without coupons.

*   *   *   *

So that some future generation which may be exempt from rationing may know with what we had to be content, not only during the six years' war but also afterwards, here are some things to enlighten them. Meat ration, 1s. 2d. a week (some canned, if necessary); butter minimum, 2 oz. a week; cheese, 2 oz.; bacon, 2 oz.; cooking fats, 1 oz.; jam or other preserves, 1 lb. a month; tea, $\frac{1}{2}$ lb. a month.

Things like canned fish, fruit, peas and beans, dried peas and beans, rice (when obtainable), dried fruits, and biscuits were on " points," and any marked run on a particular article was usually countered by an increase in " points " value, to divert demand to something which was less attractive but temporarily more plentiful. Sweets were rationed by a " personal points " scheme, after some retailers had adopted their own rationing system.

Coal, coke, gas and electricity were never actually rationed, but if a 1943 appeal for a voluntary cut in consumption had not been heeded some drastic action would have followed. There was an immediate drop in consumption and the situation was tided over . . . temporarily. In the following years, however, the mining situation became so critical that coal, coke, and patent fuel were put on an allocation basis, which meant " if available." The maximum allowance for a household was 34 cwts. a year. There was no guarantee that even that quantity would be available.

If an old proverb is to be believed, the war did not encourage an approach to godliness, for soap was a commodity that was rationed. Shaving soap was exempt, so some women bought that.

Eggs were an " allocation," on the basis of one a month. There were months when not even the one egg made an appearance. In consequence, many housewives became poultry keepers. Lack of experience did not seem to affect their success.

To supplement the official rations there were some unrationed foodstuffs. Where they went puzzled many people, for they were rarely to be had in the shops. Even fresh fish was sometimes practically unobtainable, except for privileged back-door customers, and the humble bloater and kipper became almost forgotten.

Children grew up without knowledge of a banana, and when they did reappear in March, 1946, for children only, some children needed much persuasion to try this novelty. Oranges became an allocation, tomatoes became an allocation. There were times when there wasn't an onion for the kitchen, times when in regard to many things we just had to " do without."

Clothes rationing was so severe that two major articles for the wardrobe could not be bought in a year. A man's suit needed 26 coupons, which were more than were available in the first rationing, and more than half the year's issue. Other coupon values were :—Overcoat, 18 ; raincoat, 16 or 18 ; shoes, 9 ; pyjamas, 8 ; shirt and two collars, 7. Underclothing, socks, pullovers, gloves, ties, handkerchiefs, all called for coupons ; everything wearable, in fact, except hats.

It was much the same with ladies ; Costumes and coats took 18, raincoats 15, and slacks 8. If they were extravagant with stockings, as many were until they joined the bare-legged brigade, they had to go without other things. Household linen, referred to earlier, was all on coupons, it suffered considerable wear and tear in the course of the six years, and there were no separate coupons for its replacement.

The slogan of the times was " make do and mend." Where people had " made do " with the minimum before clothes rationing came in, as they were officially urged to do, they had to do the maximum of mending afterwards. The wearer of new clothes became conspicuous and to an extent embarrassed. To go shabby became a virtue.

The Red Cross and St. John

THE war efforts of the Luton detachments of the British Red Cross Society and of the Luton Corps of the St. John Ambulance Brigade ran on parallel lines in many respects, while in others they became a joint effort. To many the Red Cross may suggest merely a women's nursing organisation and the St. John Ambulance Brigade a band of men volunteers who, in emergency, are always at hand to help the physically distressed. Yet the intensity of their joint work under war conditions and its far wider ramifications made up a contribution of the highest value to the nation.

*   *   *   *

Members of the men's Red Cross detachment in Luton put in many thousands of hours on voluntary duties during the war. They made it their particular duty to relieve the porters at Luton and Dunstable Hospital during the weekends. Every Saturday night two members reported to the Hospital for this purpose, and from 1939 onwards they put in a total of 8,000 hours. Members also reported to the Hospital when there were raid incidents, day or night, and, following the rocket incident in Biscot Road, they were on duty at the Hospital from the time the casualties arrived until the following morning, assisting in the operating theatre. Four men were also on duty every night for stretcher-bearing and fire-watch in emergency.

Between 1939 and 1945 members put in over 35,000 hours on fire-watch duty, and over 17,000 hours' duty at public events. In addition they did 3,000 hours of A.R.P. duty, plus an average of 2,300 hours a year at the Red Cross surgery.

Cadet duties in 1944 and 1945 alone totalled 13,730 hours.

The war effort of the Women's detachment of the British Red Cross Society really began in 1938, when members helped to fit gas masks during the November crisis. Lectures in anti-gas measures had started early that year, and of the 250 women who attended, 35 became new members of the Red Cross, while others went on to the A.R.P. reserve.

Numbers so increased that the original detachment, becoming unworkable, was divided into three, each with an average of 40 members. They trained for the Civil Nursing Reserve, working 50 hours in Luton and Dunstable Hospital. Some worked in First Aid Posts, on Mobile and Light Mobile units, at the Blood Transfusion Depot, at the Ray Therapy Institute, and in industrial nursing.

In the 1939 'flu epidemic members helped to nurse sick Service personnel in halls and at a sick bay in Brantwood Road. The latter proved too small, so " Uplands," London Road, was taken, and for sixteen months Red Cross officers and members worked there, only giving up when R.A.M.C. personnel took over.

In conjunction with the magnificent work done jointly by the Red Cross and St. John for prisoners of war, a Next-of-Kin Bureau was opened in October, 1942, when so many Luton homes had menfolk in the hands of the Japanese, and news of them was so hard to obtain. Located at the St. John Ambulance headquarters in Barbers Lane, it was open weekly for relatives of prisoners to meet there for information and advice, and it served a very valuable purpose. Its activities did not end until early 1946, when practically all the prisoners who had been freed in the Far-East had come home.

Those from the Continent who were home much earlier had found it a place where they could get some much-needed things at less than the customary price, although they still had to surrender coupons. This form of service was even more valuable for the later arrivals from the Far East, as they had particular need of extra supplies of warm underclothing, etc.

Two parties were also arranged for homecoming war prisoners.

Joint efforts by the Red Cross and the St. John Ambulance Brigade for the Prisoners of War Fund produced about £6,000 from street collections, while collections at local cinemas added another £2,406.

* * * *

The earliest war activities of Luton members of the St. John Ambulance Brigade were of an anticipatory character. As early as 1937, officers from Luton were specially trained at the London headquarters to become instructors in air raid and anti-gas precautions. This was followed by two years of intensive training of large numbers of A.R.P. volunteers and of the general public, both in the town and in the large works, in first-aid and anti-gas treatment.

Brigade members were appointed official instructors in all branches of the Casualty and Ambulance services, and assisted in training air wardens, the police, and the Home Guard. When the Luton A.R.P. Service was formed, all members of the Brigade immediately volunteered for service in one form or another, and from the start of the war the first-aid posts and stations were largely manned by them.

In the first-aid parties the men rendered valuable service during the bombing of Luton in 1940 and 1941. Later these parties were combined with the Rescue Service, and Brigade members continued regular stand-by duties throughout the war, attending all incidents. Certificates of merit were presented to two members in recognition of specially meritorious service at the last incident of all, when a rocket did such damage in Biscot Road. About 130 members were attached to the rescue parties in 1943-44, several holding principal executive positions.

Stretcher-bearer parties provided for Luton and Dunstable Hospital not only served during bombing incidents, but also carried out a regular rota of orderly duties.

In spite of the large amount of time taken up by their Civil Defence duties, normal duties were not neglected. Members continued their

ABOVE: *Dame Beryl Oliver, D.B.E., R.R.C., who was in charge of Red Cross personnel, inspecting local V.A.D.'s during her visit to Luton on January 10th, 1943.*

BELOW: *Lady Louis Mountbatten, Lady Superintendent in charge of the Nursing Divisions of the St. John Ambulance Brigade, inspecting members of a Luton unit during the same month.*

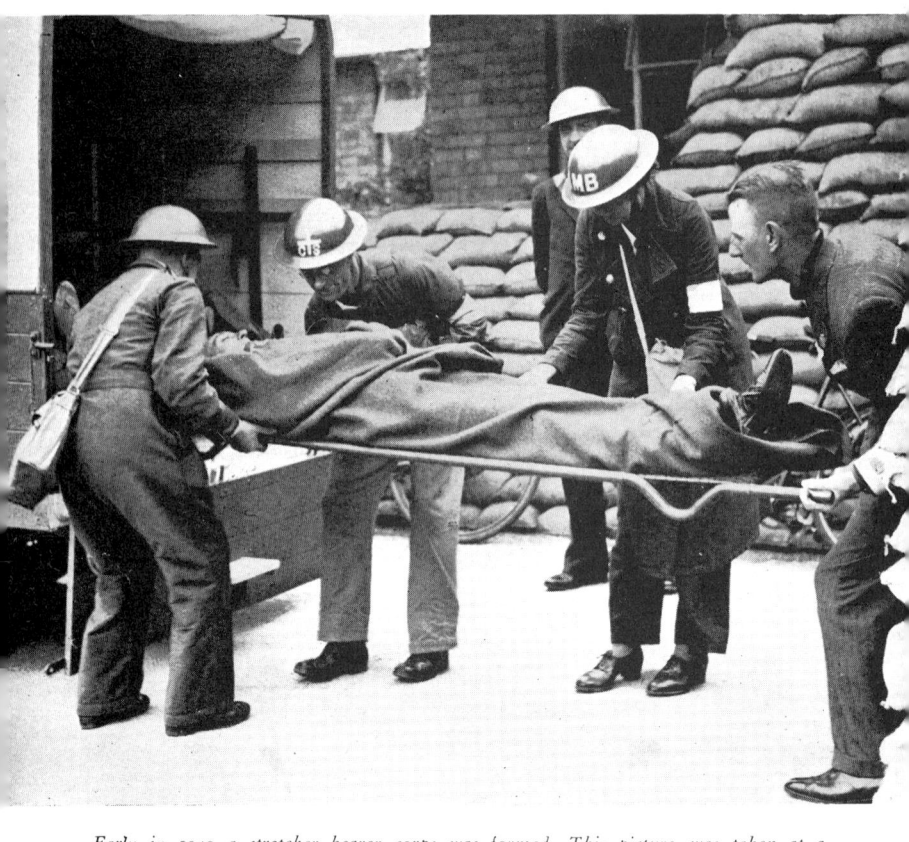

Early in 1940 *a stretcher bearer corps was formed. This picture was taken at a practice, but they were later called upon to carry out the real thing when bombs began to fall on the town.*

attendance at cinemas—a particularly important service during the raid periods—at football matches, sports meetings, and the Open Air Pool. They were always on duty where there was any big public assembly, and the Holidays-at-Home seasons created extra duties. All this was carried on despite the fact that mobilisation in September, 1939, had taken away those members who were in the Military Hospital Reserve or the Royal Naval Sick Berth Reserve.

Figures of the wartime growth of the Brigade are illuminating. In 1939 there were four ambulance (men's) divisions in Luton. These were combined in 1941, together with one nursing division and two cadet divisions, to form the Luton Corps. Since then, and in spite of the call-up of men for the Services, the Corps has continued to grow. Now there are eight ambulance divisions, four nursing divisions, and six cadet divisions—plus an independent Corps at Vauxhall Motors, Ltd.

All the activities connected with Civil Defence were continued until the Stand Down, and the services of the Brigade in that connection were so well appreciated that two trophies originally presented for competition among A.R.P. personnel have been passed on to the Brigade for their peacetime competitions. The Burgoyne Trophy will in future be a stimulus for the ambulance divisions, and the Pakes Cup for the nursing divisions.

*   *   *   *

The nursing personnel also found the war years a period of great activity, which was reflected in membership. At the beginning of 1939 there was one division with 44 members. At the end of the war there were four divisions with a total strength of 108, peak membership having been 140 in 1944.

Many women in local factories were trained in first-aid, and some increased their knowledge by attending lectures on home nursing and A.R.P. Certificates awarded to women candidates included 505 Senior First Aid, 262 Senior Home Nursing, and 66 A.R.P. St. John instructors gave 110 lectures on first-aid to W.V.S. members alone, and as a result of the interest aroused several members of the W.V.S. joined the Brigade.

During 1939 and 1940 many members trained at Luton and Dunstable Hospital for the expected emergency. This enabled a rota to be on call for bomb incidents, day and night, so that in their special capacity they could render service as valuable as the men's section were trained to render. Later a similar rota was formed for St. Mary's Hospital, and members continue to supplement the nursing service at both hospitals in the evenings and on Sundays.

Women members of St. John were attached to all first-aid posts during the whole of the war, some on full-time work, but the majority as part-time volunteers. In many cases they also staffed factory first-aid posts. Like the men, they also still carried on their peacetime activities, attending cinemas on busy evenings, doing duty at the

299

Swimming Pool in the season, establishing first-aid posts for all big public events and during the Holidays-at-Home seasons, while during the VE and VJ-Day celebrations, posts were maintained at the Electricity Showrooms and at Wardown Park throughout each day and night.

* * * *

Although, in view of the operations of the Luton Nursing Association, and the fact that in an industrial town few members are available until the evening, it is not possible to establish in Luton the Nursing Aid Scheme which is found of much value in some places, the voluntary worker of the St. John Ambulance Brigade still goes on. The Medical Comforts Depot in Barbers Lane is still open three times a week to issue comforts in case of illness, the articles there made available having been in great demand during the period when there was such an evacuation from London to Luton. Training classes for recruits are another continuing activity.

* * * *

In addition to the good war work done by Luton members of the Red Cross and of the St. John Ambulance Brigade, as separate organisations and jointly, Luton people can also feel justifiably proud of what they themselves did for the Duke of Gloucester's Red Cross and St. John Appeal.

Principally through what was known as the Penny-a-Week Fund although few gave the minimum and many willingly doubled their regular contributions when D-Day made even greater liabilities probable, an original collection of £28 in the first month was developed until by the end of 1944 it was over £1,000 a month.

In January, 1945, the £50,000 mark having been passed, there was a special celebration. To this came Lord Iliffe, chairman of the Appeal. He considered it " a wonderful success," and probably a record for the country on a population basis, as it represented over a penny a week from everybody, including infants.

It was emphasised by Lady Keens, the then Mayor, that the £50,000 had been raised without deduction of a penny for expenses, and acknowledgment was made of the great help received from the schools, and particularly the elementary schools.

That celebration was not to be the end of things, but a spur to further effort. In fact, £70,000 by the end of the year was regarded as practicable, the £3,000 of the first year having been quadrupled in 1944. However, the sudden ending of the world war resulted in the appeal being closed in August, 1945, and the Luton effort ended with its pennies having totalled £65,000.

They Went to War

IT is officially estimated that by the time the war ended 12,000 Luton men and women had joined the Services. There would have been 12,001, but one man who received his calling-up papers for September 22nd, 1939, and duly reported to Kempston Barracks as directed, was sent home again. The military authorities did not regard him as likely to make a useful soldier . . . he was 86.

From the days when the British Expeditionary Force went to France until the end of the war with the Japanese, Luton men were fighting on and under the sea, in the air, and on every land front. For an inland town Luton seemed to have an extraordinary number of young men with a preference for the sea. They chose it even before the R.A.F., numerous as were the volunteers for the latter.

The war was an epic of desperate adventure. Convoys to Russia battled their way through the bitter gloom of the Arctic night. Tankers and food ships ran the gauntlet of U-boats in tropic waters. Ceaseless patrols kept watch and ward over the drear Antarctic wastes. With them all were Luton men.

Hitler's Fortress of Europe stood menacing behind seeming impregnable ramparts while patient fearless men were probing, ever probing for the weaknesses they knew were there. Snakes stirred in the hot foetid slime of the insect ridden Burmese jungle. The merciless sun beat down in brassy waves of heat on the long road from Alamein to Tunisia. Luton men were there.

High in the black night air, penetrating deeper and ever deeper into the Third Reich were the bomber aircrews of the R.A.F. Luton men were with them too.

These men, trained in a new technique of war, proved themselves possessed of all the skill and resource needed to combat the obstacles they had to overcome. Some who were away in lonely outposts like Iceland, the Faroes, and the Azores, even if their contribution was less spectacular, were nevertheless playing an essential role in the master strategy which led surely, if more slowly than could have been desired, to the ultimate goal.

Losses from a smaller Luton, in the four-and-a-half-years of the 1914-18 war, are commemorated by 1,285 names on the Memorial which stands in front of the Town Hall. The total for the six years of the Second World War was much smaller, and, on the whole, Luton men and women came through those six years with extreme good fortune.

*   *   *   *

Two months before war broke out a new militia was brought into being. It was really the beginning of general conscription, but it did not start as such. It was to be a preparatory step in the training of young men, and it began with the compulsory registration, under the Military Training Act, of the 20-year-olds. The date fixed for the first registration was Saturday, June 3rd, 1939, and it was announced that after June 2nd no one in that category could join the Territorials.

This did more to stimulate local recruiting for the Territorials than all the propaganda of the between-war years. Many young men made certain of getting into the Territorial unit of their choice while they could, rather than chance where they would be sent after registration. The first batch of those who did register was called up for training on July 15th, 1939, and Luton men were among the first to report at the depot of the County Regiment at Kempston.

Whether men had enrolled in the Territorials, or were compulsorily registered for the new militia, in fact made very little difference two months later. Before the second batch was due to register for the Militia in the October, the Territorials were on a war footing . . . active participants in a struggle which was to prove for this country the longest within living memory.

In due course the Military Training Act was succeeded by National Service Acts. Men of more and more mature years were brought in as also were the youngsters as they reached Service age. Eventually, also, they conscripted women.

*   *   *   *

After the first batch of Militia had reported for training, the reservists were the next to be on their way. They were recalled from their peace-time occupations when war, though not declared, was considered inevitable. The Territorials were mobilised, although this did not necessarily mean that they all went off immediately.

The Territorials of 1939 were somewhat different from those who left Luton in August, 1914. Then they were the 5th Bedfords, a company of Royal Engineers, and the Eastern Mounted Brigade Field Ambulance, R.A.M.C. They all took part in the Gallipoli adventure, and afterwards in the successful Palestine campaign.

When, after that war, the Territorial Force was re-established as the Territorial Army, Luton was again a base for the 5th Bedfords and an R.E. Company, but the R.A.M.C. unit ceased to exist. Instead, there was a battery of Field Artillery. Yeomanry, as a cavalry force, were deemed to have had their day, the Bedfordshire Yeomanry were transformed into the 105th (Beds. Yeo.) Brigade, R.F.A., and Luton, which in earlier years had provided only a few men for the Dunstable Troop of the Yeomanry, produced the 420th Battery. Other changes followed when, in a complete re-organisation, the Royal Horse Artillery, Royal Field Artillery, and Royal Garrison Artillery, had to abandon their separate identities and become just Royal Artillery. A somewhat anomalous result was the creation of Artillery Regiments within the Regiment. To this end batteries were combined, and, when the Luton battery went off to war it went, not as a battery, but, in conjunction with the Dunstable battery, as a Field Regiment of Artillery.

This, however, was not the only respect in which the 1939 Territorials differed from those of 1914. Under Mr. Hore-Belisha's scheme for the expansion of the Territorial Army, the 5th Bedfords had expanded into the 5th and 6th, the 5th being allotted the northern half of the county, and the 6th the south. Similarly, the 249th Field Coy. R.E., had the 289th Field Park Coy. as offshoot. There was also an R.A.S.C. Coy., only a few months old when the war started. There was a not-much-older company of W.A.T.S., later to become just A.T.S. It was one of the first companies of women Territorials in the country.

All these were units, but they were not all. There was also a preliminary training centre for the R.A.F.V.R., whence Luton men, with some training as pilots, air gunners, observers, and navigators were gradually absorbed into squadrons, and only as individuals could afterwards be traced. Many of them became very successful members of aircrews, and as such collected a substantial number of decorations. They became scattered all over the world. Of some, alas, their story ended when an " aircraft did not return."

* * * *

The war history of the units which went away as units varied very considerably. They did not even remain in the same higher formation. For instance, the Artillery went to Singapore. Other Luton units did not, but the 5th Bedfords, who had the sticky job at Gallipoli in the previous war, also landed into the Singapore fiasco. If the fortunes of the Artillery and the 5th Bedfords, whose subsequent experiences were so terrible, are therefore reviewed as one, the general story may also be told of many other Luton men who, having originally joined the Bedfords, found themselves transferred to other infantry battalions brigaded with the Bedfords—the Royal Norfolks, Suffolks, and Cambridgeshires. They all went through the same preliminary of ranging up and down the country, combining defence with further training. When they embarked for the Far East, they all went in convoy, by a route which took them right across the Atlantic on the way to the Cape, they had a brief break in India, then on to Singapore where they all landed when matters had become hopeless.

Orders to go abroad as part of the 18th Division were received on September 24th, 1941, and they sailed from Liverpool on October 29th. First port of call was Halifax, Nova Scotia, the next Port of Spain, Trinidad ; then on to the Cape, for a three-days' shore break and a taste of South Africa's boundless hospitality. It was believed, and apparently correctly at the time, that they were bound for the Middle East, but plans must have undergone a sudden change, for the next stop was Bombay. Then Singapore, too late for other than a brief part in a battle which was already lost, too late for everything except years of terrible experience and endurance as prisoners of the Japanese.

The 5th Bedfords were the first to land. They reached Singapore on January 29th, 1942, and when the order to cease fire was given on

February 15th, many in the battalion had not even seen a Japanese soldier. This was because the battalion was split up after arrival, to meet the urgencies of various local situations. It was understood that they would reassemble later and go into action as a battalion, but that time never arrived. There were only two brigades of fresh troops. These two brigades, with units split up, and further handicapped by always meeting tired troops who were being driven back and back by an enemy who knew everything about jungle warfare and camouflage, could do very little. The only consolation was that in the fighting in which some were permitted to engage the casualties were very few. The major casualties were to come in those grim years while they were prisoners.

The Artillery fared no better. Major C. H. B. Grotrian, who commanded the Luton Battery until he left for other duty, was subsequently killed in action in Burma. Major W. H. Merry, who commanded at Dunstable, was killed in the fighting at Singapore while endeavouring to reorganise some other troops who were in a bad way. The maps available for the Gunners were very unreliable. The Gunners did their best—that was all they could do—before they, like the 5th Bedfords, were driven off into the years of captivity.

*   *   *   *

After Singapore was all over, and formal official notification had been received by relatives that their men were " missing," months passed without news. Then came brief official notification that men were prisoners. It was April, 1943, when this news began to filter through and much later before the men themselves were allowed to send printed cards. These cards contained very cheering messages, the general tenour being that everything was as it should be, that they were working for pay, and that there was no cause for any anxiety. Relatives, however, were advised not to put too much faith in these statements. Evidently there was reason for the authorities to believe that conditions in the prison camps were anything but what they should be, and although there was an apparent official desire not to cause despondency, there was still the suggestion that any cheerful messages from prison camps, and particularly those in Malaya and Siam, should be taken with reserve.

Later revelations proved only too fully how bad things really were. The conditions under which prisoners had to live and work in the jungle caused far more casualties than were sustained in the fighting, and the men who managed to survive had some grisly stories to tell. The real fate of some could only be ascertained, or assumed, when there had been searching investigations after the war with Japan had ended. The lot of the prisoners was made still worse by the prolonged refusal of the Japanese to let Red Cross relief workers have access to the camps, either to provide comforts or investigate conditions, and the prisoners, in addition to having to wait an almost unbearable time for their first mail from home, were also denied those things which helped to make life bearable in the prison camps of Germany. Their ultimate release, too, was longer deferred.

Of what they suffered in the meantime there are innumerable stories. It will be sufficient to give one or two as typical. Here is what a young officer of the 5th Bedfords said when he came home :—

" There were bad periods—as bad as they could be—especially when the big push to build the Siam-Burma railway was nearing the climax. The Japanese policy was summed up in a remark I heard from one Japanese area commandant to whom protests had been made. He said, ' If prisoners working on this railway die, it does not matter. There are still thousands more to take their place.'

" Prisoners at that time were pushed beyond the limit of endurance, and no humanitarian considerations were allowed to interfere with the progress of the railway. Sick prisoners were evacuated to camps where conditions and food were a bit better, and under the care of Allied doctors who were among the prisoners, and who did magnificent work under terrible conditions, many of the sick men recovered their health, only to lose it again when sent back for a further period of forced labour."

A Luton Gunner sergeant was able to keep a copy of an order issued at another camp by a new commandant, one of those later charged with atrocities. It was a camp of ill-fame, and the effect of the order was that prisoners only continued to live at the goodwill of their captors, that ill-health was really their own fault, and therefore no excuse for not doing enough work. The day after this order was issued 14 men died from malnutrition. That day's diet consisted of half-a-pint of " rice pap ", half-a-pint of rice with a bit of dried fish, and another half-a-pint of rice with pumpkin water. On this diet men had to work from 6 a.m. till 4 a.m. next day. At another camp where this sergeant spent some time there was a list of things for which prisoners could be shot. No. 1 on the list was " Man who pretends to be sick and does not work." Many were sick unto death. There was no need to shoot them. In fact, of about 650 gunners of this Regiment alone taken prisoner, 251 died in captivity.

These were the experiences not alone of men in the two units specifically mentioned, but shared commonly by men of all arms whose fate it was to be prisoners of the Japanese, and while those who had to work on the construction of the " Death Railway " fared worst of all, there were none who escaped grievous treatment. Many who lived to be released were in such pitiable plight that they could only be brought home by easy stages, and then had to go into hospital. Even those who were in better shape had to be safeguarded against themselves on the homeward journey, lest the ample food should do them harm. There were few who had not lost many stones in weight. A strange yellowness of countenance had not disappeared on the journey. Only too often men gave the impression that they were still in fear and afraid to express their thoughts. Pausing in the middle of some-

U

thing they were saying, they would lose the thread entirely, and be unable to continue.

The authorities recognised that these men had suffered even more than those who had been prisoners in Europe, and merited special consideration. Because of this, when their home-coming leave had expired they were all automatically demobilised, whereas prisoners from Europe who had returned earlier had to rejoin their units until their due demobilisation date, even though their active service was over. There were some who after return to this country died in hospital from the effects of their treatment in their jungle prisons. Some were a long time in recovering their health sufficiently to be able to resume their normal occupations. It is good to be able to say that there were some who appeared to make a quick recovery, but time alone will show to what extent they have been prematurely aged by their three-and-a-half-years in the hands of the Japanese.

Tribute to the 5th Bedfords who had returned was paid at a county gathering at Bedford on December 16th, 1945. The survivors paraded under their commanding officer, Lieut.-Col. D. R. Thomas, O.B.E., M.C., and marched through crowded streets to St. Paul's Church, opposite the Town Hall, for a memorial and thanksgiving service. The church was packed, and the service was relayed to a crowd outside. The service was followed by a march past, the Lord Lieutenant, Lt.-Col. D. C. Part, O.B.E., taking the salute. With him were the Mayors of all three boroughs in the county, Bedford, Luton and Dunstable, General Sir Henry Jackson, Colonel of the Regiment, and many high military officers. Two returned prisoners who had each lost a leg were provided with special seats on the dais.

For the Artillery a similar service was held at Dunstable Priory Church on Saturday, January 12th, 1946. The men paraded under their Commanding Officer, Col. S. C. Harris, and marched to church from Grove House Gardens through flag decorated streets. They came principally from Luton, Dunstable and Leighton Buzzard, and all the local authorities in the area were well represented in the congregation. In the subsequent march past the salute was taken by Major-General C. W. Norman, C.B.E., Commanding the East Central District, who, with the civic heads of Luton, Dunstable and Leighton Buzzard, was among the principal guests at a reunion dinner in the evening.

*   *   *   *

While the Field Regiment of Artillery was training for their Far East adventure, a Heavy Regiment, which was a development in the northern part of the county as part of the expansion of the Territorial Force, went to France with the B.E.F. Those who got back from Dunkirk were for a long time scattered on coastal defence duty. From coastal artillery it was reconstituted as a Heavy Regiment for the Normandy invasion. It took part in the assault on the Arromanches beaches, in the subsequent attack on Mount Pincon, helped

Taken at Kempston Barracks less than a month after they had been called to the colours . . . in July 1939, these militiamen, many of whom were from Luton, already had a bearing of which the Army could be proud.

Locally stationed troops using the Moor as a training ground.

ABOVE: *Budding pilots of the Luton Town Centre of the Royal Air Force Volunteer Reserve taking instruction on an aircraft compass shortly before the outbreak of hostilities.*

BELOW: *Naval air cadets who later became pilots with the Fleet Air Arm received part of their training at Luton Airport. The instructor is explaining the mechanism of a machine gun.*

*Members of the Sergeant's Mess of the
289th Field Park Company, R.E., during
the training period in East Anglia before
the Company went to Normandy.*

*Some of the men of the 249th Field Coy.,
R.E., Luton, who became Airborne
R.E.'s for the Normandy landing.*

Officers of the 5th Battn., Beds. and Herts. Regiment, then under the command of Lieut. Col. A. D. Gaye, photographed at their last pre-war camp, just before the Battalion was divided in order that the 6th Battn. should be created.

to reduce Falaise, and supported the 43rd Division in the crossing of the Seine. After a period in reserve it supported the Guards' armoured push up the Nijmegen corridor in the attempt to relieve the airborne troops at Arnhem. It was said afterwards by the commander of the 1st Airborne Division that the artillery support was a deciding factor in the survival of the Division for the nine days it spent north of the Rhine.

Other big responsibilities were helping to stem Rundstedt's Ardennes offensive, participation in the 1,000-gun barrage which opened the battle of the Reichswald Forest, and the ultimate attack on the Wesel bridgehead. To take part in the attack on Bremen the regiment covered 160 miles in one day. Hamburg was due for attention, but was declared an open city soon after shelling began. Occupational duties later took the regiment to Brunswick Luneberg, where it was disbanded in April, 1946. Maybe in its reorganised form it had little more association with the county than its name and battery numbers, but it did add one more chapter to the modern history of the Bedford-shire Yeomanry.

*   *   *   *

The 6th Bedfords on formation had as a nucleus the Luton and Dunstable rifle companies of the 5th Battn., and on this foundation recruited to build up a separate unit. They left Luton on November 1st, 1939, for Woodbridge, Suffolk, under their original Commanding Officer, Lieut.-Col. C. H. Miskin, M.C., who had served with the 5th Bedfords in the Gallipoli and Palestine Campaign. At Wood-bridge more recruits were received, and one company went to Bawdsey to do guard duty at a big radio station.

From Woodbridge the Battalion went to Northumberland, where Col. Miskin left the unit, the first of several changes in command. The next move was to Toddington and Winchcombe, Gloucestershire ; where the battalion was held as G.H.Q. reserve, preliminary to being stationed much nearer home at Aylesbury, as War Office reserve. Afterwards it was the East Anglian coast again, for coast defence and other duties. Then came a move to Caterham, where the Battalion took over the Guards' Depot for about seven months. There was still another move to come, to Beckenham, in the London District. The battalion had been brought up to a very high pitch of efficiency, and having been earmarked for independent brigade operations in connection with D-Day, at last had a prospect of going into the fray as a unit. It was therefore a cause of great disappointment to those who had been responsible for building up the battalion into a fine fighting force when a personal representative of the Commander-in-Chief came in July, 1944, with a message of regret that the battalion would have to be split up and used to strengthen battle trained units which were short of reinforcements.

As a result, when the Dorsets won fame in the thick of the fighting at Arnhem, one of their companies was actually "A" Company from

311

the 6th Bedfords, under its original company commander, Major Grafton ; but any credit they won at Arnhem will go down in regimental history as belonging to the Dorsets and not the Bedfords. Such is the fortune of war. Another company went almost in its entirety to the Seaforth Highlanders, and the rest of the battalion was split among about fifteen different units. The officers were similarly scattered, and when the battalion was finally disbanded in August, 1944, there remained only one officer who, with the exception of a period with the 2nd Herts., had been with the 6th Bedfords from beginning to end—Major G. Hickson, a Harpenden man who is with B. Laporte, Ltd., Luton, and who in pre-war days was with the Dunstable company of the 6th. At the time of disbandment he was second-in-command.

From beginning to end the battalion had only two commissioned Quartermasters, Capt. C. H. White, M.B.E., who later went in the same capacity to North Africa and Italy with the 30th Bedfords, and Lieut. C. Richards, who succeeded him. Both returned to Luton on leaving the Service, and both found a peacetime occupation with the same Luton firm.

*　　*　　*　　*

The 249th Field Company, R.E., having shed enough of its surplus personnel to enable the 289th Field Park Company to be formed, went off under Major J. B. Smyth-Wood to Denham, Norfolk, to work on coastal defences. The C.R.E. of the companies in the group was Lieut.-Col. R. Briars, M.C., of Luton, who had previously commanded the 249th Field Company. Lt.-Col. Briars resigned owing to ill-health in 1940, and died at Luton in 1943.

At Denham five members of the company were selected to join a small force which went to Norway on a demolition job. They returned after ten days . . . " job completed."

From Denham the company went on to Morpeth and Ashington, to work on North-East coastal defences, and continued this job from winter quarters at Prudhoe. Then there was a move to Northleach, near Cheltenham, for special training, and participation in the " Bumper " and " Spartan " Army exercises, where they covered much the same ground as the 289th Field Park Company and other units in which they had an interest. They even passed through Harpenden, where they slept one night in the streets. Then they settled again for a time in East Anglia. They were stationed at Bungay, and concerned with the coastal defences of Lowestoft, Oulton Broad, and Thorpeness, where they had to clear the beaches of mines brought ashore by bad weather.

Then the company began to split up for some of the newer forms of warfare. Most of them went for training as Airborne troops. Some went to a Parachute Regiment. Others, generally those whose age was regarded as too high for those two spheres of activity went to Assault Squadrons of R.E.s.

The Airborne people went to Bulford for glider training; the Parachute troops went to Ridgeway, Yorks. to practise jumping. Glider training at Bulford went on until D-Day, when two platoons of the company, as part of the 6th Airborne Division, were the first R.E.'s down at Caen. The other platoons went by sea. They were expected to be back quite soon, to prepare for another operation. In fact, they had three months in Normandy before they came back. The men from the company who went to the parachute Regiment took part in the Arnhem adventure, and when late in 1944 the Germans attempted the Ardennes break the glider people had another job at Nijmegen and on the Maas. They eventually went on into Germany, to Brunswick and Hanover.

In the meantime there had been many other changes in the company. Major Smyth-Wood left for another appointment in 1943. Capt. Wadsworth, who had been second-in-command, left to take command of No. 556 Company at Wallingford. Ultimately the commanding officer was Major W. May, a grandson of the late Sir Walter Kent. Associated with the company from 1939, he had been second-in-command, and finally held a staff appointment in Germany.

*   *   *   *

The 289th Field Park Company, R.E., came into existence as a separate Territorial unit in Luton on September 3rd, 1939. Under the Hore-Belisha scheme for the expansion of the Territorial Army the 249th Field Company had recruited until it was almost 100 per cent. over establishment. On that morning it marched to Pope's Meadow. The 249th Field Company and 289th Field Park Company marched back to the Drill Hall. Curiously enough, it was the offshoot company which was to go through the war as a company, and the parent company which was to be broken up. The first Commanding Officer of the new company was Capt. (later Major) W. H. Wakeham, who had been a subaltern in the 249th Field Company in earlier years, had left Luton in the interim and returned when war was imminent. He was the only original officer of the company to stay until 1943, and when he left he was presented with an inscribed silver salver from all ranks.

The new company spent its first two months in Luton, getting over its teething troubles, and then went to Bury St. Edmunds, where training became more intensive and, under the watchful eye of C.S.M. Charles H. Wilmott, some of the mysteries of explosives and general field engineering were made plain.

Subsequent moves took the company all over England and Wales, and twice into Scotland. On two major Army exercises, " Bumper " and " Spartan ", the company found itself very near Luton ; on other occasions they actually passed through the town, which was very tantalising to the Luton men still in the unit.

Climax to strenuous years of training came on June 6th, 1944, when the company was at Loddon, Norfolk. They had four hours' notice to move, and began a journey which did not end until, through Normandy, Belgium and Holland, they reached Arnsberg, in Germany. In Normandy, with 23rd Bridging Platoon, R.E., attached, they became the " Sappers' Shop " of the 49th (Polar Bear) Division. At the start there were few bridging problems, but after the break-out there were the rivers Vire, Dives and Toques to be crossed, and the demand for Bailey bridging material suddenly assumed enormous proportions.

During the crossing of the Antwerp-Turnhout Canal an enthusiastic " harbouring party " put down signs, " Reserved for 48 " (The company code number) in a cement factory on the far bank. Returning next day, it was discovered that overnight the Germans had re-occupied the factory and captured the unit harbour signs—an event unique in the Divisional R.E.

The advance through Roosendal to Willemstadt brought an additional problem to the Field Park Company. Besides supplying bulldozers and bridging material, numerous craters in the forward area required to be filled or by-passed, and a steady stream of tipping lorries had to be kept filled with sleepers and other material.

During a long stay in Nijmegen the Workshops Platoon did a great work in producing gadgets designed to aid " island warfare." Company records show that they also made over 5,000 signs of various kinds, while their mobile shower baths were a great boon to many units. The Stores Platoon issued 3,500 tons of R.E. stores, while the Bridging Platoon issued 6,720 feet of Bailey Bridge.

The company command had changed several times after Major Wakeham left. C.S.M. Wilmott left in 1940, and was succeeded by C.S.M. J. D. McIlroy, who was a sticker until transferred to the 2nd Army R. E. School in August, 1944. The company ceased to exist on December 20th, 1945, those not then due for demobilisation being transferred to other R.E. units. During the six years of its existence it was a happy company. Its members have many grand memories, and a record of which they can well be proud.

*   *   *   *

The 534th (Ammunition) Company, R.A.S.C., was a Territorial unit which had existed but a few months when it went off from Luton to take part in the war. It was started only in March, 1939, because one of the three existing R.A.S.C. companies in the East Anglian Division which had its headquarters at Barking had been converted into an anti-aircraft unit. Bedfordshire was regarded as the best recruiting ground for the establishment of an entirely new company, Luton as the best spot in the county, and the company was largely built up of men who were in the motor industry or were competent drivers of heavy vehicles. Perhaps this was why, although it was such a new unit, so many of the men in it got into the war very quickly. While other local Territorials were combining coast defence with further training, many of the men in the new R.A.S.C. company found themselves in France with the B.E.F. The company as such became the 4th Division Ammunition Company, and retained that identity at home until the end of 1941. Then it became a Tank Transportation Company, and in this capacity did very good work in North Africa, and subsequently in Italy. Long before that, however, because of the number of drafts the company had provided, and their replacement by a general intake, it had lost practically all the Luton men who joined it on formation, but to the end of hostilities little groups of those originals were still sticking together in some company or other. Some of them will have lasting memories of leaving Dunkirk in the *Lancastria*. They got home. The *Lancastria* did not. If in later days any of the original members of the company looked for their original headquarters in Old Bedford Road, they looked in vain. Badly damaged in an air raid incident, they had to be completely demolished.

*   *   *   *

Members of the Luton Town Centre, R.A.F.V.R., received the call to service on September 1st, 1939. It was a broadcast announcement which also required Navy and Army reservists to rejoin. It was assumed that the Air Volunteers, most of whom held rank as sergeants, would be posted away almost immediately for training. It involved one important decision, to sell the remaining stock of beer in the Sergeant's Mess at 1d. a pint ! The beer was sold, but the Volunteers stayed on.

No. 29 Elementary and Reserve Training School, as it was officially known, came into existence in Luton in August, 1938. Part of a reservist training scheme announced in Parliament two years before, it was one of a number of similar schools formed at civil flying fields throughout the country. The original intention at Luton was to train 100 men. A Town Centre, opened in George Street West, was soon found inadequate, and larger premises were obtained in Bute Street, with ample room at that time for offices, lecture rooms, and a Sergeants' Mess. Most of the ground training was carried on there during the week, volunteers being expected to attend on two evenings for lectures by Service and civilian instructors, under the supervision of the Commandant, Wing-Commander Waller, of Harpenden. At week-ends they went to the Airport for flying training on Miles Magister aircraft, and later on advanced trainers of the Hawker Hart series.

After the Luton School had been open two months there were 25 pilots under training. Some had gone solo and another 40 had passed the Selection Board. Munich put a different complexion on things. During the last few months of 1938 numbers steadily rose, and early in 1939 it was announced that there were no more vacancies for pilot training.

About this time two further categories for air crew were opened, for observers and air-gunners. The Bute Street premises became overcrowded, and a factory in John Street was taken for lectures.

A little later volunteers were called for ground duties in a number of trades. Again the response was good. Week-end training for ground crews was mostly at Henlow Camp, and evening training at the Luton Centre.

In the summer of 1939 the pilots went to " practice camp " at Luton Airport for a fortnight's continuous training, but there were no facilities for other categories.

Following the call to service on September 1st, the Luton volunteers had to report daily. Amid the suspense and anticipation, there was a good deal of drilling in the L.N.E.R. station yard. Only a few of the pilots had uniforms, the rest still wore civilian clothes.

As September drew to a close the first batches were sent to training stations. Some of the pilots went to an Initial Training Wing at Hastings ; observers were posted to Staverton, between Cheltenham and Gloucester. At first the Regulars with whom they had to mix were a little disgruntled at this intrusion into their ranks, but during the testing days of 1940 many were the gaps that had to be filled by " week-end flyers." Although most of the observers, air gunners, and ground crew were rapidly posted away, some pilots had to wait for training facilities, and temporarily returned to their civilian occupations. The Town Centre was still in existence, but the spirit of the " week-end flyers " had departed.

Some of the Luton V.R. ground crew found their way to France before the year was out. They were followed later by a few observers and air gunners. One air gunner from Luton " baled out " twice from his Lysander in the few months before Dunkirk.

By the spring of 1940 a large percentage of the air crew members had joined operational squadrons, and took part directly with the fighters or indirectly with the bombers, in the Battle of Britain. Many of the " week-end flyers " paid the supreme sacrifice or were taken prisoner in this period and the years that followed. Those who were more fortunate carried on. Commissions were granted to the greater number, and a few reached senior rank. Between them they obtained quite a number of decorations.

With the war over, pre-war volunteers have met to talk over old times, but many faces are missing. Now the R.A.F.V.R. is to be born anew, and it is probable that Luton will again be a centre.

*   *   *   *

The 12th Bedfordshire Company, W.A.T.S., was mobilised on September 1st, 1939, and left Luton for Aldershot, where in time it lost its county status, and became just A.T.S. Formed about November, 1938, it was one of the earliest units of its kind—so early, in fact, that the service numbers of members were in the first thousand. When recruiting was started Mrs. R. M. Primett was appointed Junior Commander, the company was given headquarters at the Drill Hall, and for drill attached to the 249th Field Company, R.E. The N.C.O.'s of that company had the unusual job of putting the women through

The men who came back. Men of the 5th Bedfords, survivors of the Singapore calamity celebrated their return from captivity, and remembered those they had left behind, at a thanksgiving and memorial service at St. Paul's Church, Bedford, in December, 1945. Above are some of the officers.

ABOVE : *A section of the men marching to the service.*

BELOW : *Officers and men of the Bedfs. Yeomanry, 148 Field Regiment, R.A., also survivors from the Far East, at the dinner held in their honour at Dunstable Town Hall in January, 1946.*

The Corn Exchange Canteen, one of the two opened for British and Overseas troops in Luton, became a popular rendezvous for serving men and women. Here are some of the voluntary workers preparing for an invasion of hungry souls. At the extreme right is Mrs. Grace Goring, who was the controller from the day the canteen opened in 1940, until the last cup of tea was served in 1946.

their foot drills and marching exercises. Originally it was intended that it should be purely a Luton company, but later Dunstable was added to its recruiting area. When on mobilisation the company went to Aldershot it was attached for duty to the R.A.O.C., and there, in October, 1939, it had the distinction of being the first A.T.S. Company to be inspected by the King. With the expansion of the A.T.S. an increase in the establishment of companies, transfers and the normal wastage of personnel, the company largely lost its Luton associations, but there were some of the Luton originals still with the company till the end of the war.

*　　　*　　　*　　　*

The 1st Bedfords were in Cairo when the war started, but during the autumn they went back to Palestine, which they found quieter than before. There they guarded prisoners taken in General Wavell's advance, but some picked personnel went off to Abyssinia on " hush-hush " jobs. Later these were heard of at Mombasa. In March, 1941, the battalion went to occupy the island of Lemnos, near the entrance to the Dardenelles, to ensure its safety as an R.A.F. base, but with the approach of the Germans to Athens it was withdrawn to Alexandria. Orders to reinforce the Crete garrison having been cancelled just before the fall of that island, the next move was to Syria. There, the Vichy French agreeing to an armistice, they had only one accidental casualty. In October, 1941, orders were received to proceed to " an unknown destination." This proved to be Tobruk. After Tobruk it was Syria again, then India, the Arakan, and finally into the Burmese jungle behind the Japanese lines as part of the famous Chindit Force.

*　　　*　　　*　　　*

The 2nd Bedfords went to France as part of the original B.E.F. After Dunkirk they had a strenuous time training at home for they knew not what. It proved to be the landing in Tunisia. With the North African campaign successfully completed, they took part in the invasion of Italy. After the war in Europe had ended the battalion had to go to Greece to help check internal disorders, and they were still there during the Greek elections of early 1946.

*　　　*　　　*　　　*

The 30th Bedfords, a category unit which originated from the 7th Bedfords, mobilised at Ampthill, and went to North Africa in August, 1942. There they were responsible for train and dump guards. In January, 1945, they crossed to Italy for the same kind of duty, and were eventually disbanded early in 1946. They were one of 10 Bedfordshire battalions which existed during the war years, compared with 21 in the 1914-18 war.

*　　　*　　　*　　　*

The 1st Hertfords spent some time on garrison duty at Gibraltar, during the period when it was feared that the Rock might become a major object of enemy attention, and then went into the Italian campaign, taking part in some of the fiercest fighting in the Gothic Line. The 2nd Hertfords found that their way into battle lay across the Normandy beaches. They eventually reached Palestine.

*　　*　　*　　*

During the six years of war county regiments lost much of their local association, and although men might be Bedfords when they joined as recruits there was no guarantee that they would remain Bedfords. Nor was there any guarantee that they would be Bedfords at all. It depended on what regiment happened to be most in need of new men. This accounted for the presence of a considerable number of Luton men in the Buffs at Malta throughout the blitz. Unfortunately they went afterwards to Leros, and then into captivity. A number of Luton men managed to keep together in an R.A.F. unit commanded by Sqdn.-Leader R. B. Waller, O.B.E., of Luton. With the Eighth Army in ill-fortune and good, they constituted an Air Force Park which, having had experience of moving in retreat, turned and travelled the whole length of the Desert Front, went across to Sicily, were taken from there to Italy in a landing craft which had Lieut. Rex Sanders, of Luton, as one of its two officers, and could claim to be the only Air Force Park established in front of the Army's field guns, which fired over them at Salerno. There were other instances of Luton men keeping together through long periods of service.

Newer fighting formations like the Parachute Regiment and the Commandos naturally attracted many volunteers. It was really surprising how many Luton men " dropped in " at Arnhem during the great adventure of 1944. The technical units which kept the Army moving were also very popular with those who had an engineering training, and a lot of Luton men so qualified found their way into the R.E.M.E. when this organisation was created.

*　　*　　*　　*

One most significant change with the passing of the war years was the fading-out of conscientious objectors. They were numerous in the early stages of the war. The question was raised as to whether they ought to be retained in the service of public authorities. Sometimes their appeals against military service were heard in London, sometimes in Cambridge. A considerable number appealed successfully, although exemption from armed service was usually conditional on service in a non-combatant unit, or working on the land. It is a remarkable fact that nothing was heard of conscientious objectors among the younger classes called up in the latter stages of the war. On the other hand, cases are known of men who, after obtaining exemption, changed their minds after learning of some of the things done in the name of Nazism or Fascism, and threw in their lot with their fellows in the common struggle against these evils.

As registration of women for the Services had not come into operation in the period when the tribunals had to sit most frequently to hear claims to exemption on conscientious grounds, no women appeared before them, and there is no record of Luton having produced a woman objector of Service age.

*   *   *   *

Unlike August, 1914 when almost as soon as the Luton Territorials marched off to their training area in East Anglia the North Midland Division descended on Luton and spread itself over the town and neighbourhood, there was no great friendly invasion of this kind in September, 1939, or afterwards. In 1914 the streets of Luton became parade grounds. Whole battalions were billeted in close proximity. There were whole streets where every house had to take in several soldiers. There were not enough open spaces for their drills. Sergeant-majors exercised their lungs in public, to the great edification, among others, of some small boys who became mascots, complete with uniform, and who in the latest war may themselves have become sergeant-majors.

But if there was no such wholesale invasion by troops who would later apply Luton place-names to trenches they dug on the battlefields of France, Luton nevertheless had some interesting Service visitors. In the early days of the war a Tank Regiment was the most notable. The men in it regarded themselves as a grade above soldiers. They were technicians. Their tanks may not have been very good, for tanks had not then become commonplace, but the men prided themselves on their job, and made many friends before they went to the Far East. Those in command exercised a thoughtfulness in one direction which might well have been shown by others, but wasn't. If a pavement had to be crossed from parking ground to highway, it was not permissible to leave the pavement muddy, no matter what the weather. The pavement was cleaned immediately, and again when the tanks had returned from an exercise. This example was not followed by other units which used Pope's Meadow, and often left that part of Old Bedford Road in a terrible mess.

Throughout the war period quite a variety of units came and went. For a long time Luton accommodated a big R.A.S.C. training school. The personnel of this were the most permanent visitors of their time. Later a Smoke Company of the Pioneer Corps stayed a long time, but with the disappearance of the smoke canisters they also disappeared. There was a considerable period when a Bomb Disposal Company went every day from Luton on their dangerous jobs. The Fleet Air Arm trained at the Airport until it was decided to transfer this activity to Cheshire, and so make the Airport available as an Air Transport Auxiliary Centre. There was a ring of searchlight batteries in and round the town, but these seemed to change periodically. Some Defiants were stationed at the Airport for a time, although it seemed a toss-up whether at night they scared off or attracted enemy planes. They moved on, as they had done several times before they came here, but even after they had gone night fighters from somewhere seemed to

321

v

be in the air over Luton just as quickly after the sirens had sounded. Apart from light machine guns on the roofs of some factories, that was pretty much the extent of Luton's opposition to air attack.

Usually there were one or two infantry battalions quartered in the outer areas of the town, generally using unoccupied houses as billets, the Army Fire Service had a post here for some time, and after the creation of the R.E.M.E. Luton was one of the headquarters of this new organisation. There was also an A.T.S. headquarters, one reason why, in addition to the familiar " Redcaps," one section of which kept a particular eye on the driving on military vehicles, it became a fairly common sight to see A.T.S. " Redcaps " patrolling in pairs.

The approach of D-Day, however, brought some of Luton's most interesting Service visitors. Tank transporters, all " waterproofed," almost blocked some of the streets. Some had taken part in earlier landings. In due course most of them disappeared. They were followed by a new lot of transporters each carrying a " Buffalo "— apparently a sky-blue combination of turretless tank and paddle boat. They in turn went away, to ferry troops across the Seine, the Rhine, and many lesser rivers. Their special tracks acted as paddle wheels while waterborne, and then served to climb out of the water and advance on land, no matter how marshy the ground was.

For D-Day, also, Luton was the assembly point of the first Field General Hospital to land in Normandy. Many of the personnel had already seen service in North Africa or Italy. Their strength was made up by others to whom landing on a hostile coast was to be a new experience. The doctors were not conspicuous. The nursing sisters were, in the grey and scarlet which in the field gives place to khaki battle dress. They landed in Normandy. Later a similar party left Luton for Burma.

There were no such picturesque visitors in the streets afterwards. Small parties of troops continued to come to one or other of the technical training schools, although the Salvage Training School had vanished, and about the only distinguishing feature of uniforms subsequently seen was a black " flash " which indicated, as did their goat mascot, that the unit was one which had its normal headquarters in the Principality.

*   *   *   *

Wherever there were troops there had to be canteens. Voluntary canteens at the Electricity Showrooms and the Corn Exchange were very popular with the troops stationed in and around Luton. They were originated by the late Alderman C. C. Dillingham. In his forceful way he told some of his friends that they would help him, and relieved them of some of the necessary capital. The canteens started in a modest way, developed as time went on, and although their standard of comfort was never very luxurious, the ladies in charge at least made their patrons feel very welcome. After Ald. Dillingham's death the canteens became the responsibility of a welfare committee.

Accommodation, heat and light were provided free by the Town Council, choirs, orchestras, concert parties and individual artistes attended from time to time to entertain the troops, and things served over the counter were mostly sold at cost. Cups of tea were about the only source of a small profit, but even from this margin it was found possible to do something to improve the lot of the men and women at searchlight stations round the town.

Started in 1940, the canteen at the Electricity Showroom was originally in charge of Mrs. C. C. Dillingham, with Mrs. G. Wistow Walker as deputy. When Mrs. Dillingham retired Mrs. Walker became Controller, and, with Mr. R. Collier as deputy, carried on the canteen until it was closed at Christmas, 1945. At the Corn Exchange, Mrs. Grace Goring was Controller throughout, with Mrs. Blake as deputy, and when this canteen closed on March 31st, 1946, Mrs. Goring had not missed one night's attendance in six years.

An interesting sidelight on this canteen which was subsequently given was that takings during the six years totalled £19,000. That represented quite a lot of work by the voluntary staff, some of whom were with Mrs. Goring from start to finish. It was largely the product of serving two million cups of tea.

*   *   *   *

A welcome, though unofficial, form of welfare work was undertaken by readers of *The Luton News* through what was known as the " Warm Greetings Fund." This was started in the first winter of the war, when opposing armies looked at one another but did not fight. A Luton artillery sergeant in France wrote asking whether something could be done to make the winter a little brighter and more bearable for his men. Woollies and things like that were wanted. They were sent, and that was why it was called the " Warm Greetings Fund." In those days woollen comforts were easy to obtain. Wool was not then on coupons. Some good people quickly formed themselves into knitting circles, bought their own wool, and kept the fund supplied with pullovers, Balaclava helmets, scarves, gloves, socks, etc. Little money was necessary at that time, except to pay the postage on the parcels, but money also came along. It made possible the inclusion of other acceptable things, then also easily obtainable. They were sent not only to local men in France, but to those in the Navy, at isolated air stations, and anywhere where Luton men were known to be serving. In that first winter, too, a bulk gift was sent to France for the 2nd Bedfords. Even wireless sets, sports equipment, musical instruments, and a variety of other bulky things were sent. In those days they could be had for the asking.

Similarly, if a searchlight battery near Luton wanted something, the need had only to be mentioned. What was wanted came along or, if heavy, could be fetched. Such gifts ran to armchairs, tables, china, and even pianos.

In later days, when the North African desert was the principal scene of fighting, it was possible to send some things which would otherwise have been quite unobtainable by the recipients, or would have involved paying a fantastic price. And always, whatever else was sent, there was a demand for books. As the war dragged on and life became more austere, the character of the gifts which could be sent had to change somewhat. A repetition of the gift of thousands of cigarettes by the wholesale tobacconists of Luton as a body could not be expected. Many other things which had regularly been bought became scarce in the shops, but there were some good trade friends who saw that when the things which were most wanted were available, those responsible for running the fund had first opportunity to buy. The money was always there. Except in the early days that was never a problem. In some places there were regular collections. Some individuals sent regular monthly contributions. Towards the end it was possible to announce that, with the end actually in sight, no more money would be needed, there being ample already in hand to carry on right to the end of 1945.

In the closing stages recipients in home units generally received a money gift, to apply as they thought fit, and postage stamps. Those abroad still received a parcel of articles which were certain to be acceptable, plus a postal order. It was found that the parcels were appreciated all the more because they were unexpected. They made men feel that, although far from home, they were by no means forgotten.

In all, 5,328 men and women from Luton who were in the Services received individual gifts, quite apart from what was done for units.

The Eagle's Brood

IT was our American friends who discovered Luton as a holiday resort.

Some may question the level of intelligence which induced them to choose Luton ; but they had their reasons, and the better the type of American, the better his reasons. They came, and came again.

It began quite early. They were still a long way from the war. The day of mass raids by Liberators and Flying Fortresses had yet to come. The same camp routine, the same faces day after day, irked them. In time everybody on the camp knew everybody else. They did the same things, at work or during their leisure. They spoke the same language.

When they had 48 hours' leave, their impulse was to get clear of camp. Who first discovered Luton we shall never know, but the word must have gone round quickly that in Luton there were sociable and hospitable people.   More and more came.

Take a look at three typical G.I.'s.   Late one evening they arrived from the Midlands, strangers in a blacked-out town.   They found hotel accommodation a problem they hadn't expected, but they dug in somewhere quickly enough to have a good time at a dance.   They were at a dance the second night.

The third night they absolutely had to leave by a train about 9.30, or invite trouble at camp.   Uncertain where the " Depot " was in the blackness, they hung on till practically the last minute, the most staid member of the trio keeping an anxious eye on the clock.   They accepted on trust an absolute stranger's offer to deliver them at the station in time.   They caught their train with a minute to spare. They left, loud in praise of the good time they had had, and full of assurances that Luton would see them again.

There were many such parties.   They didn't all want London all the time.   They were not all from the big cities of the West.   They wanted to see something less artificial, something more representative of the real folk of this England, even if they didn't quite understand them.   So they came.   Not many Luton people would choose to travel such distances to spend a week-end at a strange place which to them had no more claim than Luton to be a holiday resort.

Most of our visitors, of course, belonged to the U.S. Army Air Force.   Not all were flying officers or even top-sergeants.   Many were just technical personnel.   Some were very smart.   Some, less smart, made us wonder how they managed in their own wide open spaces, with no buildings to prop up.

" Ah," we were told, " they are not the pick of the U.S. Army. They are draftees.   The regulars, the really smart men, are all out in the Pacific."   And that dictum we had to accept.

*   *   *   *

Some could have been put into British Service dress, and been mistaken for the real thing.   Others, no matter what their dress, would still have shown that their forbears originated from Middle Europe, and that not many generations ago.   Of the coloured element Luton saw little except grinning black faces and white teeth as their owners drove convoys of trucks through the town.

All G.I.'s seemed well provided with money.   They would sometimes deny this, and stress that they were only allowed to draw part of their authorised pay.   But they seemed able to buy everything they and their lady friends wanted if it was on sale.   Perhaps they were sometimes a little too greedy and insistent, but they were a long way from home.

What was particularly noticeable was the change some of these men underwent through staying here a year or two.   Of the first who arrived, many were very akin to the first American arrivals on the Continent in the previous war.   Then they arrived full of assurance that they were the outfit who could finish the job in a twinkling. They were not at all pleased when they found themselves attached to British units " for instruction." They found that war as it was then being waged was a job they had to learn anew, from people who really did know.

Similarly, a good many arrived this time, full of the same assurance. They remained to realise that in this country we knew something, at least, about the job, having managed to stay in the fight quite a long time on our own. Then these particular visitors became much less vocal, and really human.

*   *   *   *

To the leave men, of course, there were added those stationed at airfields not far from the town. They rolled in at night, in fleets of buses and Service trucks. They were going to have a gayer night than camp offered.

But some of the most interesting were those who came for reasons of family sentiment.

There was the man who came from the far North, with only a few hours to spend here . . . When he got back home he wanted to be able to talk to his father about Luton. First he had to find Bute Street, and see whether the place where his father once worked still existed. If not, he wanted to be able to tell father why, and what else had happened in Bute Street. He wanted to know about other places which his father would recognise if he could re-visit the town of his birth ; if they had gone, he wanted to know why, and what had taken their places.

His was a well-known Luton name, and he was told where he might find some probable relatives. But the train service did not permit. Provided with pictures of the Luton his father would remember, he went back to the North rejoicing.

*   *   *   *

The one main grouse of those able to stay awhile was that their own authorities had not provided a hostel. Eventually the American Red Cross did establish a club in George Street, with Miss Isobel Lee in charge, but this was not until June, 1944. The Donut Club became very popular—may it be suggested that it was because it was so largely staffed by Luton ladies ? But it did not cater for the bed and breakfast so many wanted. Americans, in fact, often slept in the air raid tunnels when they could find no better accommodation. The club did not open until 10 a.m., and they badly felt the need of a clean-up before that. The meal question was not so difficult, if they were content with one of the many cafés which sprang up in Luton during the war years.

True, a number of people set out to cash in on this need, and some gave the Americans a very square deal. Others, if the comments of the Americans themselves were well-founded, seemed to aim at getting the most cash for the minimum they could be induced to

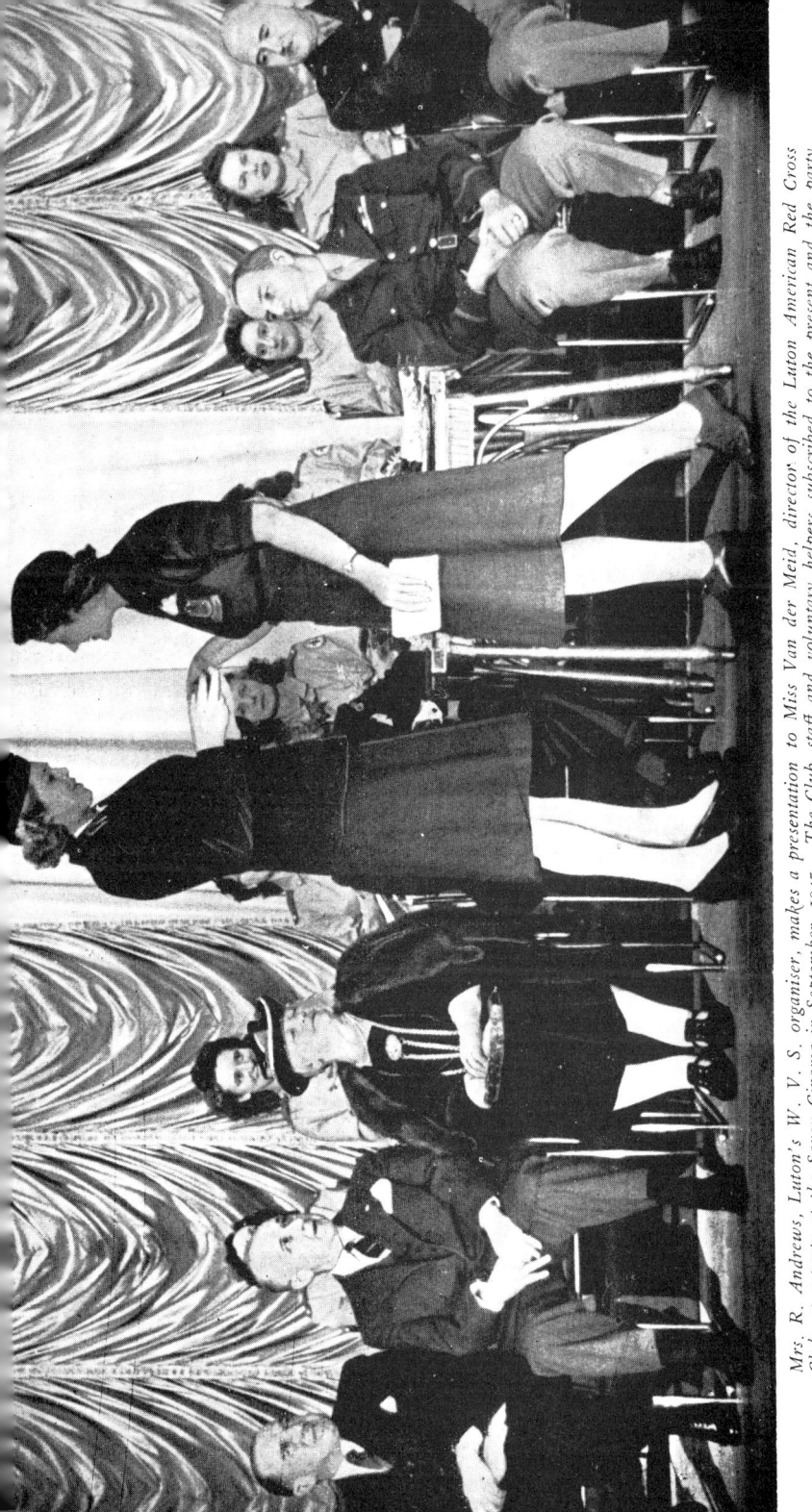

Mrs. R. Andrews, Luton's W. V. S. organiser, makes a presentation to Miss Van der Meid, director of the Luton American Red Cross Club, at a party at the Savoy Cinema in September, 1945. The Club staff and voluntary helpers subscribed to the present and the party was given by the American Red Cross and United States Army, as an expression of thanks to the staff, and to the people of Luton for their hospitality to American Servicemen.

LEFT: *An American host pours the lemonade at a party at the American Red Cross Club, Luton. Nearly one hundred children who had not been able to attend any party during the season were entertained.*

ABOVE: *Some of the guests enjoy a doughnut at the American Red Cross Club, Luton, when an "Open Day" was held on November 23rd, 1944 . . . America's Thanksgiving Day. In the centre of the picture is Miss Isobel Lee, the first Director, with Mrs. Venniker, in charge of local voluntary helpers, and Mrs. M. Plasom, staff assistant, on her right.*

RIGHT: *British wives of American serving men with their babies, at a Baby Show held in the Club, shortly before it closed.*

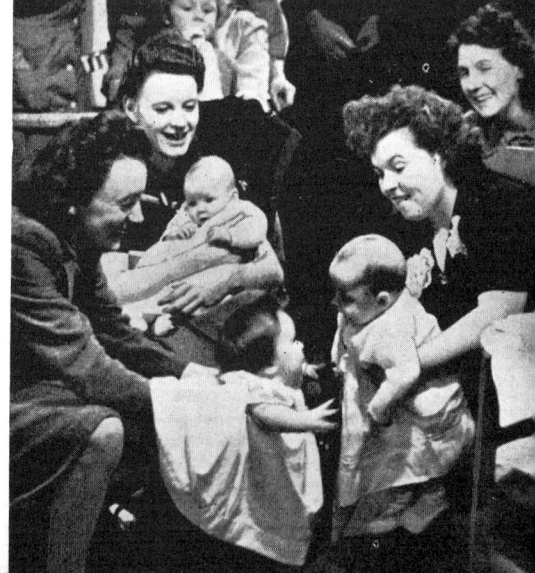

ABOVE: *Service with a smile as Miss Henrietta Christian, captain in charge, serves her first customer at the refreshment bar of the American Red Cross Club in George Street, opened in June, 1944.*

LEFT: *Cpl. Nichols L. McKay was the first customer to check in at the "Donut Dug-out," as the Club became known to the Americans. Standing behind the counter is a member of Luton W.V.S.*

BELOW: *Coffee and doughnuts for some of the first G.I.'s to make use of their club, which had recreational facilities and an information bureau.*

provide. Then the G.I.'s grouse about the lack of a hostel became really vehement.

*   *   *   *

After a few months the authorities did something about it. They provided dormitory accommodation for 50 at the Donut Club. Simultaneously they opened 46 and 48, Downs Rd., with a local lady in charge, one house accommodating 50 and the other 75. All three dormitories were used to capacity until the Americans began to move homewards ; after that, only week-ends found them in full demand.

Running such dormitories was not without incident. There was the occasion, for example, when one young man decided that to mark his 21st birthday he would get tight—very tight. He was very young and, as we would say, very " browned-off." Home was a long way away. It was all so different from what he had planned back among the bright lights before 1941. He knew no one here. What he wanted was liquor and more liquor.

They tried to dissuade him but somehow he succeeded and got past the fuddled stage. The dormitory warden somehow got him to bed, but he was restless and unpredictable. She stayed with him, sitting by the side of his bed for a long time, and she talked to him patiently. She talked to him of his family and his mother across the other side, of his friends and his home town. Eventually he fell asleep. The next morning he was a pleasant boy again and when he saw the warden he was so grateful.

*   *   *   *

The Donut Club, with Miss Van der Meid as successor to Miss Lee, continued very popular right to the end, and when, because so many of those for whom it was intended had gone home, a closing date was fixed, there was such an outcry by those still using it that sentence was suspended, but only for a few weeks. It closed its doors on November 20th, 1945.

Local ladies who gave so much voluntary service there will remember one special occasion. Determined to show their appreciation, the Americans themselves threw a party for the canteen helpers, donned aprons, served refreshments and did all the washing-up, and then proceeded to demonstrate how to make a party go.

*   *   *   *

In the latter days it was interesting to meet men who having completed or exceeded the number of operational flights which entitled them to go home, came to have a last look at Luton.

If a man came from one of the Southern States, he didn't think any more of our summer weather than we do. In fact, his primary reason for being glad of a chance to go home early, even if it was midsummer, was that at home he would at least be able to feel warm again.

But there were others not so anxious to go home in a hurry. They wanted to have a good look round, in case they could never come again.

330

They were quite content to stand aside in favour of other, and perhaps younger, men, who were to go on to the Far East after home leave.

*   *   *   *

It was to be expected that international marriages would be fairly numerous. Prospective brides were not deterred by the warning that they did not acquire American citizenship, that they would have to wait a long time before they could go to the States, and that if and when they did arrive the conditions of the new life awaiting them might be not at all to their liking. Marriages continued to take place. Husbands went back, their brides, left behind, started agitations and formed deputations about the lack of transportation for them. They still had to wait. They formed a " Columbus Club " ; held their own baby show.

And still more marriages took place. By the end of 1945 the transportation problem seemed to have been solved, for it was announced that they would all be out of this country by the following February. Reception centres were established where, with their children, if any, the G.I. Brides assembled before being taken to Southampton and put on a boat for the States. They were on their way.

*   *   *   *

Now we see no more of the white-belted, white-spatted, white-gloved " Snowdrops " who had their own peculiar methods of dealing with such of their countrymen as were unruly.

Nor can parties of ultra-smart Americans come to represent their country at some ceremonial parade, as they did during the war years.

But if they continue to have more money in the States than we do here, despite how much they may have lent to us, we shall see some of those Americans again. They will come, although not in uniform.

And some are certain to come to Luton.

The Rising Generation

IF little or nothing was done by the nation in the first twelve months of the war to tap the potential of the youth of Britain, it was not because the existence of these latent energies and enthusiasms was not realised. Boys and girls of what is now colloquially known as the " teen-age " classes were in 1939 an unknown factor. From 14 to 16 they were either of senior school age or had already moved into industry, which was accelerating its service to the nation. At any rate they were creatures with minds and wills of their own. From 16

331

until the ages when the call up operated, boys and girls had become young men and women who were productive assets to industry.

What was their reaction to war? That was not long in doubt. The teen-agers showed themselves consistent in their reasoning and persistent in their devotion to the national cause. They soaked up knowledge like sponges, docketed it, and produced it without effort. They were authorities on the most abstruse technical matters connected with the fighting services. Their enthusiasms were phenomenal and lasting. Boys of 16 fought their way into the Home Guard through a maze of regulations and by all manner of subterfuges. Once in they displayed a quick-wittedness that astounded their older comrades. No job was too menial. No job was skimped. Their physical and mental stamina was astounding.

Youth could easily have been conscripted, trained and disciplined from a very early age, but the horrid example of Hitler Youth, of children bereft of the finer human attributes, was anathema to the British mind. Youth must not be regimented, yet it must be encouraged, carefully yet vigorously, to use its tremendous energies where most needed.

So it fell out that youth was given a very definite place in activities arising out of the war, quite apart from any useful war work in which the young people who had left school were engaged during the day.

Until December, 1941, it was largely left to the young people themselves to seek membership of one or other of the existing youth organisations, but after that until the end of 1945 they had to register at the age of 16, so that information could be obtained as to their leisure-time interests. The intention was not that those who were apparently at a loose end should be *directed* into some suitable organisation. It gave an opportunity to recommend them to join an organisation.

It gave an additional impetus to recruiting for the three pre-entry training organisations, although it may be said that most of the young people who joined these, or became members of the cadet divisions of the Red Cross Society or St. John Ambulance Brigade, or the N.F.S. messenger service, did not need much guidance.

* * * *

In Luton, as in other places, the war severely handicapped the older youth organisations like the Boys' Brigade, the Church Lads' Brigade, the Scouts, and Luton Boys' Club, by taking away many of their enthusiastic leaders, and in other ways by making it difficult for the remaining leaders to carry on. But it also brought other youth organisations into being, and it was natural that those which provided pre-entry training for the three Services should exercise the greatest appeal. The very fact that these youths were provided with smart uniforms which, except in size, were indistinguishable from the real thing, was an added stimulus to recruiting, if one were needed, and nothing was so heartening as the way these young people reacted to

Service discipline. They enjoyed it. They studied it, practised it with fervour. In the result, when they were eventually called to the fighting Services proper they had already learned responsibility and leadership. The doors to promotion were quickly opened to them.

*   *   *   *

It was only natural that of the pre-training organisations which came into existence during the war, the Air Training Corps should make the greatest appeal to youth. When it came into existence on February 1st, 1941, the thrilling deeds of the R.A.F. in the Battle of Britain were fresh in the public memory. Among youth there was a general ambition not only to fly in some capacity or other, but to play the same stirring part as did the Battle of Britain heroes.

In Luton the Air Training Corps inherited a valuable legacy. A Luton squadron of the pre-war Air Defence Cadet Corps had been formed in 1938 under the auspices of the Air League of the British Empire. Luton was one of the first towns in the country to form such a squadron, which was registered as No. 10 (Founder) Squadron. Mr. Frank Facer, the first Luton man ever to fly—and that was pre-1914—was in charge. He and other pioneers of the Youth Air Training Scheme did much hard work, and many members of the squadron later joined the R.A.F., and built up very creditable war records. Notable among the early entrants from the A.D.C.C., as it was known, were five lads who spent almost every moment of their spare time in making themselves proficient as wireless operators. They were completely successful, and after a special examination at an R.A.F. Station they were accepted into the R.A.F., as special-entry wireless operators some months earlier than they would otherwise have been eligible to join.

By the end of 1940 the need for aircrews had become of vital importance, and the Air Ministry decided to assume complete responsibility for all pre-entry R.A.F. training. The wisdom of this decision was more than justified by later events.

February, 1941, then, saw the birth of the Air Training Corps as an integral part of the R.A.F. The Luton response to the call for volunteers was really remarkable. An organising committee, a nucleus of officers under Mr. H. T. Rushton, with a number of civilian instructors, quickly got to work. The officers, although granted commissions in the R.A.F.V.R., worked on a purely voluntary basis, and from the earliest days gave all their spare time to the organisation and training of the cadets. The local unit took over the No. 10 (F) Squadron, A.D.C.C. as a nucleus, became the 10(F) Squadron, A.T.C., and recruiting went ahead rapidly. In a very few weeks more than 200 cadets had been enrolled, and they were augmented by many enlisted airmen who, on joining the R.A.F. proper, had been sent back temporarily to their jobs. These were " deferred service " airmen, and they reported for pre-entry training with the A.T.C. pending actual call-up. By May of that year the strength of the squadron had reached 300, and it had become necessary to hold classes on every night of the week except Saturday. In the early days the instruction was confined mainly to drill, P.T., signals, air navigation and calculations, interspersed with lectures by serving R.A.F. officers. As training got under way there were also visits to airfields, mainly with a view to giving the cadets a little Service " atmosphere," and many other courses were added, such as aircraft recognition, theory of flight, engines, armament, wireless mechanics, and so on.

Numbers continued to grow, in spite of the fact that cadets were already passing into the Services, and it was inevitable that a second squadron (No. 1979) should be formed. To this end a certain number of officers and cadets were transferred from the parent squadron. Mr. H. R. Waller had by this time taken over from Mr. Rushton, who had taken a higher appointment with the A.T.C., and Mr. R. A. Gibbs went to 1979 Squadron. The two Luton squadrons then took under their wing the newly-formed Toddington Flight, and initiated a Works Flight at Vauxhall Motors, Ltd. A few months later the latter attained a strength sufficient to justify the formation of yet another Luton squadron, which became No. 2122 (Vauxhall) Squadron, under Mr. W. J. Hunter. In time Mr. C. Miller succeeded Mr. Gibbs in command of 1979 Squadron.

Until well into 1944 A.T.C. training went on without a halt. Each year saw many of the cadets go off for a week's course, which included flying in Service machines, at an R.A.F. Station. Practically everyone had already done some flying, and many had passed proficiency examinations set by the Air Ministry. Ex-members on leave, wearing wings or air crew brevets, were a frequent sight at A.T.C. headquarters at Waller Street School.

Not so common, but gradually increasing in numbers, were ex-cadets who had gained commissions, sometimes in the other fighting Services.

By mid-1944 the demand for air crews became considerably less, and many members of the local squadrons, who had devoted a lot of time to training to fit themselves for aircrew duties, found they were being called for service as R.A.F. ground staff, or for the Navy or Army, or even for the mines. There was some dissatisfaction with high policy on this matter, and the inevitable result was a falling off in numbers.

After the cessation of hostilities the incentive to train disappeared, and No. 1979 Squadron was eventually re-absorbed into No. 10 (F) Squadron which continues.

Luton may well be proud of the part its squadrons of the Air Training Corps played during the war. They passed between 600 and 700 semi-trained youths and men into the Services. Of these at least fifty were granted commissions, and it is known that at least three were awarded the Distinguished Flying Cross.

Sport was greatly favoured as part of the cadets' training, and in spite of the war the Luton A.T.C. squadrons sponsored four highly successful swimming galas. No. 10(F) Squadron also did well on the football field, winning the Eastern Command Trophy in two successive years and reaching the final in the following season.

The A.T.C. were also the first local pre-training unit to have a fully equipped band, which became in great request.

Tribute must be paid to the civilian instructors who so willingly gave, and still give, their services without stint to help the youths in the squadrons. Without their help the corps could hardly have existed. The results would certainly not have been the same. Nor would a high standard of discipline have been so quickly obtained but for the influence of Mr. Edmund Canterbury, a South African veteran who had won a Long Service award even before he went into the Gallipoli Campaign, and who saw in the A.T.C. an opportunity for still further useful service.

*   *   *   *

The Luton unit of the Sea Cadet Corps, which became a popular pre-training organisation for many boys, was really the successor of the Navy League Sea Cadet Corps, which had been in existence for many years prior to the war. Not until 1942, however, did the Admiralty take it under its wing as an official recruiting agency for the Royal Navy, and decide on a large expansion, with Luton as the centre of a unit.

Admiral Sir Lionel Halsey, who is so well known throughout the county, and who is Commodore of the Sea Cadet Corps of the whole of the British Isles, contacted the late Mr. C. C. Dillingham, and the Luton unit was formed. It was fortunate in having for its first commanding officer Lieut.-Commander T. H. Keyes, who had had long experience in the Royal Navy, and through his connection with George Kent, Ltd., was closely in touch with some of Luton's youth. Other original officers were Lieut. W. S. Hyde (No. 1), and Sub-Lieuts. G. H. Bone, E. G. Baker, T. C. Gregory, and F. Gowing (Administrative Officer). Three of the originals have now left, and the work is now carried on by Lieut. Hyde, as commanding officer, and Sub-Lieuts. Bone, Gowing and Warwick.

The unit was given an establishment of 100, and held its first parade on June 1st, 1942, at its headquarters, Beech Hill School. Cadets are trained in seamanship, signalling, squad drill, etc., and sport plays an important part in training. A football team plays in a local league, and Luton has won the swimming competition once, and the athletic competition twice, in the last two years in competition with its neighbours at Dunstable, Bedford, Hitchin, Welwyn and Biggleswade.

In 1945 the Luton unit organised a parade of ten units from Bedfordshire and Hertfordshire on the Wardown Sports Ground, where they were inspected by Admiral Sir Lionel Halsey. They afterwards marched through the town, the salute being taken at the Town Hall.

But competitions and ceremonial parades, however useful and successful they may be, are not the be-all and end-all of the movement. Its essential aim is to give boys a preliminary training for a life at sea. That it is fulfilling this primary purpose is shown by the fact that by early 1946 it had passed 44 boys into the Royal Navy, six to the Fleet Air Arm, and 15 to the Merchant Navy, while three had succeeded in gaining commissions. Letters are frequently received from ex-cadets now scattered all over the seven seas, and when on leave they always call at headquarters to renew old friendships.

Summer camps are held at Naval establishments under Service conditions and Admiralty supervision.

The Luton Sea Cadets certainly had no cause for unhappy memories of Victory Day, June 8'h, 1946. The pouring rain which spoiled the pleasure of the celebrations mattered not at all to them while they were exploring the mysteries of *H.M.S. Diadem*, the second ship adopted by Luton during the war. It was an exceptional opportunity for them. *Diadem* was lying in the Thames off Greenwich for public inspection on the two days following V-Day. The Sea Cadets had a private view on V-Day, at the invitation of Captain Knapp. They had the run of the ship—and a grand tea.

*   *   *   *

The Army Cadet Force came into existence in Luton as a pre-service unit in February, 1942. The first Company was formed by Lieut. V. Russell in connection with Luton Boys' Club, Park Street. Very soon afterwards Luton Grammar School, then known as Luton Modern School, established a second unit, with Lieut. S. J. Pointing as its first commanding officer. The movement increased in popularity among the youth of Luton, and in July of the same year a further unit was formed for Leagrave and Limbury, under the command of Lieut. F. H. Rowe. Lt.-Col. R. Briars, M.C., had much to do with the organisation of the A.C.F. in Luton in its preliminary stages until persistent ill-health compelled him to relinquish the work. He died in 1943.

Like so many other organisations, the Army Cadet Force movement in Luton suffered from lack of suitable accommodation. By 1944 conditions at Park Street had become very difficult, and a move was made to Williamson Street, where the Boys' Club Section was re-formed as the Luton Town Company. With the stand down of the Home Guard, this later found its way to more spacious premises at the Drill Hall, Old Bedford Road.

Changing personnel somewhat retarded the progress of the Cadet Force until, their other duties having ceased, a number of Home Guard officers and instructors found the Cadet Force provided them with a new field of service. Through the hard work and interest of Major F. G. Harmer, M.M., an up-to-date social club for the cadets was provided at the Drill Hall and, with a committee of voluntary workers, it became a very popular place with the " young soldiers."

The Sea Cadets—training for the Royal Navy—had a strong war-time Corps in Luton. In the picture above a signals class is receiving a semaphore message.

Officers and cadets of the Luton Sea Cadet Corps photographed during the war years.

...ol. A. J. Mander inspecting Luton Army Cadets in July 1943.

ABOVE: *A squad of the Luton Grammar (then Modern) School Army Cadet Corps put in some foot-slogging in the playground.*

BELOW: *Councillor J. Burgoyne then Mayor of Luton, pinning th first gold medal for gallantry to b awarded by the Air Defence Cade Corps (later the A.T.C.) on t the tunic of Cadet H. G. Pyper, o No. 10 F. Squadron, for hi heroism in rescuing a five-year-ol boy from the River Ouse at Bedford.*

BELOW: *Six Luton Air Cadets, who, although under 18, were accepted for special entry into the R.A.F. in January, 1941, after passing a signalling test at 20 words a minute. With them is their instructor, Sgt. Day, of the Home Guard, who later became an A.T.C. officer, and assumed command of No. 10 F. Squadron in 1946.*

Air Chief Marshal Sir Robert Brooke-Popham inspecting the band of Nos. 10 F. and 1979 Squadrons, Luton A.T.C. On his right is Squadron Leader H. T. Rushton, and on his left Flight Lieutenant H. R. Waller.

Heading the parade through the town, the band of Luton A.T.C. Squadrons march through George Street, shortly after its formation at the end of 1942.

Members of the Girls' Training Corps swing past the saluting base at the Boys' Brigade Diamond Jubilee parade in June 1943.

BELOW: *This bucket-swinging quintet were off to fetch the water at a week-end camp for Luton patrol leaders, guides and rangers, held in Stockwood Park in August 1943.*

ABOVE: *Four G.T.C. girls get down to a spell of morse practice.*

During the war period very successful camps were held at Bedford and at Ampthill Park, and a series of week-end camps and courses proved very popular, while for 1946 a seaside camp was found practicable, for training under something very approaching service conditions. As compulsory service for the youth of the country is to continue, the wider training which cadets now receive should be even more valuable than that received by the earlier cadets, a large percentage of whom passed into the Services, where they found that even such A.C.F. training as they had been able to receive was very helpful in their new life.

For cadets of a technical bent special courses were arranged at the Luton R.E.M.E. School, under Capt. A. Driver, and here they were able to obtain a very practical form of instruction.

The sporting side received special attention, and District and Command finals of the A.C.F. Boxing Championships were staged at the Electrolux Canteen, through the kindness of the management of the company.

During War Savings weeks the cadets rendered very useful service, and in Youth week they provided demonstrations. Now, organised in close association with the County Regiment, the Army Cadet Force goes on, and will continue to attract lads who can appreciate the value of pre-entry training for the service to the country which they will be called on to render in due course.

*   *   *   *

Founded as the Whittlesey Club in the years following the first World War, Luton Boys' Club put up a record of service in the Second of which it may well be proud.

After Munich a number of senior members joined the Territorials and the R.A.F.V.R., and were mobilised immediately war was declared. The calls of Civil Defence made further inroads on the leisure of many of the older members, and parties of all ages joined in sandbagging, the provision of shelters, and the other hasty provisions of those hectic days. Evacuation also brought its problems, and London schools billeted in the area were allowed to use the club premises during part of the evenings for games for their boys. The Air Training Corps, in its earliest days, also used part of the club as temporary headquarters. The first Army Cadet Force unit in Luton was also formed at the club, and was an immediate success. Later it was absorbed into a local battalion and moved to the Drill Hall.

Meanwhile more and more members had been conscripted with their age groups, and as far as can be ascertained the total reached over 250. Others, although on war work, gave a vast amount of time to all branches of Civil Defence. The bombing incidents in the Park Street district cost the club considerable damage to property and equipment. At these times it was used by the police and Civil Defence as an information post.

All through these difficult times the club remained open and active.

Leaders and Old Boys were all serving in one cause or another, yet time was found to keep the flag flying. Games and other activities were naturally not anywhere near pre-war standard, but members on leave found the place a mine of information about old friends, where they were, and what they were doing. News, good and bad, arrived and filtered out.

War casualties cost the club many popular lads, for 23 gave their lives, two with the Navy, seven in the Army, and 14 with the R.A.F., while two came back each minus a leg. The ending of the war in the Far East brought the return of a number who had been prisoners, but some who did not return have found their last resting place many thousands of miles from home.

*   *   *   *

Some 100 officers and boys of the Luton and District Battalion, Boys' Brigade, were called to the Colours, and five made the supreme sacrifice. In spite of the loss of officers to the Services, and the fact that the remaining leaders were on shift work, doing overtime, or engaging in some other phase of the national effort, membership almost trebled during the war years. This would not have been possible without the fine work of the senior boys.

The boys of the companies rendered valuable service in many ways. When the L.D.V. was started, they made up a rota of members to attend at L.D.V. headquarters from early evening till late at night, taking out urgent messages to members of the L.D.V. who were wanted for duty out of their turn because some others had to put overtime or Sunday work on urgent jobs even before their L.D.V. duty. Messenger work for the police and the N.F.S. was also undertaken throughout the war.

Headquarters instituted a National Service badge. To qualify for this, boys had to render at least 100 hours of voluntary, unpaid service. Besides messenger duty, many did fire-watch in their streets or at their school; some did organised work in the Dig-for-Victory Campaign, or systematic collecting for the Red Cross. First aid is always part of B.B. training, but during the war larger numbers than ever attended classes. Now it is quite common to see the National Service badge among the badges worn within the battalion.

*   *   *   *

The Church Lads' Brigade, like many other organisations, suffered considerably in Luton through the effects of war. During 1939 and 1940 many of its officers and instructors volunteered for the Services. Then came the greatest difficulty of all—the problem of uniforms and equipment. Supplies became very short, and the senior section of the local unit found it impossible to carry on. Biscot, the parent company in Luton, closed down for the time being, but Leagrave and Stopsley bravely kept their junior sections going, in spite of the drawbacks of the blackout and raid warnings, and the fact that most of the church premises were heavily taxed by the needs of the Services or the local authority. Now, with the return of many old members, the release of equipment, and supplies of uniforms in prospect, it is hoped that the C.L.B. will rise again, and take a prominent place among Luton's youth organisations.

*   *   *   *

" Carry on, but Forward," was the Girls' Life Brigade motto during the war years, and the Luton and District Battalion can be proud of their endeavours to fulfil this motto. Like other·organisations, they had many difficulties. Officers and other prospective leaders were called to the Women's Services or became nurses in hospitals, and although their G.L.B. training in discipline, home nursing, etc., served them well, their departure made things harder for those left to carry on. They had to spend much time which would normally have been devoted to Brigade activities at work on munitions, driving ambulances, firewatch, etc.

Moreover, halls used for Brigade meetings were commandeered, with the result that some companies had to close down temporarily or meet in very inadequate premises. The introduction of clothing coupons was also a blow, making " uniform " a trying problem, and one which long after the cessation of hostilities was a continuing problem.

In spite of these handicaps the Battalion grew in size. Six new companies, including three which now form part of the new Dunstable and District Battalion, were affiliated, increasing the number of active companies to twelve. This increase cannot be attributed to the registration of young people for guidance into youth groups, as the majority of members recruited were under fourteen. This was mainly due to the fact that lack of officers precluded the running of Pioneer Sections (girls of sixteen and over) in many companies. It was also found that girls in the higher teens, with no previous Brigade experience, preferred mixed clubs.

In view of the greatly increased interest in youth activities during the last five years, however, it is certain that had helpers been available the work of the Girls' Life Brigade, with its four-square programme—spiritual, physical, educational and social—would have been greatly extended in spite of prevailing difficulties. But much was done, and is being done, by the Luton Battalion. Ordinary activities were continued in spite of raid warnings. Keen competition was roused between the companies by the introduction of P.T., general efficiency, and other competitions. Interest in First-Aid lectures, which pre-war had been regarded as " rather boring," resulted in the institution of a First-Aid competition, and incidentally led to many members joining First-Aid units. Many knitting badges were won by knitting for the Forces, and, later, for China's children. Money was raised for deserving causes by displays, collections, etc. Members helped farmers, looked after evacuee children, hemmed bandages, searched for moths in stored clothing for bombed-out families, and did not let the "good

343

work " cease with hostilities.   Under the G.L.B. post-war reconstruction scheme, members raised money to help European countries. Bibles for Norway, groats for French babies, funds for the reconstruction of Continental Sunday Schools, were provided.

*　　　*　　　*　　　*

Luton Boy Scouts' Association, which now includes Sea Scouts and Air Scouts, lost 136 members to the Services.   Of these, 12 gained commissions, 11 were killed, 10 wounded, and one listed as " missing." Scoutmaster Alec Brown was subsequently awarded the Medal of Merit for the way he carried on his Scouting life " under the most terrible conditions " while in the hands of the Japanese at the Changi Prison Camp.

The Civil Defence Services claimed 88 members, of whom two were killed.   The George Medal was awarded to the Scoutmaster of the St. Peter's Troop, Section Officer S.A. Wright, N.F.S., for bravery during the blitz on Thames Haven.

Younger Scouts collected 35 tons of salvage, erected 85 air raid shelters for other people, and put in 4,040 hours on harvesting and other farm work, 1,030 hours for the emergency medical service, 351 hours on Home Guard duties, and also found time to assist with evacuees.

*　　　*　　　*　　　*

Some Luton girls found an opportunity to " do their bit " when in May, 1942, the Luton Girls' Service Company, affiliated to the Luton High School Company of Service, was formed.   A year later it became the Girls' Training Corps, with Mrs. Evans, a High School mistress, as commandant.   Service ranks were instituted.

The G.T.C., though termed a youth organisation, was more than that.   Many of its members filled important posts as N.F.S. and W.V.S. messengers in connection with raid incidents, did secretarial work for the Luton Army Cadet Force, and assisted in the Youth Headquarters' canteen.

They studied a variety of subjects which were of much use to those who afterwards joined the women's Services.   Drills and parades were naturally held, other subjects including A.R.P. lectures, aircraft recognition, morse, first aid, hygiene and crafts.   Dr. F. Grundy, Luton's Medical Officer, himself gave a series of lectures on health.

The social side of the organisation was not neglected, and the girls held dramatics, sports, hikes and socials.   Talks on current events were also given.

Membership of the G.T.C. naturally varied, but the peak was about 80 girls.   The closure of the women's Services on certain occasions throughout the war, and the declaration of peace, affected members, but 775 Corps of the G.T.C. still carries on in Luton.

*　　　*　　　*　　　*

But as the war progressed there were still numbers of boys and girls who remained outside these organisations.   Their leisure was a pretty

ABOVE: *Luton Sea Scouts being inspected by Lt. Col. D. C. Part at a church parade in July, 1945.*

BELOW: *The President of the Luton Battalion of the Boys' Brigade, Mr. A. E. Harris, carries out an inspection of one of the Luton companies.*

ABOVE: *Cheers from some Luton Boy Scouts who were taking part in District Competitions in March, 1945.*

Members of Beech Hill Youth Centre in a physical training demonstration at an open evening in May, 1941.

Some of the leaders and members of the High Town Youth Centre photographed in May, 1942.

aimless thing. To induce them to apply it a little more beneficially, if only to themselves, Youth Centres were opened. They were financed and controlled by the County Education authority, acting through an area committee, which had Mr. H. O. Crouch as secretary. The Centre Leaders did not have an easy job, but they got down to it, activities were arranged to be interesting as well as instructive, and in time a useful work developed.

The centres and their leaders were :—High Town (at Hitchin Road Girls' School), Miss K. V. Wilson ; Beech Hill, Mr. A. D. McMullen ; Chapel Street, Mr. R. Eling ; Stopsley, Mr. A. C. Benson.

The High Town Centre, with 520 members, was by far the largest. Beech Hill and Chapel Street were less well attended, but ran one another very close in membership. Stopsley Centre, catering for a district where the population is much more scattered, could be excused for attracting the smallest attendance.

The work of the centres was not planned on a rigid programme which had to apply equally to each. The programme was variable according to the reasonable wishes of members, but in general the activities covered physical training, cookery, domestic science, music and the drama, and discussions, with cricket, football, rambling, and social gatherings encouraged according to the season.

It cannot be said that the older public's first impressions of the centres were altogether favourable. It was not easy to make the young people realise that the movement was intended to have a more serious background than just some additional provision for their entertainment. But that stage passed, and as some of the young people began to indicate a growing sense of responsibility they were encouraged to express their views through their own Youth Council, although this could not be more than an advisory body.

The Youth Council came into existence in July, 1942. It held its inaugural meeting in the Council Chamber at the Town Hall, and received some good advice from the Mayor. Urging the young people not to go through life just as fault-finders and grousers, he said :— " Don't wait until you have a more prominent place in this Chamber. Find yourself a job, satisfy yourself it is your job, equip yourself well, and cultivate some of the grace and courtesy which is said to be disappearing from our society."

The idea of a Youth Council was undoubtedly good, but events suggested that it was put into operation rather prematurely. There were weak points in this provision for the leisure of youth. Only registration was compulsory. There was no compulsion to join any organisation, and outside the pre-service organisations, little power to discipline any who, after joining, were inclined to be unruly. It also became clear, after central Youth Headquarters were established in Guildford Street, that there were still a good many members of youth centres still holding the view that they ought to have still more of the entertainment to which they seemed to think they were entitled, and that they were under no obligation to regard membership as a lead to any more serious application of their leisure.

Because of this, the Guildford Street headquarters, intended as a connecting link not only for the Youth Centres but for all youth organisations, came in for considerable criticism at one period. In fact, at a meeting of the County Council a Luton member alleged that the County Service of Youth was turning young people into jitterbugs instead of forming characters which would make the young people good citizens. This was not wholly admitted, but it was not denied that the crowds which gathered at Guildford Street showed that the place was not being used strictly as contemplated.

Guildford Street Headquarters had been intended for use for joint function of youth organisations and to provide facilities for occasional central meetings of voluntary clubs and organisations, but because of the free entertainment and social life that quickly developed there, it became so overcrowded at week-ends and so many were seeking admittance on Sundays, that two " houses " had to be run.

A music and dancing licence was sought but it was refused, and although one member of the responsible committee seemed to regard this as a setback, those familiar with the building realised that it was the only decision which could be reached.

There had to be a change. It was arrived at in a very amicable way. The Area Committee asked the Youth Council Executive Committee and its own executive committee to meet separately to go into the matter. They did so, published independent reports, found afterwards that they were almost of like opinion, and soon reached an agreed policy on the use of the Headquarters. Main principles were that the building should be maintained as headquarters, and not used as a club ; the premises to be available for use by any bona-fide youth organisation from Mondays to Fridays, for the purposes originally contemplated ; organised activities of at least 45 minutes per session to be arranged for Saturdays and Sundays, the Sunday evening programme to end on a serious note ; admission to be by a special card.

Although over 1,000 membership cards were ultimately issued, the average nightly attendance fell to about 150, and gradually the Headquarters reverted to its original purpose.

An additional step early in 1946 was the appointment of Mr. J. Leyshon as full-time warden. As he had been a school-master and then a warrant officer in the Army, it was reasonable to anticipate that he would be able to maintain a rather higher standard of discipline. Steps were also being taken to secure more suitable premises for headquarters. When Guildford Street was opened, it was a case of taking what could be had, and had the Co-operative Society not been helpful it might have been necessary to wait a long time before any place could be found. Future activities will centre at what was Waller Street School.

It was fitting that the youth organisations of Luton should celebrate their war effort by combining in an Empire Youth Pageant at Wardown in May, 1946. Two thousand young people, representing every Luton youth organisation took part in a march through the town. The parade was a fitting demonstration of the services given by youth to the war effort. Youth has shown that it can rise to responsibilities, that it is developing qualities of leadership and that the future of Britain will be in capable and enterprising hands.

Social Survey

THE outbreak of war had an immediate and stunning impact on the social life and habits of Luton people. Social life in general can be divided roughly into two sections, that which revolves round public or commercially provided facilities, and that which has its foundation in the good neighbourliness of little circles of people, largely families who live and move and have their being in close domestic proximity.

Theatre, cinema and publicly provided entertainment bulk largely in people's lives at all times. Their commercial development up to 1939 had led the public to place so much reliance on the excellence of their fare, that some few thoughtful people interested in sociology had wondered whether we were not in danger of losing the art of entertaining ourselves, of becoming shallow-minded, and incapable of constructive and thoughtful argument ; in short, whether we were not likely to lose some of the social virtues that sweeten the activities of the human mind.

The tempo of life had increased with the years ; the telephone, the car, the aeroplane, the stop press and the radio had stepped up the speed of human activity so that more could be got through in less time. Big business had found the remedy for a permanent mental fatigue It found that it could sell, and the public would buy, escapism at 3s. 6d., 2s. 9d., 2s., 1s. 3d. a time. The halls of glamour were filled with young and old of both sexes.

*   *   *   *

When war came, theatre and cinema alike were closed to the public from the Monday in that fateful week of early September, 1939. What the days and nights were to bring was in the lap of the gods, but it was obviously unwise to allow people still to crowd into such places of entertainment. The Government therefore imposed the ban.

There was no immediate bombing. On the Saturday of the first week of war the ban was lifted, but a closing time of 10 p.m. was fixed. The ban was not re-imposed in the worst of the blitz periods. Even when Luton was being bombed all that was done was to advise people to go to the pictures or the theatre as early in the week as possible, and so even out the attendances. At the same time a limit was imposed on the attendance at some dances, to make dispersal easier in emergency.

The 10 p.m. limit for cinemas sealed the fate of one pre-war cinema custom, but probably even those most directly affected could not readily name it. Gone is the afternoon performance when 6d. secured a seat in the stalls, and a little more the freedom of the house. Housewives were the chief patrons, but the bargain price held good for all who entered before 4 p.m., so here is a reminiscent comment by a mere man—" When I had a free afternoon I could bring the wife in by bus, go to the cinema with her, take her home by bus, and all on eighteenpence. Now, for a single seat alone . . . "

The principal performances had to start earlier ; the 6d. afternoons had to go and join other things belonging to the good old days.

However, if the war took away some possibilities of entertainment for those who must be entertained, war or no war, it provided others. To the screen came some things which would not otherwise have had a place. There were times in years gone by when the exhibition of a film which was of purely educational or interest value was a sure way of clearing the house of those who had seen the main part of the continuous programme. The war caused people to look on many a non-fictional film from a new angle. The documentary film often held their interest quite as much as one of purely entertainment value. Sometimes the documentary and the entertaining were cleverly combined.

Desert Victory was purely documentary, but it drew big audiences because so many had a personal interest in the men who won this victory. The official record on the screen showed them things which were beyond their imagining—things they could not build into a whole from the scrappy letters of relatives out there. *Coastal Command*, *Ships With Wings* and *The Big Blockade* were others in the same category. Pictures like *Went the Day Well?*, *Next of Kin*, *Millions Like Us*, and *The Moon is Down*, although primarily entertainment, all had a lesson for thoughtful patrons.

The documentary film brought war propaganda to a fine art. Its purpose was to maintain and enhance the morale of the people. It did not need to be fictional, though it often was, but it had to be technically and histrionically perfect. It had to be a vivid narrative. It had to show the starkness of war but Allied courage and perseverance in face of odds must always triumph and point the moral and the right and the magnitude of the issues at stake.

49th Parallel was a wonderful way to put across the lesson that the people of two enormous countries, Canada and United States, can live as peaceful neighbours without the necessity of any fortifications along the longest international frontier in the world, when fortified frontiers had failed to save many other countries from being overrun by an enemy. *In Which We Serve* told in a very graphic way the things which go to make a warship an efficient fighting unit. *Way to the Stars* was a notable tribute to the relationships of the R.A.F. and the U.S.A.A.F. *This Happy Breed* was another outstanding story.

The task of the Navy in safeguarding *The Western Approaches* was well brought home by this film, and people did not find it any the less interesting because it came within the strictly documentary class. *The Great Day* was another. *Sergeant York* used a true story of the 1914-18 war to drive home a great lesson, *Mrs. Miniver* had Greer Garson in the title role. It was the picture of the average middle class British mother's reaction to the dark days of 1940. Many cinemagoers hold that it was the outstanding picture of the six years of war. *The First of the Few* was another big drama. It told of the birth of the Spitfire and the Battle of Britain.

Thirty Seconds over Tokio and *I Live in Grosvenor Square* brought some of the American aspects of war to the screen.

True Glory and *Burma Victory* were other notable documentary films.

At all cinemas, of course, the news reels reached exceptional heights of interest. The risks run by the cameramen to get their pictures would have provided a documentary in themselves.

In addition to those mentioned, readers will recall that these other films also contributed much to the morale of the people and the war effort.

1939 :   *The Lion has Wings.*
1940 :   *For Freedom* (the story of the Battle of the River Plate and the Altmark rescue).
1941 :   Chaplin's *The Great Dictator* ; *Target for To-night* (the story of a bombing raid on Germany) ; *Atlantic Ferry* ; Quentin Reynolds *One Day in Soviet Russia.*
1942 :   *The Defeat of the Germans at Moscow* ; *Unpublished Story* (the London Blitz) ; *One of Our Aircraft is Missing* (the escape of a R.A.F. crew who baled out over occupied Holland) ; *Secret Mission* (about the British Secret Service).
1943 :   *Nine Men* (a Libyan Desert story) ; *The Silver Fleet* (anti-Nazi sabotage in occupied Holland) ; *Immortal Sergeant* ; *The Story of Stalingrad* ; *Commandos Strike at Dawn* ; Leslie Howard's *The Gentle Sex* (life in the A.T.S.) ; *We Dive at Dawn* (the submarine service) ; Mr. Joseph Davies' *Mission to Moscow* ; *Convoy* ; *The Battle of Britain* ; Disney's *Victory Through Air Power.*
1944 :   *San Demetrio, London* (the story of a torpedoed petrol tanker) ; Irving Berlin's *This is the Army* ; *Tunisian Victory* ; *The Nelson Touch* ; *The Way Ahead* with David Niven (the infantryman in training and at war) ; *A Canterbury Tale* ; *The White Cliffs of Dover.*

There were other films too, which, though they had no war interest, nevertheless will be remembered. In 1939 there was *Goodbye Mr. Chips.* Arthur Askey's *Band Waggon* and Will Hay in *The Ghost of St. Michael's* came in 1940 and early 1941 and later that year Leslie Howard starred in *Pimpernel Smith.* Shaw's *Major Barbara* and Ronald

Colman in *The Prisoner of Zenda* also came that year and there was a succession of Walt Disney films *Pinnocchio, Bambi, Dumbo* and *Fantasia* which were remarkable. October, 1942, brought that longest of all films *Gone With the Wind* the showing of which lasted four hours. *Happidrome* was a welcome visitor in 1943 as was *Random Harvest* with Ronald Colman and Greer Garson. 1944 was notable for *Madame Curie* and *The Song of Bernadette*.

The limitations of the stage do not debar it from competing on level terms with the screen as the medium for telling a fine story. This was shown at the Grand Theatre when *Flare Path* was presented.

*   *   *   *

In quite another field, that of music, the war also brought to Luton audiences some entertainment they otherwise would not have been able to enjoy. The B.B.C. settled at Bedford. It was comparatively easy for Stanford Robinson to bring the B.B.C. Theatre Orchestra to Luton and, having received a great welcome, to bring it again. Luton people certainly appreciated that combination and the music they put over, perhaps not highbrow enough for some, but definitely the right programmes for those for whom they were planned. In other ways, too, and not always confined to matters musical, Luton benefited by the wartime proximity of the B.B.C.

But if the B.B.C. Theatre Orchestra brought popular music, others brought something more serious, and gave Luton a chance to demonstrate that it has an audience for the Symphony concert. Orchestras normally heard only in London had for a time to look elsewhere for supporters, people being justifiably disinclined to assemble in London to hear them, even if their normal places of performance were still intact. So the orchestras came out into the country to their audiences. Often they were accompanied by some outstanding vocal or instrumental soloist. Even if such visits were only intermittent, they gave people who wanted something other than light music their chance. They did much to make Sunday concerts an established thing.

Visits of famous orchestras and artistes were not confined to events open to the public. There were many visits that went unheralded and unchronicled. Security demanded that no reference should be made in the Press to visits of conductors, orchestras, bands and variety, theatrical, and cinema personalities to big works engaged on war production. The names of these visitors were household words. In normal times their presence in Luton would have been accompanied by surging crowds of fans and packed houses. The war cloaked them with secrecy, yet in works canteens, where Ensa brought them to entertain the workers, nothing was more appreciated than the relief they brought to tired minds and bodies that had been toiling to provide the weapons of war. And it is significant that Ensa did not send only variety and theatrical stars. World-famous orchestras, conductors, pianists and violinists whose art interpreted to perfection the music of the masters, were welcomed as fervently as the cross talk comedians.

LEFT: "The Great Dictator" studies a globe of the world. Charlie Chaplin's film, which came to Luton in 1941, brought a short spell of light relief for war-weary nerves.

BELOW: A poignant scene from "Mrs. Miniver," starring Greer Garson. The family wait anxiously in their shelter as enemy aircraft thunder overhead.

The B.B.C. Symphony Orchestra were
evacuated to Bedford, and became
frequent visitors to Luton. Sir Adrian
Boult is seen conducting during one of
their concerts at the Odeon Cinema.

Luton Girls' Choir did much to put Luton on the musical map during the war
years. They are seen with their conductor and accompanist, Mr. Arthur E. Davies.

Mr. Arthur Davies conducting Luton Choral Society during one of their war-time performances at Luton Parish Church.

Gracie Fields . . .
the ever popular
" Lass from Lanca-
shire" . . . at the
microphone when she
visited Vauxhall
Motors Ltd., in Sep-
tember, 1943. Part of
the large audience of
workers in the can-
teen who saw and
heard her are shown
below.

Two Electrolux workers join Jack
Buchanan at the microphone at the
recording of a " Workers' Playtime" broadcast in November, 1942.

"Is that the meater?
I want some butch!"
Mrs. Feather (Jeanne
de Casalis) is in
trouble again as she
records a "Workers'
Playtime" from the
Skefko Works.
Luton.

Concurrently Luton Choral Society developed its activities considerably. They could not continue to perform, as for half a century before, in one hall or another not primarily built with regard to acoustics. They could and did, transfer some of their concerts to more modern surroundings; again it had to be on Sundays. They made another departure. They gave performances in the fine setting of Luton's old Parish Church, and in an atmosphere ideal for some choral works. There, also, orchestral concerts were a wartime departure from precedent.

There were many forms of locally organised entertainment that served the war effort—and served it well. Outstanding among them was the Luton Girls' Choir, founded and developed by Mr. Arthur E. Davies, who was also playing a prominent part in the Luton Choral Society. The choir had been in existence before the war, and had already raised large sums for charity. It continued during the war, and towards the end it attracted the notice of the B.B.C. and began to acquire a national fame. To-day the Luton Girls' Choir, whose harmony is " like birds singing," and the Luton Choral Society are two of Luton's most valuable goodwill exports.

*   *   *   *

From the first week of the war many other forms of social activity had to suffer a war dim out; some a total black out. A primary cause was the military requisitioning of many halls where the smaller social events were normally held. Concerts, dances, whist drives and the like, all suffered.

Annual banquets, less pretentious annual dinners, and some very cheerful annual reunions, were all abandoned at the start of the war. It was felt to be not the thing to continue them in the circumstances of the time. Later, their resumption was made difficult by rationing and by the price restrictions on public meals.

Some people may have considered this a blessing in disguise. No longer had they to suffer those speeches which were inevitably on the toast list because so-and-so had to be given the opportunity to say a few words, thus detracting from the real entertainment and conviviality of those gathered round the fleshpots.

With so many of the smaller halls not available, there was also no longer a Winter Assembly Hall for the larger gatherings. Through the war winters it continued in its summer guise of a swimming bath. It was kept as a static water tank—though it was never drawn on. It took a General Election after the end of the war in Europe, and the presumed need of a big hall where political eloquence could be let loose, to bring it back into use as an Assembly Hall. Now it will presumably alternate seasonally, as in pre-September, 1939, offering hospitality to swimmers in summer, and catering for other recreations and " letting off steam " in winter.

The closing of so many halls emphasised the inadequacy of the Assembly Hall at the Town Hall.

When the Town Hall was built, Whitehall ruled that the ratepayers of that time could not afford the fine concert and assembly hall that was part of the plan and was badly wanted by the town.

The small hall under the Council Chamber became therefore the Assembly Hall at the Town Hall but it was quite inadequate and from time to time there have been bitter complaints that " The Town Council have failed in their duty, etc." It is Whitehall that is to blame.

The site for the big Concert and Assembly Hall adjoins the Town Hall, but what the cost will be and when it can be done no one yet knows.

*   *   *   *

The black-out, the earlier closing of shops, the suspension of late buses, all combined in developing a habit of earlier home-going. So did the sirens, after Luton had been bombed. Then attendance at clubs and other places where men foregather of an evening quickly thinned out when a warning sounded. Men went home to reassure their womenfolk, and did not return. For aliens, however friendly, earlier homegoing became compulsory. They needed a permit to be out after the prescribed hour, but, if residents of old standing, did not find obtaining a permit too difficult.

If the war affected some forms of public entertainment and also public hospitality, what of its effect on private hospitality? It suffered considerably, and particularly among the many who had no canteen facilities to supplement their rations, and could not afford those off-ration extras which might have helped. But, despite these limitations, a good many people managed to extend some private hospitality to Service people, and particularly to men from overseas. It could not compare with that extended to our own men in South Africa, Canada, or the States, where life was not so austere, and the number of visitors small in proportion to the population. It was only a tithe of what would have been offered if larders had been better stocked. As one family man said—" My boy, when he comes on leave, usually brings another with him. If it's only for one meal it's not so bad, but if it's for a weekend . . . they forget we don't get Army rations . . they can eat . . . whole loaves and cakes vanish . . . we'd like to do more, but things just don't run to it in a small household."

The household was very much a self-contained unit. There was something symbolical about drawing the black-out curtains and so shutting out the dark world without and the terror by night. The eerie wail of the siren brought to all hearts an unexpressed but anxious feeling of expectancy. Many families went naturally to their own Anderson shelters. Others made a point of joining forces, a habit that subconsciously, at any rate, did serve to bolster up personal morale.

Books played a great part in the isolated, blacked-out life of the home. The war brought a spate of reading matter, some good, some indifferent in quality, but in the main it brought not only more reading but more good reading. The Library service in Luton, not only the Public Libraries but the subscription libraries, have always found a ready patronage, and they did much during the war by the maintenance of that service to help the public mind forget the hazards of everyday life. The Public Libraries experienced a phenomenal demand. During the last year of the war, according to the Borough Librarian, Mr. Frank M. Gardner, over a million books were issued. The total for 1939 was 460,000. Mr. Gardner recorded that, in the same year, over 200,000 non-fiction works were issued compared with under 100,000 in 1939. Classical authors were in much greater demand, too, Trollope, Jane Austen and Dickens enjoying a definite revival.

*   *   *   *

When public shelters were completed there developed among those who used them a queer form of communal life. They were the troglodytes, and wherever two or three families met regularly in the dark but safe world of the underground, there, without fail, was found someone who, as shelter-marshal, devoted himself to the entertainment and social intercourse of his group of shelterers. Never was better work done. While Heinkels and Dorniers ranged the skies and circled the town, the tunnel-shelter life of the townsfolk became almost an eagerly-anticipated nightly feature.

Another aspect of the neighbourly visits between families was that it was found to result in a useful economy. Fuel and light had to be watched so that no waste occurred. To share one's light and warmth and even cooking became a pleasurable duty. Many an erstwhile shy and retiring housewife became a good solo player and learnt to throw a pretty dart.

Looking back on the experiences of those six years, it may have imposed many handicaps on social life, but it has introduced much that would otherwise have been slow in coming. People generally became better mixers. Their voluntary war work was a great leveller. Truly " the colonel's lady and Judy O'Grady were sisters under the skin '

Sport during War

SPORT was one of the first of our social activities to feel the full effect of war. From the day war was declared there was a temporary blackout of sport as complete as that ordered to defeat enemy bombers. The fundamental cause was the possibility that, if the expected bombing materialised, the gathering of large crowds for League football or other major sporting events would intensify the danger. The simplest way to eliminate this danger was to ban all such assemblies for the time being, and this the Government decreed.

As with the contemporary ban on cinemas, etc., it was relaxed after a time, but as a safety precaution some attendance limits were substituted. Many sporting activities were then resumed. Their scale became more and more restricted as time went on and as more and more players went into the Services. But, on some scale or other, sport had to continue, if only for its beneficial effect on nerves frayed by other impacts of war on the life of the individual. Travel restrictions, loss of star players, problems in obtaining or renewing kit, coupons for such sport clothes as had to be bought, could not stop it entirely, and if matches with time-honoured opponents had to be suspended, there were often good Service teams eager to take the field.

In one of the early summers of the war, in fact, it was not unusual to see four Service teams playing cricket on Wardown Sports Ground, and playing some jolly good cricket, too, though, with the players in their khaki on a dull afternoon much of the atmosphere of cricket seemed to be missing.

*   *   *   *

FOOTBALL

On September 5th, 1939, all professional players' contracts were suspended, all League competitions were cancelled, and all football under the auspices of the Football Association was temporarily suspended pending further instructions. Thus the first Saturday of the war, September 9th, was completely blank from the sport viewpoint.

However, the ban on football was quickly relaxed, and clubs were permitted to arrange friendly matches, except in prohibited areas, and subject to attendance limitations. Luton was not a prohibited area, so matches were resumed. For a considerable period spectators had a grim reminder that there were more serious things than football afoot. Mounted above the grandstand, as on other buildings in Luton were machine guns manned in the expectation of air attack.

Some of the Luton Town players left the district immediately the suspension of contracts took effect, but the Town were able to field a pretty representative side in their first friendly match, which was against Brentford at Kenilworth Road on September 16th.

Players who did not leave the district found work of national importance locally, but gradually, one after the other, they went into the Services, and their record during the war bears favourable comparison with that of any other club in the country.

Four lost their lives on active service. Best known of these was Joe Coen, the first team goalkeeper for several seasons, who was killed in an air crash. Charlie Clark, a sergeant in the Army, was killed in Tunisia. Jock Gillespie was one of the many who gave their

After fixtures for the Football League, Division II, had been suspended in September, 1939, there was an interval of a few weeks and then the game went on. Supporters, however, were few and far between as our picture shows when Fred Roberts led out the Town team for a Southern Section match.

It's a goal! No, the goalkeeper has deflected the ball round the post. An incident in a wartime game on the Town Ground, when Nottingham Forest were the visitors.

ABOVE: *With a number of their younger players in the Services, Luton Town Cricket Club had a thin time during the war years. But the game went on. Arthur Fryer is seen above leading out his team to meet Welwyn in the first game of the 1945 season.*

BELOW: *The Australian XI which visited Wardown in August, 1942 to meet a combined Luton Town and Vauxhall team. In three-and-a-half hours the visitors had dismissed the Luton team for 99 runs, and scored 100 for 3 wickets to score an easy victory.*

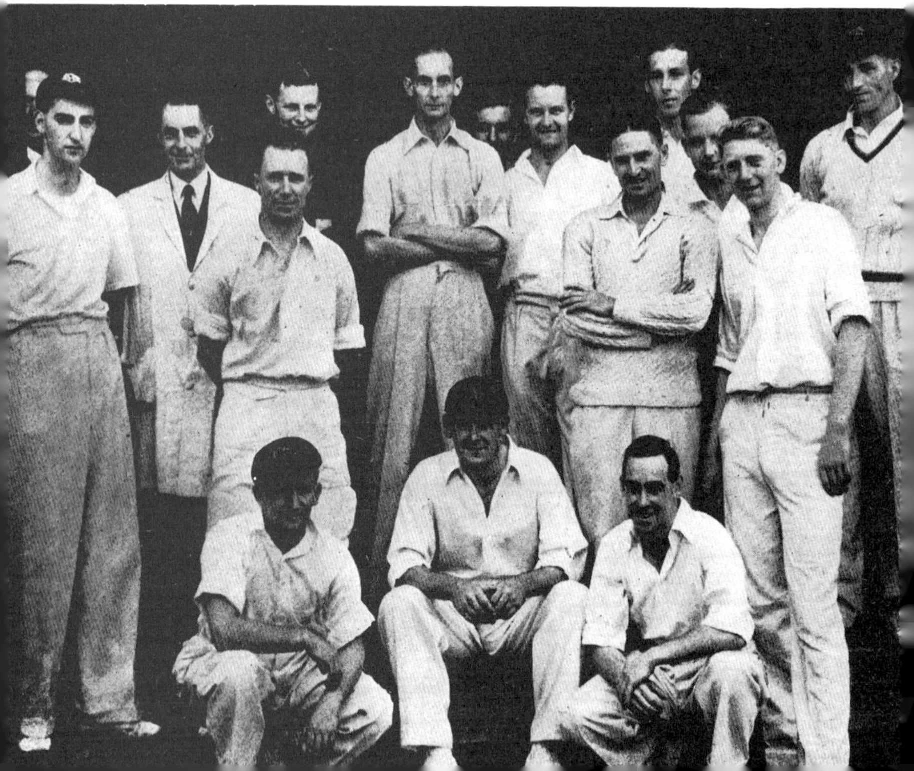

Luton Borough Police were the visitors when this picture was taken at Luton Town Bowling Club in July, 1941.

Organisers and visitors at a darts match at Castle Street Hall, Luton, in April, 1945, when a Luton team entertained the "News of the World" champions.

ABOVE: *Outdoor boxing on the Luton Town Football Ground was a feature of the town's "Holidays at Home" programme. This picture was taken at a six-contest tournament on July 25th, 1942.*

BELOW: *Waiting for the pistol at the start of the 100 yards at a triangular athletic contest between Luton Grammar (then Modern) School, the Old Boys and an R.A.S.C. team. £50 was raised for the British Red Cross Society.*

lives at Dunkirk. C. J. Ladd, a full-back of much promise, joined the Navy, and was killed in H.M.S. Hood.

Another player, Doug. Gardiner, was a prisoner of war for some years after being shot down over Germany, but was freed when Germany was overrun, and resumed the Town colours with credit. Others who joined the Services quite early on, including Billington, the centre-forward, were retained in the Services so long that they could only make very occasional appearances for the Town even after the end of hostilities, and it was almost the end of the 1945-46 season before the Town could regularly field a side which could be anything like a regular team. Even when that season ended there were still many players on the Town books who could not be seen on the Town ground because they were in the Services.

Friendly matches had only a short spell, and then gave place to Regional Leagues. Luton Town were in the Midland Section, with the Wolves, Northampton, Birmingham, Walsall, Coventry City, Leicester City, and West Bromwich Albion. Each club played the other four times, but while these matches aroused a certain amount of interest among supporters, it was far below that of normal times, and at Luton, at any rate, did not create any need for an attendance limitation.

As time went on the player position became increasingly difficult, and the Town were forced to follow the example of other clubs and utilise " guest " players, a system which permitted a player to appear for a club other than his own, always provided his own club gave permission. Among those who played for Luton under these circumstances was Eddie Hapgood, English International and Arsenal star. It was not unknown at an away match to have to borrow a man from the home club. Local youngsters also got a chance and, with an eye to the future, Luton began to take a greater interest than ever in rising talent in the immediate neighbourhood.

Conditions became even more trying as the years went on. Added to the shortage of players were the difficulties of travel and the shortage of playing kits and footballs. One thing which also caused the Town management many headaches was the almost impossible job of obtaining gatemen. Gates generally were considerably lower than pre-war, but as players' wages dropped, most clubs managed to avoid adding to their liabilities, and some even made modest profits.

In the 1940-41 season Luton were included in the Football League South Region, but when the London clubs broke away and formed a competition of their own the Town got together with such clubs as Portsmouth, Watford, Brighton and Cardiff, and the League South "C" was formed. There was also the Midland Cup Competition and the Football League Cup. In the following season the London clubs extended their league, but Luton remained under the Football League, in a competition in which clubs arranged their own matches.

The London clubs returned to the fold for the 1942-43 season, and Luton was included with them to form the Football League South,

an arrangement which continued for the two following seasons.   On
the whole this Regional football filled the gap well.   It was the best
that could be done while travelling difficulties were so great.   Making
cup ties a matter of home and away matches, and depending on the goal
aggregates of the two meetings, was also a wartime innovation.

The Luton District and South Beds. League shared the fate of all
other competitions and closed down, but the Executive Committee
began a subsidiary competition of three divisions as soon as permission was given for competitive football to be resumed.   The
League managed to continue throughout the war, and had much to do
with maintaining a high standard in local junior football.   The Minor
League also ran successfully.   The Bedfordshire F.A. saw to it that
the clubs had cup competitions, and the pre-war competitions were
maintained right throughout the war.   Amateur clubs, of course, had
all sorts of wartime worries and troubles, and it was only enthusiasm,
fine team spirit, and hard work by the officials, that enabled many of
them to survive the disadvantages of the time.

Both the leading local amateur clubs, Vauxhall Motors and Luton
Amateur, joined the Herts. and Beds. Combination which was formed
shortly after the beginning of the war.   This competition was ill-
starred, and fell through at the beginning of 1941, mainly owing to the
inadequate number of clubs and the travel restrictions.   After that,
both teams played friendly matches for charity.   They also ran teams
in the subsidiary competition of the Luton District and South Beds.
League.

In the latter war years some important Service matches were seen
on the Town Ground, but their appeal was largely confined to Service
supporters.

*   *   *   *

CRICKET

In the 1940 season Luton Town C.C. cut down the number of teams
fielded each Saturday from four to two, and on this limited basis had
quite a good season.   In later years, in common with all other sports
clubs, they experienced such difficulties in finding players that they
considered themselves fortunate if able to field one strong side a week.
They had other difficulties.   The pavilion was taken over as an A.R.P.
post, and players had to change on the verandah.   The opposing
players could not have their time-honoured social interval over
tea, for the provision of tea became impossible, and players who
wanted tea had to take it with them in a flask.

Equipment became very scarce, any replacement of boots or flannels
or sweaters involved surrendering precious coupons, and road transport was next to impossible.   But even under these conditions the
game went on, chiefly through the efforts of a handful of club stalwarts
who simply would not give give it up even temporarily.

Vauxhall Motors kept their first XI and their Sunday XI going
throughout the war years.   During that period many notable cricketers

visited the Vauxhall ground with Service teams. They included the Rev. E. T. Killick, England and Middlesex; Leslie Todd, Kent; L. G. Berry, Leicestershire; F. Buse, Somerset; and Spencer, Kent. The first attempt by the club to arrange a two-day match was in June, 1943, when the Royal Australian Air Force Overseas H.Q. brought down a strong XI. The match was notable for high scoring. Vauxhall made 412 for four wickets, T. Clark and R. Hills each contributing a century, and there was a first wicket stand of 183. The Australians improved on this, running up 265 for the first wicket. Workman and Sheidow each reached three figures, and the side's total was 361 for seven wickets. In all, three two-day matches were played against the Australians, and it was not until 1945 that the visitors were able to claim a victory.

Another match that caused much interest, and produced a big sum for charity was when a British Empire XI came to play a strong side chosen by Mr. J. E. D. Moysey. It was staged on the excellent ground of Kent's Athletic. But such matches were the exception, interesting as they were. The really local " derbies " of the war years were the matches played between the Town Club and Vauxhall on Whit Monday and August Bank Holiday in each year. These matches were arranged as part of the Holidays at Home programme.

Many of the smaller clubs in the town carried on gallantly in spite of their many handicaps, and it can be said that local cricket came through its greatest testing time with credit.

*   *   *   *

BOWLS

Luton Town Bowling Club, like the Town Cricket Club, had their pavilion invaded, only in this case the invaders were the Army. For a long time it was used as a sergeants' mess, and club members had to be content with the use of one odd corner. Even the small building on the opposite side of the green was taken over by the Army, for use as a food store. The other clubs with private greens escaped any such requisitioning.

County competitions and inter-County matches had to lapse during the war years, but all the local clubs managed to remain active and to continue club competitions and reasonable match lists, although some old fixtures had to be dropped because of travel difficulties. Keeping the greens in condition was by no means easy, but, whatever the drawbacks, bowlers continued to trundle the wood, and at times to put the Red Cross and other organisations in their debt.

*   *   *   *

HOCKEY

After the first few weeks of war Luton Town Hockey Club was able to function more or less normally for the rest of that season, but the number of players leaving to join the Services forced clubs generally to do some hard thinking about the future. Accordingly, in the 1940-41 season Luton Town, Old Dunstablians, and Kent's joined forces and pooled their playing resources. The combination was named The Remnants, the moving spirit being the late Mr. J. J. Payne. After his unfortunate death much of the work of the club devolved on the shoulders of Mr. J. A. R. Oliver, who also captained the side.

The Remnants were able to put an excellent team into the field, and can point with pride to their record of not once having had to cancel a match. They were honoured, too, by a visit to their ground at Wardown by a Hockey Association XI, an occasion which provided a big day for local hockey enthusiasts.

Vauxhall Motors were able to carry on independently, and gained much success.

* * * *

RUGBY

Luton Rugby F.C. managed to complete the 1939-40 season, but then found the difficulties facing them were overwhelming, and suspended activities until the 1945-46 season.

Vauxhall Motors, better placed as regards availability of players, carried on and fielded one team regularly throughout the war years. Most of their matches were against Service teams, chiefly from neighbouring R.A.F. Stations. Apart from this, local rugby was definitely pushed into the background by the war.

* * * *

GOLF

Both golf clubs catering for Luton players had to manage without a professional during the greater part of the war, and to maintain their courses as best they could with the minimum of ground staff. Loss of members to the Services, and transport restrictions, meant that county championship meetings and inter-club matches had to be abandoned; major trophy competitions were discontinued for a time, and the Luton and District Banks and the Vauxhall Golfing Societies ceased to function.

South Beds, having spent thousands on preparations to transfer part of the course to new land, on seeding it and constructing new greens, had this land requisitioned for agriculture; but, unlike 1914-18, when a large part of the then course became a rifle range, members were able to continue playing over 18 holes. Dunstable Downs had to shorten their course somewhat, but with the expert assistance of a farmer member, made quite a good profit out of farming their spare land.

Ball shortage was the greatest handicap in the closing stages of the war. There were no new balls, but those who could scrape up a dozen old ones could send them away, and expect to receive nine playable " remakes " in return. The life of a " remake " had no guarantee. Sometimes, in fact, it was very short. But with these most players had to be content, while as to buying new clubs, the best thing to do was to wait.

However, despite all handicaps, members managed to keep the

clubs going, to offer hospitality to players in the Services, and to raise considerable sums for war and other charities ; and 1946 opened with prospects so good that South Beds. felt warranted in increasing the subscription to meet rising costs, and to reimpose an entrance fee, while Dunstable Downs membership was so full that there was a waiting list.

*　　*　　*　　*

GREYHOUND RACING

Greyhound racing is dependent on artificial lighting for evening meetings. That, of course, was out of the question. For three weeks there were no meetings at Luton Stadium. Then the management began to stage meetings on Monday afternoons. Later, meetings were also held on Friday afternoons, but in 1942, the Government stopped mid-week meetings because it was felt workers might be tempted to lose precious hours from vital jobs, and for the rest of the war greyhound racing at Luton Stadium was on Saturday afternoons only. Despite staffing difficulties and transport restrictions, which prevented owners from bringing dogs long distances, racing continued successfully on a one meeting a week basis until conditions had so changed that an evening meeting could be added.

*　　*　　*　　*

DARTS

Darts played a big part in the indoor recreational life of Luton during the war, and the Luton Clubs' League made rapid strides. The Licensed Victuallers' League, finding their clubs could not raise teams during the early part of the war, discontinued activities until 1944, which was a bumper year. Members of both Leagues raised large sums for war charities, and an open competition in aid of comforts for the troops was a big success. Darts was probably the most popular of all war-time recreations. Wherever there was a Home Guard post, an A.R.P. post, a firewatcher's room, there one could always find a darts board occupying an honoured place on a pitted wall. In pubs and clubs, in the kitchens and the halls of thousands of homes, there was the darts board.

*　　*　　*　　*

BILLIARDS

The war caused a break in the Luton Billiards League's long run of successful seasons. Those concerned with the League decided to suspend activities for the first winter of the war. In fact, it remained dormant until the autumn of 1945, when activities were resumed on much the same lines as in pre-war years, the only notable difference being that the teams were reduced from six to four players.

In the various clubs the cup competitions which were a feature of the winter season were also suspended, but it was found possible to arrange exhibitions by notable professionals and amateurs for various war charities, and the demonstrations given by some lady experts were

369

Y

particularly good, not only with the cue, but in the way they relieved spectators of charity money.

*   *   *   *

BOXING

In the amateur field some really good performances were put up during the war years by members of the Boxing Sections of the Vauxhall and Electrolux Recreation Clubs, and members of these clubs won honours in national championships. At both places facilities were also provided for interesting Service displays, and for these local support was always forthcoming, but professional boxing as staged in Luton during that period was by no means the popular venture it is in some towns.

New Brooms

TIRED of Coalition politics after the 1914-18 war, Luton, a traditional Liberal seat, swung over to Conservative representation. During the ensuing years it wobbled from time to time between Liberalism and Conservatism and then settled down as a National Liberal constituency. But during the inter-war years Labour as a political force had been growing and out of the 1945 elections, Luton emerged with its first Labour M.P.

The 1945 Elections were a landslide ; the biggest political landslide since 1906. When places like Bedford, Hitchin and St. Albans, regarded as essentially safe Conservative seats, went Labour in keeping with the general trend of things, who could be surprised to find that an industrial town like Luton had also voted Labour ? And particularly so when regard is paid to the fact that the electorate had been swelled in the latter pre-war years by large numbers of people from the North, Clydeside and Wales ; from many places where for long Labour had been the dominant political party. It is reasonable to assume that many of the younger men who had reached electoral age while in the Services also voted Labour, in the belief that Labour might advance the country one stage nearer the Utopia which has been promised for years. They believed that the time was ripe for a change of Government, and certainly, they thought, such a change could not make things worse ; it might make them better.

*   *   *   *

From the beginning of the war party politics were nominally in suspense. Towards the end of 1944, however, portents of victory became more marked, and attention began to centre on domestic issues which would revive party divisions. Mr. E. L. Burgin had been Luton's M.P. since 1929. He was elected as a Liberal. The succeeding brief Labour administration resulted in some party ties going to the melting pot. In the 1931 election, with no Conservative opponent, he was re-elected as a Liberal National, with a 24,000 majority over Labour. From then onwards he retained the support of Conservatives, and in 1935 was again re-elected. His Labour opponent on that occasion, Mr. F. L. Kerran, succeeded in reducing Mr. Burgin's majority to about 13,000, the first sign of the political change which was taking place.

Mr. Burgin had an eventful career at Westminster. First a Charity Commissioner, then Parliamentary Secretary to the Board of Trade, and then Minister of Transport, in 1939 he was appointed the first Minister of Supply. It was a somewhat thankless job at that period, for the productive capacity of the nation had still to be developed. In office he had many critics, and when, in the dark days of 1940, Mr. Churchill became Prime Minister and re-shuffled the Government, Mr. Burgin joined the ranks of the ex-Ministers. Nevertheless, as an eminent international lawyer, his specialist help was much in demand by the Government during the war years, but by early 1945 his health was causing concern. At the time of the election in July he was gravely ill and could not have contested the seat. He died in August at the age of 58.

Labour had been looking for a new candidate since 1944 and in December of that year they fixed on Mr. William N. Warbey, who since 1941 had been Chief English Press Officer to the Norwegian Government in its exile in this country. Mr. Warbey wasted little time. Early in the New Year he launched his campaign.

The Labour campaign was working all through the early months of 1945, but it was late May before it was known to the Liberal and Conservative Co-ordinating Committee that they also would have to find another candidate. The General Election had already been fixed for July 5th. Barely a month remained for campaigning when Lieut.-Col. Leonard Graham Brown, M.D., F.R.C.S., was announced as a National Candidate. Senior ear, nose, and throat specialist at Charing Cross Hospital, and winner of the M.C. in the 1914-18 war, he was new to the political platform. Against highly expert opponents, quick to seize on everything which would react to the advantage of the Labour campaign, he found himself at a great disadvantage, a disadvantage which persisted throughout the campaign. Labour was all out for social legislation of the kind which has since hit the country almost as a tidal wave. Against this Dr. Graham Brown could do little beyond declare himself an opponent of Socialism, and urge electors to back Mr. Churchill.

Both sides introduced some big names for their chief meetings in the Winter Assembly Hall. Lord Teviot, Lord Simon and Mr. A.

T. Lennox-Boyd, a Conservative who successfully defended his own seat in Mid-Beds., came in support of Dr. Graham Brown. Mr. Warbey's advocates included Hannen Swaffer and Professor Harold Laski.

Polling took place on July 5th, 1945, on a register hastily prepared for the election, and far from satisfactory. Many people had failed to take precaution to ensure that they were included, and both sides complained bitterly of anomalies, such as children's names appearing and parents' being omitted. One result was that a revised and much more accurate register was prepared for the subsequent municipal elections.

For the result of the election there was a wait of nearly three weeks, to ensure that the votes of people in the Services overseas arrived.

Ballot boxes were kept in police custody until July 25th, and then taken to the Winter Assembly Hall, where most of one day was occupied by a preliminary check to ensure that no Service voter had voted both by post and by proxy. Next day Labour optimism was justified. Mr. Warbey was Luton's first Labour M.P. His majority was 7,421. Actual voting was :—Warbey, 39,335 ; Brown, 31,914. 74.9 per cent. of those entitled to had voted. That evening Labour had a big celebration at the Winter Assembly Hall. Ward Associations followed with Victory Socials.

*   *   *   *

Success in the General Election stimulated the Labour party throughout the country to go all out in an effort to secure control of municipal authorities in the following November. At Luton, although the Labour Co-operative group on the Town Council was small in 1939, and any casual vacancies which occurred while elections were suspended during the war years had been filled on the basis of maintaining the *status quo*, Labour considered that there were distinct prospects of their obtaining a majority for the first time. It was anticipated that, as after the end of the 1914-1918 war, a number of the senior members of the Council would retire. It was known that some would have done earlier had there been no war. Room for fresh blood was therefore certain. In addition, those who by being co-opted during the war had found the road to municipal honours easy had all to seek electoral approval of their continued membership. This meant 14 vacancies in the nine wards to be filled on November 1st.

The constitution of the Council was : Liberal 14, Conservative 12, Labour Co-operative Group 9, Independent 1. Four Liberal or Conservative aldermen out of the nine, including Lady Keens, the Mayor, were due to retire on November 9th. Of the retiring councillors, 12 were in the Liberal-Conservative group, one was a co-opted Labour member, and one the Independent.

As early as February the Labour party had announced two prospective candidates, and others were introduced at later ward meetings. The naming of the first Liberal-Conservative candidate in April was

LEFT: *Dr. Graham Brown, Liberal National candidate for Luton in the General Election of July 1945, chats to stallholders in Luton market.*

RIGHT: *Luton Labour supporters give a cheer. Front centre is Mr. W. N. Warbey, newly elected M.P. for Luton, with Mrs. Warbey.*

BELOW: *The scene at the counting of the votes inside the Winter Assembly Hall.*

followed by a Ratepayers' Association declaration that they also intended running candidates, and when the Communists also began to talk about entering the field there was prospect of a free-for-all. Labour made it clear that they were going into the fight on strict party lines. Individualism would count less than ever, they declared. The Liberal-Conservative group, declaring that the ratepayers were only concerned with efficient service, pooled their resources and called their nominees " People's Candidates." The announced candidates of the Ratepayers' Association did not all materialise, while the one announced Communist candidate, instead of handing in nomination papers by 5 p.m. on the appointed day, discovered that 9 a.m. next day was too late.

Even so there were 32 candidates. Labour put forward 14—one for every vacancy ; Liberals, 7 ; Conservatives, 5 ; Ratepayers' Association, 4 ; and there were two Independents. The use of the Parliamentary register gave the vote to many who had never before voted in municipal elections because they were not rated occupiers of property, and equally so to all who had newly come of electoral age. Altogether some 20,000 more were eligible to vote.

Labour gained six seats, Independents, two. The Ratepayers' Association nominees were all defeated. 48 per cent. of the electorate voted.

*   *   *   *

Labour now had 15 councillors out of 27 . . . not a majority of the whole Council, but a majority of councillors, and councillors were the only members entitled to vote in the election of aldermen. To get an absolute majority they could either elect four Labour aldermen from their councillors and rely on winning the resultant by-elections, or they could adopt an easier course. The Local Government Act enables aldermen to be chosen from outside the Council. Labour could do this, gain their objective, and avoid the expense and possible risk of defeat in by-elections. There were few instances on record of such a course having been adopted, but the opportunity was there, and they took it. The Labour-Co-operative group, with their councillors in majority, elected Councillor W. G. Roberts as Luton's first Labour Mayor, voted off the Council Lady Keens, who had just completed her term as Mayor, and also Alderman A. E. Ansell, the other two aldermen due to retire having intimated that they did not desire re-election. They then elected as aldermen four non-members of the Council of whom two had been unsuccessful at the polls eight days earlier. This was a point not overlooked by many critics of this method of securing political control. The strong feeling aroused, however, found no reflection in the voting when two by-elections were held within a few weeks, following the resignation of Councillor T. H. Knight, a Co-operative member, and Councillor A. W. Gregory, Conservative. Labour nominees won both seats. They increased their majority on the Council to four.

When County Council elections followed in March, 1946, Labour did better in Luton than anywhere else in the county. There were 18 Luton seats to fill, and only four retiring members seeking re-election. Labour put forward 18 candidates. Luton's one previous Labour member was re-elected, two secured seats without opposition, and six others were successful at the poll, against an opposition again largely composed of " People's Candidates."

The one Communist candidate failed.

Final Victory

V ICTORY in Europe gave to Luton its first taste of one of the four great freedoms that the Atlantic Charter envisaged—Freedom from Fear.

From the announcement on September 3rd, 1939, that this country was again at war with Germany, the town had known many fears—the fear of invasion and all that it implied ; the fear that a loved one in the armed forces would find torture or death in a far-off land ; the fear that a home painstakingly put together would be shattered in an instant, and the fear that German bombing would snatch from its homes the children for whom the future was planned.

But from the beginning of 1945 there surged strongly in every heart the hope and expectation that the end was near. The Armies of Liberation had swept across France almost to the Rhine, the last Nazi counter-offensive in the Ardennes had proved abortive, the V. sites had been overrun, the Russians had liberated Budapest and stood at the gates of Warsaw. Surely, surely, only a few more months remained.

And it was natural that thoughts should turn to the most fitting manner in which the return of peace to Europe should be celebrated. When it was first announced that the Town Council proposed to spend up to £2,000 in providing entertainment a storm of protest was raised. Recalling that many soldiers had returned as cripples, that others still languished in Japanese prison camps, and that more were still fighting in the Far East, there were many who thought Luton should " weep rather than sing." They derided the suggestion that people should dance in the streets, and felt that rejoicing should be delayed until the entire world had returned to peace and sanity.

Others argued that the occasion should not pass unrecognised, and their opinion was the view of the majority. They acknowledged the devastation the war had caused in many homes ; the grief occasioned by personal loss; and the sorrow that came with remembrance of thousands still in the hands of the Japanese, whose torture of prisoners had revolted the civilised world.

The voice of the majority grew louder and reached its culmination in the utterance of a woman who asked, " Shall I weep on V-Day because I no longer need to listen for the siren, no longer need to dash downstairs with my children to the shelter?

" Shall I weep when I find the worry and strain of the war with the Germans over at last, and my children and other children can look forward to the normal existence I had as a child?

" No, I shall not, unless they are tears of joy. I hope I shall sing and dance, whether in George Street or in my own home. My first thoughts will be to thank God, and everything I do will be in thanks to God and our dear boys who will have made this wonderful thing possible.

" Must we make our boys who have lost their lives or limbs ashamed of us by being miserable on the glorious day, or can we show them that what they have done has been worth while?

" Let us all, when V-Day comes laugh, sing and be happy, and wipe out the bitterness of the last five years.

" For many it will not be easy, but with prayers and courage in our hearts, songs and smiles on our lips, it can be done."

*   *   *   *

On May 7th, 1945, came the news that Germany had surrendered unconditionally. Momentarily the town stood still. Its people had waited so long for that news, and too often had their soaring hopes of its imminent arrival been dashed. They hesitated to accept its full portent. They had expected the first news of Germany's defeat to come from the Prime Minister, but when a late announcement declared that the following day was to be VE-Day and that the Prime Minister would broadcast, then all doubts vanished, and Luton had its first night free from fear.

Varied emotions surged through the minds of all. Memories of those who gave their lives so that the town might enjoy that day temprred the celebrations in many homes, but the thought that a father or son who had helped to carry retribution right into the heart of Germany might soon return added to the happiness of many more. The conflict between sorrow and joy, however, was submerged by the wave of thankfulness and relief that arose from every heart.

This was the dominant note of all celebrations—celebrations which were rightly regarded as but an intermediate stage on the road to complete and final victory. It was the end of a major task, however, and Ltuon in common with the rest of the country found time to count its blessings and snatch a few brief hours from the dreary task of making war.

The town did not await the dawn of VE-Day to begin its celebrations of the overthrow of Nazi oppression and tyranny. No sooner was it made known that the next day—May 8th—was to be the day of national thanksgiving than the drab, grey streets of war-time became avenues of colour in profuse array, enriched in darkness by beams of light from countless windows and the flickering flames of many bonfires. It was the end of more than five years of war-darkened streets, the end of the fear and havoc of the then seemingly unceasing nightly terror raids. No longer was it necessary for mothers to rouse their sleeping children and dash for safety to the cold and cheerless shelters. They could retire for the night and sleep until a natural awakening. It was the occasion to celebrate—the winning of a dearly bought victory.

Luton's first big cheer for victory was heard at the Town Hall, from which the news that hostilities in Europe had ceased was relayed. It was the spontaneous outburst of pent-up emotions—feelings that had long lain dormant and subdued under the staid exterior of the so-called prosaic and unimaginative Britisher. But that night, Luton gave the lie to the phrase. It celebrated as a victor should, and though outwardly carefree it remembered those who had suffered, with a deep and abiding respect that has outlived those transitory outbursts of joy.

The cheer that greeted the victory report was momentarily hushed while the then Mayor, Lady Keens, announced that the celebrations next day would commence with a service of thanksgiving which she and members of the Town Council would attend.

Afterwards bonfires were lighted, and the people danced and sang in the streets. Music was hastily improvised, one householder going so far as to drag a piano from his home and play for a jubilant crowd of neighbours.

Greatest scenes of animation, however, were in the immediate vicinity of the Town Hall—the nerve centre of the town throughout the war. Complete strangers joined hands to dance in the Palais Glide, British and American troops mingled with carefree camaraderie among the jostling and cheering throng. It was the climax of hope frustrated for many years, and the merriment continued until VE-Day was born.

The slightest incident that night was made the occasion of good-humoured banter and cheers. The majesty of the law was forgotten by more than one of the milling crowd. Two policemen had a lively chase before they could recover helmets snatched from their heads by revellers and quickly hand-passed through a scrum of several hundreds. They seemed to relish the chase, though another of their comrades wore a slightly embarrassed look when two light-hearted maids, evidently appreciative of the temporary waiving of dignity, implanted their over-elaborately painted lips on his blushing cheeks. A soldier was similarly decorated, rather more willingly, and had a V-sign in lipstick drawn on his forehead.

Luton awakened slowly from its unexpected outburst of cheer. It was rather forcibly reminded that though Germany had bowed the knee, some war-time restrictions must remain.

Housewives were early afoot, queueing for bread and other perishable goods before shops put up their shutters for days of long-awaited rejoicing. Earlier still, however, were the thousands of workers, who, confused by the unexpected method of the peace announcement, caught their usual bus to make sure that they really had the day off. At Vauxhall Motors, Ltd., more than 1,000 reported for work. The firm, appreciating that they had turned up to honour arrangements announced on notices throughout the works, decided to grant them an extra day's holiday with pay. Eventually all Luton appreciated that VE-Day was a reality, and that a holiday had been declared.

*   *   *   *

The official opening of the borough's celebrations was at the Parish Church, where hundreds, unable to get inside, waited in the churchyard in a downpour of rain to join in a service relayed through loudspeakers. Inside, the Mayor and Corporation, who had walked in procession from the Town Hall, sat in the crowded Church, where both before and after the service, the bells rang joyous peals proclaiming victory.

It was a proud occasion for the many mothers, wives and sweethearts, most of whom wore red, white and blue rosettes, with regimental and other service badges, as they heard the Vicar, Canon W. Davison, R.D., voice the thanks of all for the victory of righteousness over the forces of evil.

" Let us," the Vicar said, " not relax our efforts now, and let us resist temptation to become cynical and despairing.

" This hour of victory, this day of rejoicing, will be an empty spectacle, a mere piece of emotional satisfaction, unless it spurs us on to greater efforts.

" Let it also be a day of rededication as we bow our heads in memory of the gallant dead.

" Then let us go on in the same spirit as we have continued the struggle, with courage undiminished and with strength renewed, to the still greater tasks that lie ahead."

Later in the day services were held in Chapel Street Methodist Church and at the Sports' Ground, where several thousands, led by Luton Band, raised their voices in the singing of " Abide with Me."

Speaking after the morning service, the Mayor, from the bandstand at the Town Hall, said the day had given her the proudest moment of her life, adding, " We are full of thanksgiving to God for having brought us through to victory. We grieve for our friends who have lost loved ones, but we rejoice with those whose loved ones are returning.

" We have seen the powers of darkness put to flight. We have seen the morning break."

Later, Lady Keens wrote, " Our first thought must be one of thank-

*Peace in Europe . . . The scene in George Street, look-
ing towards the floodlit Town Hall on the night of VE
plus 1.*

ABOVE: *Luton Parish Church was filled to capacity for the V.E. Thanksgiving Service.*

BELOW: *Many who were unable to gain admission listened in to the loudspeakers which relayed the service in the church-yard*

ABOVE: *Hundreds of people packed George Street on V.E. Day to listen to the band, and generally air their feelings.*

LEFT: *Waitresses from a nearby restaurant join in the dancing in George Street.*

BELOW: *V.J. Day, too, brought the revellers to the town centre, where rejoicing went on through the evening, and into the night.*

Lady Keens, Mayor of Luton, is in the centre of this happy group at the Blundell Road V.E. Party . . . one of the many street parties held in the town.

Bonfires in the streets marked the end of a happy day on V.J. Day . . . let the tar melt, who cares!

fulness to God that we have been granted the victory for which we have striven so hard and so long.

" The people of Luton have played a proud part in this struggle—on the field of battle, in the air, on and under the sea, in the factories and in the home. I have seen at first-hand some of the immense amount of voluntary service which has ungrudgingly been given by men, women—yes, and children, too. A common danger united us, a common aim bound us all together as never before.

" In this hour of triumph we remember those who have fallen, and those who are sick in mind and body. I hope our actions in the coming years will show that this remembrance is not mere lip-service, but a real and living thing.

" With the end of the war in Europe one great cloud has been lifted from our town and our country. I wish I could say that all the clouds had been lifted. There remains the war in the Far East, with all the anxieties it must bring to those households in Luton which have, or will have, men fighting out there. And there are those, always in our thoughts, whose men have been the prisoners of the Japanese since 1942.

" We must back up our men in the Far East as we have backed up their comrades from the dark days of Dunkirk until the day of victory.

" I am sure Luton will do it. There is the fine tradition of these last five and a half years to guide us—a tradition of hard work, of splendid voluntary service, of willingness to do the little extra in the larger cause.

" And when the war in the Far East is over, when we can celebrate the total victory and turn all our energies to solving the problems of reconstruction, I hope we shall retain a large measure of the good neighbourliness and understanding that carried us through times the like of which we hope never to see again."

*   *   *   *

The lighter side of Victory celebrations was continued with unabated vigour—dancing in the streets was resumed, with joyous voices continually raised in song and light-hearted banter. The gaily decorated streets presented a scene unparalleled in the history of the town.

Elderly women with ribbons in their hair vied with younger women in a colourful array of dress, while small children wore flag-fashioned frocks.

There were also scenes of incongruity that brought smiles to the straightest face—a man wearing a boiler suit and top hat being escorted home by his wife brought the biggest laugh, though a soldier wearing a straw boater ran him close as a mirth-producer.

In the dazzling glare of peace-time lighting the celebrations again continued until a late hour. The Town Hall tower was floodlit, coloured lights twinkled in the trees in New Bedford Road and V-signs etched in electric bulbs could be seen all over the town.

Traffic was diverted from the main streets, and from George Street to Wardown Park thousands jostled, danced, sang and whistled, while bells, rattles and a few fireworks made a varied contribution of sound and vigorously contested the right to be heard with the music of bands and recordings relayed from the Town Hall.

As the night advanced, bonfires were again lighted in all quarters of the town, and in no small number of them Hitler's effigy came to an appropriate end.

In the Selborne Road district there was no doubt as to the residents' idea of Hitler's " last territorial claim." A scaffold was erected and the execution of Der Fuehrer carried out, while an effigy of Goering swung from a near-by lamp-post, lighted up by the rays of the lamp he had helped to keep extinguished so long. In other districts, Mussolini met a similar fate.

Even after midnight the revelry continued unabated in the vicinity of the Town Hall, where many, well-nigh exhausted, sat on the steps and watched those who had still the energy to sing and dance.

Greatest memory of the day, however, was the hush that fell on the rejoicings when the King and the Prime Minister broadcast. When Mr. Churchill ended, the huge crowd spontaneously sang " There'll always be an England." It was a grand and moving spectacle.

The scenes on VE-Day were renewed with no less exuberance on the following day, and that night the whole front of the Town Hall was floodlit and the rejoicings continued.

Though extensions of licences had been granted to public houses throughout the town, the supply was not equal to the demand, and many had closed their doors at a very early hour. In the circumstances a sailor who paraded Williamson Street with a bucket of beer and dispensed it by the cupful was a cheering sight.

That night searchlights raked the sky, and passing aircraft flashed the V-sign to the jubilant townspeople.

The days did not pass without some casualties, but though nineteen persons were taken to the Luton and Dunstable Hospital no one was seriously injured. Indeed, so well did Luton behave that the Chief Constable, Mr. Ronald Alderson, publicly thanked the people through the Press.

" I am grateful to everyone," he said. " It was a credit to the town. The people enjoyed themselves well, and did so in a manner that considerably lightened the police duties on such an occasion."

*　　*　　*　　*

Eight babies were born in Luton on VE-Day, which was commemorated in the names of two. One, whose surname begins with E, was christened Vivienne and the second was called Veronica Edith.

Nor were the children forgotten in the greater realisation by their parents of what the day meant to all. Streets all over the town became banqueting halls where, at flower-decked trestle tables, thousands of children were entertained. Nothing was spared to give them the day of their lives.

They were visited by the Mayor, who was greeted with tumultuous cheers and the singing of " For she's a jolly good fellow," as she made a tour of the parties to speak, and cheerfully sign autographs.

The children also had fancy-dress parades, sports, entertainments, and at night out-lasted their parents in revels around bonfires as fireworks crackled and sparkled to seemingly unending cries of delight.

Accompanying the Mayor was the Chief Constable, who remarked, " This is the sort of thing we want our children to remember, not the experiences they have undergone in the past five years."

Luton's love of children, shown in pre-war days by the number of parties given for them, was re-born in the dawn of peace in Europe.

*   *   *   *

Seven bands took part in Luton's victory parade and thanksgiving service on the following Sunday, when the Town was given an inspiring picture in perspective of its war effort.

It was a proper perspective too, for Luton was not pushing herself to the fore. As a tribute to the United States, American soldiers, with the Stars and Stripes and their regimental colours, headed the procession, led by the Luton Band.

Next came British troops with a golden-horned goat mascot, followed by the A.T.S. and the R.A.F.

Then the procession assumed its more intimate local aspect—all sections of the Civil Defence organisations were there, with the Home Guard and N.F.S. Special Constables paraded with the police and the War Reserve force, together with the Women Auxiliaries.

The great share women had taken was symbolised by their sections of the Civil Defence, the Red Cross, St. John Ambulance and kindred contingents. Besides the Women's Voluntary Services there was also the Women's Land Army and the Women's Section of the British Legion, with women war workers in their overalls.

There were the pre-Service units too, and older organisations for girls and boys, trade union and guild representatives.

The parade took half-an-hour to march past. Cheer upon cheer came from the crowds along the route from the Manor Road Recreation ground to the Town football ground. Many in the crowds wore medals or medal ribbons, but it was in the procession that medals were most conspicuous, though some wore only ribbons.

Two policemen who were Old Contemptibles led the procession, while many more were included in its ranks.

Reminders of Luton's bombing ordeals were two Luton George Medallists—Supt. Sear at the head of the police, and Major J. C. Cunningham, D.S.O., with the Home Guard.

The Luton Band played for the march past the Mayor, who was

385

z

accompanied by most members of the Council. The service was conducted by the Rev. G. H. Woodham, president of Luton Free Church Council, the Vicar of Luton, Canon Wm. Davison, R.D., giving the address.

The celebrations gradually drew to a close, though children's parties continued for many days, and controversy, so loud when the planning for victory was taking place, stilled completely when the Town Council announced that the celebrations cost only £440 out of the £2,000 allowed.

*　　*　　*　　*

Luton again went back to work to win, this time, world peace, and three months and a week later stopped to celebrate again the achievement of its aspirations—It was VJ-Day, August 15th.

Once again the Town celebrated a great and joyous occasion in a thoroughly decent way, and though there was again plenty of noise and quite a few bonfires and fireworks, there were no excesses.

Thousands of people, in exuberant mood, thronged the streets by night and day, but there was not a single incident requiring police attention.

Luton fittingly began its celebrations of world peace with a service of thanksgiving in the Parish Church, to which the Mayor and Corporation in their robes marched in procession through streets once more beflagged.

In the church, which was again inadequate for the many who wished to participate in the service, seats were specially reserved for Forces' personnel and for relatives of men killed in the Far East or prisoners in Japanese hands.

The Vicar, Canon Davison, struck a note of hope and expectation in his address, when he commented, " Our hearts are full of thanksgiving that this time of suspense, this nightmare of agony, has at last passed, and that our loved ones in the Far East will soon be released."

" World peace can be effected by men of resolution working towards that end. The idea of isolationism must now be shattered for ever."

After a morning of drizzling rain the sun came out, and crowds again filled the main streets to sing, dance and make merry. The celebrations continued in the same strain as on VE-Day, bonfires glowed red against the night sky, and the flashing and sparkling of fireworks mingled with the brilliance of floodlighting as the people brought to a reluctant close the first of their two VJ holidays.

The rejoicings were again hushed to hear the King's speech broadcast from the Town Hall, and the crowd joined lustily in singing the National Anthem, before they resumed their laughter and making cheer.

During the speech the Mayor, Lady Keens, stood in the Town Hall balcony with Mr. W. N. Warbey, M.P. for Luton, who travelled from the opening session of the new Parliament to join in the town's celebrations. He also attended several children's parties, which were again a feature of the town's rejoicing.

So well did the people enjoy themselves on the first VJ-Day, however, that the remaining celebrations were tame by comparison. The tempo of events increased only in the late afternoon of the following day, and again revelry ruled to a late hour.

But the first flush of Victory had gone, and while children's parties continued to hold daily sway, a feeling of sober relief and thankfulness seemed to pervade the thoughts of adults. It was as though Luton had said, " We have won the war, now let us make sure that we win the peace." Her eyes seemed to peer deeply into the future in search of the day—

> " *When the war-drums beat no longer,*
> *And the battle-flags are furled* ;
> *In the Parliament of man,*
> *The Federation of the world.*"

The Roll of Honour

ABEL, SIDNEY, 4, St. Paul's Road, Luton. Sgt.-Pilot, R.A.F. Killed on active service, May 1st, 1943.

ABBOTT, LESLIE CHARLES, 134, Turners Road, Luton. Pte., 4th Royal Norfolks. Killed in action, Paula Uban Island, Singapore, February 8th, 1942.

ABBOTT, ROBERT, 17, Corncastle Road, Luton. Spr., R.E. Died on active service, Cairn Ryan, Scotland, March 25th, 1942.

ABRAHAMS, ROBERT CHARLES, 8, Cumberland Street, Luton. Rfmn., K.R.R. Died of wounds, Sangro, Italy, May 13th, 1944.

ADAMS, RONALD BERTRAM THOMAS, 212, Dunstable Road, Luton. Pilot Officer, 174th (Rocket Typhoon) Squadron, R.A.F. Presumed killed on operations, Osnabruck, Germany, February 24th, 1945.

ADDISON, ERNEST, 1, Dunstable Close, Luton. Chief Cook, M.V. *San Vittorio* (Tanker). Lost at sea, May 16th, 1942.

AINSWORTH, STANLEY, 15, Villa Road, Luton. F/Sgt., 51st Squadron, R.A.F. Killed on operations over Leipzig, Germany, December 4th, 1943.

AITCHISON, JOHN FREDERICK, 4, Ferndale Road, Luton. Cabin Boy, Merchant Navy. Died as P.O.W., Japanese prison camp, after sinking of SS. *Kirkpool*. Place and date of death unknown.

AITKEN, JAMES MCLAUGHLIN, 41, Solway Road, Luton. Spr., R.E. Accidentally killed on active service, Newcastle-on-Tyne, June 15th, 1940.

ALLEN, CLIFFORD CHAS., 54, Cambridge Street, Luton. Gnr., 133/41st Light A.A. Regt., R.A. Killed in action, Middle East, October 17th, 1943.

ALLEN, CYRIL, 16, Vernon Road, Luton. Cpl., 8th Royal Warwicks. Regt. Died on active service, October 27th, 1942.

ALLEN, DONALD BERTIE, 178, North Street, Luton. Boy (First Class), R.N. Lost at sea, Crete, May 22nd, 1941.

ALLEN, JONATHAN WILLIAM, 29, Drury Lane, Houghton Regis, and B. Laporte, Ltd., Luton. Bdr., R.A. Died as Prisoner-of-War, Japanese Prison Camp, 1944.

ALLEN, OLIVER JAMES, 54, Windsor Street, Luton. Cpl., 2nd Battn. Bedfs. and Herts. Regt. Killed in action, Cessena, Italy, November 21st, 1944.

ALLEN, RONALD WILLIAM, 25, Collingdon Street, Luton. Tpr., Reconnaissance Corps. Killed on active service, November 12th, 1942.

ANSELL, GLADYS, 58, Old Bedford Road, Luton. Killed by enemy action, at Luton, October 14th, 1940.

ANSELL, HORACE GEORGE, 2a, Dordans Road, Luton. Sgt., R.A.F. Missing, presumed killed, France, August 17-18th, 1943.

ANSTEE, JACK, 111, Ashburnham Road, Luton. F/Officer, R.A.F. Missing, presumed killed, night operations over Germany, January, 1944.

APPLEBY, FREDERICK WILLIAM, 109, Cambridge Street, Luton. Spr., R.E. Killed in action, Italy, April 1st, 1944.

ARCHER, HARRY, 16, Leicester Road, Luton. Killed by enemy action, at Vauxhall Motors, Ltd., Luton, August 30th, 1940.

ARDLEY, GUY, 52, Lemsford Road, St. Albans, and Hayward-Tyler & Co., Ltd., Luton. F/Officer, R.A.F. Missing on operations, September, 1944.

ARLIDGE, FRANK, 25, Rondini Avenue, Luton. Killed by enemy action at De Havillands, Hatfield, October 3rd, 1940.

ARMITAGE, HAROLD WILLIAM, 8, Hayes Close, Stopsley, Luton. Able Seaman, R.N., H.M.S. *Cornwall*. Died of wounds, Bay of Bengal, April 5th, 1942.

ARMSTRONG, PERCY, 1, Hayes Close, Luton. Gnr., R.A. Lost at sea while prisoner of Japanese, November 18th, 1942.

ARNOLD, EDWARD FRED, 9, Overstone Road, Luton. Died of injuries caused by enemy action at Vauxhall Motors, Ltd., August 30th, 1940.

ARNOLD, SIDNEY ALLEN, 90, Ash Road, Luton. Pte., Suffolk Regt. Died as prisoner of Japanese, No. 4 Camp, Siam, July 16th, 1943.

ASHDOWN, CECIL JOSEPH, 18, High Street, Houghton Regis, and Home Counties Newspapers, Ltd., Luton. Died as prisoner of Japanese while working on Burma-Siam Railway, July 23rd, 1943.

ATKIN, AUBREY CYRIL WILLIAM, 2, St. Paul's Road, Luton. Dvr., R.E. Killed in action, Singapore, February 13th, 1942.

ATTFIELD, ALFRED JAMES. Killed by enemy action at Vauxhall Motors, Ltd., Luton, August 30th, 1940.

ATTWOOD, HAROLD ERNEST EDWARD, 21, Faringdon Road, Luton. Flt/Sgt., R.A.F., att. No. 423 R.C.A.F. Squadron, Coastal Command. Killed on operations, North Sea, November 13th, 1943.

AUSTIN, JOHN PRESCOTT, 216, Cutenhoe Road, Luton. F/Officer, Bomber Command, R.A.F. Killed in action, Northern France, August 18th, 1944.

AXBY, LESLIE FREDERICK, 77, Milton Road, Luton. Sgt./Pilot, No. 466 Squadron, R.A.A.F. Missing, presumed killed, January 30th, 1943.

BACON, LESLIE BERNARD, 16, Chaul End Lane, Luton. Pte., Suffolk Regt. Died as prisoner of Japanese in Siam, November 1st, 1943.

BACON, LESLIE WILLIAM, 64, Leicester Road, Luton. Sgt. Obsvr., R.A.F. Killed on active service, air operations, 1941.

BADRICK, CYRIL EZRA, 20, Maidenhall Road, Luton. Stoker, First-Class, R.N., H.M.S. *Dulverton*. Lost at sea, November 17th, 1941.

BADRICK, ROBERT EDWARD, 26, Tower Road, Luton. A/Seaman, R.N. Killed on active service, Normandy Beaches, June 8th, 1944.

BAILEY, GEORGE ALFRED, 93, Trent Road, Luton. Pte., Suffolk Regt. Died as prisoner of Japanese, Sonkrai, Siam, August 7th, 1943.

BAKER, FREDERICK WILLIAM, 34, Denbigh Road, Luton. Royal Corps of Signals. Killed on active service, Palestine, May 26th, 1946.

BAKER, NORMAN JOHN, 194, Strathmore Avenue, Luton. Spr., 288th Field Coy., R.E. Killed whilst laying land-mines, September 22nd, 1940.

BALL, SIDNEY A., 126, Hartley Road, Luton. Gnr., Commandoes. Killed in action, December, 1942.

BARFORD, SIDNEY WILLIAM, 30, Edward Street, Luton. Pte., Cambs. Reg. Died as prisoner of Japanese, August 15th, 1943.

BARFORD, W., 10, Derwent Road, Luton. Able Seaman, R.N. Killed in action, 1940.

BARKER, LESLIE, 40, Windermere Crescent, Luton. Paratrooper, Parachute Regt. Parachuted behind German lines in Normandy before D-Day. Died of wounds, June 28th, 1944.

BARKER, MARCUS EDGAR, 44, London Road, Luton. Flt/Sgt., 221st Squadron, R.A.F. Missing after operations off coast of Italy, February 2nd, 1943.

BARNES, ARTHUR CHARLES JACK, 50, Turners Road, Luton. Lt., Loyal Regt. and 1st Somerset L.I. Died on active service, Burma, March 4th, 1944.

BARNES, HENRY CHARLES, 14, Gillam Street, Luton. Gnr., R.A. Died on active service, January, 1940.

BARNES, William Henry, 46, Linden Road, Luton. Cpl., R.E. Killed in action, Boulogne, France, September 17th, 1944.

BARRETT, John James, 46, Charmouth Road, St. Albans, and B. Laporte, Ltd., Luton. Lt., R.E. Killed in action, North Africa, 1943.

BARTON, Norman Richard, 170, Cutenhoe Road, Luton. Gnr., 148th Field Regt., R.A. Killed as result of air operations while prisoner of Japanese, Indo-China, April 9th, 1945.

BATCHELOR, William, 15, Alder Crescent, Luton. Pte., 6th Battn. Bedfs. and Herts. Regt. Died on active service, India, April, 1942.

BATES, Arthur F., 16, The Crescent, Toddington, and Luton Co-operative Society, Ltd. Tpr., 53rd Reconnaissance Regt. Died of wounds, Normandy, August 18th, 1944.

BATES, Francis Robert, 18, Strathmore Avenue, Luton. Sgt., R.A.S.C. Died of wounds, Middle East, February 18th, 1942.

BAVISTER, Joseph, 74, Dumfries Street, Luton. Gnr., 412th Batty., 148th Field Regt., R.A. Lost at sea while prisoner of Japanese, September 12th, 1944.

BAXTER, George, 14, Portland Road, Luton. Pte., Cambs. Regt. Died as prisoner of Japanese, Siam, June 18th, 1943.

BAYNHAM, Mrs., 83, Biscot Road, Luton. Killed by enemy action at Luton, November 6th, 1944.

BEALES, Rex, 7, Abingdon Road, Luton. Sgt./Pilot, R.A.F. Died on active service, August 2nd, 1940.

BERRESFORD, Benjamin, 44, Conway Road, Luton. O/Seaman, R.N., H.M.S. *Martin*. Lost at sea, presumed killed in North Africa landings, November 11th, 1942.

BETTS, Alan Victor, 64, Bramingham Road, Luton. Stoker (First Class), R.N. Lost at sea, off French Coast, July 20th, 1944.

BILEY, Jack, 139, New Town Street, Luton. L/Cpl. Died as prisoner of Japanese, No. 2 Camp, Siam, June, 1943.

BIRD, Alfred Henry, 82, Cobden Street, Luton. Pte., R. Norfolk Regt. Missing, presumed killed, Dunkirk, May, 1940.

BIRD, Kenneth Sydney, 94, St. Peter's Road, Luton. F/Officer, R.A.F. Killed on air operations over France, April 17th, 1943.

BIRD, Sidney Frederick, 124, Langley Street, Luton. Cpl., 1st Battn. Royal Norfolk Regt. Killed in action, Caen, July 8th, 1944.

BLACK, Archibald William, 93, Russell Rise, Luton. P/Officer, R.A.F., No. 91 (Spitfire) Squadron. Missing on air operations south-west of Boulogne, November 17th, 1941.

BLACKWELL, William Alfred, 27, Whitecroft Road, Luton. Sgt. W/Op. A.G., R.A.F. Killed on operations over Germany, May 27th, 1943.

BLATCHFORD, J., 256, Biscot Road, Luton. Sgt./Pilot, R.A.F. Killed on active service, December, 1940.

BLIGH, Rex William, Icknield Way, Luton. Flt./Sgt., R.A.F. Died on active service, India, January, 1944.

BLINDELL, David, 25, Talbot Road, Luton. Flt./Mech., R.A.F., Bomber Command. Killed in flying accident in Canada, August 11th, 1943.

BLOW, Kenneth Leslie Owen, D.F.C., 390, Dunstable Road, Luton. W/Officer, R.A.F. Killed on operations, Holland, December 10th, 1943.

BLOWER, Douglas Roger, 293, High Town Road, Luton. Pte., Queen's Royal Regt. Died of wounds, El Alamein, October 24th, 1942.

BLOY, Charles Robert. Killed by enemy action, at Vauxhall Motors, Ltd., Luton, August 30th, 1940.

BLYTHE, Thomas Francis, 135, Harcourt Street, Luton. Sgt. W/Op. A.G., R.A.F. Killed in action, November 27th, 1942.

BOND, Victor Cyril, 100, Castle Street, Luton. Sgt., 203rd Squadron, R.A. Died from injuries and burns received on active service, Egypt, October 9th, 1942.

BONE, James Reginald, 9, Woodland Avenue, Luton. Pte., R.A.M.C. Died on active service, February, 1946.

BONNER, Maurice Norman, 61, Bury Park Road, Luton. L/Cpl., R. Norfolk Regt. Died as prisoner of Japanese, Thanbyuzayat, Burma, September 17th, 1943.

BONNER, Reginald William, 7, Willow Way, Luton. Gnr., Heavy A.A. Regt., R.A. Killed in action, Italy, January 21st, 1944.

BONNICK, Reginald George, 102, Cambridge Street, Luton. Died September 2nd, 1940, as result of enemy action at Luton, August 30th, 1940.

BORLAND, Isabel, 15, Highbury Road, Luton. Killed by enemy action, at Luton, October 14th, 1940.

BOSS, Kenneth, M.C., 117, Farley Avenue, Luton. Capt., R.A. Died of wounds, N.W. Europe, July, 1945.

BOSTON, Brian James, 58, Clarendon Road, Luton. F/Officer, R.A.F., Bomber Command. Killed during operations over Germany, August 26th, 1944.

BOURNES, Arthur Bowland, 44, Brunswick Street, Luton. Fatally injured while on fire watch, Luton and Dunstable Hospital, November 2nd, 1941.

BOWERS, Donald, 24, Sherwood Road, Luton. Airborne Unit. Killed in action, Normandy, July, 1944.

BRACEWELL, Jim E., 118, Bishopscote Road, Luton. Gnr., 420th Battery, R.A. Died as prisoner in Japanese hands, Pratchai, Kirakan, Siam.

BRANSOM, Lewis Egbert, 37, Whitefield Avenue, Sundon Park Estate, Luton. Stoker i/c. R.N., H.M.S. *Harvester*. Lost at sea, Mid-Atlantic, March 11th, 1943.

BRAY, Ronald, Gresham Assurance Coy., Luton. Sgt.W/Op., A.G., R.A.F. Killed in raid on Brest, 1941.

BREEZE, Evan John, 88, Chester Avenue, Luton. Killed by enemy action, at Vauxhall Motors, Ltd., Luton, August 30th, 1940.

BRIARS, Ronald Albert, 458, New Bedford Road, Luton. L/Cpl., Cambs. Regt. Died as prisoner of Japanese, Malaya, June 29th, 1943.

BRIGHT, Sidney J., 54, Park Street, Luton. L/Cpl., Corps of Military Police. Killed in action, Italy, December 17th, 1944.

BROWN, Donald H., 1, Ridgway Road, Luton. Sgt./Obs., R.A.F. Killed on active service, air operations, Far East, September, 1942.

BROWN, Douglas, 248, Dunstable Road, Luton. Lt., Bedfs. & Herts. Regt., att. Royal Warwicks. Regt. Killed in action, Western Front, October, 1944.

BROWN, Harold, 153, Dallow Road, Luton. Sgt., R.A.F. Killed in action, Far East, January 26th, 1942.

BROWN, Peter Charles, 22, Newark Road, Luton. Sgt. W/Op. A.G., R.A.F., Coastal Command. Killed in action, air operations, March, 1944.

BRYANT, Frank Dennis Widdows, 107, Shelley Road, Luton. Second Officer, Merchant Navy, S.S. *Whitford Point*. Lost at sea, Irish Sea, October 20th, 1940.

BUGG, Eric John, 65, Lincoln Road, Luton. Pte., 1st Battn. Northants. Regt. Killed in action, Dangyin, Burma, April 20th, 1945.

BURCHMORE, William Robert, 97, Harcourt Street, Luton. Killed by enemy action, at Luton, August 30th, 1940.

BURNS, Kenneth J., 57, Durham Road, Luton. Sergt., No. 211 Squadron, R.A.F. Died as prisoner of Japanese, Moena Island (Celebes), November 1st, 1944.

BURR, William Henry, 172, Blundell Road, Luton. Volunteer, 4th Bedfs. Battn. Home Guard. Killed on exercises, June 15th, 1941.

BURROWS, George, 16, Midland Road, Luton. Killed by enemy action, at Luton, September 5th, 1942.

BUSHBY, Stanley G., 46, Conway Road, Luton. Killed by enemy action, at Luton, October 14th, 1940.

BUSSEREAU, Victor Roque, 120, Leagrave Road, Luton. Lt., R.C.N.V.R. Missing, presumed killed, H.M.S. *Rajputana*, May, 1941.

BUTCHER, THOMAS DERRICK, 14, Inkerman Street, Luton. W/Officer, No. 24 Squadron, R.A.F. Killed in air accident, Llanfair, nr. Ruthin, Wales, July 17th, 1942.

BUTLER, THOMAS WALTER, 11, Applecroft Road, Luton. Cpl., K.R.R. Killed in Egypt, August, 1941.

BUTTERFIELD, RONALD ALFRED, 33, Cambridge Street, Luton. Pte., Bedfs. and Herts. Regt. Killed in action, Italy, June 28th, 1944.

BUXTON, CYRIL CHARLES WILLIAM, 8, North Street, Luton. Pte., Oxon. and Bucks. Light Infantry. Died of wounds, Hamilkein, Germany, March 24th, 1945.

CAFFELL, GORDON W. J., 26, St. Margaret's Avenue, Luton. L/Bdr., 148th Field Regt., R.A. Died as prisoner of Japanese, Siam, January 31st, 1944.

CAIN, ANTHONY RICHARD, 20, The Close, Kinsbourne Green, and Vauxhall Motors, Ltd., Luton. Sgt./Navigator, R.A.F. Killed in action, June, 1941.

CAIN, LESLIE, 81, Ashcroft Road, Luton. Tpr., 142nd Regt., R.A.C. Died of wounds, Algiers, July 2nd, 1943.

CAIN, ROBERT WILLIAM, 5, Hart Lane, Luton. Cfm., R.E.M.E. Killed on active service in Irak, August 15th, 1944.

CANHAM, REX, 18, Rothesay Road, Luton. Gnr., Light A.A. Battery, R.A. Died as prisoner of Japanese, Kuomoto Camp, Japan, January 16th, 1943.

CARD, FRANCIS AUSTIN WILLIAM, 506, Hitchin Road, Luton. Sick Berth Attendant, R.N., H.M.S. *Curacoa*. Lost at sea, October 2nd, 1942.

CARR, ROBERT, 30, Kingsley Road, Luton. Pte., 2nd Battn. Duke of Wellington's Regt. Killed in action, Burma, June 4th, 1944.

CARTER, BERYL, 77, Biscot Road, Luton. Killed by enemy action, at Luton, November 6th, 1944.

CARTER, CLIFFORD JACK, 24, Montrose Avenue, Luton. Able Seaman, Merchant Navy. Lost at sea through enemy action, March, 1941.

CARTER, EDWARD GEORGE, 16, Kingsway, Luton. Cpl., Royal Signals (Paratrooper). Killed at Bosnia, Yugo-Slavia, August 15th, 1944.

CARTER, GEORGE, 1, Preston Path, Luton. Gnr., R.A. Missing from Japanese transport after fall of Singapore, 1942.

CARTER, HARRY G., 24, Medina Road, Luton. Killed by enemy action, at Luton, October 14th, 1940.

CARTER, REGINALD A., 37, St. Peter's Road, Luton. Gnr., R.A. Killed on active service, August, 1941.

CASE, NORMAN, 72, Selbourne Road, Luton. Able Seaman, R.N. Died, August 27th, 1943.

CASTLETON, ALEXANDER GORDON, 28, Lyndhurst Road, Luton. Sergt., Royal Corps of Signals. Died on active service, May 14th, 1946.

CATLIN, HERBERT EDWARD, 113, Beechwood Road, Luton. Pte., Pioneer Corps. Lost at sea with S.S. *Lancastria* during evacuation from Dunkirk, June 17th, 1940.

CATO, CYRIL GEORGE, 178, Dallow Road, Luton. Sergt., 289th Field Park Coy., R.E. Died after invaliding from Germany, July 15th, 1946.

CATO, FREDERICK GEORGE BERT, 289, Dallow Road, Luton. Pte., 5th Battn. Bedfs. and Herts. Regt. Lost at sea on board the *Hofoko Maru* as prisoner of Japanese, September 21st, 1944.

CHALKLEY, HORACE FREDERICK, 49, Lyndhurst Road, Luton. Sgt., 148th Field Regt., R.A. Lost at sea in the Pacific as prisoner of Japanese, September 12th, 1944.

CHALKLEY, JOHN, 52, Mayne Avenue, Luton. Sgt.-W/O., R.A.F. Missing on operations, Berlin, August 23rd-24th, 1943.

CHAMBERLAIN, ERNEST JOHN, 31, Cannon Lane, Stopsley, Luton. Pte., 5th Battn. Bedfs. and Herts. Regt. Lost at sea as prisoner of Japanese, September 21st, 1944.

CHAMBERLAIN, GLADYS, 3, Hitchin Road, Luton. Killed by enemy action, at Luton, October 14th, 1940.

CHAMBERLAIN, MARION A., " Sarina," Turners Road, Luton. Killed by enemy action, at Luton, October 14th, 1940.

CHAMBERS, ALFRED GEORGE, 101, Milton Road, Luton. Cpl., R. Norfolk Regt. Killed in action, Battle of the Imphal Road, Burma, June 9th, 1944.

CHAMBERS, FRANK H., 48, Avondale Road, Luton. Killed by U.S. bomb lorry explosion, Offley, January 8th, 1945.

CHAMBERS, GEORGE HARRY. Killed by enemy action, at Vauxhall Motors, Ltd., Luton, August 30th, 1940.

CHAMPKIN, DOUGLAS GEORGE, 42, Lincoln Road, Luton. Sgt.-F/Engr., 460th Squadron, R.A.F. Killed on operations ; buried at Lahr, Baden, Germany, April 27th-28th, 1944.

CHANCE, PHILIP JAMES, 74, Durham Road, Luton. Gnr., Light A.A. Batty., R.A. Died at sea while prisoner of Japanese, November 13th, 1942.

CHAPPELL, PETER C., 5, Oakley Road, Luton. P/Officer, R.A.F., Bomber Command. Killed on operations, Abingdon, July 28th, 1941.

CHERRY, HAROLD ARTHUR, 3, Douglas Road, Luton. Lieut., R.A., att. Tactical Air Force. Killed in Italy, February 26th, 1945.

CHERRY, KENNETH EDWIN, 48, Castle Hill Road, Totternhoe, and Percival Aircraft, Ltd., Luton. L/Cpl. Died of wounds, Greece, December 27th, 1944.

CHESHAM, AMELIA, 4, Mountfield Road, Luton. Killed by enemy action, at Luton, October 14th, 1940.

CHESHIRE, SIDNEY JAMES, 32, Harcourt Street, Luton. Tpr., Reconnaissance Regt. Killed on active service, April 24th, 1942.

CHOTE, ARTHUR HAYDN FREDERICK, 38, Marston Gardens, Luton. F/Sgt. 14th Squadron, R.A.F. Killed on active service, near Chester, August 3rd, 1942.

CHURCH, FREDERICK JAMES, 89, Putteridge Road, Luton. A/Seaman, H.M.S. *Isis*, R.N. Died on war service from exposure at sea, July 20th, 1944.

CLARIDGE, ALBERT EDWARD, 62, Talbot Road, Luton. F/Officer, R.A.F. Died, May 31st, 1944.

CLARIDGE, CYRIL CHARLES, 5, Alfred Street, Luton. Pte., 4th Battn. Suffolk Regt. Killed in action, Singapore, April 22nd, 1942.

CLARIDGE, SIDNEY GEORGE JAMES, 31, Brooms Road, Luton. Pte., Suffolk Regt. Died as prisoner of Japanese, Japan, February 3rd, 1944.

CLARINGBOLD, LEON JACK, 2, Crescent Road, Luton. A/Seaman, R.N. Lost at sea, May 23rd, 1941.

CLARK, DAVID, 15, Derwent Road, Luton. Sgt. (O), R.A.F. Killed on active service, Scotland, December 10th, 1941.

CLARK, WILLIAM HENRY, 10, Tower Road, Luton. F/Sgt., Security Police, R.A.F. Accidentally killed on active service, Burton-on-Trent, February 18th, 1945.

CLARKE, BRIAN EDWARD, 56, Lyndhurst Road, Luton. Sgt. W/Op.-A.G., 576th Squadron, R.A.F. Killed on operations, Kollerbecke, near Detmold, Germany, January 14th, 1944.

CLARK, DAVID, 29, Montrose Avenue, Luton. Sgt./Observer, R.A.F. Bomber Command. Killed on active service, December 10th, 1941.

CLARK, JOHN F. S., 41, Cavendish Road, Luton. Died, India, 1941.

CLARK, RONALD ERNEST, 79, St. Augustine's Avenue, Luton. Pte., Royal Scots. Killed on active service, May, 1945.

CLEARY, ALBERT EDWARD, 35, Chester Avenue, Luton. Sgt., R.A.F. Missing, presumed killed, South Atlantic, August 17th, 1941.

CLINTON, BASIL, 251, New Bedford Road, Luton. P/Officer, R.A.F. Killed on active service near Cape Hotham, Australia, July 31st, 1945.

CLOUGH, R. A. Died as result of enemy action at Vauxhall Motors, Ltd., Luton, August 30th, 1940.

AA

COCKS, WALTER HENRY. Killed by enemy action, at Vauxhall Motors, Ltd., Luton, August 30th, 1940.

COEN, JOSEPH LEO, Beechwood Road, Luton. Sgt., R.A.F. Killed on active service, October 15th, 1941.

COKER, J. W., 28, Curzon Road, Luton. Spr., R.E. Died as prisoner of war in Japanese Camp, Siam, 1943.

COLE, HENRY WILLIAM, 175, Biscot Road, Luton. Gnr./Dvr., 217th Batty., R.A. Killed in action near Bremen, Germany, May 1st, 1945.

COLE, ROBERT ARNOLD, 38, Reginald Street, Luton. F/Sgt., R.A.F. Killed on operations over Leverkusen-Wesdorf, Germany, July 30th-31st, 1943.

COLEMAN, EWART REGINALD, 23, St. Michael's Crescent, Luton. Gnr., R.A. Died of injuries on active service, May 16th, 1944.

COLEMAN, HENRY, 130, Wenlock Street, Luton. Pioneer Corps. Killed on active service, December, 1940.

COLEMAN, JOHN, 47, Whitecroft Road, Luton. Pte., The Buffs. Died as prisoner of war, Germany, July 24th, 1944.

COLEY, JOHN WILSON, 47, Russell Rise, Luton. L/Sgt., R.E. Killed in action, N.W. Europe, November 8th, 1944.

COLLINGS, DONALD HERBERT, 93, Russell Rise, Luton. Sgt./Pilot, 6th (P) Adv. Fighter Unit, R.A.F. Killed on active service, September 18th, 1943.

CONISBEE, GORDON H. C., Sgt. (N), R.A.F. Killed on active service, Walney Island, Barrow-in-Furness, September 30th, 1944.

CONLEY, CECIL VERNON, " Hazelmere," Icknield Way, Luton. Sapper, R.E. Died on active service, Basra, Irak, June 19th, 1942.

COOK, ALFRED, 40, Belmont Road, Luton. Pte., 5th Battn. Bedfs. and Herts. Regt. Died as prisoner of Japanese, Krian-Krai, September 10th, 1943.

COOMBES, HARRY, 73, Latimer Road, Luton. Pte., R. Berks. Regt. Died of wounds, C.M.F., February 14th, 1944.

COOP, GEORGE, 122, Fourth Avenue, Sundon, Luton. Killed by enemy action, at Luton, November 6th, 1944.

COOPER, CHARLES SAMUEL, 58, Cobden Street, Luton. Killed in action, Italy, November 4th, 1943.

COOPER, GEORGE WILLIAM, 1, Ferndale Road, Luton. O/Seaman, R.N. Lost with H.M.S. *Boadicea* off Normandy, June 13th, 1944.

COOPER, JAMES EMERTON, 9, Beech Road, Luton. Sgt./Pilot, R.A.F. Killed in action, September, 1941.

COOPER, LESLIE WILLIAM, 122, Beechwood Road, Luton. Gnr., R.A. Died as prisoner of Japanese, Malaya, October 26th, 1943.

COOPER, NORMAN F., 7, Wenlock Street, Luton. Sgt./Pilot, R.A.F. Killed on active service, July 27th, 1940.

COOPER, RUSSELL C., 55, Arundel Road, Luton. Cpl., R.A.S.C. Invalided out died July 30th, 1943.

COOTE, BERT GEORGE, 71, Bury Park Road, Luton. Tpr., North Irish Horse R.A.C. Died of wounds, Italy, August 5th, 1944.

CORKE, JOHN FREDERICK, 92, Somerset Avenue, Luton. L.A.C., R.A.F. Killed on active service, Middle East, August, 1941.

CORNISH, ALFRED JOHN, 15, St. Catherine's Avenue, Luton. L/Bdr., R.A. Killed in action, May 27th, 1940.

COULTISH, GEORGE WILLIAM, 16, Devon Road, Luton. Pte., 1/5th Battn. Welch Regt. Killed in action, Germany, March 3rd, 1945.

COWLEY, RONALD, 29, Cavendish Road, Luton. Tpr., Royal Tank Regt. Killed in action, Southern Tunisia, April 25th, 1943.

COX, FRANK, 182, Biscot Road, Luton. Pte., R. West Kent Regt. Killed in action, Italy, November 30th, 1943.

COX, RALPH, Vauxhall Motors, Ltd., Luton. R.A.F. Killed in action, 1940.

CRABTREE, JACK COLIN, 13, St. Margaret's Avenue, Luton. Lieut., Green Howards. Killed in action, Arnhem, April 21st, 1945.

CRAWLEY, ALBERT EDWARD, 20, Whitecroft Road, Luton. Pte., 5th Battn. Bedfs. and Herts. Regt. Lost on board the *Hofoku Maru* as prisoner of Japanese, September 21st, 1944.

CRAWLEY, EDWARD ALBERT. Killed by enemy action, at Vauxhall Motors, Ltd., Luton, August 30th, 1940.

CREW, CHARLES, 155, Park Street, Luton. Killed by enemy action, at Luton, September 22nd, 1940.

CREW, GLADYS, 155, Park Street, Luton. Killed by enemy action, at Luton, September 22nd, 1940.

CREW, LOUISA, 155, Park Street, Luton. Killed by enemy action, at Luton, September 22nd, 1940.

CREW, REUBEN, 149, Park Street, Luton. Killed by enemy action, at Luton, September 22nd, 1940.

CRUISE, ARTHUR, 180, Wellington Street, Luton. Sgt./Pilot, R.A.F. Died of wounds, December 22nd, 1940.

CULBERTSON, GEORGE ANDREW YPRES, 48, Dudley Street, Luton. Died as result of enemy action, at Luton, September 2nd, 1940.

CUNNINGHAM, RICHARD FULTON, 71, Wellington Street, Luton. O/Seaman, R.N., H.M.S. *Hood*. Killed in Action, North Atlantic, May 24th, 1941.

CURRANT, P. NORMAN, 9, Elliswick Road, Harpenden, and Currant & Creak, Ltd., Bute Street, Luton. Major, Seaforth Highlanders. Killed in action, Western Front, September, 1944.

CURCHIN, R. T., Gibraltar Cottages, London Road, Luton. L/Stoker, R.N. Missing, presumed killed, March, 1942.

CURTIS, CLIFFORD SIDNEY, 42, Stanford Road, Luton. Killed by enemy action, at Vauxhall Motors, Ltd., Luton, August 30th, 1940.

DANIELS, LAURENCE RUFUS, 9, Ashton Road, Luton. L/Bdr. R.A. Died as prisoner of Japanese, Siam, October 23rd 1943.

DARBY, KENNETH ROY, 62, Pondwicks Road, Luton. Dvr., R.A.S.C., att. 87th H.A.A. Regt., R.A. Died on active service, Habbaniya, Irak, December 2nd, 1941.

DAVENPORT, HAROLD, 5, Roman Road, Luton. L/Cpl., Royal Corps of Signals. Died of wounds, Burma, March, 1944.

DAVIES, EDWARD WHELAN, 50, Naseby Road, Luton. Sgt., R.A.F. Killed on operations over Paris, December 12th, 1944.

DAVIES, HENRY GEORGE, 88, Chapel Street, Luton. Gnr., Light A.A. Batty., R.A. Died as prisoner of Japanese, Singapore, March 5th, 1943.

DAVIES, REGINALD THOMAS, 53, Windmill Road, Luton. Gnr., 79th (Scottish Horse) Med. Regt., R.A. Died of wounds, January 20th, 1944.

DAVIS, CLIFFORD FRANCIS CHARLES, 38, Belmont Road, Luton. F/Sgt. Engr., R.A.F. Killed on operations, Nuremberg, March 31st, 1944 ; buried at Schweinfurt.

DAY, ALFRED, formerly of Claremont Road, Luton. F/O., R.A.F. Missing, presumed killed, in operations over Stettin, Germany, January 5th-6th, 1944.

de GRENIER-SMITH, ELVIN HENRY, 110, Oakley Road, Luton. Able Seaman, Merchant Navy. Lost at sea, June 29th, 1941.

DEAN, ALFRED JAMES, 12, Warren Road, Luton. Killed by enemy action at Vauxhall Motors, Ltd., Luton, August 30th, 1940.

DEARMAN, DERICK ROY, D.F.C., 93, Putteridge Road, Luton. P/Officer, R.A.F. Killed on operations, Paris, April 21st, 1944.

DENTON, AUBREY RONALD, 55, Tavistock Street, Luton. Gnr., 148th Field Regt., R.A. Died as prisoner of Japanese, Torsao, Siam, July 6th, 1943.

DENTON, JAMES, 7, Argyll Avenue, Luton. Tpr., 4th Reconnaissance Regt., R.A.C. Died of wounds, Italy, July 13th, 1944.

DEPLEDGE, DENNIS SYDNEY, 77, Roman Road, Luton. Petty Officer, R.N. Killed in action and buried at sea in Gibraltar Bay, January 30th, 1943.

DEWAR, JACK, 45, Talbot Road, Luton. Sgt., R.A.F. Killed on active service March 13th, 1941.

DICKENS, CHARLES FREDERICK, 51, Chase Street, Luton. Gnr., R.A. Killed in action at sea, off Greece, April 28th-29th, 1941.

DIGGINES, ALBERT E., 84, Pondwicks Road, Luton. Cpl., 2nd K.R.R.C. Killed in action, Western Front, March, 1945.

DILLINGHAM, HORACE CHARLES, 52, Chandos Road, Luton. P/Officer, R.A.F. Killed on operations over Menden, Germany, July 4th, 1943.

DIMMOCK, LESLIE CHARLES, 10, Bury Park Road, Luton. Pte., Bedfs. and Herts. Regt. Died on active service, India, May 20th, 1942.

DIXON, ERIC C., 37, Clifton Road, Luton. Dvr., R.E. Missing, presumed killed by enemy bombing, Alexandra Hospital, Singapore, February, 1942.

DIXON, MAURICE, 37, Clifton Road, Luton. Killed in action at Tobruk.

DOBBS, GEORGE, 22, Beaumont Road, Luton. S/Sergt., R.E.M.E. Died in Middle East, May 17th, 1944. Buried at Tel-el-Kebir.

DRAKE, 'ANTHONY GERARD, 88, Hartley Road, Luton. Gunner, R.A. Died from injuries on active service, July 4th, 1941.

DRAPER, ALEC VERNON, 31, Grange Avenue, Luton. Driver, Royal Corps of Signals. Killed in action, El Alamein, August 31st, 1942.

DRAPER, CHARLES WALTER, 31, Grange Avenue, Luton. Tpr., Queen's Bays. Killed in action, France, May 27th, 1940.

DUMPLETON, JOHN STEPHEN, 45, Waller Avenue, Luton. L/Cpl., 2nd Cambs. Regt. Killed in action, Malaya, January 26th, 1942.

DYNE, CHARLES FORBES, 63, Marlborough Road, Luton, and Santa Cruz, Teneriffe. Cpl., R.E. Died as prisoner of Japanese, in Japan, June, 1943.

EAMES, WILLIAM JOHN, 97, Kent Road, Luton. Pte., Bedfs. and Herts. Regt. Died after repatriation from German prison camp, March 6th, 1944.

EAST, DERRICK ARTHUR, 13, Roman Road, Luton. Radio-Telegraphist, R.N. Killed by enemy action, North Atlantic, November 1st, 1944.

EDWARDS, ROBERT, 23, Chesford Road, Luton. Pte. Died in Burma, May 22nd, 1944.

EDWARDS, RONALD, 308, Dunstable Road, Luton. Lieut., 1st Battn. Hampshire Regt. Killed in action, Catania, Sicily, July 26th, 1943.

EDWIN, EDWARD FRANCIS, 131, Turners Road, Luton. Sgt./Pilot, R.A.F. Died on active service, November 15th, 1940.

EICHEN, H., 48, Castle Street, Luton. Pte., 7th Suffolk Regt. Killed in action, Western Front, February 15th, 1945.

ELLIS, ALBERT WALTER, formerly 31, Roman Road, Luton. Pte. Killed in action, North Africa, April 13th, 1943.

ELLIS, JAMES, 68, Chester Avenue, Luton. Sgt., R.A.F. Died on active service, June, 1943.

ENDERBY, HAROLD FREDERICK, 187, Dunstable Road, Luton. Pte., Essex Regt. Died as prisoner in Germany, on or after October 26th, 1942.

ENGLEDOW, WILLIAM GEORGE VERDUN, 46, Maidenhall Road, Luton. Cpl., 1st Parachute Regt. Killed in action, N. Africa, February 3rd, 1943.

ENGLISH, ERIC DONALD, 56, Cowper Street, Luton. LAC. (M.T.), R.A.F. Lost at sea, November 7th, 1944.

EVANS, ANDREW, Vauxhall Motors, Ltd. Flt./Sgt., R.A.F. Killed on active service, March, 1941.

FAGE, RONALD THOMAS, 55, Rutland Crescent, Luton. Sgt., 15th Operational Training Unit. Killed on operations over Bremen, Germany; buried in Holland, June 25th, 1942.

FAIREY, LEONARD ROBERT, 63, St. Martin's Avenue, Luton. Killed by enemy action, at Vauxhall Motors, Ltd., Luton, August 30th, 1940.

FARMER, THOMAS CYRIL, 19, Bolton Road, Luton. Pte., Duke of Wellington's Regt. Killed in action, France, June 21st, 1944.

FARR, GEORGE HERBERT, 31, Argyll Avenue, Luton. Sigm., Royal Corps of Signals. Died on active service, Altrincham, June 16th, 1940.

FARR, Vernon Clifford, 31, Argyll Avenue, Luton. Sigm., Royal Corps of Signals. Died as prisoner of Japanese, Siam, August 10th, 1943.

FARROW, Frank, 42, Inkerman Street, Luton. Pte., 1st Suffolk Regt. Died of wounds, Falaise Gap, Normandy, August 23rd, 1944.

FAUNCH, William Gerald, 173, Cutenhoe Road, Luton. Died after being flown home from Italy, April 1st, 1946.

FELTON, Fernley George. Killed by enemy action, at Vauxhall Motors, Ltd., Luton, August 30th, 1940.

FENSOME, George, 39, Chobham Street, Luton. Fusilier, R.F. Killed in action, France, August 9th, 1944.

FENSOME, Harold Victor, 58, Lyndhurst Road, Luton. Gnr., R.A. Died as prisoner of Japanese.

FENSOME, John Stanley, 102, Bishopscote Road, Luton. Sgt., R.A.F. Killed on active service, January, 1941.

FICKEN, Norman J., 27, Windsor Street, Luton. LAC., R.A.F. Killed off Prince Edward Island, November, 1941.

FIELD, Reginald, 27, Elmore Road, Luton. Gnr., R.A. (Searchlights). Died on active service, September 14th, 1944.

FISH, William J., 10, Albion Road, Luton. Pte., R.A.S.C. Died in Calcutta Hospital following service in Burma, June, 1945.

FISHER, James Gordon, 3, Moat Lane, Luton. Stoker First Class, H.M.S. *Laforey*, R.N. Killed at sea, March 30th, 1944.

FISHER, Julia, 157, Park Street, Luton. Killed by enemy action, at Luton, September 22nd, 1940.

FLANIGAN, Michael Joseph, 65, Gardenia Avenue, Luton. Dvr., R.E. Field Company. Died as prisoner of Japanese, Changi Camp, May 16th, 1942.

FLINT, Ronald Renshaw, 2, Bishopscote Road, Luton. P/Officer, R.A.F. Killed on active service, March 24th, 1942.

FLITTON, Arthur, 14, Princess Street, Luton. Pte., R.A.M.C. Died in India, April 26th, 1942.

FLITTON, Derek Noel, 40, Stratford Road, Luton. Flt./Sgt., 408 Squadron, R.A.F. Killed on operations over enemy territory, June 8th, 1944.

FORSTER, Robert, 30, Tower Road, Luton. Tpr., 13th Reconnaisance Regt., R.A.C. Killed in action, Le Mesnil Patry, Nr. Caen, France, July 17th, 1945.

FOUNTAIN, Jack Heath, 68, Connaught Road, Luton. Cpl., R.A.F. (Dental Branch). Died on active service, October 26th, 1941.

FOWLER, Arthur, 19, Oakley Road, Luton. C.S.M., Pioneer Corps. Died in Germany after being injured by mine explosion, May 23rd, 1945.

FRANCIS, Ernest George, 41, Avondale Road, Luton. P/Officer, R.A.F. Killed on operations, Holland, April, 1944.

FRASER, Kenneth, 14, St. Margaret's Avenue, Luton. L/Seaman, R.N. Missing at sea, presumed killed, February 5th, 1944.

FREAK, Roy, 96, Oakley Road, Luton. Sergt., R.A.F. Killed on operations, April, 1942.

FREEMAN, Alfred George, 110a, Bury Park Road, Luton. Sgt., R.A. Died on active service in Germany, July 10th, 1945.

FREEMAN, George Edward, 1, Beaumont Road, Luton. Pte., 1st Battn. Suffolk Regt. Killed in action, Normandy, July 4th, 1944.

FRENCH, Douglas, 124, Leagrave Road, Luton. Cfm., R.E.M.E. Killed in action, Tunisia, April 6th, 1943.

FROST, Leslie Harold, 36, Broad Mead, Luton. Gnr., 148th Field Regt., R.A. Died as prisoner of Japanese, Singapore, November, 1943.

FULLER, Harry William, 74, Elmwood Crescent, Luton. F/Officer, 170th Squadron, R.A.F. Killed on operations, near Brunswick, Germany, March 7-8th, 1945.

FULLER, Jim, 18, Mansfield Road, Luton. Pte., R.A.S.C. Missing, presumed killed, Singapore, February, 1942.

GALE, Leonard, 79, Albert Road, Luton. Pte., Army Fire Service. Killed in action, Western Front, April, 1945.

GANDERTON, Robert, 47, St. Paul's Road, Luton. L/Stoker (Submarine), R.N.V.R. Killed on war service in H.M.S. *Oxley*, off Norway, September 10th, 1939.

GARRETT, Leonard V., 13, Guildford Street, Luton. Pte., Queen's Royal Regt. Killed in action, Italy, December 4th, 1943.

GATWARD, Derrick George, 110, Westmorland Avenue, Luton. LAC., R.A.F. Died on active service, New Delhi, August 11th, 1945.

GAYE, A. D., Lieut.-Col., formerly commanding 5th Battn. Bedfs. and Herts. Regt., Luton. Died, December 2nd, 1941.

GAUNTLETT, Glyndwr, 29, Weatherby Road, Luton. Gnr., R.A. Died as prisoner of Japanese, 1943.

GEE, Elizabeth Ethel, 159, Wellington Street, Luton. Killed by enemy action, at Luton, August 30th, 1940.

GEORGE, Ernest Walter, 33, Cambridge Street, Luton. Sigmn., Royal Corps of Signals. Died of wounds, North Africa, January 2nd, 1943.

GEORGE, Frederick, 36, Baker Street, Luton. Cpl., 5th Bedfs. and Herts. Regt. Died as prisoner of Japanese, Singapore, May 22nd, 1942.

GEORGE, W. F., 134, New Town Street, Luton. Cpl., Bedfs. and Herts. Regt. Died as prisoner of Japanese, Singapore, May 22nd, 1942.

GIBBONS, Samuel, 82, Church Street, Luton. Cpl., R.A.F. Died in hospital, India, March 18th, 1941.

GIBSON, William Maurice, 543, Hitchin Road, Luton. Sgt. Rear Gunner, R.A.F. Killed in action while returning from operations over Nuremberg, Germany, March 3rd, 1944.

GIDDINGS, Gertrude E., 17, William Street, Luton. Killed by enemy action, at Luton, October 14th, 1940.

GILBERT, Frederick Charles, 66, Wigmore Lane, Luton. Killed by enemy action, at Vauxhall Motors, Ltd., Luton, August 30th, 1940.

GILL, James V., 54, Weatherby Road, Luton. Sgt., 115th Squadron, R.A.F. Killed on operations, Germany, July 2nd, 1941.

GILLESPIE, James, 25, Rothesay Road, Luton. Killed in action, Belgium, June, 1940.

GILLETT, Arthur James, 100, Trinity Road, Luton. Pte., 5th Battn. Bedfs. and Herts. Regt. Died in hospital, Warwick, after return from Japanese prison camp, April 6th, 1946.

GLANCY, John Charles, 60, Bradgers Hill Road, Luton. Sgt., R.A.F. Missing, presumed killed, on operations, July 6-7th, 1944.

GLENISTER, Rex Brian, 58, Salisbury Road, Luton. Killed by enemy action, at Luton, November 6th, 1944.

GLOVER-PRICE, Leonard John, formerly of Luton. Sgt., R.A.F. Killed on operations, Dusseldorf, June, 1943.

GOODE, Leslie George, 77, Leagrave Road, Luton. Pte., 5th Battn. Bedfs. and Herts. Regt. Died as prisoner of Japanese, Malaya, August, 1943.

GOODMAN, Jack Lionel, 25, Tower Road, Luton. Able Seaman, R.N. Lost at sea, December 11th, 1944.

GOODWIN, John Anthony, 270, Old Bedford Road, Luton. Paymaster Sub-Lieut., R.N.V.R. Died on active service, Bombay, November, 1940.

GOSLING, Paul John Betts, 6, Austin Road, Luton. Tpr., 13/18th Royal Hussars, R.A.C. Killed in action, Bray et Lu, France, August 29th, 1944.

GRAVES, Cyril, C. C., 161, High Town Road, Luton. Yeoman of Signals, R.N. Lost with H.M.S. *Fleur-de-Lys*, October 14th, 1941.

GRAVES, Thomas Allan, 26, Bailey Street, Luton. Tpr., 7th Royal Tank Regt., R.A.C. Died on active service, October 25th, 1943.

GRAY, Victor, 191, Runley Road, Luton. Able Seaman Gnr., R.N. Lost in action at sea, June 19th, 1944.

GREEN, ALBERT EDWARD. Killed by enemy action, at Vauxhall Motors, Ltd., Luton, August 30th, 1940.

GREENWOOD, G. E., 124, Argyll Avenue, Luton. Sgt. (Flt./Engr.), R.A.F. Killed on operations over Berlin, January 27-28th, 1943.

GREGORY, HARRY GOODE, 58, Old Bedford Road, Luton. Killed by enemy action, at Luton, October 14th, 1940.

GRESTY, WILLIAM JOHN, 157, Connaught Road, Luton. Killed by enemy action, at Vauxhall Motors, Ltd., Luton, August 30th, 1940.

GRIGG, GEORGE STANLEY, 20, Rothesay Road, Luton. L/Sgt., R.A. Died of wounds, Far East, February 14th, 1942.

GROTRIAN, CHARLES HERBERT BRENT. Major, R.A., formerly commanding 420th Field Battery, R.A., Luton. Killed in action, Burma, May, 1944.

GUNN, ARTHUR ERNEST, 9, Mount Pleasant Road, Luton. Sgt., R.A. Killed in action, France, June 25th, 1944.

GUY, JENNIE, 45, Seymour Road, Luton. Killed by enemy action, at Luton, August 30th, 1940.

HACKSLEY, HERBERT HORACE, 18, Bailey Street, Luton, and Oxford. LAC., R.A.F. Died on active service, Kansas City, U.S.A., August 31st, 1942.

HADAWAY, NORMAN JACK, 38, Ryecroft Way, Stopsley, Luton. Pte., Bedfs. and Herts. Regt. Died, December 30th, 1939.

HALES, SIDNEY JAMES, 56, Cutenhoe Road, Luton. Killed by enemy action, at Vauxhall Motors, Ltd., Luton, August 30th, 1940.

HALFPENNY, ARTHUR CHARLES, 13, Vicarage Street, Luton. Pte., R. West Kent Regt. Killed in action, El Alamein, September 3rd, 1942.

HALL, JOHN GEORGE, 168, Wellington Street, Luton. Lieut., Pioneer Corps. Killed in action, Western Europe, January 27th, 1945.

HALSEY, RONALD WILLIAM, 63, Russell Rise, Luton. Able Seaman, R.N. Drowned while on active service, November, 1942.

HANCOCK, CHARLES, 38, River Way, Luton. Killed by enemy action, at Luton, November 6th, 1944.

HARDEN, MICHAEL LANGLEY, 135, New Bedford Road, Luton. Sub-Lt. (A), Fleet Air Arm. Killed on active service, October, 1942.

HARDING, HAROLD RONALD, 35, Brooms Road, Luton. Pte., Queen's Royal Regt. Killed in action, El Alamein, October 24th, 1942.

HARP, ALBERT FRANK EDWIN, 2, Farley Avenue, Luton. Cpl., 3rd Battn. Grenadier Guards. Killed on active service, and buried at Cesena, Italy, April 15th, 1945.

HARPER, JACK ABRAHAM, 56, Grove Road, Luton. Killed by enemy action, at Vauxhall Motors, Ltd., Luton, August 30th, 1940.

HARRIS, Ex-Sgt. THOMAS JAMES, D.C.M., 62, Dane Road, Luton. Killed by enemy action, at Vauxhall Motors, Ltd., Luton, August 30th, 1940.

HARRISON, CHRISTOPHER BASIL, 236, Old Bedford Road, Luton. Sgt./Pilot, R.A.F. Killed in action, Brest, September 30th, 1941.

HARRISON, GEORGE, 3, Browning Road, Luton. Pte., 1/4th Battn. Essex Regt. Killed in action, Forli-Rimini, Italy, November 8th, 1944.

HARROWER, ALEX AITKEN, 244, Beechwood Road, Luton. Killed by enemy action, at Vauxhall Motors, Ltd., Luton, August 30th, 1940.

HART, ERNEST HERBERT, 77, Butlin Road, Luton. Cpl., 5th Battn. Suffolk Regt. Died as prisoner of the Japanese, August 1st, 1943.

HARTUP, ARTHUR, 157, Park Street, Luton. Killed by enemy action, at Luton, September 22nd, 1940.

HARTUP, FLORENCE EMILY, 157, Park Street, Luton. Killed by enemy action, at Luton, September 22nd, 1940.

HASWELL, JAMES, 69, Turners Road, Luton. Killed by enemy action, at Luton, November 16th, 1940.

HATHAWAY, ARTHUR WILLIAM, 46, St. Lawrence's Avenue, Luton. Sgt.-Flt. Engineer, R.A.F., Bomber Command. Missing, presumed killed, on operations, Nuremberg, March 16-17th, 1945.

HATTON, Ronald Charles, 134, Leagrave Road, Luton. L/Cpl., R.E. Lost at sea while prisoner of Japanese, September 12th, 1944.

HAUGHTON, Derek Basil, 1, Cannon Lane, Stopsley, Luton. Pte., 5th Battn. Bedfs. and Herts. Regt. Died as prisoner of Japanese, No. 2 Camp, Siam, August 13th, 1943.

HAWKES, Arthur Bert, 146, North Street, Luton. Sgt., R.A.S.C. Killed by enemy action, Casalbordino, Italy, November 24th, 1943.

HAWKES, Tom Bailey, 21, Shirley Road, Luton. Sgt., R.A.F. Killed in action, December 17th, 1943.

HAWKINS, Cyril Kenneth, 80, Maple Road, Luton. Able Seaman, R.N. Lost at sea, Simonstown, South Africa, on V-J Day, August 15th, 1945.

HAWKINS, Frederick Charles, 78, Icknield Road, Luton. P/Officer, R.A.F. Killed on operations over Germany, October 7th, 1944.

HAWTHORN, John, 18, Hartley Road, Luton. L/Cpl., Coldstream Guards. Missing, later reported killed, Dunkirk, 1940.

HAYLEY, Douglas Andrew Ross, 7, Liscomb Road, Dunstable, and formerly of Luton. Sgt., R.A.F. Killed by enemy action, Singapore, February 12th, 1942.

HAYWARD, Alfred Harold, 64, Westbourne Road, Luton. Sgt., R.E.M.E. Died on active service, Central Mediterranean Forces, 1944.

HAYWARD, Edward, 10, Brache Street, Luton. Pte., Sussex Regt. Died as prisoner of war, Germany.

HEARN, Charles Edmund, 32, Wellington Street, Luton. Gdsm., Grenadier Guards. Killed in action, Italy, January 22nd, 1944.

HEASLEY, Alexander, 45, Farley Avenue, Luton. S/Sgt., R. Scots Fusiliers. Died of wounds, Italy, December 17th, 1943 ; buried at Sangro River Cemetery.

HIBBERT, Keith, 144, Argyll Avenue, Luton. Flt./Sgt., Pathfinder Force, R.A.F. Missing, presumed killed, over Kiel, Germany, July 24th, 1944.

HIGGINS, Albert Marshall, 58, Cavendish Road, Luton. Tpr., 59th Training Regt., R.A.C. Died on active service, October 19th, 1941.

HIGGINS, A. R., 40, South Road, Luton. Sgt., Bedfs. and Herts. Regt. Died on active service, July, 1942.

HIGGINS, Walter, 40, South Road, Luton. O/Seaman, R.N. Missing on Convoy duties, October, 1942.

HILL, Harold Denis, 120, Oak Road, Luton. Pte., 5th Battn. Wiltshire Regt. Killed in action, Mont Pincon, France, August 7th, 1944.

HILL, Lewis Albert, 452, Hitchin Road, Luton. Flt./Sgt., R.A.F. Killed on active service, October 18th, 1941.

HILL, Richard Dockrill, 70, Boyle Street, Luton. Lieut., Herts. Regt. Killed in action, Italy, September 29th, 1944.

HILLMAN, William Major, of Tredegar, and 10, Fitzroy Avenue, Luton. Gnr., 420th Field Battery, R.A. Died as prisoner of Japanese, Siam, 1943.

HINDS, William Victor, 9, Edward Street, Luton. W/Officer, R.A.F. Missing, presumed killed, S.E. Asia, April, 1942.

HOBBS, Frederick William, 76, Russell Rise, Luton. Cpl., H.Q. Staff, R.A.F. Died as prisoner of Japanese, Sandakan Camp, Borneo, May 23rd, 1945.

HOLLINSHEAD, Sidney, 54, St. Ethelbert's Avenue, Luton. Bdr., 51st Light A.A. Regt., R.A. Killed in action, Italy, July 13th, 1944.

HOLMES, Rex Alec, formerly of Stuart Street, Luton. 2/Lt., 4th Battn. Suffolk Regt. Killed in action, Singapore, February 14th, 1942.

HOLT, Herbert Thomas, 11, East Avenue, Luton. O/Seaman, R.N., H.M.S. Barham. Lost at sea, Mediterranean, November 25th, 1942.

HOLTON, Ralph, 43, Newcombe Road, Luton. Driver, R.A.S.C. Died on active service, Italy, July 16th, 1945.

HORN, Jack, 34, Ivy Road, Luton. Gunner, att. Yorks and Lancs. Regt. Killed in action, Burma, July 3rd, 1944.

HORTON, John William, 13, Welbeck Road, Luton. Gnr., R.A. Killed in action.

HOSKINS, Trevor, 398, Dunstable Road, Luton. Midshipman, R.N., H.M.S. *Waterwitch*. Died on active service, February, 1946.

HOUGH, Iris Olive, 176, Selbourne Road, Luton. Killed by enemy action, at Vauxhall Motors, Ltd., Luton, August 30th, 1940.

HOUGHTON, Albert E., 88, Albert Road, Luton. Pte., Cambs. Regt. Lost at sea as prisoner of Japanese.

HOUGHTON, Wilfred, 43, Saxon Road, Luton. Tpr., R.A.C. Killed in action, Italy, May 22nd, 1944.

HOUSDEN, Phyllis, 24, Applecroft Road, Luton. Pte., A.T.S. Died on active service, July 14th, 1945.

HOUSLEY, Constance Mary, of Doncaster. Killed by enemy action, at Luton, September 5th, 1942.

HOWARTH, James, 15, Newcombe Road, Luton. Sgt. Killed on active service, November, 1940.

HOWELLS, Emrys George, 43, Arundel Road, Luton. Cpl., 110th Squadron, R.A.F. Killed in action, Wattisham, Suffolk, November 1st, 1940.

HUBBLE, James Claude, 1, Windmill Road, Luton. P/Officer, R.A.F. Died on active service, Tern Hill, Shropshire, October 12th, 1944.

HUGHES, John Eynon Wynne, 56, Seymour Road, Luton. Died of wounds caused by enemy action, at Luton, August 30th, 1940.

HUME, Frederick Calvin, 85, Somerset Avenue, Luton. Pte., 6th Battn. Bedfs. and Herts. Regt. Died on active service, Indian theatre of war, December 24th, 1942.

HUMFREY, Robert Albert, 107, Neville Road, Luton. Gnr., R.A. Lost at sea while prisoner of Japanese, September 12th, 1944.

HUNT, Arthur George, 39, Wenlock Street, Luton. B.Q.M.S., 148th Field Regt., R.A. Died as prisoner of Japanese, July 3rd, 1943.

HURVID, Clifford W., 86, Highbury Road, Luton. Fusilier, 9th Battn. R.F. Died of wounds, Salerno, Italy, September 9th, 1943.

HUTCHINS, John, 26, Midland Road, Luton. Killed by enemy action, at Luton, September 5th, 1942.

HYNE, William Taylor, 25, Alexandra Avenue, Luton. Assistant C.E. to Admiralty at Simonstown, South Africa. Lost at sea by enemy action en route Liverpool-Cape Town, December 6th-7th, 1942.

IMPEY, Ronald Cecil. Killed by enemy action, at Vauxhall Motors, Ltd., Luton, August 30th, 1940.

INGREY, William Edward, 94, Argyll Avenue, Luton. Cpl., Oxf. and Bucks. L.I. Killed in action, Normandy, August 13th, 1944.

IRESON, Frank Lewis Thomas, 63, Ferndale Road, Luton. Sgt., R.A.F. Killed on operations, Holland, July 25th, 1941.

ISAAC, Ronald, 190, Leagrave Road, Luton. C.S.M., 249th Field Coy., R.E. (Airborne). Died of wounds, Normandy, June 10th, 1944.

ISAACS, William Henry, 85, Whitefield Road, Sundon, and Felt & Fibre Co., Ltd., Luton. Gnr., R.A. Died as prisoner of Japanese, Tarsao, Siam, March 17th, 1944.

JACKSON, Francis Charles, D.F.M., 23, Felstead Way, Luton. Sgt. Flt. Eng., R.A.F. Killed on active service, December, 1942.

JACKSON, Leslie Horace, 806, Dunstable Road, Luton. Killed by enemy action, at Vauxhall Motors, Ltd., Luton, August 30th, 1940.

JACKSON, William, 97, Blundell Road, Luton. Killed in action, May 22nd, 1940.

JAMES, Dennis Nelson, 13, Stratford Road, Luton. Stoker First Class, R.N. Killed in action at sea, October 1st, 1944.

JAMES, William Douglas, 37, Saxon Road, Luton. Flt./Sgt., 61 Squadron, R.A.F. Killed in action in raid on Magdeburg, Germany, January 21st, 1944.

JANES, Clifford Lloyd Brown, " Green Hills," New Bedford Road, Luton. Sgt./Pilot, R.A.F. Killed in action, Middle East, 1943.

JANES, Frederick William, 17, Pondwicks Road, Luton. P/Officer, R.A.F., att. R.C.A.F. Killed on air operations, believed at Ahrenfelde, near Berlin, February 14th-15th, 1944.

JARVIS, Frank, 57, Langley Street, Luton. Sgt. Died in India, August, 1943.

JEFFERISS, James Leslie, 34, Lyndhurst Road, Luton. AC2, R.A.F. Died following road accident, 96th General Hospital, North Africa, September 13th, 1943.

JEFFS, Kenneth Frank, 13, Lincoln Road, Luton. Lieut., R. Norfolk Regt. Killed in action, Malaya, February, 1942.

JEFFS, Philip John, 13, Lincoln Road, Luton. Sgt./Flt. Eng., R.A.F. Killed on air operations, Germany, May 25th, 1944.

JENKINS, Edward Bertram Douglas, 68, Hampton Road, Luton. Sgt./Pilot, R.A.F. Killed on active service, December 28th, 1940.

JENNINGS, E. Ralph, 38, Sundridge Avenue, Luton. Pte., Suffolk Regt. Died in Burma, July 16th, 1944.

JESTY, Raymond George, 98, Richmond Hill, Luton. W/Officer, R.A.F. Killed on active service, August 27th, 1943.

JONES, Anthony, 65, Ivy Road, Luton. Pte., Suffolk Regt. Died of wounds, Middle East, December 9th, 1941.

JONES, Elizabeth, 79, Biscot Road, Luton. Killed by enemy action, at Luton, November 6th, 1944.

JONES, H. A. M., 15, Brooms Road, Luton. Pte., South Wales Borderers. Died of wounds, Indian theatre of war, August 10th, 1944.

JONES, Henry, 63, Chester Avenue, Luton. Pte., 2nd Border Regt. Died of wounds, Burma, February 3rd, 1945.

JONES, James Julius, 31, Burr Street, Luton. Pte., Queen's Royal Regt. Killed in action, Italy, September 28th, 1944.

JONES, John Flood, 67, Clarendon Road, Luton. L/Seaman, R.N.R., i/c naval guns, s.s. *Beaverbrook*, Merchant Navy. Missing, presumed killed, April 1st, 1941, Battle of the Atlantic.

JONES, Robert J., 15, Brooms Road, Luton, 6th Battn. South Wales Borderers. Died of wounds, Burma, March 10th, 1944.

KAY, George, 100, Alder Crescent, Luton. Sgt., 1st Airborne Reconnaissance Squadron, R.A.C. Killed on active service, Norway, June 3rd, 1945.

KEAST, Stanley George, 2, Lincoln Road, Luton. L/Sgt., 2nd Battn. Bedfs. and Herts. Regt. Killed in action, Italy, June 30th, 1944.

KEATES, Charles Francis, 3, Warwick Road, Luton. LAC., R.A.F. Died on active service, Persia, December 14th, 1942.

KEECH, William Frederick. Killed by enemy action, at Vauxhall Motors, Ltd., Luton, August 30th, 1940.

KEELY, Mary Julia, 24, Avondale Road, Luton. Killed by enemy action, at Luton, November 4th, 1940.

KEEN, Joyce, 26, Shirley Road, Luton. Killed by enemy action, at Luton, October 14th, 1940.

KEMP, Sidney, 147, High Town Road, Luton. Pte., Durham L.I. Killed in action, N.W. Europe, August 9th, 1944.

KENT, Leslie George, 3, Gardenia Avenue, Luton. Gnr., R.A. Died on active service, April, 1940.

KENYON, Redvers, 16, Milton Road, Luton. Sgt. A.G., 50th Squadron, R.A.F. Lost on operations over Norway, October 28th-29th, 1944.

KIGHTLEY, Ernest John, 113, Boyle Street, Luton. Cpl., 6th Battn. R. Welch Fusiliers. Killed in action, Hertogenbosch, Holland, October 24th, 1944.

KIGHTLEY, Herbert, 118, Dunstable Road, Luton. LAC Armourer, R.A.F. Died on service, March 19th, 1946.

KILBY, John Andrew, 64, Crawley Green Road, Luton.   Killed by enemy action, at Vauxhall Motors, Ltd., Luton, August 30th, 1940.

KILBY, John Charles, 85, Clarendon Road, Luton.   Sgt./Pilot, R.A.F.   Killed on active service, Addo, nr. Port Elizabeth, S. Africa, January 14th, 1945.

KILBY, Percy Ewart, 3, Stockwood Crescent, Luton.   Sick Berth Attendant, Motor Rescue Launch, R.N.   Lost at sea on active service off Isle of Lewis, Hebrides, February 7th, 1943.

KIMBER, Walter Daunt, Bishops Stortford, and London Road, Luton. Sgt./Pilot, R.A.F.   Killed on active service, February, 1941.

KING, Alec Percy, 80, Wenlock Street, Luton.   Flt./Sgt., 274 Squadron, R.A.F. Killed on active service, August 26th, 1943.

KING, Cecil Robert, 73, Clarendon Road, Luton.   R.A.M.C.   Died after return from B.A.O.R., February 10th, 1946.

KING, Charles Henry.   Killed by enemy action, at Vauxhall Motors, Ltd., Luton, August 30th, 1940.

KING, Charles William, 30, Church Street, Luton.   Sgt., 7th Battn. Hampshire Regt.   Killed in action, Holland, September 25th, 1944.

KING, Robert Joseph, 18, Lincoln Road, Luton.   Gunner, Field Regt., R.A. Killed on active service, July 31st, 1941.

KING, Sidney, 152, Selbourne Road, Luton.   L/Bdr., R.A.   Killed after escaping from German prison camp near Dresden, May 11th, 1945.

KINGHAM, Ernest Arthur, Gladstone Avenue, Luton.   P/Officer, R.A.F Killed on operations over enemy-occupied territory, June, 1944.

KINGSNORTH, Frank William, 28, Pomfret Avenue, Luton.   L/Sgt., Anti-Tank Regt., R.A.   Lost at sea while prisoner of Japanese, December 9th, 1944.

KNOWLES, Ian, 3, Ludlow Avenue, Luton.   Rfm., R. Inniskilling Fusiliers. Killed on active service, May, 1944.

LACEY, Alexander William, 8, Lansdowne Road, Luton.   F/Lt., R.A.F. Killed on active service, December 21st, 1941.

LACEY, Ralph, 157, Graham Gardens, Luton.   Killed by enemy action, at Vauxhall Motors, Ltd., Luton, August 30th, 1940.

LAMB, Cyril Edward, 6, Latimer Road, Luton.   Spr., R.E.   Died as prisoner of Japanese, Siam, June 21st, 1943.

LAND, Herbert John, 74, Wenlock Street, Luton.   Pte., 5th Battn. R. Norfolk Regt.   Killed in action, Singapore, February 14th, 1942.

LANE, Ronald Ernest, 230, Marsh Road, Luton.   Spr., R.E.   Died of wounds, Anzio Beach Head, Italy, February 26th, 1944.

LANG, Jack, 1, Latimer Road, Luton.   Pte., 6th Airborne Division (Parachutist). Died on active service, Palestine, December 29th, 1945.

LARGE, Horace William, 25, Dorset Street, Luton.   Dvr., R.A.S.C.   Died on active service, Middle East, May 31st, 1942.

LARGE, Leslie William, 88, Stapleford Road, Luton.   First Class Stoker, R.N. Killed by enemy action, Northern Waters, November 13th, 1944.

LAW, Harold John, 8, Kent Road, Luton.   L/Sgt., 419th Batty. 148th Field Regt., R.A.   Lost at sea as prisoner of Japanese, September 12th, 1944.

LAWRENCE, Derek, 10, Northview Road, Luton.   AC., R.A.F.   Died at sea, April, 1941.

LAWRENCE, James, 246, Biscot Road, Luton.   L/Bdr., R.A.   Died as prisoner of Japanese, Siam, September 6th, 1943.

LAZELL, Oliver John, 61, Solway Road, Luton.   Killed by enemy action, at Luton, August 30th, 1940.

LEMMON, Douglas James William, 74, Ferndale Road, Luton.   Pte., 5th Battn. Bedfs. and Herts. Regt.   Lost at sea as prisoner of Japanese, September 21st, 1944.

LETTING, Bernard, 23, Fitzroy Avenue, Luton.   137 Squadron, R.A.F.   Died on active service off Kastrup, Copenhagen, June 14th, 1945.

LEWIS, Ivor Rees, 36, Tennyson Road, Luton. P/Officer, R.A.F. Killed on operations over the Baltic, August, 1943.

LITTLE, John Frederick, 427, Dunstable Road, Luton. W/Officer-Pilot, R.A.F. Presumed killed on operations over Dusseldorf, Germany, August 29th, 1943.

LOCKEY, Roy Cecil Sale, 3, Finsbury Road, Luton. L/Cpl., Suffolk Regt. Killed in Burma, June, 1944.

LONG, Ronald, 14, Adelaide Street, Luton. Gnr., R.A. Presumed died of wounds, Singapore, February, 1942.

LONG, Sidney James, 49, Whitecroft Road, Luton. Died as result of enemy action at Luton, August 31st, 1940.

LOVELOCK, Maurice, 114, Bishopscote Road, Luton. Pte., 1st Battn. Worcester Regt. Killed in action, Cleve, Germany, February 17th, 1945.

LUBBOCK, Cecil Alfred, 437, Dunstable Road, Luton. Tpr., 3rd Dragoon Guards, R.A.C. Killed in action, Burma, May 8th, 1944.

LUSTY, Arthur David, 66, St. Ethelbert's Avenue, Luton. Cpl., 1/7th Queen's Royal Regt. Killed in action, El Alamein, October 24th, 1942.

McALLISTER, James, 8, Bolton Road, Luton. Gnr., R.A. Died of wounds, Singapore, February 15th, 1942.

McCAULEY, Ronald James, 110, Kingsway, Luton. AC.2, 656 Squadron, R.A.F. Killed on active service, Ramrae Island, Burma, January 25th, 1944.

McCRACKEN, James, 23, Whitefield Avenue, Sundon, and Adamant Engineering Co., Ltd., Luton. L/Bdr., R.A. Died as prisoner of Japanese, Kanburi, Siam, December 12th, 1943.

McDADE, Edward Albert, 59, St. Peter's Road, Luton. Cpl., R.E. Died as prisoner of Japanese, Siam, January 21st, 1944.

McGEORGE, John Sydney, 52, Montrose Avenue, Luton. Driver, R.A.S.C., att. R.A. Killed by Allied bombing while war prisoner, Stalag XVIIIa, Wolfsberg, Austria, December 18th, 1944.

McMANUS, Patrick, 77, Church Street, Luton. Sgt., R.E. Died on active service, Middle East, November, 1943.

MANLEY, Ralph, 35, Wellington Street, Luton. Cfm., R.E.M.E. Died of wounds, Germany, April 30th, 1945.

MANN, Richard Stephen, 11, Farley Avenue, Luton. Killed by enemy action, at Vauxhall Motors, Ltd., Luton, August 30th, 1940.

MANT, Kenneth Victor, 102, Westmorland Avenue, Luton. Sgt. W/O., R.A.F. Missing on operations, May 12th-13th, 1944.

MARSHALL, Frederick E. W., 39, Corncastle Road, Luton. Driver, R.E. Killed in action, Italy, October 26th, 1943.

MARSHALL, William Charles, 65, Fountains Road, Luton. Sgt. W/Op. A.G., 18th Squadron, R.A.F. Missing on operations, Malta, December 26th, 1941.

MATHESON, David Black, 218, Ashcroft Road, Luton. Pte., R.A.S.C. Lost at sea with the *Ceramic*, Atlantic, December 6th, 1942.

MAUGHAN, John, 10, Roman Road, Luton. Gnr., R.A. Killed in action, Italy, October 22nd, 1944.

MEAD, Ernest, Luton. Gnr., R.A. Died on active service, January 31st, 1945.

MEDCRAFT, Cyril, 110, Lea Road, Luton. Pte., 1/4th K.O.Y.L.I. Killed in action, N.W. Europe, June 25th, 1944.

MELDRUM, Bernard Richard, " Dawnaday," Taunton Avenue, Luton. Cpl., R.A.S.C., att. 16/2nd H.A.A. Batty. R.A. Missing, presumed killed, Greece, April 28th, 1941.

MERCER, John, 5, Seymour Road, Luton. L/Cpl. Killed in action, Burma, February 2nd, 1945.

MERCER, Wilfred, 89, Summerfield Road, Luton. Pte., Suffolk Regt. Died as prisoner of Japanese, Burma, September, 1943.

MILES, Henry William, 7, Gloucester Road, Luton. Killed by enemy action, at Luton, August 30th, 1940.

MITCHELL, SAMUEL, 75, Kent Road, Luton. Bedfs. and Herts. Regt. Died on active service in Germany.

MITCHENER, CHARLES, "Westlea," Walcot Avenue, Luton. F/Officer, R.A.F. Missing, presumed killed, in operations over Hamburg, July 26th-27th, 1942.

MOCK, CHARLES ALBERT, 28, Tower Road, Luton. Leading Telegraphist, R.N. Lost at sea as prisoner of the Japanese, June 26th, 1944.

MOORE, NORMAN JAMES, 27, Court Road, Luton. Killed by enemy action, at Luton, November 6th, 1944.

MORGAN, WILLIAM, 7, Dunstable Close, Luton. Stoker, 2nd Class, R.N., H.M. Corvette *Bluebell*. Lost at sea, homeward bound from Russia, February 17th, 1945.

MORRIS, REGINALD FRANCIS, 67, Hazelbury Crescent, Luton. Chief Petty Officer, R.N. Killed in action, Far East, December, 1942.

MORRISON, MARGARET JEAN, 93, Harcourt Street, Luton. Killed by enemy action, at Luton, August 30th, 1940.

MORSLEY, RICHARD WILLIAM, Birmingham, and formerly Crescent Rise, Luton. Killed by enemy action, April, 1941.

MORTLOCK, CAROLE ROSEMARY, 81, Biscot Road, Luton. Killed by enemy action, at Luton, November 6th, 1944.

MOSS, REGINALD ERNEST, 86, Runley Road, Luton. L/Cpl., R.E.M.E. Killed in action, Burma, February 11th, 1944.

MOSS, RONALD EDWARD, 85, Langley Street, Luton. Pte. Killed in action, Italy, September 17th, 1944.

NELSON, CHARLES RICHARD, 42, Selbourne Road, Luton. Pte., Suffolk Regt. Died as prisoner of Japanese, Samoa, December 18th, 1942.

NEWTON, GEORGE SHEPHERD, 52, Hampton Road, Luton. Cpl., Seaforth Highlanders. Missing, believed killed, place and date unknown, 1940.

NIELAND, JAMES HENRY, 38, Bolton Road, Luton. Killed by enemy action, at Vauxhall Motors, Ltd., Luton, August 30th, 1940.

NORMAN, ROY, 74, Stratford Road, Luton. Gnr.-D.R., 419th Field Regt., R.A. Missing, presumed killed, Singapore, February 14th, 1942.

NORTHWOOD, ERIC, 165, Dallow Road, Luton. Marine. Died on active service, June, 1942.

NORTHWOOD, R., 148, Milton Road, Luton. Sgt., R.A.F. Missing, presumed killed, July, 1941.

NUNN, SILAS HENRY, 42, Inkerman Street, Luton. Tpr., 1st Royal Tank Regt., R.A.C. Killed on active service, Ellon, France, July 12th, 1944.

O'BRIEN, LEONARD DAVID, Limbrick Hall, Harpenden, and B. Laporte, Ltd., Luton. Lt., Hertfordshire Regt. Died of wounds, N.W. Europe, September, 1944.

O'DELL, EDWIN, 1, Burrs Passage, Langley Street, Luton. L/Sgt., Royal Corps of Signals. Killed in action, Sicily, July 17th, 1943.

O'FLAHERTY, DERRICK EDWARD, 13, Luton Road, Cockernhoe, Luton Boys' Club, and G. F. Farr, Collingdon Street, Luton. Sgt./Pilot, R.A.F. Killed on active service, October 23rd, 1940.

O'NEILL, GEORGE EDWARD, 141, Chester Avenue, Luton. Sgt. W/Op., R.A.F. Missing, presumed killed, on operations, Dommartin, France, May 3rd-4th, 1944.

OAKLEY, RICHARD HINES, 473, Dunstable Road, Luton. Sgt./Pilot, No. 1 Squadron, R.A.F. Killed on active service, Purdis Croft, near Felixstowe, October 21st, 1941.

ODELL, DENNIS WALTER, 15, Jubilee Street, Luton. Sgt. A/G. W/Op., 37th Squadron, R.A.F. Killed in action, Orvieto, Italy, June 7th, 1944.

OGGLESBY, FREDERICK, 11, Stuart Street, Luton. L/Cpl., Wiltshire Regt. Died of wounds received in Germany, February 18th, 1945.

OLIVER, DOROTHY WINIFRED, Hexton and Leagrave Post Office. First Class Airwoman, W.A.A.F. Accidentally killed, Wellington, Shropshire, August 23rd, 1942.

ORCHARD, Dennis Malcolm, 45, Trent Road, Luton. Killed by enemy action, at Vauxhall Motors, Ltd., Luton, August 30th, 1940.

ORDISH, Charles Brian, D.F.C., 39, Ludlow Avenue. F/Lieut., R.A.F. Killed on operations, December, 1943.

OSBORNE, Frederick William, 26, Rothesay Road, Luton. Pte., East Yorks. Regt. Killed in action, Tunisia, April 6th, 1943.

OWEN, Brinley D., 173, Toddington Road, Luton. Gnr., 419th Field Battery, R.A. Lost at sea as prisoner of Japanese, September 12th, 1944.

OWEN, Stanley James, 418, Leagrave Road, Luton. Killed by enemy action in London, August 8th, 1944.

OWLES, Aubrey Ernest, formerly of Luton, and late of 86, Poynters Road, Dunstable, and Vauxhall Motors, Ltd. Sgt./Pilot, R.A.F., 18th Squadron. Killed in air battle, August 31st, 1940.

PAGE, Sydney Lewis, 5, Edward Street, Dunstable, and Vauxhall Motors, Ltd., Luton. Gnr., R.A. Died as prisoner of Japanese, Siam, April 13th, 1943.

PAIN, Ronald George, 38, Clevedon Road, Luton. Sgt., 35th Squadron Pathfinder Force, R.A.F. Missing, presumed killed, on operations over Kiel, Germany, August 26th-27th, 1944.

PAIN, Stanley Edward, 38, Clevedon Road, Luton. Pte., 2/7th Queen's Royal Regt. Killed in action, Forli, Italy, September 27th, 1944.

PALMER, Thomas Sidney, 51, Dudley Street, Luton. Air Mechanic, Fleet Air Arm. Lost with H.M.S. *Hermes*, Indian Ocean, April 9th, 1942.

PARKER, Charles O., 344, Beechwood Road, Luton. Gdsm., Grenadier Guards. Killed on active service, April 13th, 1945.

PARKER, Edward John, 21, Boyle Street, Luton. Cpl., Corps of Military Police. Died as prisoner of Japanese, Siam, June 9th, 1943.

PARKER, Kenneth George, 484, Dunstable Road, Luton. Sgt./Pilot, R.A.F. Killed on active service, November, 1941.

PARR, Herbert Joseph, 81, Saxon Road, Luton. Sgt., 279th Field Unit, R.E. Killed in action, Liessem, Holland, November 2nd, 1944.

PARROTT, Eric Horace, 58, The Avenue, Luton. S/Ldr., R.A.F. Missing from air operations, August, 1943.

PARSONS, Frederick William, 150a, North Street, Luton. LAC., R.A.F. Died at sea while prisoner of Japanese, November 8th, 1944.

PATEMAN, Vera Winifred, 18, Midland Road, Luton. Killed by enemy action, at Luton, September 5th, 1942.

PAYNE, Harold Victor, 24, Beech Road, Luton. Spr., R.E. Killed at sea, Benghazi Harbour, December 28th, 1942.

PEACOCK, J., Beechwood Road, Luton. L/Cpl., R.A.C. Killed in action N. Africa, May, 1943.

PEARSON, W. L., 162, Marsh Road, Luton. Gnr., R.A. Died as prisoner of Japanese, Siam, 1944.

PEDDER, Robert Edward, 67, Ridgway Road, Luton. Flt./Sgt., R.A.F. Killed on operations, Germany, October 22nd, 1943.

PEPPER, Harvey, London Road, Woburn, and Vauxhall Motors, Ltd., Luton. Pte., 2nd Battn. Bedfs. and Herts. Regt. Killed in action, Western Front, May 20th, 1940.

PERRY, Edward Francis Edwin, 17, Stockingstone Road, Luton. Sgt./Pilot, R.A.F. Killed on operations, November, 1940.

PERRY, Samuel, Breachwood Green and Percival Aircraft, Ltd., Luton. L.A.C., R.A.F. Killed on active service, Rangoon, November, 1945.

PHILLIPS, Herbert Llewellyn, 13, Churchill Road, Luton. L.A.C., R.A.F. Killed on active service, Hadera, Palestine, January 17th, 1944.

PINNEY, Donald Frederick, 139, Old Bedford Road, Luton. Air Mechanic, Fleet Air Arm. Killed on active service, January 14th, 1945.

PINNEY, George Robert, 34, St. Lawrence's Avenue, Luton. Pte., Suffolk Regt. Died as prisoner of Japanese, Chunkie, Siam, October 13th, 1943.

PITKIN, Archibald Henry, 159, Selbourne Road, Luton. Killed by enemy action, at Vauxhall Motors, Ltd., Luton, August 30th, 1940.

POLLARD, George Thomas, 112, Cowper Street, Luton. Gnr., 355/111th H.A.A. Regt., R.A. Killed on active service, Germany, November 29th, 1945.

POLLARD, Leslie Arthur, 29, St. Margaret's Avenue, Luton. Gnr., 148th Field Regt., R.A. Died as prisoner of Japanese, Siam, July 5th, 1943.

PORTER, Frederick Arthur, Swindon and Luton. Killed by enemy action, at Vauxhall Motors, Ltd., Luton, August 30th, 1940.

POTT, Ernest Charles, 22, Albion Road, Luton. Pte., R.A.O.C. Lost at sea while prisoner of Japanese, November 14th, 1942.

POULTON, Hubert William, 18, Kenilworth Road, Luton. Killed by enemy action, at Luton, September 25th, 1940.

POWELL, Edward Roy, 115, Marsh Road, Luton. Royal Marine, Landing Craft. Lost at sea, Walcheren Island, Holland, November 1st, 1944.

POWER, William Peter, 402, Dunstable Road, Luton. Gnr., R.A. Died as prisoner of Japanese, Batavia, September 1st, 1942.

PRATT, Arthur P., 18, Browning Road, Luton. Cpl., R.A.F. Died as prisoner of Japanese, Harrokoe Island, June 23rd, 1943.

PRATT, Walter William, 9, Windermere Crescent, Luton. Sgt.-Major, R.E.M.E. Killed on active service, Middle East, August, 1943.

PROCTOR, Richard George, 81, Blundell Road, Luton. Pte. Killed in action, Italy, April 7th, 1944.

PRUDAN, Noel, 7, Onslow Road, Leagrave, Luton. 1st Manchester Regt. Died on active service, August 10th, 1941.

PRUDAN, Raymond, 7, Onslow Road, Leagrave, Luton. Pte., 1st Manchester Regt. Died as prisoner of Japanese, August 13th, 1943.

PRYOR, Leslie Walter, 44, Devon Road, Luton. Sgt./Pilot, 17th Operational Training Unit, R.A.F. Died at Dalton, Lancashire, as result of war operations, May 21st, 1941.

PUGH, Cedric Ronald, 6, Limbury Road, Luton. L/Cpl., Corps of Military Police. Died on active service, August 14th, 1943.

RADDON, Edward C., "The Chalet," Derby Road, Luton. Third Officer, Merchant Navy. Missing at sea, Mediterranean, May, 1941.

RAINES, Elsie May, 58, Biscot Road, Luton. Killed by enemy action, at Luton, November 5th, 1944.

RAISBECK, Kenneth, 65, Blenheim Crescent, Luton. A.C.1, R.A.F. Killed on active service while training as pilot, Oswego, Kansas, U.S.A., June 26th, 1944.

RANCE, Derrick P., 92, Ashton Road, Luton. Sgt. W/Op. A.G., R.A.F. Coastal Command. Lost at sea, January 28th, 1944.

RANDALL, Frederick James, "Sugar Loaf," Leagrave, Luton. Major, 18th Reconnaissance Corps. Died of wounds, Alexandra Hospital, Singapore between February 5th and 15th, 1942.

RANDALL, Maurice Dean, 89, Alexandra Avenue, Luton. F/Lieut., R.A.F. Killed on active service, India, October, 1944.

RANDALL, Sidney, Trinity Road, Luton. Lost with H.M.S. *Exmouth*, January, 1940.

RAYMENT, Clifford George, 17, Tower Road, Luton. Pte., 2nd Battn. Devonshire Regt. Killed in action, N.W. Europe, August 12th, 1944.

RAYMENT, Harold Edward, 103, St. Margaret's Avenue, Luton. Pte., Bedfs. and Herts. Regt. Died as prisoner of Japanese, Siam, June 30th, 1943.

RAYNER, Sidney Francis, 66, Russell Street, Luton. Major, 2nd Battn. Bedfs. and Herts. Regt. Died of wounds, Italy, May 21st, 1944.

REES, Mrs. A., 83, Biscot Road, Luton. Killed by enemy action, at Luton, November 6th, 1944.

REID, David, 17, Hampton Road, Luton. Marine. Lost with H.M.S. *Royal Oak* September, 1939.

REYNOLDS, Frederick Horace, 6, Rosslyn Crescent, Luton. Pte., 6th Battn. D.L.I. Killed in action, San El Minerva, near El Alamein, July 27th, 1942.

RHODES, Thomas Geoffrey. Killed by enemy action, at Vauxhall Motors, Ltd., Luton, August 30th, 1940.

RICHARDS, Derrick Sidney J., 135, Dallow Road, Luton. Sgt./Pilot, R.A.F., Bomber Command. Missing, presumed killed, January 14th, 1944.

RICHARDS, John Thomas, 8, Medina Road, Luton. Flt./Sgt., R.A.F. Missing, presumed killed on operations, November, 1943.

RICHARDS, Wallace, 6, St. Augustine's Avenue, Luton. F./Lieut., R.C.A.F. Killed on active service, Canada.

RICHARDS, Walter Philip, 11A, Dunstable Road, Luton. P./Officer, R.A.F. Killed on operations, Torsken, Senja Island, Norway, May 21st, 1940.

RICHARDSON, Douglas Cameron, The Mount, New Bedford Road, Luton. Bdr., R.A. Drowned as prisoner of Italians when ship from Tripoli was sunk, November, 1942.

RICHARDSON, Joseph George, 74, Cromwell Road, Luton. Sgt., 101st Squadron, R.A.F. Killed in action, retruning from operations over Germany, August 19th, 1941.

RICHES, Leslie P., formerly Curate at All Saints' Church, Luton. Chaplain to the Forces. Missing, believed drowned, Dunkirk, June, 1940.

RICKARD, Sarah, 70, Biscot Road, Luton. Killed by enemy action, at Luton, November 6th, 1944.

RIGGS, George E., 33, Brook Street, Luton. L.A.C., R.A.F. Killed in action, August 30th, 1940.

RIXON, Cyril Jack, 74, Biscot Road, Luton. Died as result of enemy action, at Luton, November 6th, 1944.

ROBERTS, Alec Frederick, 258, Dallow Road, Luton. Dvr., H.Q., 4th Indian Corps, R.A.S.C. Died on active service, Bareilly, India, June 11th, 1943.

ROBINSON, John, 11, Court Road, Luton. Fusilier. Died of wounds, Italy, October 23rd, 1943.

ROE, Dennis Edward, 27, Cambridge Street, Luton. Driver, R.A.S.C. (Airborne). Missing, presumed killed in action, Western Europe, June 7th, 1944.

ROE, E. J., 323, Manor Road, Caddington, and 40A, Buxton Road, Luton. P./Officer, R.A.F. Missing, presumed killed, in air operations over enemy-occupied territory, June, 1944.

ROE, Harold William, 17, Dordans Road, Luton. Driver, R.A.S.C. Killed in action, Celle, Germany, April 13th, 1945.

ROOKWOOD, John William, 251, Dallow Road, Luton. Telegraphist, R.N., M.T.B. Killed in action, Mediterranean, July 17th, 1943.

ROSE, Carl, 19, Cardigan Street, Luton. Pte., Cambs. Regt. Died as prisoner of Japanese, Siam, June, 1943.

ROSS, James, 101, Selbourne Road, Luton. Killed by enemy action, at Luton, October 14th, 1940.

ROWE, Horace, 82, Argyll Avenue, Luton. 1st Class Stoker, R.N., H.M.S. Acheron. Lost at sea, December 17th, 1940.

ROWLAND, Albert H., 31, New Town Street, Luton. Pte. Died on active service in India, July 15th, 1944.

RUDD, Colin James, M.C. and Bar., 164, Dunstable Road, Luton. Captain, Northants. Regt., att. Staffords, and later att. Wiltshire Regt. Killed in action, Cleve, Germany, February 10th, 1945.

RUDD, Frank, 31, Biscot Road, Luton. Killed by enemy action, at Luton, November 6th, 1944.

SALE, Stewart George, 17, Avondale Road, Luton, and Lane End, High Wycombe. War Correspondent (Reuters). Killed in Italy, September 28th, 1943.

SALTER, Henry Ernest Richard, 107, Crawley Green Road, Luton. Gnr./Driver, R.A. (Field). Died as prisoner of Japanese, Burma, September 30th, 1943.

SAMWELLS, William Alfred, 42, Hazelbury Crescent, Luton. Army Pay Corps. Died on active service, May 15th, 1942.

SANDERS, Ernest Henry, 69, Maidenhall Road, Luton. Pte., 1st Battn. Dorset Regt. Killed in action, Caen, Normandy, 1944.

SAUNDERS, Albert James, 47, Sundon Road, Luton. Pte. Killed in action, Italy, October, 1943.

SAUNDERS, John H., Wingfield Close, Bedford, and Douglas Stratford & Co., Luton. Flt./Sgt., R.A.F. Killed on active service, October, 1944.

SAUNDERS, Kenneth Albert, 52, Trinity Road, Luton. L/Bdr., 75th Anti-Tank Regt., R.A. Died on active service, near Bremen, Germany, June 4th, 1945.

SAUNDERS, Leonard A., 43, Beech Road, Luton. Gunner, R.A. Missing at Singapore, 1942.

SAVAGE, Arthur, 25, Summerfield Road, Luton. Pte., 4th Battn. King's Shropshire L.I. Killed in action, Overloon, N.W. Europe, October 15th, 1944.

SAVAGE, George, 19, Grove Road, Luton. Pte., Army Catering Corps. Killed in action, Ainsy, Normandy, July 6th, 1944.

SAXBY, Albert J. W., 101, Third Avenue, Sundon, and formerly of Luton. Sgt., R.A.F. Killed on operations over Denmark, February, 1944.

SCALES, Barbara, 61, Wardown Crescent, Luton. Killed by enemy action, at Luton, October 14th, 1940.

SCALES, Henry Percy, 89, Hartley Road, Luton. Gnr., R.A. Died as prisoner of Japanese, Siam, August 6th, 1943.

SCOTT, Sidney R., 78, Dordans Road, Luton. Pte., 2nd Battn. Bedfs. and Herts. Regt. Killed in action, Florence, Italy, August 7th, 1944.

SCRIVENER, William George, 94, Pomfret Avenue, Luton. Accidentally killed while serving as a dispatch rider, Swindon, June, 1940.

SEAR, Joseph, 31, Lea Road, Luton. O/Seaman, R.N. Died on convoy duty, Mediterranean, April, 1942.

SHARP, George Ralph, 38, Rothesay Road, Luton. Sgt., 7th Squadron, R.A.F. Killed on operations over Berlin, January 29th, 1944.

SHAW, Arnold, 8, Stratford Road, Luton. Signm., R.N. Lost with H.M.A.S. *Vampire*, Colombo, April 9th, 1942.

SHAW, Gerald Charles Francis, 139, Beechwood Road, Luton. Able Seaman, R.N., H.M. Submarine P.165. Killed in action, April 18th, 1943.

SHAW, Ronald Bertie, 96, Lea Road, Luton. Sapper, R.E. Died on active service, January 14th, 1942.

SHEPHERD, Arthur, 28, Chobham Street, Luton. Gnr., R.A. Killed by mine explosion, December 24th, 1941.

SHEPHERD, Sidney, 28, Chobham Street, Luton. Gnr., R.A. Killed by mine explosion, Kent, January, 1945.

SHOTBOLT, Reginald Arthur John, 50, Winsdon Road, Luton. L.A.C., 6th Squadron, R.A.F. Killed on active service, Gunters Field, Alabama, U.S.A., April 7th, 1942.

SHUTTLEWORTH, Frank, Oldham, and Commer Cars, Ltd., Luton. Dvr., R.A.S.C. Died on active service, North Africa, October, 1943.

SILVER, Maurice, 64, Farley Avenue, Luton. Sgt./Navigator, R.A.F. Killed on active service, June 6th, 1944.

SIMKINS, Lizzie, 91, Althorp Road, Luton. Killed by enemy action, at Luton, November 6th, 1944.

SIMMONDS, Willis, 49, Trent Road, Luton. Bdr., 148th Field Regt., R.A. Lost at sea while prisoner of Japanese, September 12th, 1944.

SIMPSON, Charles William, Saxon Road, Luton. Gnr., R.A. Died on active service, June, 1940.

SINFIELD, John, 197, Biscot Road, Luton. Gnr., 148th Field Regt., R.A. Died as prisoner of Japanese, Siam, March 29th, 1945.

SING, Henry Lee, 13, Princess Street, Luton. AC/1, R.A.F. Killed on active service, Colombo, December 12th, 1945.

SKELTON, IVAN GEORGE, 45, Windmill Road, Luton. F/Officer, R.A.F. Missing, presumed killed, on operations over Germany, October 18th, 1944.

SKELTON, JOHN ANDREW GUTHRIE, 150, Wardown Crescent, Luton. Killed by enemy action, at Luton, August 30th, 1940.

SKINNER, FRED, 71, Trinity Road, Luton. Died on active service, July 15th, 1944.

SLATER, RAYMOND GORDON, 494, Dunstable Road, Luton. L/Sgt., 420th Field Battery, R.A. Died at sea as prisoner of Japanese, September 14th, 1944.

SMART, HAROLD ALFRED STEPHEN, 144, Richmond Hill, Luton. Bdr., 148th Field Regt., R.A. Died as prisoner of Japanese, Central Siam, December 31st, 1943.

SMITH, ALFRED ARTHUR, 47, Stanley Street, Luton. Pte., 2nd Battn. The Buffs. Killed in action, El Alamein, September 30th, 1942.

SMITH, AUBREY J., 16, Cardiff Grove, Luton. Pte., Suffolk Regt. Died as prisoner of Japanese, October, 1943.

SMITH, CHARLES, 11, New Town Street, Luton. Gnr., R.A. Died on active service in India, November, 1943.

SMITH, CHARLES EDWARD, 106, Willow Way, Luton. Sgt., R.A.F., Bomber Command. Killed returning from air operations, November 19th, 1943.

SMITH, DAVID, Barton, and Cundall Folding Machine Co., Luton. Gnr., R.A. Died as prisoner of Japanese, 1944.

SMITH, EDGAR GORDON T., 9, Conway Road, Luton. P/Officer, R.A.F. Killed on operations over Germany, December, 1941.

SMITH, FRANK, 19, Stockingstone Road, Luton. R.N. Lost with H.M.S. *Rawalpindi*, off Iceland, November, 1939.

SMITH, FREDERICK, 10, Hampton Road, Luton. Gnr., R.A. Killed in action, Italy, January 17th, 1943.

SMITH, GEOFFREY ARCHIBALD, 14, Broad Mead, Luton. Sgt. F/Engr., 15th Squadron, R.A.F. Missing on operations, presumed killed, September 10th, 1942.

SMITH, HAROLD WILLIAM, 9, Dudley Street, Luton. Gnr., R.A. Killed in action at sea, July 15th, 1941.

SMITH, JOHN HOLMES, 123, Runley Road, Luton. Killed by enemy action, at De Havillands, Hatfield, October 3rd, 1940.

SMITH, LESLIE, 9, Dudley Street, Luton. Gnr.-Dvr. i/c, R.A. Died of wounds, Italy, November 2nd, 1942.

SMITH, SHEILA ELIZABETH, 95, Harcourt Street, Luton. Killed by enemy action, at Luton, August 30th, 1940.

SMITH, STANLEY E. T., 30, Norton Road, Luton. Gdsm., Irish Guards. Died of wounds, Western Front, December, 1944.

SMITHAM, DANIEL, 35, Shaftesbury Road, Luton. Third Engineer, Merchant Navy. Lost at sea by enemy action, 1942.

SMYTH, WILLIAM J., 30, Dale Road, Luton. Gnr., R.A. Lost at sea as prisoner of Japanese.

SNOW, RICHARD JAMES, Warden Hill, Luton. Cpl., Cambs. Regt. Killed in action, Far East, January 28th, 1942.

SNOXELL, CHARLES HENRY, 45, Woodside Road, Luton, and employed at Luton Brewery. AC/1, R.A.F. Lost at sea, between Java and Japan, while prisoner of Japanese, November 23rd, 1942.

SNOXELL, GERALD JAMES THOMAS, 137, New Bedford Road, Luton. F/Officer, No. 1 O.T.U., R.A.F. Died on active service, January 13th, 1943.

SOTON, HENRY P., 21, Harefield Road, Luton. Killed by U.S. bomb lorry explosion, Offley, January 8th, 1945.

SPICER, JOHN ROBERT, 13, Letchworth Road, Luton. Pte. Died on active service in France, August 1944.

SQUIRE, LAWRENCE FRANCIS, 97, Wardown Crescent, Luton. P/Officer, R.A.F. Killed on active service, December, 1940.

SQUIRES, R. R., 20, Newbury Lane, Silsoe. Killed by enemy action, at Commer Cars, Luton, November 6th, 1944.

STADDON, ALFRED, 245, New Bedford Road, Luton. Signm., R.N. Lost with H.M.S. *Janus*, Mediterranean, February, 1944.

STANGHAN, ROBERT HORACE, 67, St, Catherine's Avenue, Luton. Sgt. A.G., R.A.F. Killed on operations, Northern Germany, June 23rd, 1942.

STOKES, FREDERICK CHARLES ALBERT, 29, Roman Road, Luton. Sgt. F/Engr., 427th Squadron, R.A.F. Killed on operations, Hamburg, Germany, July 29th, 1944.

STOUGHTON, LEONARD JOHN, 203, Cutenhoe Road, Luton. Killed by enemy action, at Vauxhall Motors, Ltd., Luton, August 30th, 1940.

STRATTON, BRUCE ALBERT, 104, Stanford Road, Luton. F/Sgt. W.Op., R.A.F. Killed on operations over Germany, February 20th, 1944.

STRONELL, NORMAN JOHN, 45A, Buxton Road, Luton. F/Officer, R.A.F. Killed on operations over Stettin, Germany, August 30th, 1944.

SUMNER, STANLEY ROBERT, 60, Runley Road, Luton. Sgt./Pilot, R.A.F. Killed on active service, October 16th, 1940.

SWAIN, DOUGLAS PHILIP, 23, Argyll Avenue, Luton. Sgt./Pilot, R.A.F. Killed on active service, at Tiddim, Burma, September 12th, 1945.

SWANNICK, NORMAN HARRY, 162, Baker Street, Luton. W/Bdr., R.A. Died of wounds, Italy, May 23rd, 1944.

TANSLEY, HIRAM JOSEPH, 46, Maidenhall Road, Luton. 1st Class Stoker, R.N. Killed on active service, N. Africa, August 23rd, 1943.

TAYLOR, DAVID ARTHUR, The Flat, Luton Town Hall. Sgt./A.G., R.A.F. Killed on active service, March 23rd, 1941.

TAYLOR, ROBERT C., 23, Moor Street, Luton. Sgt., Loyal Regt. Died of wounds, Italy, August, 1944.

TAYLOR, WALTER, 37, Duke Street, Luton. Pte., Cambs. Regt. Died as prisoner of Japanese, Siam, June 1st, 1943.

TEARLE, RAYMOND JOHN., 85, London Road, Luton. P/Officer, R.A.F. Accidentally killed on active service, near Sheerness, May 17th, 1941.

THOMAS, DOUGLAS A., 35, Ridgway Road, Luton S. Flt./Engr., R.A.F. Missing, presumed killed, on operations, August, 1943.

THOMAS, JOHN GLANFFRWD, 111, Chester Avenue, Luton. Killed by enemy action, at Vauxhall Motors, Ltd., Luton, August 30th, 1940.

THOMAS, PETER ANTHONY, 67, Elmwood Crescent, Luton. Sgt. W/Op. A.G., R.A.F. Missing, presumed killed, North Sea, February 25th, 1942.

THOMAS, PHILIP EDGAR, 67, Elmwood Crescent, Luton. Sgt. W/Op. A.G., R.A.F. Missing, presumed killed, Mediterranean Sea, July 25th, 1942.

THOMPSON, ANNIE ELIZABETH, 77, Biscot Road, Luton. Killed by enemy action, at Luton, November 6th, 1944.

THOMPSON, ARTHUR JOHN. Killed by enemy action, at Vauxhall Motors, Ltd., Luton, August 30th, 1940.

THOMPSON, BARBARA GLADYS, 79, Farley Avenue, Luton. Killed by enemy action, at Luton, August 30th, 1940.

THOMPSON, IAN WILLIAM, 79, Farley Avenue, Luton. Died, September 2nd, 1940, as result of enemy action at Luton.

THOMPSON, MATTHEW, 54, Ridgway Road, Luton. Pte., Pioneer Corps. Died on active service, September 17th, 1945.

THOMPSON, MAY, 79, Farley Avenue, Luton. Killed by enemy action, at Luton, August 30th, 1940.

THOMPSON, PETER DESMOND, 11, Morley Crescent, Edgware, and formerly of Luton. Sgt./Pilot, R.A.F. Killed on active service, October, 1941.

THORNTON, GEORGE FREDERICK, 86, Runley Road, Luton. L/Cpl., 17/21st Lancers, R.A.C. Killed in action, North Africa, April 8th, 1943.

TICKNER, WILLIAM THOMAS, 82, St. Michael's Crescent, Luton. Petty Officer, R.N. Killed on active service at sea, March 27th, 1943.

TOOLEY, Trevor James Francis, 219, New Bedford Road, Luton. Lieut., Suffolk Regt. Killed in action, Normandy, June 6th, 1944.

TOYER, George Frederick, 5, Stuart Place, Luton. Gnr., R.A. Lost at sea while prisoner of Japanese, September 12th, 1944.

TOYER, Reginald George, 22, Neville Road, Luton. Gnr., R.A. Died of wounds, Burma, March 6th, 1944.

TOYER, Ronald, 20, Maidenhall Road, Luton. A/Seaman, R.N. Lost in action at sea, September 19th, 1943.

TOYER, Ronald Derrick, 97, Boyle Street, Luton. Gnr., R.A. Died as prisoner of Japanese, Siam, August 19th, 1943.

TURNER, Harry Boyd, 87a, Albert Road, Luton. Sgt., 148th Field Regt., R.A. Lost at sea as prisoner of Japanese, September 12th, 1944.

TURNER, John, 106, Oak Road, Luton. Pte., Pioneer Corps. Died on active service, March, 1941.

TURNER, Rex, 159, Tennyson Road, Luton. Tpr., 10th Hussars, R.A.C. Killed in action, Libya, May 29th, 1942.

TYREMAN, Alan, B.E.M., 12, Durbar Road, Luton. Lieut., Royal Marines. Died on active service, May 23rd, 1945.

TYREMAN, Norman Allen, 33, Linden Road, Luton. Sgt., R.A.F. Killed on operations over Germany, September 3rd, 1943.

TYSOM, Ronald Francis, 12, Ivy Road, Luton. Gnr., 510 H.A.A. Regt., R.A. Died on active service, April 30th, 1943.

UNDERWOOD, C. F. W., 23, Durbar Road, Luton. P/Officer, R.A.F. Missing on air operations, September, 1942.

UPTON, Edward, " Sunnybank," Little Bramingham, Luton. Sgt. W/Op. A.G., R.A.F. Killed by enemy action, at sea, January 8th, 1942.

VARNAM, Frederick Leslie, 29, Dale Road, Luton. Pte., R.A.M.C. Killed on active service, Bayeux, France, September 13th, 1944.

VENTHAM, Reginald William, 52, Ivy Road, Luton. Pte., 2nd Battn. Royal Scots. Killed in action, Florence, Italy, September 3rd, 1944.

VEREY, Leslie Howard, formerly of 50, Newcombe Road, Luton. Spr., R.E. Killed during air raid while prisoner in Germany, December 2nd, 1944.

VERRAN, Reginald Stanley Edward, D.F.C., 78, Talbot Road, Luton. F/Officer, R.A.F. Killed on active service, Luneberg, Germany, October 17th, 1945.

VERRAN, Robert Claude, D.F.M., 18, Carlton Close, Luton. Sgt./Observer, R.A.F. Killed on operations, Catania, Sicily, January, 1941.

VICKERS, Frank, Luton Borough Treasurer's Department. Capt., R.A. Killed on active service, Germany, March, 1946.

WADDINGTON, William, 116, Runley Road, Luton. Killed by enemy action, at Luton, August 30th, 1940.

WAINWRIGHT, Alec George, 52, Old Bedford Road, Luton. P/Officer, 73rd Squadron, R.A.F. Missing, presumed killed in action, North Africa January 21st, 1941.

WALKER, William Charles, 17, Chester Close, Luton. Invalided from R.N died January, 1945.

WALLER, Eric Gordon, 10, Hillborough Road, Luton. Sgt., R.A.F., Bomber Command. Missing, presumed killed, Langensalza-Tour, March 23rd, 1944.

WALLINGTON, Raymond Arthur, 33, Harcourt Street, Luton. Gnr., 102nd (North Hussars) Field Regt., R.A. Killed in action, Tunisia, April 4th, 1943.

WALLIS, Alfred, 35, Essex Street, Luton. Killed by enemy action, at Luton, August 30th, 1940.

WANTLING, Arthur, 49, Bradley Road, Luton. Sgt. Killed in Normandy, July, 1944.

WARD, Eric Percy, 43, Selbourne Road, Luton. Killed by enemy action, at Vauxhall Motors, Ltd., Luton, August 30th, 1940.

WARDILL, John N., Stoneheaps, Kimpton, and formerly of Luton. Sub.-Lieut. (A), Fleet Air Arm. Missing, presumed killed, on operational duty, October, 1943.

WARDILL, Wilfred G., 16, Brantwood Road, Luton. Killed by enemy action, at Norwich, January, 1942.

WARNER, Cecil Charles, 42, Clarendon Road, Luton. Pte., Somerset L.I. Died of wounds, Western Front, October, 1944.

WARREN, Kenneth Henry, 106, Wardown Crescent, Luton. L/Bdr., R.A. Died of wounds, North Africa, April 30th, 1943.

WARREN, Ronald, 87, Russell Rise, Luton. Sgt./Pilot, R.A.F. Killed on active service, March, 1941.

WARREN, Wilfred Robert, formerly of Dunstable Road, Luton. Fleet Air Arm. Killed on active service, May, 1942.

WAYWELL, Gordon, 122, Dunstable Road, Luton. Cfmn., R.E.M.E. Died on active service, Bone, N. Africa, May 17th, 1943.

WEATHERLEY, Alfred William, 75, Limbury Road, Luton. R.Q.M.S., 5th Training Battalion, R.E. Died on active service, March 4th, 1943.

WEBB, John Henry, 29, Kingsland Road, Luton. L/Cpl., R. West Kent Regt. Killed in action, Italy, January 8th, 1945.

WEDDELL, Irene Constance, 45, St. Martin's Avenue, Luton. Killed by enemy action, at Luton, October 14th, 1940.

WEEDEN, Henry John, 3, Chester Avenue, Luton. Died in hospital as the result of enemy action, at Luton, August 30th, 1940.

WEEDON, Douglas Henry, 30, Waller Avenue, Luton. Pte., Hampshire Regt. Killed in action, N.W. Europe, June 13th, 1944.

WEEDON, Jack William, 30, Waller Avenue, Luton. Gnr., 234th Battery, 77th H.A.A., R.A. Died on active service, September 4th, 1941.

WEEDON, Reginald Francis, 130, Waller Avenue, Luton. F/Officer, R.A.F. Killed on operations ; buried at St. Trond, Belgium, April 25th, 1944.

WELHAM, Robert William Charles, 9, Belmont Road, Luton. L/Bdr., R.A. Lost at sea as prisoner of Japanese, September 12th, 1944.

WELLS, Victor Charles, 142, Blundell Road, Luton. Naval Airman, Fleet Air Arm. Died on active service, June 30th, 1944.

WELLS, William (John), 8, Blyth Place, Luton. L/Bdr., 418th Field Regt., R.A. Died as prisoner of Japanese, Siam, December 12th, 1942.

WEST, Derrick, 6, Pirton Road, Luton. Killed by enemy action, at Vauxhall Motors, Ltd., Luton, August 30th, 1940.

WEST, Victor, 34, Marsh Road, Luton. R.A.F. Killed on active service, October 27th, 1940.

WEST, Walter Roy, 7, Welbeck Road, Luton. Killed in action, June 6th, 1942.

WHALLEY, George Thomas, 48, Gillam Street, Luton. Pte., 2nd Battn. Herts. Regt. Killed clearing minefield, Caen, Normandy, July 28th, 1944.

WHITE, E., 82, Lea Road, Luton. Pte. Killed in action, January 1st, 1945.

WHITE, George Robert, 461, Dunstable Road, Luton. Gdsm., 6th Battn. Grenadier Guards. Killed in action near Mareth Line, Tripoli, North Africa, March 17th, 1943.

WHITE, John Henry, 106, Hart Lane, Luton. Pte., 2nd Battn. Bedfs. and Herts. Regt. Killed in action, North Africa, April 13th, 1943.

WHITE, R. F., Rushden, and formerly of Luton. Lieut. (Leading Supply Asst.), R.N. Died on active service, June, 1942.

WHITELOCK, Robert Henry, 16, Essex Street, Luton. R.A.S.C. Died on active service, September 24th, 1942.

WHITTAKER, Arthur Thomas, 21, Oakley Road, Luton. Killed by enemy action, at Vauxhall Motors, Ltd., Luton, August 30th, 1940.

WHITTLES, Arthur Ernest, 114, Graham Gardens, Luton. Pte., R.A.M.C. Killed in action, N.W. Europe, June 10th, 1944.

WILCOCKSON, ROBERT, 29, Felstead Way, Luton. Sgt., R.A.F. Killed on operations, N.W. France, 1943.

WILLIAMS, DAVID GARFIELD, 35, Neville Road, Luton. Tpr., 15th Reconnaissance Regt. Died on active service, April 9th, 1943.

WILLIAMS, GLYN, Putteridge Park, Luton. F/Officer, R.A.F., 140 Wing 2nd T.A.F. Missing, presumed killed in action over Holland, December 3rd, 1944.

WILLIAMS, PHYLLIS MARJORIE, 120, Cowper Street, Luton. Killed by enemy action, at Luton, August 30th, 1940.

WILSON, ARTHUR GEORGE, 242, Crawley Green Road, Luton. Gnr., 419th Batty., 148th Field Regt., R.A. Died as prisoner of Japanese, Siam, September 16th, 1943.

WILSON, DENIS, 41, Lilley, and Geere & Co., Luton. Pte., Suffolk Regt. Died as prisoner of Japanese, Singapore, January 1st, 1944.

WILSON, FRANK, 24, Colin Road, Luton. Stoker, R.N., H.M.S. *Kingston Galena*, Dover Patrol. Lost at sea, July 24th, 1940.

WILSON, ROBERT, 42, Midland Road, Luton. Died September 6th, 1942, following injuries caused by enemy action, at Luton, September 5th, 1942.

WISE, DERRICK GEORGE, 125, High Town Road, Luton. Royal Marine Commando. Killed in action in Normandy, D-Day, June 6th, 1944.

WISE, PETER JOHN, 31, Biscot Road, Luton. Killed by enemy action, at Luton, November 6th, 1944.

WISEMAN, REGINALD WILLIAM, 65, Crawley Road, Luton. Dvr., Ayrshire Yeomanry R.A. Killed in action, Italy, August 7th, 1944.

WOOD, RONALD WILLIAM, 7, Chandos Road, Luton. Sgt., R.A.F., Bomber Command. Missing, presumed killed, February 25-26th, 1944.

WOODBRIDGE, FRANCIS ALLAN, " Woodville," Humberstone Road, Luton. Pte., 4th Battn. R. Norfolk Regt. Died as prisoner of Japanese, Taiwan, Formosa, January 1st, 1944.

WOODFIELD, RONALD GEORGE, 16, Belmont Road, Luton. Sgt., R.A.F. Killed in action, Denmark, April 4th, 1943.

WOODFINE, JOHN EDWARD, 56, St. Ethelbert's Avenue, Luton. Died as the result of enemy action, at Vauxhall Motors, Ltd., August 31st, 1940.

WOODS, RICHARD ANTHONY, 93, Selbourne Road, Luton. L/Cpl., R.A.S.C. Killed in action at sea, February 5th, 1942. Buried at Keppal Harbour, Singapore.,

WRIGHT, DENNIS WILLIAM, 102A, Midland Road, Luton. Flt./Sgt. Navigator R.A.F. Killed on operations, Stuttgart, July 25th, 1944.

WRIGHT, GEORGE J., 77, Pembroke Avenue, Luton. Dispatch Rider, Lothian Border Regt. Killed on active service, July 17th, 1940.

WRIGHT, JACK, 3, Clevedon Road, Luton. Pte., Highland Light Infantry. Killed in action, Germany, February 14th, 1945.

WRIGHT, KENNETH EDWIN, 67, Spencer Road, Luton. Pte., 2/5th Queen's Royal Regt. Died of wounds, Italy, December 6th, 1943.

WRIGHT, WILLIAM JOHN, 140, Kingsway, Luton. L/Bdr., R.A. Killed on grenade practice, Northumberland, January 20th, 1943.

YORK, HERBERT, 46, Cavendish Road, Luton. L/Bdr., R.A. Lost at sea as prisoner of Japanese.

YOUNG, J. H., 1, Albion Road, Luton. Tpr., Royal Tank Regt. Missing, presumed killed in action, Middle East, June 15th, 1941.

ZASTROW, W. R., 38, Fitzroy Avenue, Luton. Sgt. Flt./Eng., R.A.F. Missing on air operations, December, 1943.

Awards and Decorations

(The following is a list of Lutonians who have gained awards and decorations, either in the Services or in civilian life, during the war. In addition to the usual abbreviations, the initials M.D. are used to denote a " Mention in Despatches ").

ADAMS, H. S. B., 1, High Point, Farley Hill, Luton. Capt. **M.B.E.,** 1945, Italy.

ADAMS, NORMAN MARCUS, c/o Douglas Stratford & Co., Luton. Sergt./ Surveyor, 7th Survey Regt., R.A. **M.M.,** 1944, Holland and N.W. Europe.

ALDRED, R. A., Chas. Clay & Sons, Ltd., Luton. Lt.-Comm., R.N.V.R. **M.D.,** 1945 ; **D.S.C.,** 1946, Minesweepers.

ANDERSON, ERIC, 72, Adelaide Street, Luton. Tpr., R.A.C. **George Medal,** 1945, Italy.

ARNOLD, CECIL C., Wardown Crescent, Luton. F/Lt., R.A.F. **M.D.,** 1945.

AUSTIN, RUPERT FRANCIS, 216, Cutenhoe Road, Luton. Capt., R.E.M.E. **M.B.E.,** 1945, Italy.

BAKER, ALBERT HENRY, 13, Boyle Street, Luton. L/Cpl., 317th Coy. R.A.S.C., Att. R.A. **M.D.,** 1945, Italy.

BAKER, S. H., Luton. L/Cpl., R.A.S.C. **M.D.,** 1944, Italy.

BANKS, LESLIE J., Shell Mex & B.P. Oil Co., Luton. Lt.-Col., R.A.S.C. **M.D.,** 1943, North Africa.

BARRINGER, HAROLD WM., 25, Mixes Hill Road, Luton. L/Cpl., 77 (Br.) General Hospital (Field), R.A.M.C. **M.D.,** 1944, Normandy.

BARTLETT, CHARLES JOHN, Managing Director, Vauxhall Motors, Ltd., Luton. **Knighthood,** 1944.

BARTON, JAMES SYDNEY, 135, Beechwood Road, Luton. A/Ldg. Seaman, D.E.M.S., R.N. **M.D.,** 1943, N. Africa.

BATCHELOR, FRANK, 115, Alder Crescent, Luton. Able Seaman, R.N. **D.S.M.,** 1945.

BELL, ERNEST GEORGE, 55, Montrose Avenue, Luton. Signalman, R.N. **M.D.,** 1944, Normandy Invasion.

BENNETT, R., Luton. F/Lt., R.A.F. **Air Efficiency Award,** 1942.

BENSON, JOHN H., 111, Farley Hill, Luton. Sgt., R.A.F. **M.D.,** 1945.

BINGHAM, CYRIL, 71, Cambridge Street, Luton. Cpl., Suffolk Regt. **M.M.,** 1944, N.W. Europe.

BIRCHMORE, ROY BERTRAM, 25, Sunridge Avenue, Luton. F/Lt., 1940 (Meteor, Recon. and Special Duties) Flight, Pathfinder Force, R.A.F. **D.F.C.,** 1944 ; **Bar to D.F.C.,** 1945, Germany.

BLEANEY, ALBERT EDWARD, 17, Henry Street, Luton. Sergt., R.E. **M.D.,** 1946, N.W. Europe.

BLEANEY, BERNARD FREDK., 28, Woodland Avenue, Luton. Warrant Mech., H.M.S. *Valiant*, R.N. **M.B.E.,** 1945, S.E.A.C.

BLOW, KENNETH LESLIE OWEN, 390, Dunstable Road, Luton. Warrant Officer, R.A.F.V.R. Awarded **D.F.C.** Subsequently killed.

BOLTON, SAMUEL, 16, Bolton Road, Luton. Petty Officer, R.N. **D.S.M.,** 1942, Oran, North Africa.

BONNER, RALPH JACK, 73, Harcourt Street, Luton. Capt., 53rd Field Regt., R.A. **M.C.,** 1945, Italy.

BOOT, LESLIE, 69 Roundwood Lane, Harpenden and L.M.S. Goods Office, Luton. Staff-Sergt. R.E. **B.E.M.,** Egypt and Palestine.

BOSS, KENNETH, 117, Farley Avenue, Luton. Capt., R.A., Forward Observation Unit (Airborne). **M.C.,** June, 1945, N.W. Europe. Subsequently died of wounds.

BOULTON, FRANK PERCY, 44, Kimpton Road, Luton. Chief P.O. (E.R.A.), R.N., H.M.S. *Eskimo*. **D.S.M.,** 1944, N. Africa ; **B.E.M.,** 1944, Sicily.

BOYD-STEVENSON, Donald, 45, Chatsworth Road, Luton. S/Ldr., 104th Squadron, R.A.F. **D.F.C.**, 1943, Middle East.

BROWN, Gordon Percy, 63, Wychwood Avenue, Luton. Major, 1st Battn. Leics. Regt. **M.D.**, 1945, N.W. Europe ; **M.C.**, 1946, N.W. Europe.

BROWN, Willie Calvert, 90 St. Catherine's Avenue, Luton. Sergt., R.A.F. **M.D.**, 1943.

BRUMPTON, Charles Edward, 205, Runley Road, Luton. Cpl., Royal Marines (Combined Operations). **D.S.M.**, 1944, Normandy.

BURGOYNE, Ald. John, 228, Stockingstone Road, Luton. Chairman of Luton Emergency Committee. **O.B.E.**, 1946.

BUNNAGE, Ronald T., 63, Fountains Road, Luton. B.Q.M.S., R.A., No. 4 Military Dispersal Unit. **B.E.M.**, 1946.

BUNYAN, Reginald Arthur, 5, Trent Road, Luton. F/Sgt., No. 61 Squadron, R.A.F. **D.F.M.**, 1944.

BUXTON, S. L., Luton. Capt., 17/21st Lancers, R.A.C. **M.C.**, 1942, Middle East.

CARRUTHERS, Donald, 11, Brook Street, Luton. F/O., No. 35 Sq., R.A.F. **D.F.M.**, 1944, France and Germany.

CAWLEY, Alfred, 108, Graham Gardens, Luton. L/Sgt., No. 1 Air Support Signals Unit, Royal Signals (Army). **M.D.**, 1944, Italy.

CHANDLER, Geoffrey Graham, 222, Dunstable Road, Luton. Sgt/Artificer, R.A. **M.M.**, 1944, Italy.

CHANDLER, Graham H., Chiltern House, Markyate. Naval Armament Supply Officer, R.N. **M.B.E.**, 1942, Gibraltar.

CHESHIRE, Hettie, 30, Chandos Road, Luton. Chief Petty Officer, W.R.N.S. **M.B.E.**, 1945.

CLARK, William Henry, 10, Tower Road, Luton. Flt./Sgt., Security Police, R.A.F. **M.D.**, 1942. Subsequently killed.

COLEMAN, Arthur, 7, Dunstable Road, Caddington, and Percival Aircraft, Ltd., Luton. W/Officer, R.A.S.C. **M.D.**, 1945, Far East ; **B.E.M.**, 1946, S.E. Asia.

COLLIER, James Patrick, 98, Gardenia Avenue, Luton. Captain, 74 E. and M. Platoon, R.E., 21st Army Group, B.A.O.R. **M.D.**, 1945, N.W. Europe.

COLLINS, George Edwd., 29, Ivy Road, Luton. W/Sergt., 2902 Civil Labour Unit, Pioneer Corps. **M.D.**, 1945, Italy.

COOK, Leslie, 80, Kingston Road, Luton. Sub-Conductor (W.O.I.), R.A.O.C. **M.D.**, 1943, North Africa.

COOKE, John Douglas, 11, Douglas Road, Harpenden, and George Street West, Luton. Capt., Royal Corps of Signals. **M.D.**, 1940, Dunkirk.

COOPER, Philip Leslie George, formerly of 126, Oak Road, Luton, and now of 12, Beechcroft Gardens, Abington, Northants. Cpl., 5th R. Inniskilling Dragoon Guards. **M.M.**, 1945, Western Front.

COOPER, Philip Sidney, 160, Stockingstone Road, Luton. Cpl., Inniskilling Dragoons, R.A.C. **M.M.**, 1944, Normandy.

COOPER, Ronald, c/o Commer Cars, Ltd., Luton. C.P.O. (Ldg. Wireless Mechanic), R.N. **M.D.**, 1943, Far East.

CORNES, Geoffrey F., 319, New Bedford Road, Luton. Squadron Leader, R.A.F. **D.F.M.**, 1942, Battle of El Alamein ; **M.D.**, 1945, Western Europe.

COULSON, Leonard, 56, Chatsworth Road, Luton. Coder, R.N. **French Croix de Guerre,** 1944, Normandy.

COX, Kenneth Victor, 45, Newark Road, Luton. F/Lieut., R.A.F. **D.F.M.**, 1941, Western Desert.

CRADDOCK, Joseph Percy, 31, Whitecroft Road, Luton. Sgt., R.A. **M.D.** 1944, Italy.

CRAIN, Frederick Chas., 6, Chandos Road, Luton. Cpl., No. 120 Sq., R.A.F., Coastal Command. **M.D.**, 1945, Battle of the Atlantic.

CROWNE, J. G., 16, Downs Road, Luton, and Eastex, Ltd., Guildford Street, Luton. Major, Nigerian Regt. **M.B.E.**, 1945, Chindits, Burma.

CRUTTENDEN, G. H., 83, Manton Drive, Luton. Major, R.A.O.C. **M.D.,** 1946, Central Mediterranean Forces.

CUNNINGHAM, JOHN CRAWFORD, D.S.O., 45, St. Margaret's Avenue, Luton. Major, 7th Bedfs. Battn. Home Guard, and Security Officer, Percival Aircraft, Ltd., Luton. **George Medal,** 1941, Parachute Mine incident.

CURRANT, CHRISTOPHER, "Two Gables," West Common, Harpenden, and Currant & Creak, Ltd., Luton. W/Comm., R.A.F. **D.F.C.,** 1940, Battle of Britain ; **Bar to D.F.C.,** 1940, Defence of London ; **D.S.O.,** 1942, Northern France ; **Belgian Croix de Guerre,** 1942.

CURRANT, ERIC JAMES, Currant & Creak, Ltd., Luton. Lt.-Col. Indian Army Medical Corps, 14th Army. **M.D.,** 1944, Arakan.

DANDY, WILLIAM ROBERT I., 51, Ludlow Avenue, Luton. Chief Special Constable of Luton. **M.B.E.,** 1945.

DANES, BRAMWELL JOSEPH, 51, Alton Road, Luton. L/Bdr., 23rd Field Regt., R.A. **M.D.,** 1945, Italy ; **American Bronze Star,** 1945, Italy.

DAY, RONALD WM., 27, Douglas Road, Luton. T/Sergt., H.Q. 2nd Tactical Air Force, and H.Q., B.A.F.O., Germany. **M.D.,** 1945, Europe. **B.E.M.,** 1946, Europe.

DEAN, R., 9, Holland Road, Luton. Staff-Sergt., No. 8 General Transport Column, R.A.S.C. **M.D.,** 1945, Italy.

DEARMAN, DEREK ROY, 93, Putteridge Road, Luton. P/O, R.A.F. **D.F.C.** 1944. (Previously killed in action).

DELLER, SYDNEY STEWART, 24, Ryecroft Way, Stopsley, Luton. Tpr., Northant. Yeomanry. **M.D.,** 1945, N.W. Europe.

DELME-MURRAY, G. B., 28, Conway Road, Luton. Major, 17th Dogra Regt. **D.S.O.,** 1945, Burma.

DENTON, REGINALD, 25, Althorpe Road, Luton. Sergt., No. 156 Sq., R.A.F. **M.D.,** 1944.

DERBYSHIRE, ALFRED HORLEY, Dunstable Road, Caddington and R. Colin Large, Ltd., Luton. F/O., R.A.F. **M.D.,** 1942.

DUDLEY, ERIC GEO., 4, Greenhill Avenue, Luton. F/O., 44 Sq., R.A.F. **D.F.C.,** 1943.

DUNHAM, PETER B., formerly Stockingstone Road, Luton. Major, R.E. **M.D.,** 1945, Rhine and N. Holland.

EBERLIE, ELIZABETH MARY FRANCES, 57, Crawley Green Road, Luton. Junior Comm., A.T.S. **U.S. Army Bronze Star,** 1945, S.H.A.E.F.

EGAN, EDWIN PHILIP JAMES, "The Sportsman," Stopsley, Luton. Seaman, R.N. **D.S.M.,** 1944.

ELLIS, EDWARD SYDNEY, 263, Marsh Road, Luton. F/Lt., R.A.F. **C.G.M.,** 1943, "Battle of Berlin " ; **D.F.C.,** 1944, Germany ; **M.D.,** 1945 Heavy Conversion Unit.

ELLWOOD, WILLIAM CYRIL, 6, St. Mary's Road, Luton. Sgt., Commandos. **D.C.M.,** 1943, Italy.

EMERY, FREDERICK WILLIAM DOUGLAS, 4, High Mead, Luton. F/Officer, 76 Squadron, R.A.F. **D.F.C.,** 1945.

EVANS, EVAN A. C., Clerk to Luton Rural District Council. **M.B.E.,** 1946.

FALLER, FREDERICK, 170, Beechwood Road, Luton. Works Superintendent, Commer Cars, Ltd. **M.B.E.** (Civil Division), 1943.

FAUNCH, SIDNEY CHAS., 74, Wychwood Avenue, Luton. L/Cpl., 240th Field Coy., R.E. **George Medal,** 1944, Normandy Invasion.

FARMER, DERRICK, 100, Montrose Avenue, Luton. W.O.I., R.A.S.C. **M.D.,** 1946, North Africa and Italy.

FENSOME, HUBERT HEDLEY, 79, Kent Road, Luton. L/Stoker, R.N. **M.D.** 1945, Northern France.

FIELD, ALBERT GEORGE, 11, Crescent Rise, Luton. Sgt., Lancers R.A.C **B.E.M.,** 1942, North African Convoy.

FLITTON, STANLEY CHARLES, 25, Kingsland Road, Luton. A/Seaman, R.N. **M.D.,** 1944, Normandy Landing and Germany.

417

FRANKLIN, William Edward, 171, Dunstable Road, Caddington. Lieut., 7th Bedfs. Battn. Home Guard, Luton. **M.B.E.**, 1944.

FRANKS, Percy R., 72, Bury Park Road, Luton. Capt., Royal Signals. **M.D.,** Burma, 1945.

FREEMAN, Nelson Thos., 66, St. Ethelbert's Avenue, Luton. F/Sgt., R.A.F. **M.D.,** 1943.

FREER, Walter John Patrick, 148, Wellington Street, Luton. Sgt., 13/18th Royal Hussars (Queen Mary's Own), 10th Armoured Division. **M.D.,** 1944, N. Africa.

FRENCH, John W. L., Messrs. French & Co., Cardiff Road, Luton. F/Lt., R.A.F. **D.F.C.,** 1945.

FULLER, Desmond Chas., 136, Runley Road, Luton. S.Q.M. Sgt., 51st Royal Tank Regt. **M.D.,** 1945, Italy.

FYSON, P. A., Vauxhall Motors, Ltd., Luton. F/O., R.A.F. **D.F.C.,** 1944.

GAWLEY, Samuel, Woodside. Pte., 4th Bedfs. Battn. Home Guard, Luton. **B.E.M.,** 1944.

GINN, Robert James, 193, Cutenhoe Road, Luton. S/Ldr., R.A.F. **M.B.E.,** 1943.

GLANCY, J., Luton. Parachute Regt. **M.M.,** 1944, Northern France.

GLOVER, Thomas W., 21, Hastings Street, Luton. C.S.M., R.E. **M.D.,** 1945, Rhine Crossing.

GODDARD, Edmund, Lawn End, Harpenden, and Commer Cars, Ltd., Luton. Chief P/O., R.N. **C.G.M.,** 1944, Midget Submarine attack on the *Tirpitz*.

GODFREY, George Leslie, 37, Alton Road, Luton. L/Seaman, R.N. **D.S.M.,** 1940, Dunkirk Evacuation.

GOODMAN, F. Arthur, Commer-Karrier, Ltd., Luton. Lt.-Col., R.A.O.C. **M.C.,** 1940, s.s. *Lancastria*.

GRAVES-MORRIS, Philip H., Upper George Street, Luton. Lt.-Col., 2nd Worcs. Regt. **M.C.,** 1941, Middle East ; **D.S.O.,** 1945, Chindits, Burma.

GRIDLEY, John, Luton. Sgt., Wiltshire Regt. **M.M.,** 1944, Italy.

GRIFFITHS, Gerald, 37, Russell Rise, Luton. F/Sgt., R.A.F. **D.F.M.,** 1944, Berlin.

HAFNER, John Charles, 694, Dunstable Road, Luton. Lt., R.N.V.R. **Norwegian War Medal,** 1945, North Atlantic.

HANDFORD, Leslie, 57, Wardown Crescent, Luton. Capt., R.E.M.E. **M.D.,** 1946, N.W. Europe.

HARE, Louis William, 70, Blundell Road, Luton. Petty Officer, R.N. **M.D.,** 1943, Minelaying Operations.

HAWKINS, Austin Ralph, 58, Wardown Crescent, Luton. Major, Royal Marines. **M.D.,** 1943, M.E.F. ; **M.D.,** 1945, N.W. Europe.

HERBERT, Aston Arthur, 46, Butlin Road, Luton. Cpl., Royal Marines. **M.D.,** 1945, N.W. Europe.

HICKS, William Jas., 25, Mayne Avenue, Luton. Sergt., Bedfs. and Herts. Regt. **Belgian Croix de Guerre, (1940) with Palms** for service with 1st Battn. Belgian Fusiliers, 1946.

HILL, Arnold M., 17, Richmond Hill, Luton. F/Lt., R.A.F. **D.F.C.,** 1943.

HITCH, James E., 333, Dallow Road, Luton. Sgt., R.A.S.C. **M.D.,** 1946, Italy.

HOAR, Kenneth Sidney, 34, Carlton Crescent, Luton. W/Officer, R.A.F., Coastal Command. **M.D.,** 1944.

HOBBS, Peter Henry, 1, Brook Street, Luton. Major, R.A.V.C. **M.B.E.,** 1945, Burma.

HOBBS, Robert Brian, 20, Ashton Road, Luton. Petty Officer, H.M.S. *Belfast*, R.N. **B.E.M.,** 1942, Russian Convoys ; **American Purple Heart,** 1946, Normandy Invasion.

HUGHES, Clarence Lindsay, 30, Malvern Road, Luton. F/O., R.A.F. **D.F.C.,** 1944.

HUNTINGFORD, Frederick George, 44, Hawthorn Avenue, Stopsley, Luton. L/Seaman, R.N. **M.D.,** 1944, Light Coastal Forces ; **D.S.M.,** 1945.

HUTTON, D. J., B. Laporte, Ltd., Luton. S/Lt., R.N.V.R. **D.S.O.,** 1940, Dunkirk.

HYDE, W. J., Luton G.P.O. Major, R.E., i/c A.P.O. **M.D.,** 1945, N.W. Europe.

JENNINGS, BERNARD JAMES, Luton. Sgt., R.A.F. **D.F.M.,** 1941.

JENNINGS, FRANK, 341, Beechwood Road, Luton. Lt.-Comm., R.N.R. **M.D.,** 1945, Normandy Invasion.

JOBLING, JOSEPH, 4, Wingate Road, Luton. Welding Shop Foreman, Electrolux, Ltd., Luton. **B.E.M.,** 1945.

JOHNSON, MICHAEL BRITTON, 11, Bedford Gardens, Luton. Major, 34th Amphibian Assault Regt., Royal Marines. **M.B.E.,** 1945, Normandy Invasion.

JACKSON, FRANCIS CHAS., 23, Felstead Way, Luton. Sgt. (E.), R.A.F. **D.F.M.,** 1943. (Previously killed in action).

KEEN, MICHAEL WILLIAM, 97, St. Ethelbert's Avenue, Luton. Major, R.E.M.E. (Airborne). **M.D.,** 1945, N.W. Europe.

KELL, JOHN, 38, Alexandra Avenue, Luton. Sgt., R.A.F. **B.E.M.,** 1946.

KING, RONALD WILFRED, 33, Argyll Avenue, Luton. F/O., R.A.F. **D.F.C.,** 1943, Anti U-Boat Patrol.

KING, WILLIAM JAMES, Luton. Sgt., R.A.F. **D.F.M.,** 1941, North Africa.

KINGHAM, JACK, 464, Hitchin Road, Luton. F/Sgt., No. 115 Sq., R.A.F. **M.D.,** 1944, Germany.

KIRBY, WALTER JAS. FREDK., 26, Brooms Road, Luton. Pte., 2nd Battn. Bedfs. and Herts. Regt. **M.M.,** 1944, Battle of Cassino.

KITCHENER, RONALD D., 51, West Hill Road, Luton. Lt. (E.), R.N.V.R. **M.D.,** 1944, Normandy Invasion.

LAMB, JAMES THOMAS, 29, St. Lawrence's Avenue, Luton. L/Sgt., 2nd Battn. R. Norfolk Regt. **M.D.,** 1944, Assam.

LARKMAN, RICHARD WILLIAM, 72, Wychwood Avenue, Luton. Capt., R.A.O.C. **M.D.,** 1943, North Africa, followed by second mention.

LATHWELL, REGINALD, 135, Farley Hill, Luton. Staff Sgt., R.A.S.C. **M.D.,** 1945, Normandy Invasion and Rhine Crossing.

LEGGATT, HENRY JOHN, 10, Tudor Road, Luton. L/Sgt., 6th Field Regt., R.A. **M.D.,** 1945, N.W. Europe.

LOOKER, E. M., Studham (formerly of Luton). Tpr., The Bays, Royal Tank Regt. **M.D.,** 1945, Italy.

LUCAS, SYDNEY EDWARD, 18, Grange Avenue, Luton. P/O., R.A.F. **D.F.C.,** 1944.

MacGEORGE, JACK STEPHEN, 123, North Street, Luton. Marine. **M.D.,** 1945.

MALSTER, WALTER JOHN, Divisional Commander, N.F.S., Luton, and Sub-Area Commander, Bedfordshire. **M.B.E.,** 1943, for general leadership during Eastern Region Blitz.

McPHEE, JAMES, 80A, Castle Street, Luton. F/Lt., R.A.F. **A.F.C.,** 1944.

McPHEE, THOMAS, 80A, Castle Street, Luton. S/Ldr., R.A.F. **D.F.M.,** 1941 ; **D.F.C.,** 1944.

MANDER, ARTHUR JOHN, 9, Ashburnham Road, Luton. Colonel Commanding Beds. South Sector, Home Guard. **O.B.E.,** 1941.

MANDER, STEWART TOM, 21, Blundell Road, Luton. S/Ldr., P. and S.U., 84 Group, R.A.F. **M.D.,** 1945, France and Germany ; **M.B.E.,** 1946, France, and Germany.

MANN, RUSSELL FRANK, 22A, Norton Road, Luton. Sgt., Pioneer Corps· **B.E.M.,** 1943, Phillippeville.

MANSTOFF, A., Luton. F/Sgt., R.A.F. **D.F.M.,** 1944.

MARLOW, WILLIAM THOS., 97, Boyle Street, Luton. R.S.M., Grenadier Guards, and Corps of Military Police. **B.E.M.,** 1945.

MARTIN, J., Luton. Sgt., 1st King's Dragoon Guards, R.A.C. **M.M.,** 1943, Middle East.

MASON, FRANK, 110, Alexandra Avenue, Luton. F/Lt., R.A.F. **D.F.C.,** 1942, Middle East.

MATTHEWS, DENNIS EDWARD, 61, Manor Road, Caddington, and Geo. Kent, Ltd., Hibbert Street, Luton. F/O., R.A.F. **D.F.C.,** 1945.

MAYES, DEREK LEONARD, 277, New Bedford Road, Luton. F/O., R.A.F. **D.F.C.,** 1943.

MAYLIN, John Horace Daniel, 3, Gloucester Road, Luton. C.S.M., 534th Tank Transportation Coy., R.A.S.C. **M.D.**, 1945, Africa.

MELLS, George Edward, Luton. L/Cpl., R.E. **B.E.M.**, 1944, Normandy.

MILLER, W. H., 97, Cowper Street, Luton. Sgt., R.A.C. **M.D.**, 1945, Italy.

MOCKERIDGE, Frederick Claude, 6, Montague Avenue, Toddington Road, Luton. C.S.M., Corps of Military Police. **M.M.**, 1940, Dunkirk.

MOODY, Leslie, 88, Elmwood Crescent, Luton. Major, Bedfs. & Herts. Regt., att. Monmouthshire Regt. **M.C.**, 1944, Albert Canal.

NUNN, Ronald A., 64, Crawley Road, Luton. Signalman. **Royal Victorian Medal**, 1945.

ORDE, Norman, 182, Beechwood Road, Luton. Sgt., 16/5 Queen's Lancers, R.A.C. **M.M.**, 1945, Italy.

ORDISH, Charles Brian, 39, Ludlow Avenue, Luton. F/Lt., R.A.F. **D.F.C.**, 1943. (Previously killed in action).

OWEN, Brian John, 78, Lea Road, Luton. F/O., R.A.F. **D.F.M.**, 1944, Germany.

PAILING, Rex, 199, New Bedford Road South, Luton. L/Bdr., 6th Searchlight Regt., R.A. **Belgian Croix de Guerre (1940) with Palm**, 1944, B.L.A.

PARFITT, D. W., 1, St. Margaret's Avenue, Luton. Capt., R.A.S.C. **M.D.**, 1945, N.W. Europe.

PARROTT, D. F., 134, North Street, Luton. L/Signalman, R.N. **M.D.**, 1940, Battle of the River Plate.

PARTRIDGE, J. E., Vauxhall Motors, Ltd., Luton. F/Lt., R.A.F. **D.F.C.**, 1942 ; **Bar to D.F.C.**, 1942 ; **D.S.O.**, 1943, Germany.

PEARSON, John, 1, Rothesay Road, Luton. M.S.M., R.A.S.C. **M.D.**, 1945, Italy.

PECK, David J., 99, Strathmore Avenue, Luton. Cpl., R.A.F. **M.D.**, 1944.

PHILPOTT, Reginald H., 35, Hartley Road, Luton. Driver, R.A.S.C. **M.M.**, 1946, N.W. Europe.

PICKFORD, James Thomas, 52, Browning Road, Luton. F/Sgt., R.A.F. **D.F.M.**, 1943.

PINKERTON, George Eustace, Limbury Manor, Luton. Capt., R.A.M.C. att. 1st Battn. K.O.Y.L.I. **M.C.**, 1944, Italy.

PLATER, Albert Jack, 57, Liverpool Road, Luton. Gnr., 99th Field Regt., R.A. **M.D.**, 1942, Western Desert.

PRATT, George Edward, 5, The Meads, Luton. Cpl., 111 Wing, R.A.F. **M.D.**, 1946, N.W. Europe.

PRIMETT, Ronald Murray, 137, Old Bedford Road, Luton. Lieut.-Col., R.A.O.C. **M.D.**, 1945, Italy.

PRYDE, Herbert Marshall, 31, Cardiff Road Luton. Master-at-Arms, R.N. **D.S.M.**, 1943, Malta Convoy.

PUNTER, Derek Hubert, 74, Manton Drive, Luton. Major, H.Q., 30 Corps District, R.A.O.C. **American Bronze Star**, 1944, B.A.O.R. ; **M.D.**, 1945, B.A.O.R.

RAMSAY, David B., 36, Castle Street, Luton. Capt., R.A.M.C. **M.D.**, 1944, Middle East.

REEVE, Leslie Frederick William, 7, Austin Road, Luton. L/Seaman, R.N. **M.D.**, 1945, Light Coastal Forces, Italy.

RICHARDSON, Keith R., 11, Humberstone Close, Luton. F/O., R.A.F. **D.F.C.**, 1945, Rhine Crossing.

RING, J. P., 76, Bradley Road, Luton. Cpl. **M.M.**, 1940, North Africa.

ROBERTSON, Ian Alex., 31, Felstead Way, Luton. S/Ldr., R.A.F. **D.F.C.**, 1941.

ROBINSON, Albert Edward, " Greenhills," Orchard Way, Luton. Capt., 15th Vehicle Park., R.A.O.C. **M.D.**, 1945, Italy.

ROBINSON, James, 40, Smart Street, Luton. Tank Shop Foreman, Vauxhall Motors, Ltd. **B.E.M.**, 1943.

RUDD, Colin Jas., 164, Dunstable Road, Luton. Capt., Northants. Regt. **M.C.**, 1944, N.W. Europe ; **Bar to M.C.**, 1944, Nijmegen-Arnhem Crossing, N.W. Europe. (Subsequently killed in action).

RUMBLE, Albert Edward, 10, East Avenue, Luton. S/Ldr., Special Duties List, att. M.A.P. **A.F.C.**, 1946, Test Pilot Duties.

SAUNDERS, William, St. Paul's Road, Luton. Sgt., R.A.S.C. **M.D.**, 1940, France.

SAVAGE, Arthur, 25, Summerfield Road, Luton. Pte., 4th Battn. King's Shropshire L.I. **M.M.**, 1944.

SAVAGE, John, 50, Chester Avenue, Luton. Sgt., Hampshire Regt. **D.C.M.**, 1944, Italy.

SEAR, Albert Joseph, Deputy Chief Constable of Luton. **George Medal,** 1941, Parachute Mine Incident at Percival Aircraft, Ltd., Luton.

SHANE, David Thos. Patrick, 1, Runfold Avenue, Luton. Able Seaman, Naval Diving Party " P " 2443, R.N. **M.D.**, 1946, Under-water Bomb Mine Disposal, Bremen, June, 1945.

SHARP, Leslie Alfred, 9, Surrey Street, Luton. Gunner, R.A. **M.M.**, 1942, Tobruk.

SIMKINS, Edward Wickens, 140, Cutenhoe Road, Luton. F/O., R.A.F. **D.F.C.**, 1944.

SINCLAIR, F. G., 95, Turners Road, Luton. Cpl., R.E.M.E. **M.D.**, 1946, Mediterranean.

SKELTON, Graham Clyde, 59, High Town Road, Luton. Flt./Lieut., 467 Squadron, R.A.F. **D.F.C.**, 1945.

SMITH, Walter R. S., 103, Chesford Road, Stopsley, Luton. Comm., R.N.V.R. **D.S.C.**, 1944, Normandy Invasion.

SMYTH, David P. W., 21, Walcot Avenue, Luton. Sgt., R.A. **M.M.**, 1943, North Africa.

SPIRES, John Henry, 11, Denbigh Road, Luton. F/Lt., R.A.F. **D.F.M.**, 1941, Malta and Middle East ; **D.F.C.**, 1944, France and Germany.

STANGHAN, Percy W., 74, St. Michael's Crescent, Luton. F/Sgt., R.A.F. **M.D.**, 1944.

STOKES, Cecil Sydney, " Bedfordia," Bramble Road, Luton. Sgt., R.A.F. **M.D.**, 1944.

STOTT, Gordon, 18, Alexandra Avenue, Luton. Sergt., No. 1 B.P.O., R.A.F. **M.D.**, 1944, M.E.F.

STRINGER, George, 98, Crawley Green Road, Luton. Senior Progress Man, Vauxhall Motors, Ltd. **B.E.M.**, 1945.

STYGALL, John Samuel, 29, Avenue Grimaldi, Luton. Assistant Production Engineer, Geo. Kent, Ltd., Luton. **B.E.M.**, 1946.

TAYLOR, Douglas, Town Hall, Luton. Sergt., 6th Armoured Divisional Signals. **M.D.**, 1943, Africa.

TEMPLEMAN-ROOKE, Basil Arthur, 49, Bishopscote Road, Luton. Wing Commander, R.A.F., formerly Leader of 576 and 150 Squadrons. **D.F.C.**, 1943, **Bar to D.F.C.**, 1945, and **D.S.O.**, 1945, all presented at one Investiture, 1945.

THOMSON, John, Inspector, Luton Borough Police, in charge of A.R.P. Department. **B.E.M.**, 1944.

THORNE, Frank Jas., 15, Priory Gardens, Luton. Captain, 31st Group, Pioneer Corps. **M.D.**, 1946, N.W. Europe.

TILDSLEY, William McKee Griffith, 45, Wimborne Road, Luton. W/Officer, 119th Coy. Pioneer Corps. **M.B.E.**, 1945, N.W. Europe.

TOFIELD, Claude Cecil L., 475, Dunstable Road, Luton. Col., R.E.M.E. **C.B.E.**, 1946.

TOWNSEND, Nigel H., 8, Priory Gardens, Luton. Capt., R.A.S.C. **M.D.**, 1945, Rhine Crossing ; **American Bronze Star,** 1945, Holland.

UNDERWOOD, Alan, 12, Durbar Road, Luton. Lieut., Royal Marines. **B.E.M.**, 1941, for bravery in air raid. Subsequently died on service.

VERGE, John, 16, Gardenia Avenue, Luton. Lt. and Q.M., 10th Hussars, R.A.C. **M.B.E.**, 1943, North Africa.

VERRAN, Reginald Stanley Edward, 78, Talbot Road, Luton. F/Officer, R.A.F.V.R. **D.F.C.,** June, 1945. Subsequently killed.

VERRAN, Robert Claude, 18, Carlton Close, Luton. Sgt./Obs., R.A.F. **D.F.M.,** 1940 ; **M.D.** Subsequently killed in action.

VINCENT, H. C., Luton Borough Treasurer's Staff. Capt., R.A. **M.D.,** Burma.

WALLER, Robert Bruce, " Fairholme," Hart Hill, Luton. S/Ldr., 418, A.S.P., R.A.F. **M.D.,** 1943, Western Desert ; **M.D.,** 1944, Sicily and Italy ; **O.B.E.,** 1945, Corsica and Southern France.

WALTHEW, Harry F., 6, Manland Avenue, Harpenden, and Vauxhall Motors, Ltd., Luton. Lt.-Col., Herts. Regt. **O.B.E.,** 1946.

WEATHERLEY, Alfred Wm. Geo., 75, Limbury Road, Luton. Sergt., Special Forces (Airborne Signals). **M.M.,** 1944, Greece.

WELCH, Roy Hector, 12, Carlton Close, Luton. F/Lt., R.A.F. **A.F.C.,** 1944.

WELLS, Horace Guy, 8, Blyth Place, Luton. Capt., 15th Parachute Regt. **M.D.,** 1942, N. Africa.

WERNHER, Lady Zia, Luton Hoo. Leicestershire County President, St. John Ambulance Brigade. **O.B.E.,** 1946.

WHITE, Charles Henry, 66, Frederick Street, Luton. Capt. and Q.M., Bedfs. and Herts. Regt. **M.B.E.,** 1942.

WHITEHEAD, John Francis, 60, Newcombe Road, Luton. Warrant Supply Officer, R. New Zealand Navy. **B.E.M.,** 1942, Indian Ocean.

WHITMORE, Edward Randolph, 105, Montrose Avenue, Luton. Automatic Shop Foreman, Shefko Ball Bearing Co., Ltd., Luton. **B.E.M.,** 1945.

WICKHAM, Charles Sydney, 52, Sundon Park Road, Luton. LAC., 220 Squadron, R.A.F. **M.D.,** 1945, Azores.

WOODBRIDGE, Percy Henry, 121, Toddington Road, Luton. F/Sgt., R.A.F. **M.D.,** 1944.

WOODCRAFT, Ernest, 183, Selbourne Road, Luton. Sgt. **M.D.,** 1944, Middle East.

WOODS, Charles Mason, 8, Weatherby Road, Luton. Stoker Petty Officer, R.N. **D.S.M.,** 1944, Battle of the Atlantic.

WOOLLFORD, Roy, 4, Beverley Road, Luton. W/Officer, R.A.F. **D.F.C.,** 1944, Germany.

WRIGHT, Sidney Arthur, 22, St. Monica's Avenue, Luton. Part-time A.F.S. Section Officer. **George Medal,** 1940, Thames Haven Oil Wharves.

Acknowledgments

The publishers wish to acknowledge their indebtedness

To Mr. A. F. Pope, of *The Luton News*, who personally supervised the compilation of this book. His rich store of local knowledge, gained through close personal contact over many years with all phases of Luton life, has been invaluable.

To Alderman John Burgoyne, O.B.E., (Mayor of Luton through the greater part of the war), to officers of the Corporation of Luton, local officials of Government departments, ministers of religion, educationists, industrialists, traders, social workers, and all others who, as leaders of some branch of the local war effort, have willingly given valuable help in the provision and checking of information.

To those members of the Editorial staff of *The Luton News* who undertook the responsibility of writing articles, and were thereby involved in much painstaking research among records, published and unpublished, during the last eight years.

To their colleagues of the Photographic staff, whose daily work throughout the war provided some thousands of pictures of all aspects of Luton's war-time life, from which most of the illustrations reproduced here have been selected.

To the Photo-Engraving staff of Home Counties Newspapers, Ltd., and the staff of Gibbs, Bamforth & Co. (Luton), Ltd., whose craftsmanship contributed to the technical production of the book.